MW01012890

ALSO BY AMERICA'S TEST KITCHEN

Five-Ingredient Dinners

The Complete Plant-Based Cookbook

Vegetables Illustrated

The Complete Salad Cookbook

The New Cooking School Cookbook: Fundamentals

One-Hour Comfort

Cook for Your Gut Health

The Ultimate Meal-Prep Cookbook

The Complete One Pot

Bowls

The Chicken Bible

The Side Dish Bible

Foolproof Fish

Meat Illustrated

The Complete Autumn and Winter Cookbook

The Complete Summer Cookbook

Cooking for One

100 Techniques

How Can It Be Gluten-Free Cookbook Collection

Easy Everyday Keto

Everything Chocolate

The Perfect Pie

How to Cocktail

Spiced

The Ultimate Burger

The New Essentials Cookbook

Dinner Illustrated

America's Test Kitchen Menu Cookbook

Cook's Illustrated Revolutionary Recipes

Tasting Italy: A Culinary Journey

Cooking at Home with Bridget and Julia

The Complete Mediterranean Cookbook

The Complete Vegetarian Cookbook

The Complete Diabetes Cookbook

The Complete Cooking for Two Cookbook

The Complete Slow Cooker

The Complete Make-Ahead Cookbook

Just Add Sauce

How to Braise Everything

How to Roast Everything

Nutritious Delicious

What Good Cooks Know

Cook's Science

The Science of Good Cooking

The Perfect Cake

The Perfect Cookie

Bread Illustrated

Master of the Grill

Kitchen Smarts

Kitchen Hacks

100 Recipes: The Absolute Best Ways to Make the True Essentials

The New Family Cookbook

The Cook's Illustrated Baking Book

The Cook's Illustrated Cookbook

The America's Test Kitchen Family Baking Book

America's Test Kitchen Twentieth Anniversary TV Show Cookbook

The Best of America's Test Kitchen (2007–2022 Editions)

The Complete America's Test Kitchen TV Show Cookbook 2001–2022

Mediterranean Instant Pot

Healthy and Delicious Instant Pot

Healthy Air Fryer

Toaster Oven Perfection

Cook It in Your Dutch Oven

Vegan for Everybody

Sous Vide for Everybody

Air Fryer Perfection

Multicooker Perfection

Food Processor Perfection

Pressure Cooker Perfection

Instant Pot Ace Blender Cookbook

Naturally Sweet

Foolproof Preserving

Paleo Perfected

The Best Mexican Recipes

Slow Cooker Revolution Volume 2: The Easy-Prep Edition

Slow Cooker Revolution

The America's Test Kitchen D.I.Y. Cookbook

The Cook's Illustrated All-Time Best Series

All-Time Best Brunch

All-Time Best Dinners for Two

All-Time Best Sunday Suppers

All-Time Best Holiday Entertaining

All-Time Best Soups

Cook's Country Titles

Big Flavors from Italian America

One-Pan Wonders

Cook It in Cast Iron

Cook's Country Eats Local

The Complete Cook's Country TV Show Cookbook

For a Full Listing of All Our Books

CooksIllustrated.com

AmericasTestKitchen.com

PRAISE FOR AMERICA'S TEST KITCHEN TITLES

"An exhaustive but approachable primer for those looking for a 'flexible' diet. Chock-full of tips, you can dive into the science of plant-based cooking or just sit back and enjoy the 500 recipes."

Minneapolis Star Tribune on *The Complete Plant-Based Cookbook*

"The book's depth, breadth, and practicality makes it a must-have for seafood lovers."

Publishers Weekly (starred review) on *Foolproof Fish*

"Another flawless entry in the America's Test Kitchen canon, *Bowls* guides readers of all culinary skill levels in composing one-bowl meals from a variety of cuisines."

BuzzFeed Books on *Bowls*

Selected as the Cookbook Award Winner of 2019 in the Health and Special Diet Category

International Association of Culinary Professionals (IACP) on *The Complete Diabetes Cookbook*

"Diabetics and all health-conscious home cooks will find great information on almost every page."

Booklist (starred review) on *The Complete Diabetes Cookbook*

"This is a wonderful, useful guide to healthy eating."

Publishers Weekly on *Nutritious Delicious*

"*The Perfect Cookie*. . . is, in a word, perfect. This is an important and substantial cookbook. . . . If you love cookies, but have been a tad shy to bake on your own, all your fears will be dissipated. This is one book you can use for years with magnificently happy results."

The Huffington Post on *The Perfect Cookie*

Selected as one of the 10 Best New Cookbooks of 2017

The LA TIMES on *The Perfect Cookie*

"The sum total of exhaustive experimentation . . . anyone interested in gluten-free cookery simply shouldn't be without it."

Nigella Lawson on *The How Can It Be Gluten-Free Cookbook*

"True to its name, this smart and endlessly enlightening cookbook is about as definitive as it's possible to get in the modern vegetarian realm."

Men's Journal on *The Complete Vegetarian Cookbook*

"If you're a home cook who loves long introductions that tell you why a dish works followed by lots of step-by-step hand holding, then you'll love *Vegetables Illustrated*."

The Wall Street Journal on *Vegetables Illustrated*

"A one-volume kitchen seminar, addressing in one smart chapter after another the sometimes surprising whys behind a cook's best practices. . . . You get the myth, the theory, the science, and the proof, all rigorously interrogated as only America's Test Kitchen can do."

NPR on *The Science of Good Cooking*

"The 21st-century *Fannie Farmer Cookbook* or *The Joy of Cooking*. If you had to have one cookbook and that's all you could have, this one would do it."

CBS San Francisco on *The New Family Cookbook*

"Some 2,500 photos walk readers through 600 painstakingly tested recipes, leaving little room for error."

Associated Press on *The America's Test Kitchen Cooking School Cookbook*

"The go-to gift book for newlyweds, small families, or empty nesters."

Orlando Sentinel on *The Complete Cooking for Two Cookbook*

"Some books impress by the sheer audacity of their ambition. Backed by the magazine's famed mission to test every recipe relentlessly until it is the best it can be, this nearly 900-page volume lands with an authoritative wallop."

Chicago Tribune on *The Cook's Illustrated Cookbook*

"This impressive installment from America's Test Kitchen equips readers with dozens of repertoire-worthy recipes. . . . This is a must-have for beginner cooks and more experienced ones who wish to sharpen their skills."

Publishers Weekly (starred review) on *The New Essentials Cookbook*

"A one-volume kitchen seminar, addressing in one smart chapter after another the sometimes surprising whys behind a cook's best practices. . . . You get the myth, the theory, the science, and the proof, all rigorously interrogated as only America's Test Kitchen can do."

NPR on *The Science of Good Cooking*

More Mediterranean

225+ NEW PLANT-FORWARD RECIPES

ENDLESS INSPIRATION FOR EATING WELL

AMERICA'S TEST KITCHEN

Library of Congress Cataloging-in-Publication Data has been applied for.

ISBN 978-1-948703-88-8

AMERICA'S TEST KITCHEN
21 Drydock Avenue, Boston, MA 02210

Printed in Canada
10 9 8 7 6 5 4 3 2 1

Distributed by Penguin Random House Publisher Services
Tel: 800.733.3000

Pictured on Front Cover Roasted Salmon Fillets (page 359), Horta (page 127), White Bean Hummus with Herb and Olive Salad (page 299), Skillet-Roasted Carrots with Za'atar Bread Crumbs and Cilantro (page 130)

Pictured on Back Cover Chraime (page 336), Crispy Artichoke Salad with Lemon Vinaigrette (page 22), Couscous-Stuffed Acorn Squash (page 105), Creamy Hawaij Cauliflower Soup with Zhoug (page 69), Grilled Tofu and Vegetables with Rose Harissa (page 309)

Editorial Director, Books Adam Kowit

Executive Food Editor Dan Zuccarello

Deputy Food Editor Stephanie Pixley

Executive Managing Editor Debra Hudak

Senior Book Editor Sacha Madadian

Senior Editors Leah Colins, Camila Chaparro, Joseph Gitter, Sara Mayer, Russell Selander

Associate Editor Sarah Ewald

Test Cook Carmen Dongo

Assistant Editor Emily Rahravan

Design Director, Books Lindsey Timko Chandler

Book Designer Sarah Dailey

Photography Director Julie Bozzo Cote

Photography Producer Meredith Mulcahy

Senior Staff Photographers Steve Klise and Daniel J. van Ackere

Staff Photographer Kevin White

Additional Photography Joseph Keller and Carl Tremblay

Food Styling Joy Howard, Catrine Kelty, Chantal Lambeth, Gina McCreadie, Kendra McNight, Ashley Moore, Christie Morrison, Marie Piraino, Elle Simone Scott, Kendra Smith, and Sally Staub

Photoshoot Kitchen Team

    Photo Team and Special Events Manager Alli Berkey

    Lead Test Cook Eric Haessler

    Test Cooks Hannah Fenton, Jacqueline Gochenouer, and Gina McCreadie

    Assistant Test Cooks Hisham Hassan and Christa West

Senior Manager, Publishing Operations Taylor Argenzio

Imaging Manager Lauren Robbins

Production and Imaging Specialists Tricia Neumyer, Dennis Noble, and Amanda Yong

Copy Editor Cheryl Redmond

Proofreader Ann-Marie Imbornoni

Indexer Elizabeth Parson

Chief Creative Officer Jack Bishop

Executive Editorial Directors Julia Collin Davison and Bridget Lancaster

Our special thanks to the following chefs, cooks, and educators for lending their expertise and helping us develop recipes for this book: Diana Abouali (Msakhan, page 374), Awad Awad (Msakhan, page 374), Tanya Cavanaugh (Msakhan, page 374), Maryam Habil (Embakbbka, page 402), Walid Hachani (Tunisian Tajine with White Beans, page 315), Sheila Sutton (Mehshi Bazal, page 394), Radia Yousef (Chorba Frik, page 208).

Contents

WELCOME TO
America's Test Kitchen

This book has been tested, written, and edited by the folks at America's Test Kitchen, where curious cooks become confident cooks. Located in Boston's Seaport District in the historic Innovation and Design Building, it features 15,000 square feet of kitchen space including multiple photography and video studios. It is the home of *Cook's Illustrated* magazine and *Cook's Country* magazine and is the workday destination for more than 60 test cooks, editors, and cookware specialists. Our mission is to empower and inspire confidence, community, and creativity in the kitchen.

We start the process of testing a recipe with a complete lack of preconceptions, which means that we accept no claim, no technique, and no recipe at face value. We simply assemble as many variations as possible, test a half-dozen of the most promising, and taste the results blind. We then construct our own recipe and continue to test it, varying ingredients, techniques, and cooking times until we reach a consensus. As we like to say in the test kitchen, "We make the mistakes so you don't have to." The result, we hope, is the best version of a particular recipe, but we realize that only you can be the final judge of our success (or failure). We use the same rigorous approach when we test equipment and taste ingredients.

All of this would not be possible without a belief that good cooking, much like good music, is based on a foundation of objective technique. Some people like spicy foods and others don't, but there is a right way to sauté, there is a best way to cook a pot roast, and there are measurable scientific principles involved in producing perfectly beaten, stable egg whites. Our ultimate goal is to investigate the fundamental principles of cooking to give you the techniques, tools, and ingredients you need to become a better cook. It is as simple as that.

To see what goes on behind the scenes at America's Test Kitchen, check out our social media channels for kitchen snapshots, exclusive content, video tips, and much more. You can watch us work (in our actual test kitchen) by tuning in to *America's Test Kitchen* or *Cook's Country* on public television or on our websites. Listen to *Proof*, *Mystery Recipe*, and *The Walk-In* (AmericasTestKitchen.com/podcasts) to hear engaging, complex stories about people and food. Want to hone your cooking skills or finally learn how to bake—with an America's Test Kitchen test cook? Enroll in one of our online cooking classes. And you can engage the next generation of home cooks with kid-tested recipes from America's Test Kitchen Kids.

Our community of home recipe testers provides valuable feedback on recipes under development by ensuring that they are foolproof. You can help us investigate the how and why behind successful recipes from your home kitchen. (Sign up at AmericasTestKitchen.com/recipe_testing.)

However you choose to visit us, we welcome you into our kitchen, where you can stand by our side as we test our way to the best recipes in America.

facebook.com/AmericasTestKitchen
instagram.com/TestKitchen
youtube.com/AmericasTestKitchen
tiktok.com/@TestKitchen
twittor.com/TestKitchen
pinterest.com/TestKitchen

AmericasTestKitchen.com
CooksIllustrated.com
CooksCountry.com
OnlineCookingSchool.com
AmericasTestKitchen.com/kids

CONTENTS

AN INTRODUCTION

The Mediterranean Sea is an incredible body of water, a geographic connector of three large continents. It's home to robust histories and diverse cultures— as well as a very healthy diet.

While we refer to a singular Mediterranean diet, Mediterranean cuisine is no monolith. The Mediterranean Basin is home to a group of countries (those with coastlines on the Mediterranean Sea), each with its own distinct cuisine. What they share is a tendency to put a daily emphasis on vegetables, beans and legumes, grains, more seafood than meat (and a modest amount of each at that), and heart-healthy olive oil. From these ingredients comes cooking that's so simply enjoyable it's hard to think of the Mediterranean diet as a diet; it's rooted in pleasure, absent of the calorie-counting, macro-tracking, or restriction associated with diets. It's about eating delicious food in satisfying, moderate portions in good company and in combination with activity. The Mediterranean way is really *a lifestyle*, one that keeps its people healthy in high numbers.

Doctors and dietitians worldwide consistently prescribe the Mediterranean diet, for good reason: It has been proven to ward off heart disease, encourage good gut health, promote positive mental health, and even prevent Alzheimer's and cancer.

These abundant health assets might have brought you to the Mediterranean diet, by doctor's recommendation or personal interest. Or maybe you just want to eat really wonderful food and try new Mediterranean dishes. You're in the right place. We've published this follow-up to *The Complete Mediterranean Cookbook*, our bestselling first book on the subject, to give you more—more recipes to add to your Mediterranean cooking repertoire but also more options.

In this book, you'll find more focus on plant-forward cooking. Vegetables, grains, and beans are the heart of this collection; we devote the first two thirds of the book to them, and use them in conjunction with eggs, fish, and meat in the last third, so making a meal that emphasizes them is simple. Vegetables play a starring role in dishes like impressive Whole Romanesco with Berbere and Yogurt-Tahini Sauce, which makes a brilliant dinner on its own. You'll see homages to powerhouse ingredients like chickpeas, which bulk up a version of shakshuka and flaunt their creamy texture and nutty flavor in Lablabi, a Tunisian soup often eaten for breakfast. And when you do cook meat, you'll find it in moderate amounts and expertly paired, as in Seared Steak Tips with Cauliflower and Zhoug.

Because any vegetable can be a valuable part of a Mediterranean diet, we've opened the Mediterranean pantry doors wide to include a broad range of ingredients, emphasizing all kinds of plants and grains in vibrant dishes and inspired combinations. Our aim is to show there isn't a limit to the variety of healthful ingredients you can cook with while enjoying the vibrant flavors of the Mediterranean. This nutritional diversity keeps the lifestyle sustainable: Eating in proper balance is effortless when you're making meals from all the vegetables of the rainbow, all the grains in your cupboard, and all the fish in the sea. It also ensures that you benefit from a wide variety of micronutrients. The contrasting flavors and textures of the Fattoush with Butternut Squash and Apple—crispy fried pita shards, sweet, creamy cubes of roasted butternut squash, crisp, bitter radicchio, and a shower of tangy sumac—will be a new go-to fall salad meal. Make sumptuous Spanish-style meatballs, albóndigas, from protein- and fiber-packed quinoa. Turn planks of tofu into grillable steaks bathed in spicy, aromatic rose harissa.

When it comes to creating a meal from the dishes in this book, you have options. You'll find plenty of one-pan and other weeknight-friendly meals. A sheet pan supper of Roasted Salmon with White Beans, Fennel, and Tomatoes, or Baharat Cauliflower and Eggplant with Chickpeas, provides all the nutritional building blocks on one rimmed baking sheet—no sides or accompaniments needed. Other dishes, like Cabbage, Kohlrabi, and Lamb Tagine with Prunes, need little more than a simple grain side. Vibrant vegetable dishes and salads like Sweet Potato Salad with Cumin, Smoked Paprika, and Almonds could be a meal with just a simple piece of seared fish, or maybe another vegetable alongside them on the plate.

Build on your repertoire of Mediterranean recipes by cooking from the different cuisines of the region and also explore layers of flavor with inspiring combinations. You'll eat every last green bean when they're charred and adorned with crunchy cracked coriander seeds, sesame seeds, oniony nigella seeds, and a lemony tahini sauce. Top sandwiches of fava bean fritters with bright batons of Pink Pickled Turnips. Give lamb chops a sweet-sour tamarind glaze to contrast the rich, deeply flavored meat. You can tell we loved cooking and eating this food—and we know you will, too.

THE MEDITERRANEAN WAY

Food, and sharing it, contributes to the quality (and longevity) of life in the Mediterranean. And what is locally accessible in this mild, temperate area of the world is not only tasty but also centers on a universally healthy concept: a daily emphasis on vegetables, fruits, beans, lentils, whole grains, seafood (more so than meat and poultry), and heart-healthy olive oil. The Mediterranean way of eating is this simple, and it guides the recipes we included in this book—plant-forward recipes that are low in saturated fat, full of fiber, and smart in protein selection.

NAMING THE DIET

The Mediterranean way became defined as a diet and a respected way of eating outside the region through the Seven Countries Study, which was launched in the late 1950s by an American physiologist named Ancel Keys. He found that the people of Crete tended to have lower incidences of coronary heart disease than participants in other countries, a fact that he attributed to their traditional diet—regionally abundant plants, fish from their waters, and plenty of olive oil, a gift of the prolific olive harvest. Today, plant-forward eating continues to support principles of good health, and populations in the Mediterranean continue to live longer than others.

CALLING ALL PLANTS

So what plants and healthful proteins will you find in this book so you can eat and live this way, too? Just about all of them. Cooks in Mediterranean countries, especially today, don't prepare only foods that originated there, and you don't need to, either. Eating a diversity of vegetables, whole grains, and legumes is best for your body because it provides the most micronutrients. Here we celebrate Mediterranean flavors and cuisines while also looking at a wide range of vegetables, from tomatoes to butternut squash, that originated the world over; we think you should eat any vegetable as much as you choose. The same goes for hearty grains from all over, like protein-packed quinoa and nutrient-rich red rice.

You'll enjoy avocado, which contains the same healthful fats as olive oil, or salmon, a freshwater fish that's packed with omega-3 fatty acids and a flavor robust enough for your Mediterranean plate. You'll savor the soybean with recipes that use tempeh served with savory condiments (see page 312) or tofu tucked into a vibrant pita wrap (see page 306).

Salmon, Avocado, Grapefruit, and Watercress Salad

You could consider most of the recipes in this book Mediterranean-inspired, incorporating a broad range of healthful ingredients. You'll love being able to cook with foods from around the world and your own backyard. It will make eating according to the Mediterranean diet not only more interesting, but also more practical, both habitual and pleasurable. If you're eating mostly plants, you're eating well.

BUILDING YOUR PLANT-FORWARD PLATE

If, in addition to eating well, you want to simplify meal planning at dinner time, this book does a lot of the work for you. Each of the three large chapters—Mostly Plants; Mainly Grains and Beans; and Meat, Fish, Tofu, and More—offers a lively mix of dishes, from cooling salads to warm, comforting roasted meals. With our advice, mix and match the dishes to create your nutritionally complete meal, or simply eat a hearty plant-forward dish alone and discover how it satisfies as your entire meal.

Recipes in the Mostly Plants chapter are not all vegetarian, but they're vegetable-heavy. When animal proteins appear they're good-for-you options: Some increase satiety, like the modest amount of smoked salmon that interweaves with carrot, grapefruit, and endive in an orange-hued salad (see page 25). Some act mainly as seasonings, lending savor to deepen verdant, earthy, or sweet vegetable-based meals. Since produce should fill up your plate, we encourage you to start with recipes in the plants chapter. Spend time also exploring the rich textures and nutty flavors of dishes in the Mainly Grains and Beans chapter. Learn how filling these can be; often, they're all you need to put on your plate. And find dishes that balance meat and vegetables for you in our Meat, Fish, Tofu, and More chapter. Think about which moderately portioned meat dishes bring out the best in the plant-based recipes on your plate. Following are a few of the many ways you can envision your plate, all balanced and nutritious. We hope they inspire you to explore the recipes in this book any night of the week.

FROM PYRAMID TO PLATE

In our first book on the Mediterranean diet, we turned to the Mediterranean Diet Pyramid originally developed in the 1990s as part of a collaboration between the Harvard School of Public Health and Oldways, a nonprofit organization whose mission is to inspire good health through cultural food traditions. While the Pyramid is a useful tool for understanding what to eat in abundance, the United States Department of Agriculture (USDA) has embraced a simple way to understand how to eat healthy meals called MyPlate. Unsurprisingly, the USDA's MyPlate model aligns closely with the Mediterranean diet.

We find that imagining food on sections of a plate is a perfect way to learn how to build a meal with the types of dishes in this book. According to this model, half your meal should come from vegetables (fruit is included here). The next largest section is for grains. The smallest section is for meat. This doesn't mean you need to eat, say, three compartmentalized dishes, or make your meal match MyPlate; it's a way to think about balancing the categories of foods in your meals (and the chapters in this book), whatever they might look like, and, most importantly, placing an emphasis on plants. Often a vegetable or grain dish is great on its own as a meal, or as a partner on the plate.

WHOLE GRAINS

VEGETABLES & FRUIT

PROTEIN

1. INSPIRED BY MYPLATE

The USDA's MyPlate model isn't the only model for eating the Mediterranean way, but it's a great healthful way of looking at your plate. Fill and color half your plate with vegetables by choosing from a number of salads and hearty sides. Then, round out the plate by combining these with a grain or bean dish, like a grain salad or warm side jeweled with fruit and nuts, and a moderate protein portion, like a fish fillet or tempeh. Recipes for simple sides (see pages 110 and 230) and protein options (see page 356) make it easy—you don't need to cook three multicomponent dishes.

Plates to Make

- Charred Green Beans with Coriander, Sesame, and Nigella Seeds (page 128) + Chickpea Salad with Carrots, Raisins, and Almonds (page 235) + Seared Tempeh (page 357)

- Parsley-Cucumber Salad with Feta, Pomegranate, and Walnuts (page 33) + Basmati Rice Pilaf (page 231) + Arrosticini (page 409)

- Spinach with Garlic and Lemon (page 112) + Red Rice and Quinoa Salad with Blood Oranges (page 180) + Roasted Salmon Fillets (page 359)

- Roasted Asparagus with Cilantro-Lime Gremolata (page 113) + White Bean and Tuna Salad (page 199)

- Riced Cauliflower with Preserved Lemon (page 123) + Perfect Fried Eggs (page 358) + Lentil Salad with Pomegranate and Walnuts (page 235)

- Shrimp Risotto (page 222) + Pan-Roasted Brussels Sprouts with Lemon and Pecorino Romano (page 111)

- Persimmon and Burrata Salad with Prosciutto (page 57) + Kamut with Carrots and Pomegranate (page 235)

2. PLANT IT FORWARD

If you're always serving a meat-heavy entrée and two sides, it's time to embrace plants as more-than-able stars that don't need much in the way of supporting cast members. A robust vegetable dish can be dinner; for example, a butternut squash steak can be eaten much like a beef steak. You might want to pair it with a simple grain (find ideas on pages 230–235) or a light green salad, a poached egg, or some crusty bread—and be done.

Plates to Make

- Whole Romanesco with Berbere and Yogurt-Tahini Sauce (page 84) + Simple Couscous (page 234)
- Mushroom Bourguignon (page 93) + Creamy Parmesan Polenta (page 233)
- Couscous-Stuffed Acorn Squash (page 105)
- Carrot and Beet Salad with Rose Harissa (page 56)
- Cauliflower Puree with Blistered Tomatoes and 'Nduja (page 116)
- Skillet-Roasted Carrots with Za'atar Bread Crumbs and Cilantro (page 130) + Perfect Fried Eggs (page 358)
- Seared Halloumi and Vegetable Salad Bowl (page 63)
- Stuffed Tomatoes with Couscous and Zucchini (page 108) + Spinach with Garlic and Lemon (page 112)

3. HALF AND HALF

Simple pairings teach you what flavors and textures complement each other in dishes. Put two things on the plate that will fill you up, and with enjoyment. Pair something from Meat, Fish, Tofu, and More with a vegetable or grain side, for example, and dinner is served in two healthful halves. This scheme works for any combination of foods from the three chapters of dishes in the book. See how to mix and match below.

Plates to Make

- Chopped Vegetable and Stone Fruit Salad (page 32) + Pan-Roasted Cod (page 360)
- Beet Salad with Spiced Yogurt and Watercress (page 27) + Roasted Salmon Fillets (page 359)
- Roasted Cauliflower and Grape Salad with Chermoula (page 60) + Pearl Couscous with Chorizo and Chickpeas (page 169)
- Braised Eggplant with Paprika, Coriander, and Yogurt (page 124) + Quinoa Pilaf with Olives, Raisins, and Cilantro (page 191)
- Cannellini Beans with Roasted Red Peppers and Kale (page 206) + Tortilla Española with Celery Root and Peas (page 318)

4. THE COMPLETE ONE-PAN MEAL

We love the previous principles for making Mediterranean meals with endless combinations of flavors that keep us interested in the kitchen. But we also love meals that require zero guesswork, so all three chapters contain recipes for hearty one-pan meals, which give you a flavorful, nutritionally balanced dinner with ease. Easy doesn't mean boring, however; these recipes range from medleys of roasted vegetables to sumptuous soups and stews. A number of risottos (of all different grains, from traditional short-grain rice to farro and barley) cook into one-pot meals, and proteins sizzle alongside vegetables all in the same skillet. Here are the one-pan meals in this book.

Plates to Make

EASY WAYS TO EAT MEDITERRANEAN EVERY DAY

Our meal ideas on pages 5–7 show you how to put together a superlatively healthful and delicious plate from the recipes in this book. In addition, we've gathered some quick helpful hints that make it easy to build a meal you love every day.

VEGETABLES FIRST

Since these nutrient-dense plants are the most important part of your diet, it's wise, fun (and perhaps contrary to your routine) to first choose a vegetable dish that appeals to you (maybe a heaping platter of spiced sweet potato noodles; see page 120), and then fill in any blanks with items that pair with the vegetables you crave.

IN SEASON AND LOCAL IF POSSIBLE

Many of us live outside of temperate Mediterranean climates, but choosing what's fresh and in season when you can will help you narrow your choices for your plate. Blink and you'll miss springtime produce—and intriguing dishes like Panzanella with Fiddleheads (page 30). Jump to use juicy summer tomatoes in Feta, Jicama, and Tomato Salad (page 43). Good-quality local, in-season produce is worthy of taking up the most space on your plate.

EASY ADDITIONS

Dinner shouldn't be difficult. If you've made a hearty dish, you don't need to make another multicomponent recipe to go alongside it (unless you want to). Tap into our collection of simple side dishes (see pages 110 and 230) or easy proteins (see page 356). Or, even easier, toss a salad of greens, lemon juice, and olive oil to accompany your phyllo pie (see page 143) or frittata (see page 314), rip up some flatbread for serving, or put an egg on something.

RETHINK YOUR PROTEIN SOURCES

Protein doesn't come just from meat or eggs or tofu. Whole grains and beans, beyond packing fiber, provide plant-based, hearty, healthful protein. Red lentil kibbeh, made from lentils and bulgur, offers just as much protein as meat versions of the dish. Reimagine how you eat hummus by serving it as a landing pad for crispy mushrooms (see page 301). Make sandwiches around plant-based foods like Ta'ameya with Tahini-Yogurt Sauce (page 287) or Quinoa Lettuce Wraps with Feta and Olives (page 168).

USE MEAT AS A FLAVORING

Meat doesn't always have to be a distinct element, and a small amount of meat can flavor meals without weighing them down. Traditionally, scarce or expensive meat was stretched further by combining it with vegetables, grains, and beans, like the chorizo that adds heat and richness to Patatas a la Riojana (page 78) or the ground meat that gives lentil and bulgur–stuffed peppers (see page 106) savor.

SERVING SIZE SLIDING SCALE

The serving sizes we offer for dishes assumes they are a part of a whole. But you can (and should) adjust how you serve up dishes based on the value they're meant to add to the plate. A Sweet Potato Salad with Cumin, Smoked Paprika, and Almonds (page 38) serves six as a side but this dish might be meal-worthy to you. Serve up larger portions at your own discretion if it's meant to be your dinner alone.

FUN WITH FLAVOR (AND TEXTURE)

You'll keep eating healthy if even the basics continue to surprise. Drizzle simple dishes with a bright herb sauce to awaken them, or shower them with nuts—the crunch will keep you coming back for more. Find more ideas for livening up your food on page 12.

THE SPICE PANTRY

Spices are potent flavorings that we use to balance (see page 12) so many dishes in this book. They're often included in a recipe's title because they give the recipe identity, tell a story of the cuisine, and simply pack a punch. The Mediterranean has always been an important spice hub. Here we honor the spices and spice blends that we turn to in this book and that we think you should keep in your cupboard for the most flavorful meals. We highly suggest purchasing spices from a single-source purveyor whose spices come from compensated indigenous farmers.

ALEPPO PEPPER

Made from dried, crushed Aleppo (or Halaby) peppers (a name that comes from the northern Syrian city), these flakes are widely used in Syria and nearby regions. Aleppo has a complex, raisin-like sweetness, tang, and slow-to-build heat with roasty notes. It's sometimes used to add finishing heat as in Spiced Eggplant and Kale Soup (page 77), against a cooling dollop of yogurt. Purchase ground dried Aleppo pepper. (For more information on Aleppo pepper, see page 50.)

BAHARAT

Baharat (the word means "spices" in Arabic) is unsurprisingly a most common Middle Eastern warm spice blend. It's sometimes called seven spice blend because, while it varies from region to region, a common iteration includes these seven spices: black pepper, coriander, cardamom, nutmeg, cumin, cloves, and cinnamon. Other spices sometimes found in baharat are dried mint (as in Turkey); dried rosebuds (as in North Africa); and chile flakes, saffron, sumac, or turmeric. It's a common rub for meat as well as a seasoning for ground meat (see page 394), it seasons roasted vegetables (see page 94), and it's used as both a cooking spice and a finishing one. (For more information on baharat, see page 132.)

CARAWAY

The ancient Greeks used caraway seeds as a cure for an upset stomach, and the seeds are still often paired with heavier foods like dishes with cheese. They're pungent and herbaceous, with a slightly bitter finish, making them a natural with robust meats. Caraway is an element of the spice blend tabil (see page 15), and sometimes a regional addition to baharat in Libya and Tunisia and to za'atar in Palestine.

CARDAMOM

Cardamom seeds are complex, flavorful seeds that come from mostly flavorless pods. They have a delicate, earthy, floral flavor with light sweetness. Green cardamom is the most commonly found variety in the United States. White cardamom is simply green cardamom that's been bleached so as not to discolor light-colored baked goods and other foods. Black cardamom (also called large cardamom) is not true cardamom but a relative. We've found that green cardamom is the most vibrant and balanced. The flavor of cardamom doesn't stick around, so buy whole pods and then remove and grind the seeds. In addition to being used alone, cardamom is a major element of ras el hanout.

CINNAMON

The savory side of cinnamon is on display in Mediterranean cuisine, and the spice adds warmth to many dishes and to spice blends. Most cinnamon sold in this country is the rolled bark of the cassia tree, not Ceylon cinnamon, which is known as "true" cinnamon. "Cinnamon" is actually an umbrella term for several different species of evergreen trees in the genus *Cinnamomum*. Moreover, different countries grow different species of trees, which is why different varieties are often named by country. Vietnamese growers, for example, cultivate *Cinnamomum loureiroi*, which is naturally higher in the volatile oils that provide heat and carry cinnamon's trademark flavors than the *Cinnamomum burmannii* grown in Indonesia. Ceylon cinnamon is grown primarily in Sri Lanka; we've found it milder than other varieties.

CORIANDER

When you buy whole coriander seeds rather than ground coriander, you're actually buying the fruit of the coriander plant (which also gives us the herb cilantro). Coriander provides a sweet, almost fruity or citrusy flavor that enhances spice rubs for meat and fish, and brings brightness that offsets the warmth of spice blends like baharat, ras el hanout, and tabil. Using the seeds whole, as in Charred Green Beans with Coriander, Sesame, and Nigella Seeds (page 128), adds a spicy crunch to dishes.

CUMIN

The ancient Greeks used it as medicine, and ancient Romans kept it on their dining tables the way modern Americans do pepper; now cumin adds depth to dishes the world over. Cumin seeds are harvested from the annual plant *Cuminum cyminum*, which is a member of the parsley family. India is the main producer of cumin, but other sources include Turkey and Iran. Cumin plays a role in numerous spice blends and chili powders. Cumin seeds, which resemble caraway, can also add toastiness, crunch, and a distinctive woodsy aroma to dishes.

FENNEL

Dried fennel seeds have an herbal, piney flavor that pairs well with rich meats. They're stronger in taste than similarly licorice-y anise seeds and taste great in very savory dishes. As every part of the fennel plant is edible, dried fennel seeds can point up the flavor of fresh fennel, as they do in our Chicken Salad with Pickled Fennel and Macadamia Nuts (page 363).

FENUGREEK

Fenugreek is a nutty seed with a unique maple-like flavor that is used in India and the Middle East. Fenugreek has an allium aroma with a burnt-sugar sweetness. It packs a punch as part of the rub for our Shawarma-Spiced Tofu Wraps with Sumac Onions (page 306).

GINGER

Ground ginger adds a warm, spicy flavor and aroma. Dried ginger is sharper and less floral than fresh; because of profound differences in moisture, pungency, and flavor, the two aren't interchangeable in recipes. Dried ginger (instead of fresh) is a nice addition to spice blends like ras el hanout.

HAWAIJ

This earthy, fragrant, bold Yemenite Jewish spice blend is golden from lots of turmeric and lightly floral, and is most notably used in liberal amounts in soups and stews, like Marak Temani (page 389). Basic versions contain black pepper, cumin, and cardamom in addition to the turmeric. There is a sweet version that's also used for coffee. (For more information on Hawaij, see page 68.)

MINT

In the Mediterranean, dried mint is used as a finisher (sometimes raw, sometimes cooked in oil); it gives a hit of fresh aroma that's concentrated enough to cut through complex flavors in a dish, like our Spiced Stuffed Peppers with Yogurt-Tahini Sauce (page 106). Some cultures also use it for its digestive properties. If dried mint isn't already a staple in your pantry, we highly recommend you stock it.

NIGELLA SEEDS

Nigella seeds (also called charnushka) are common in India and the Middle East. The seeds have an oniony bite and a slightly astringent, piney taste. You can sprinkle them on savory pastries (see page 140) in place of poppy or sesame seeds or garnish sandwiches, salads, and side dishes with them. Note: They're often mislabeled as black cumin or caraway.

NUTMEG

Heady and powerful, nutmeg is a hard, brown seed from a tropical tree. It's often used in creamy savory dishes like butternut squash soup (see page 70). It's also an element of ras el hanout. A little nutmeg goes a long way. You can grate a small amount from a whole nutmeg in almost the same time it'd take you to measure ground—and the flavor will shine.

PAPRIKA

Paprika is a generic term for a spice made from grinding dried red chile pods (and sometimes the seeds and stems as well) to a fine powder. Whether paprika is labeled sweet, smoked, or hot is determined by the variety (or varieties) of pepper used and how the pepper is manipulated. Sweet paprika is the most common. Typically made from a combination of mild red peppers, it's prized for its deep scarlet hue. Smoked paprika is produced by drying peppers (either sweet or hot) over smoldering embers. Spanish paprika has a lighter, slightly orange tint. Pimentón, as it is also known, is available in its sweet form as well as in two smoked varieties: sweet and hot. The smoked paprika is created by drying ripe red chile peppers slowly, according to tradition, over smoldering oak fires for upwards of two weeks. (Regular paprika is air-dried in the sun or by machine.) In their two simplest categories, sweet and smoked paprika both have their place, with smoked hot being more of a specialty product. Paprika is a large contributor of flavor in our harissa recipe (see page 17) and rounds out the fresh peppers in Spicy Roasted Red Pepper Whipped Feta (page 154).

RAS EL HANOUT

This North African blend delivers complex flavor from a mix of warm spices. It translates as "head of the shop" because traditionally each blend was a unique combination of some 25 spices, seeds, dried flowers, berries, and nuts determined by the spice shop's proprietor. Blends can include spices as varied as cumin, saffron, cinnamon, nutmeg, dried rose petals, galangal, and paprika.

ROSE

When we use floral rose as a spice in the test kitchen, we use it in the form of dried rosebuds, not the petals; food-grade buds are much easier to find at spice shops and specialty markets. In addition to being used for Rose Harissa (page 118), rosebuds beautifully season savory dishes like Carrot and Beet Salad with Rose Harissa (page 56).

SAFFRON

Saffron is made from the dried stigmas of *Crocus sativus* flowers; the stigmas are so delicate they must be harvested by hand in a painstaking process. (It takes about 200 hours to pick enough stigmas to produce just 1 pound of saffron, which typically sells for thousands of dollars.) Luckily, a little saffron goes a long way, adding a distinct reddish-gold color, notes of honey and grass, and a slight hint of bitterness to dishes in Spanish and Middle Eastern and North African cuisines. Though the bulk of commercially produced saffron comes from Spain and Iran, it is also harvested on a small scale in India, Greece, France, and even Lancaster County, Pennsylvania.

SESAME SEEDS

Look for these seeds on pastries (see page 140), ground into tahini, in spice blends like Za'atar (page 15), or as a finisher. These oily seeds from a sesame plant can be grayish ivory, brown, red, or black and are used in both savory and sweet recipes.

SUMAC

Ground sumac is made from dried berries that are harvested from a shrub grown in southern Europe and in the Middle East. It is an essential component of za'atar, but it's also used as an ingredient in spice rubs or sprinkled over foods as a finishing touch like in Fattoush with Butternut Squash and Apple (page 28). It's bright, with a clean, citrusy flavor and a slight raisin-y sweetness—both more balanced and more complex-tasting than lemon juice. You can find both ground sumac and sumac berries, which you can grind yourself. (For more information on sumac, see page 29.)

TABIL

This Tunisian spice blend, which means "seasoning" or simply "coriander," can go in pretty much anything. Depending on who's blending it, it can range from simple to quite complex but its flavor profile is usually a bit warm, a bit garlicky, a bit earthy, and sometimes a bit nutty and spicy, so it lends complexity to dishes like Tabil Couscous with Sardines (page 239).

TURMERIC

Most of the world's turmeric is grown in India, where it has been cultivated for centuries. The portion of the plant that's above ground is green and leafy. The edible part is the underground stem, or rhizome. It's small and knobby, with dark orange flesh and a thin brown peel. It looks similar to ginger, another rhizome in the same family. It's possible to find the fresh stuff in some markets, and we use it in a turmeric yogurt dipping sauce (page 153). A key ingredient in spice blends, slightly bitter turmeric combines well with strong spices such as cinnamon, cumin, ginger, and coriander, and we use it as much for its striking golden color (see Tofu and Chickpea Flour Frittata on page 308) as we do for its flavor.

URFA PEPPER

This pepper native to Urfa, Turkey, is a cousin to Syrian Aleppo. It can also be called by the Kurdish name, Isot pepper. The pepper flake is spicier than Aleppo with a deep, smoky, chocolaty flavor, adding nuance as a finishing flavoring. It has a slight, pleasant oiliness when browned. It contrasts the sweetness of spiralized sweet potatoes (see page 120) and adds welcome heat to the pan sauce in our Lamb Chops with Tamarind Pan Sauce (page 405). (For more information on Urfa pepper, see page 50.)

ZA'ATAR

Za'atar is an aromatic eastern Mediterranean spice blend that is used as both a seasoning and a condiment. Thyme gives it a round herbal flavor, sumac provides lemony tartness, and sesame seeds lend richness and subtle crunch. (For more information on za'atar, see page 131.)

BALANCING ACT

Balancing multifarious flavors and textures in plant-forward meals makes them endlessly exciting. After all, the lively taste of all of this food is what makes eating the Mediterranean way for life a joy.

It's helpful to think of supporting ingredients in a dish in terms of flavor (like acidity, savor, and sweetness) or texture (crunch) categories. You'll find some examples of Mediterranean ingredients in the chart below: Some items are raw ingredients, some are condiments, some are spices. Pick from any two or three categories and you're on your way to elevating any vegetable, grain, or protein dish to something exciting. We've used these principles to inspire the composed dishes in the book. You can do the same with your own meals or the simple staple sides and proteins we've provided in the chapters—they're blank slates. Here are a few combinations to get you started.

- **Acidity** + **Heat** + **Richness** (see Hasselback Eggplant with Muhammara on page 99)
- **Warmth** + **Sweetness** + **Richness** (see Butternut Squash Steaks with Honey-Nut Topping on page 88)
- **Savor** + **Acidity** + **Freshness** (see Pearl Couscous with Chorizo and Chickpeas on page 169)
- **Heat** + **Sweetness** + **Freshness** (see Lamb Chops with Tamarind Pan Sauce on page 405)

ACIDITY	HEAT	WARMTH	RICHNESS	SAVOR	SWEETNESS	FRESHNESS	CRUNCH
Citrus Juice	Fresh Chiles	Cinnamon	Yogurt	Anchovies	Orange Juice	Raw Vegetables	Pomegranate Seeds
Vinegar	Dried Chile Pepper	Allspice	Olive oil	Capers	Pomegranate Seeds	Fresh Herbs	Nuts and Seeds
Pomegranate Molasses	Harissa	Ginger	Pesto	Olives	Honey	Scallions	Crispy Shallots
Pickled Vegetables or Fruits	Zhoug	Cloves	Feta Cheese	Parmesan Cheese	Caramelized Onion	Chives	Crispy Lentils
Tomato Products	Chermoula	Coriander	Mozzarella	Tomato Products	Dried Fruits	Citrus Juice	Raw Vegetables
Sumac	Chile Oil	Cumin	Nuts and Seeds	Nigella Seeds	Fresh Fruits	Chermoula	Pickled Vegetables
Preserved Lemon	Chorizo	Paprika	Tahini	Allium	Chutney	Salsa Verde	Za'atar
Tamarind		Baharat	Fried Egg	Mushrooms		Pesto	Dukkah
Vinaigrette		Ras el Hanout	Cured Meat			Zhoug	Bread Crumbs
Chutney		Hawaij					Pita Chips
							Fried Capers

SWEET POTATO SWITCH-UPS

Plant-based foods are delicious alone, usually carrying their own predominant flavor element off which to play. Here, we show three ways you can elevate and enliven simple sweet potato wedges (see page 100) with ingredient additions that represent different flavor categories. The sweet, earthy flavors of sweet potatoes get a boost from complementary warm spices and sharp contrasts of acidity and heat. The combinations can be used with any form of sweet potatoes (spiralized, roasted, boiled, mashed). Vegetables dressed up and balanced like this will be a beautiful, flavorful central element to your plate.

(1) Spicy Sweet Potato Wedges with Tahini Sauce and Crispy Lentils

- **Richness:** Tahini sauce is rich, savory, and lemony.
- **Heat:** A garnish of thinly sliced rings of Fresno peppers provides the sweet potatoes with heat and bite.
- **Crunch:** Crispy lentils add hearty crunch.

(2) Ras el Hanout Sweet Potato Wedges with Pomegranate Molasses and Pistachios

- **Warmth:** The spice rub rounds out the sweet, earthy flavor.
- **Acidity:** Pomegranate molasses is pleasantly bright and acidic.
- **Crunch:** Sweet pistachios add complementary crunch.

(3) Sweet Potato Wedges with Feta and Sumac

- **Richness:** Feta cheese has briny richness.
- **Acidity:** A sprinkle of sumac is a quick hit of lemony, acidic flavor.
- **Freshness:** Squeezing a lemon wedge over the potatoes freshens and brightens the dish.

MEDITERRANEAN ACCOMPANIMENTS

The Balancing Act section (see page 12) shows that a spice rub, a drizzle of a vibrant sauce, or a dollop of a piquant condiment can instantly boost a dish's flavor. These are the spice blends, sauces, and condiments we reference in recipes in this book. Feel free to use them as they're called for in our recipes or experiment with them to bring complexity to your own dishes.

SPICE BLENDS

Baharat
Makes about ½ cup

Baharat, the Arabic word for "spice," is the name of a spice blend found in dishes across North Africa and the Middle East. It's often also called seven spice blend, and the seven spices featured in our blend are those most commonly found, though there are regional variations. Some other versions include allspice or have a hint of floral flavor from rosebuds; in Palestine, you may find paprika or chile in the blend; in Turkey, the blend sometimes gets herbal notes from mint, oregano, and/or bay leaves. No matter the combination, the warm blend has an intense profile that befits meat dishes, legumes, and hearty vegetables.

- 3 (3-inch) cinnamon sticks, broken into pieces
- 4¾ teaspoons cumin seeds
- 1½ tablespoons coriander seeds
- 1 tablespoon black peppercorns
- 2 teaspoons whole cloves
- 1 tablespoon ground cardamom
- 2 teaspoons ground nutmeg

Process cinnamon sticks in spice grinder until finely ground, about 30 seconds. Add cumin seeds, coriander seeds, peppercorns, and cloves and process until finely ground, about 30 seconds. Transfer to bowl and stir in cardamom and nutmeg. (Baharat can be stored in airtight container at room temperature for up to 1 month.)

Dukkah
Makes ½ cup

Dukkah is an Egyptian blend used in the Middle East that contains spices, nuts, and seeds. It's traditionally sprinkled on olive oil as a dip for bread, but it also makes a great crunchy topping for dips, vegetables, or grain and bean salads, or a garnish for soup. There are several variations; this one hits lots of flavor and texture notes.

- 1½ teaspoons coriander seeds, toasted
- ¾ teaspoon cumin seeds, toasted
- ½ teaspoon fennel seeds, toasted
- 2 tablespoons sesame seeds, toasted
- 3 tablespoons shelled pistachios, toasted and chopped fine
- ½ teaspoon flake sea salt, such as Maldon
- ½ teaspoon pepper

Process coriander seeds, cumin seeds, and fennel seeds in spice grinder until finely ground, about 30 seconds. Add sesame seeds and pulse until coarsely ground, about 4 pulses; transfer to small bowl. Stir in pistachios, salt, and pepper. (Dukkah can be refrigerated for up to 3 months.)

Hawaij
Makes about ½ cup

This golden blend is found in Israeli cooking by way of its migration with Yemenite Jews and it both warms and colors dishes. While a multipurpose blend, it has a rich history of use in soups, stews, and curries in Yemen. The spices found in this recipe are common—the color comes from the generous amount of turmeric. Cloves are optional, found only in some versions, but we love the depth a small amount adds.

2½ tablespoons black peppercorns
2 tablespoons cumin seeds
1½ tablespoons coriander seeds
10 cardamom pods
6 whole cloves
1½ tablespoons ground turmeric

Process peppercorns, cumin seeds, coriander seeds, cardamom pods, and cloves in spice grinder until finely ground, about 30 seconds. Transfer to bowl and stir in turmeric. (Hawaij can be stored in airtight container at room temperature for up to 1 month.)

Ras el Hanout
Makes about ½ cup

Ras el hanout is a complex Moroccan spice blend that traditionally features a host of warm spices—and it's a very special blend in the cuisine. The name translates to "head of shop," and the blend was historically meant to represent a selection of the very best spices. It gives robust flavor to couscous dishes, soups, stews, braises, and more.

16 cardamom pods
4 teaspoons coriander seeds
4 teaspoons cumin seeds
2 teaspoons anise seeds
2 teaspoons ground dried Aleppo pepper
½ teaspoon allspice berries
¼ teaspoon black peppercorns
4 teaspoons ground ginger
2 teaspoons ground nutmeg
2 teaspoons ground cinnamon

Process cardamom pods, coriander seeds, cumin seeds, anise seeds, Aleppo, allspice, and peppercorns in spice grinder until finely ground, about 30 seconds. Stir in ginger, nutmeg, and cinnamon. (Ras el hanout can be stored in airtight container at room temperature for up to 1 month.)

Tabil
Makes about ½ cup

The word tabil sometimes translates to "coriander," so it's no surprise that coriander is the most prominent ingredient in this spice blend used in Tunisian cuisine. It lends Tunisian dishes a beautiful complex aroma.

3½ tablespoons coriander seeds
2 tablespoons plus 2 teaspoons caraway seeds
1 tablespoon plus 2 teaspoons cumin seeds

Combine all ingredients in bowl. (Tabil can be stored in airtight container at room temperature for up to 1 month.)

Za'atar
Makes about ½ cup

Za'atar is an aromatic eastern Mediterranean blend of herbs, spices, and seeds that is used as both a seasoning for cooked dishes and a raw condiment. Try sprinkling it on almost anything that could use a bright, lemony punch.

½ cup dried thyme, ground
2 tablespoons sesame seeds, toasted
1½ tablespoons ground sumac

Combine all ingredients in bowl. (Za'atar can be stored in airtight container at room temperature for up to 1 month.)

SAUCES

Tahini Sauce
Makes about 1¼ cups

Just a light drizzle of tahini sauce is enough to give any dish that could benefit from it nutty richness cut with lemony brightness. Some garlic also ensures that the sauce has bite.

- ½ cup tahini
- ½ cup water
- ¼ cup lemon juice (2 lemons)
- 2 garlic cloves, minced

Whisk all ingredients in bowl until combined. Season with salt and pepper to taste. Let sit until flavors meld, about 30 minutes. (Sauce can be refrigerated for up to 4 days.)

Garlic Yogurt Sauce
Makes about ½ cup

Almost any dish that asks for a cooling, creamy yogurt sauce would go nicely served with this one that's flavored gently with garlic, lemon, and herbs. To make a drizzleable version of this sauce, use regular plain yogurt.

- ½ cup plain Greek yogurt
- 1 tablespoon lemon juice
- 1 tablespoon chopped fresh mint
- 1 garlic clove, minced

Combine all ingredients in bowl and season with salt and pepper to taste. Serve. (Sauce can be refrigerated for up to 4 days.)

Avocado-Yogurt Sauce
Makes about 1¼ cups

This condiment is a plush accompaniment for our Loaded Sweet Potato Wedges with Tempeh (page 100), but a dollop is an excellent addition to a roasted salmon fillet or a vegetable or grain bowl. The rich avocado gets nice tang (and reinforcing creaminess) from the yogurt and lively flavor from cumin and lime.

- 1 ripe avocado, cut into ½-inch pieces
- ¼ cup plain yogurt
- 1 teaspoon lime juice
- ½ teaspoon ground cumin
- ⅛ teaspoon table salt
- ⅛ teaspoon pepper

Using sturdy whisk, mash and stir all ingredients together in bowl until as smooth as possible. Season with salt and pepper to taste. Serve.

Tahini-Yogurt Sauce
Makes about 1 cup

A cross between a bright yogurt sauce and a nutty, garlicky tahini sauce, this creamy sauce is an especially great accompaniment to roasted vegetables of all kinds.

- ⅓ cup tahini
- ⅓ cup plain Greek yogurt
- ¼ cup water
- 3 tablespoons lemon juice
- 1 garlic clove, minced
- ¾ teaspoon table salt

Whisk all ingredients in bowl until combined. Season with salt and pepper to taste. Let sit until flavors meld, about 30 minutes. (Sauce can be refrigerated for up to 4 days.)

CONDIMENTS

Anchoïade
Makes about 1¼ cups

This anchovy-enhanced aioli-like dip from Provence has a supersavory flavor and brightness that makes it great with crudités or seafood. We use it in inspired ways, as a topping for egg tortillas (see page 318) or fideos (see page 266).

- 2 large egg yolks
- 8 anchovy fillets, rinsed, patted dry, and minced
- 2 teaspoons Dijon mustard
- 2 teaspoons lemon juice
- 1 garlic clove, minced
- ¾ cup vegetable oil
- 1 tablespoon water
- ¼ teaspoon pepper
- ¼ cup extra-virgin olive oil

Process egg yolks, anchovies, mustard, lemon juice, and garlic in food processor until combined, about 20 seconds. With processor running, slowly drizzle in vegetable oil until combined, about 1 minute. Transfer to medium bowl and whisk in water and pepper. Whisking constantly, slowly drizzle in olive oil, then season with salt and pepper to taste. (Anchoiade can be refrigerated for up to 4 days.)

Basil Pesto
Makes about 1½ cups

Basil pesto, the famous Genovese sauce, isn't just for pasta and pizza. (Find pestos of all kinds, with other herbs and greens, and even potent ingredients like tomatoes, built into the recipes in this book.) A dollop is an enriching addition to soups and stews, and it can ably coat a host of other grains and beans, or finish a simple chicken breast or fish fillet with interest. Pounding the basil helps bring out its flavorful oils.

6	garlic cloves, unpeeled
½	cup pine nuts
4	cups fresh basil leaves
4	tablespoons fresh parsley leaves
1	cup extra-virgin olive oil
1	ounce Parmesan cheese, grated fine (½ cup)

1 Toast garlic in 8-inch skillet over medium heat, shaking skillet occasionally, until softened and spotty brown, about 8 minutes. When garlic is cool enough to handle, remove and discard skins and chop coarse. Meanwhile, toast pine nuts in now-empty skillet over medium heat, stirring often, until golden and fragrant, 4 to 5 minutes.

2 Place basil and parsley in 1-gallon zipper-lock bag. Pound bag with flat side of meat pounder or with rolling pin until all leaves are bruised.

3 Process garlic, pine nuts, and herbs in food processor until finely chopped, about 1 minute, scraping down sides of bowl as needed. With processor running, slowly add oil until incorporated. Transfer pesto to bowl, stir in Parmesan, and season with salt and pepper to taste. (Pesto can be refrigerated for up to 3 days or frozen for up to 3 months. To prevent browning, press plastic wrap flush to surface or top with thin layer of olive oil. Bring to room temperature before using.)

Harissa
Makes about ½ cup

Harissa is a traditional Tunisian condiment that is great for flavoring soups, sauces, and dressings or dolloping on lamb, hummus, eggs, and sandwiches. It's a hot sauce and then some, with lots of warm spice aroma and a garlicky bite. If you can't find Aleppo pepper, you can substitute ¾ teaspoon paprika and ¾ teaspoon finely chopped red pepper flakes.

6	tablespoons extra-virgin olive oil
6	garlic cloves, minced
2	tablespoons paprika
1	tablespoon ground coriander
1–3	tablespoons ground dried Aleppo pepper
1	teaspoon ground cumin
¾	teaspoon caraway seeds
½	teaspoon table salt

Combine all ingredients in bowl and microwave until bubbling and very fragrant, about 1 minute, stirring halfway through microwaving; let cool completely. (Harissa can be refrigerated for up to 4 days.)

Rose Harissa
Makes about ½ cup

Rose is a traditional addition to harissa in Tunisia, adding further complexity to this favorite condiment. Rose flavor comes from petals and rose water. Be sure to use food-grade dried rosebuds, which you can find at spice shops and specialty markets. This recipe can be easily doubled.

- 6 tablespoons extra-virgin olive oil
- ¼ cup paprika
- 1½ tablespoons ground dried Aleppo pepper
- 1 tablespoon ground coriander
- 3 garlic cloves, minced
- ½ teaspoon ground cumin
- ½ teaspoon caraway seeds
- ½ teaspoon table salt
- 2 tablespoons crumbled dried rosebuds, stems removed
- 1¼ teaspoons rose water

Combine oil, paprika, Aleppo pepper, coriander, garlic, cumin, caraway, and salt in bowl and microwave until bubbling and very fragrant, about 1 minute, stirring halfway through microwaving. Whisk in rosebuds and rose water; let cool completely. (Rose harissa can be refrigerated for up to 4 days.)

Preserved Lemons
Makes 4 preserved lemons

Moroccan preserved lemons show how transformative salt can be. Once preserved in salt, lemon becomes an almost completely different ingredient, an incredible, versatile condiment: The lemon rinds become soft and aromatic and can be sliced thin or minced before adding to a dish. Their bright, ultralemony flavor, balanced by brininess and sourness, adds great interest to stews, salad dressings, cooked grains, sautéed vegetables, and more. Look for Meyer lemons from August through March; regular lemons can be substituted. Wash, scrub, and dry the lemons well before preserving them. You will need a 1-quart glass jar with a tight-fitting lid for this recipe.

- 12 lemons, preferably Meyer
- ½ cup kosher salt

1 Wash and dry 4 lemons. Cut lengthwise into quarters, stopping 1 inch from bottom so lemons stay intact at base. Juice remaining 8 lemons to yield 1½ cups juice; set aside any extra juice.

2 Gently stretch 1 cut lemon open and pour 2 tablespoons salt into center. Working over bowl, gently rub cut surfaces of lemon together, then place lemon in 1-quart jar. Repeat with remaining cut lemons and remaining salt. Add any accumulated salt and juice in bowl to jar.

3 Pour 1½ cups lemon juice into jar and press gently to submerge lemons. (Add reserved extra juice to jar as needed to cover lemons completely.) Cover jar tightly with lid and shake. Refrigerate lemons, shaking jar once per day for first 4 days to redistribute salt and juice. Let lemons cure in refrigerator until glossy and softened, 6 to 8 weeks. (Preserved lemons can be refrigerated for at least 6 months.)

4 To use, cut off desired amount of preserved lemon. If desired, use knife to remove pulp and white pith from rind before using.

Pink Pickled Turnips
Makes 4 cups

Refreshing and crunchy, pink pickled turnips are a staple in Middle Eastern cuisine. Because they are traditionally served with robust foods like falafel or ta'ameya (see page 287), these are mild, seasoned with just a bit of garlic, allspice, and black peppercorns. The turnips get their vibrant fuchsia hue from beets that accompany them in the brine. And the beets eventually become pickled and make for a tasty treat. The turnips need to be refrigerated for two days before serving. If using a glass storage container, be sure to fill it with hot water to warm, then drain it before packing with vegetables. The turnips need to be refrigerated for two days to allow the brine to fully penetrate and pickle the vegetable. These pickled turnips cannot be processed for long-term storage.

1¼ cups white wine vinegar

1¼ cups water

2½ tablespoons sugar

1½ tablespoons canning and pickling salt
(see page 324)

3 garlic cloves, smashed and peeled

¾ teaspoon whole allspice berries

¾ teaspoon black peppercorns

1 pound turnips, peeled and cut into
2 by ½-inch sticks

1 small beet, trimmed, peeled, and
cut into 1-inch pieces

1 Bring vinegar, water, sugar, salt, garlic, allspice, and peppercorns to boil in medium saucepan over medium-high heat. Cover, remove from heat, and let steep for 10 minutes. Strain brine through fine-mesh strainer, then return to saucepan.

2 Place two 1-pint jars in bowl and place under hot running water until heated through, 1 to 2 minutes; shake dry. Pack turnips vertically into hot jars with beet pieces evenly distributed throughout.

3 Return brine to brief boil. Using funnel and ladle, pour hot brine over vegetables to cover. Let jars cool to room temperature, cover with lids, and refrigerate for at least 2 days before serving. (Pickled turnips can be refrigerated for up to 1 month; turnips will soften over time.)

Quick-Pickled Onions

Makes 1 cup

If you keep some quick-pickled onions on hand, you'll always be able to awaken rich dishes with tartness and bite. They are easy to make, keep well, and have endless uses.

1 cup red wine vinegar

⅓ cup sugar

¼ teaspoon table salt

1 red onion, halved and sliced thin

Bring vinegar, sugar, and salt to simmer in small saucepan over medium-high heat, stirring occasionally, until sugar has dissolved. Off heat, stir in onion, cover, and let cool completely, about 1 hour. Serve. (Pickled onions can be refrigerated in airtight container for up to 1 week.)

Sumac Onions

Makes about 2 cups

These generously sized marinated onion slices are a robust sandwich or salad accompaniment. In addition to being dressed with lemon juice and red wine vinegar, the Middle Eastern condiment also gets a generous seasoning of puckery sumac. Olive oil and a little sugar and salt balance the flavors.

1 red onion, halved and sliced through
root end into ¼-inch pieces

2 tablespoons lemon juice

2 tablespoons red wine vinegar

1 tablespoon extra-virgin olive oil

1 tablespoon ground sumac

½ teaspoon sugar

¼ teaspoon table salt

Combine all ingredients in bowl. Let sit, stirring occasionally for 1 hour. (Onions can be refrigerated for up to 1 week).

Green Zhoug

Makes about ½ cup

Zhoug is an Israeli hot sauce that can be either red or green. Our vibrant green version is made with fresh herbs, chiles, and spices. We like it with fish or drizzled on soups or sandwiches.

6 tablespoons extra-virgin olive oil

½ teaspoon ground coriander

¼ teaspoon ground cumin

¼ teaspoon ground cardamom

¼ teaspoon table salt
Pinch ground cloves

¾ cup fresh cilantro leaves

½ cup fresh parsley leaves

2 green Thai chiles, stemmed and chopped

2 garlic cloves, minced

1 Microwave oil, coriander, cumin, cardamom, salt, and cloves in covered bowl until fragrant, about 30 seconds; let cool completely.

2 Pulse oil-spice mixture, cilantro, parsley, chiles, and garlic in food processor until coarse paste forms, about 15 pulses, scraping down sides of bowl as needed. (Zhoug can be refrigerated for up to 4 days.)

Mostly Plants

CRISPY ARTICHOKE SALAD WITH LEMON VINAIGRETTE

SERVES
4

40 MINS

3 cups jarred whole baby artichokes packed in water, halved, rinsed, and patted dry

3 tablespoons cornstarch

1 cup extra-virgin olive oil for frying

1 tablespoon lemon juice

¾ teaspoon Dijon mustard

¾ teaspoon minced shallot

Pinch table salt

4 teaspoons extra-virgin olive oil

2 ounces (2 cups) mizuna or baby arugula

¾ cup frozen peas, thawed

1 teaspoon Za'atar (page 15)

WHY THIS RECIPE WORKS Flower-like artichokes are beloved across the Mediterranean, where they're stuffed, steamed, and even infused into liquor. And they're fried. Taking inspiration from irresistible recipes like the ultracrispy Jewish fried artichokes of Rome and the poppable Syrian version, we bring these textural marvels to the table and turn them into a light meal that's easy and unintimidating. In Mediterranean countries, the artichoke may be so revered because of the work that goes into preparing the delicacy; here, however, we savor the taste without the work by using jarred artichoke hearts. We toss them in cornstarch and fry them until crispy but still moist. The salad gets a lot of its different flavors from vegetables alone, with the fried artichokes sitting on a bed of spicy, mustardy mizuna leaves and sweet peas in a lemony dressing. A finishing sprinkle of za'atar adds more tartness and a bit more crunch. The salad's careful balance of richness with freshness makes it a lovely light meal, or it can serve as a side to roast chicken or fish for a lively spring dinner.

1 Toss artichokes with cornstarch in bowl to coat. Heat 1 cup oil in 12-inch skillet over medium heat until shimmering. Shake excess cornstarch from artichokes and carefully add to skillet in single layer. Cook, stirring occasionally, until golden and crisp all over, 5 to 7 minutes. Using slotted spoon, transfer artichokes to paper towel–lined plate to cool slightly, about 10 minutes.

2 Whisk lemon juice, mustard, shallot, and salt together in bowl. Whisking constantly, slowly drizzle in 4 teaspoons oil until emulsified. Toss mizuna, peas, and 2 tablespoons vinaigrette together in large bowl. Transfer to serving platter and top with artichokes, drizzle with remaining vinaigrette, and sprinkle with za'atar. Serve.

*Cals 190 | Total Fat 12g | Sat Fat 1.5g
Chol 0mg | Sodium 330mg
Total Carb 16g | Dietary Fiber 3g
Total Sugars 2g | Protein 4g*

CARROT AND SMOKED SALMON SALAD

2 pounds carrots with greens attached, divided, ¼ cup greens chopped

5 tablespoons cider vinegar, divided

1 tablespoon sugar

⅛ teaspoon plus ¾ teaspoon table salt, divided

¼ cup extra-virgin olive oil, divided

¼ teaspoon pepper

1 red grapefruit

2 tablespoons chopped fresh dill

2 teaspoons Dijon mustard

2 heads Belgian endive (4 ounces each), halved, cored, and sliced ½ inch thick

8 ounces smoked salmon

WHY THIS RECIPE WORKS If carrots seem conventional, try this salad that uses all of the carrot (greens and root) in multiple ways. Carrots with their greens attached are sweeter than bagged carrots, and their feathery greens are fresh and slightly bitter, like parsley—a shame to waste. We pickle ribbons of carrots for a bite and roast the remaining carrots to bring out their sweetness. Tossing the roasted carrots with a Dijon-dill vinaigrette while slightly warm allows them to absorb a lot of flavor. We introduce smoked salmon to this mealworthy recipe, which adds flavor, salt, and welcome richness without an overwhelming presence. (Its orange color doesn't hurt the aesthetic, either.) Finally, we incorporate raw endive for its crisp bite and color contrast and grapefruit for sweet-tart flavor. The chopped carrot greens get tossed into this shining salad. Parsley can be substituted for the carrot greens. You should have about 1½ pounds of carrots after trimming the carrot greens.

1 Adjust oven rack to lowest position and heat oven to 450 degrees. Peel and shave 4 ounces carrots into thin ribbons with vegetable peeler; set aside. Peel and slice remaining carrots on bias ¼ inch thick; set aside.

2 Microwave ¼ cup vinegar, sugar, and ⅛ teaspoon salt in bowl until simmering, 1 to 2 minutes. Stir in shaved carrots, then let sit, stirring occasionally, for 45 minutes. (Drained pickled carrots can be refrigerated for up to 5 days.)

3 Toss sliced carrots with 1 tablespoon oil, pepper, and ½ teaspoon salt in bowl, then spread in single layer on rimmed baking sheet, cut side down. Roast until tender and bottoms are well browned, 15 to 25 minutes. Let cool slightly, about 15 minutes.

4 Meanwhile, cut away peel and pith from grapefruit. Quarter grapefruit, then slice crosswise into ¼-inch-thick pieces.

5 Whisk dill, mustard, remaining 1 tablespoon vinegar, and remaining ¼ teaspoon salt together in large bowl. Whisking constantly, slowly drizzle in remaining 3 tablespoons oil until emulsified. Add endive, carrot greens, roasted carrots, pickled carrots, and grapefruit and toss to combine; season with salt and pepper to taste. Arrange salmon around edge of serving platter, then transfer salad to center of platter. Serve.

Cals 210 | Total Fat 11g | Sat Fat 1.5g
Chol 10mg | Sodium 710mg
Total Carb 19g | Dietary Fiber 6g
Total Sugars 9g | Protein 9g

BEET SALAD WITH SPICED YOGURT AND WATERCRESS

SERVES 4 TO 6

50 MINS

2 pounds beets, trimmed, peeled, and cut into ¾-inch pieces

1⅛ teaspoons table salt, divided

1¼ cups plain Greek yogurt

¼ cup minced fresh cilantro, divided

3 tablespoons extra-virgin olive oil, divided

2 teaspoons grated fresh ginger

1 teaspoon grated lime zest plus 2 tablespoons juice, divided

1 garlic clove, minced

½ teaspoon ground cumin

½ teaspoon ground coriander

¼ teaspoon pepper

5 ounces (5 cups) watercress, torn into bite-size pieces

¼ cup shelled pistachios, toasted and chopped, divided

WHY THIS RECIPE WORKS Beets are mainstays of the eastern Mediterranean, and they appear frequently in yogurt-dressed salads. Some are chunky and some are more like textured purees, but these earthy-sweet vegetables benefit from the tangy richness of yogurt any way you dress them. Here, yogurt flavored with lime juice and warmed with spices is an ultracreamy landing pad for beets and watercress in a substantial salad plated with panache. Steaming cubes of beets in the microwave achieves concentrated sweetness (unlike with boiling) with speed (unlike with pan-steaming or roasting). Lightly dressing the silky, tender beets along with the watercress, piling them on our yogurt schmear, and sprinkling with pistachios makes for a stunning presentation and also keeps the colors separate. A swipe through this salad is a cool, creamy, earthy, tangy, sweet treat.

1 Combine beets, ⅓ cup water, and ½ teaspoon salt in large bowl. Cover and microwave until beets can be easily pierced with paring knife, 25 to 30 minutes, stirring halfway through microwaving. Drain beets in colander and let cool.

2 Whisk yogurt, 3 tablespoons cilantro, 2 tablespoons oil, ginger, lime zest and 1 tablespoon juice, garlic, cumin, coriander, pepper, and ½ teaspoon salt together in bowl. Slowly stir in up to 3 tablespoons water until mixture has consistency of regular yogurt. Season with salt and pepper to taste. Spread yogurt mixture over serving platter.

3 Toss watercress with 2 tablespoons pistachios, 2 teaspoons oil, 1 teaspoon lime juice, and pinch salt in large bowl. Arrange watercress mixture over top of yogurt mixture, leaving 1-inch border of yogurt mixture. Toss beets with remaining 1 teaspoon oil, remaining 2 teaspoons lime juice, and remaining pinch salt in now-empty bowl. Arrange beet mixture over top of watercress mixture. Sprinkle salad with remaining 1 tablespoon cilantro and remaining 2 tablespoons pistachios and serve.

Cals 212 | Total Fat 13g | Sat Fat 3g
Chol 8mg | Sodium 580mg
Total Carb 19g | Dietary Fiber 5g
Total Sugars 13g | Protein 9g

FATTOUSH WITH BUTTERNUT SQUASH AND APPLE

SERVES
4 TO 6

1½ HRS

2   (8-inch) pita breads,
    halved crosswise

½   cup extra-virgin olive oil,
    divided

⅛   plus ¾ teaspoon table salt,
    divided

⅛   teaspoon pepper

2   pounds butternut squash,
    peeled, seeded, and cut
    into ½-inch pieces

3   tablespoons lemon juice

4   teaspoons ground sumac,
    plus extra for serving

1   garlic clove, minced

1   apple, cored and cut into
    ½-inch pieces

¼   head radicchio, cored and
    chopped (1 cup)

½   cup chopped fresh parsley

4   scallions, sliced thin

WHY THIS RECIPE WORKS Flatbreads are a mainstay of tables across the Mediterranean, but the thin breads stale quickly, so creative dishes designed to use them up abound. Such recipes are called fatteh, derived from the Arabic word "fatta," meaning "to crumble." Pita bread salad, or fattoush, is a common example—and its appeal goes far beyond leftovers. The vibrant mix is simple but a textural marvel, combining crumbled toasted, fried, or day-old bread with summertime produce (tomatoes and cucumbers), fresh herbs, and greens, all simply dressed with lemon juice and olive oil and lavished with sumac. We thought about how to carry the experience into the colder months, when tomatoes and cucumbers aren't at their peak. We conjured a combination with distinctly fall flavors that still boasts fantastic contrasts in texture. Crisp sweet apples and slightly bitter radicchio provide fresh crunch, while roasted butternut squash gives the salad complexity and is a caramelized, soft, creamy foil to the crisp pieces of pita. We prefer a sweeter crisp apple like Pink Lady or Fuji to complement the bright lemony dressing.

1 Adjust oven racks to middle and lowest positions and heat oven to 375 degrees. Using kitchen shears, cut around perimeter of each pita and separate into 2 thin rounds. Cut each round in half. Place pitas smooth side down on wire rack set in rimmed baking sheet. Brush rough side of pitas evenly with 3 tablespoons oil, then sprinkle with ⅛ teaspoon salt and pepper. (Pitas do not need to be uniformly coated with oil.) Bake on upper rack until pitas are crisp and pale golden brown, 8 to 12 minutes. Let cool completely.

2 Increase oven temperature to 450 degrees. Toss squash with 1 tablespoon oil and ½ teaspoon salt. Spread in even layer on rimmed baking sheet and roast on lower rack until browned and tender, 20 to 25 minutes, stirring halfway through. Set aside to cool slightly, about 10 minutes.

3 Whisk lemon juice, sumac, garlic, and remaining ¼ teaspoon salt together in small bowl and let sit for 10 minutes. Whisking constantly, slowly drizzle in remaining ¼ cup oil.

4 Break cooled pitas into ½-inch pieces and place in large bowl. Add roasted squash, apple, radicchio, parsley, and scallions. Drizzle dressing over salad and toss gently to coat. Season with salt and pepper to taste. Serve, sprinkling individual portions with extra sumac.

Cals 310 | Total Fat 19g | Sat Fat 2.5g
Chol 0mg | Sodium 460mg
Total Carb 33g | Dietary Fiber 4g
Total Sugars 7g | Protein 4g

Spice with Sour

Ground sumac is made from dried berries that are harvested from a shrub grown in southern Europe and in the Middle East. It's bright, with a clean, citrusy flavor and a slight raisiny sweetness—both more balanced and more complex-tasting than lemon juice. Try adding it when dishes need pucker. Sumac can be used as an ingredient in spice rubs or sprinkled over foods as a finishing touch. Liven up dry rubs and dressings or sprinkle it over vegetables, grilled meats, stews, eggs, and even popcorn so as not to mute its bright flavor. You can find both ground sumac and sumac berries, which you can grind yourself.

PANZANELLA WITH FIDDLEHEADS

SERVES
4 TO 6

50 MINS

1   pound fiddleheads, trimmed and cleaned

½   teaspoon table salt, divided, plus salt for blanching fiddleheads

6   ounces ciabatta or sourdough bread, cut into ¾-inch pieces (4 cups)

½   cup extra-virgin olive oil, divided

1   garlic clove, minced to paste

½   teaspoon pepper, divided

¼   cup red wine vinegar

5   ounces grape tomatoes, halved

2   ounces goat cheese, crumbled (½ cup)

1/4   cup chopped fresh basil

WHY THIS RECIPE WORKS While one thinks of panzanella as a salad of fresh tomatoes and bread, early versions didn't include tomatoes. Panzanella was originally a way for Tuscans to extend the use of their precious loaves of bread; the stale bread was simply soaked in water and any vegetables were tossed in. Here is a new variation, a bread salad abundant with bright green fiddleheads that showcases the spiraled vegetable's arresting appearance and unique flavor and texture, and moves tomatoes to a supporting role. Blanching the fiddleheads first ensures that they're fully clean and also turns them a vivid green. We toss them with rich, chewy-crispy croutons, sweet grape tomatoes, and a simple vinaigrette; the sweetness and tang complement the fiddleheads. Fresh basil and creamy goat cheese finish this beautiful, hearty salad. Be sure to set up the ice water bath before cooking the fiddleheads; plunging them into the cold water immediately after blanching retains their bright green color and ensures that they don't overcook.

1 Bring 4 quarts water to boil in large pot. Fill large bowl halfway with ice and water. Add fiddleheads and 1 tablespoon salt to boiling water and cook until crisp-tender, about 5 minutes. Using spider skimmer or slotted spoon, transfer fiddleheads to ice bath and let sit until cool, about 2 minutes. Transfer fiddleheads to plate lined with triple layer of paper towels and dry well.

2 Toss bread, 3 tablespoons water, and ¼ teaspoon salt together in large bowl, squeezing bread gently until water is absorbed. Cook bread mixture and ¼ cup oil in 12-inch nonstick skillet over medium-high heat, stirring often, until browned and crisp, 7 to 10 minutes.

3 Off heat, push bread to sides of skillet. Add 1 tablespoon oil, garlic, and ¼ teaspoon pepper and cook using residual heat of skillet, mashing mixture into skillet, until fragrant, about 10 seconds. Stir bread into garlic mixture, then transfer croutons to bowl to cool slightly, about 5 minutes.

4 Whisk vinegar, remaining 3 tablespoons oil, remaining ¼ teaspoon salt, and remaining ¼ teaspoon pepper in large bowl until combined. Add fiddleheads, croutons, and tomatoes and toss gently to coat. Season with salt and pepper to taste. Transfer to serving platter and sprinkle with goat cheese and basil. Serve.

Cals 290 | Total Fat 21g | Sat Fat 4g
Chol 5mg | Sodium 360mg
Total Carb 17g | Dietary Fiber 0g
Total Sugars 1g | Protein 8g

Pretty to Eat

Fiddleheads are the most beautiful of foraged greens. These tightly coiled ferns are so-named for their resemblance to the scroll of a violin. Their brief annual appearance (two to three weeks in any given area) signals the true beginning of spring. Find these coiled greens at farmers' markets and, increasingly, supermarkets. Look for fiddleheads that are tightly coiled and bright green with no browning, with bits of their brown, papery sheath clinging to them. Store them in a plastic produce bag in the refrigerator for just a few days. Never eat fiddleheads raw; they should always be blanched before they're used in a recipe.

CHOPPED VEGETABLE AND STONE FRUIT SALAD

SERVES
4 TO 6

30 MINS

1 pound ripe but firm plums, nectarines, peaches, or apricots, halved, pitted, and chopped

½ teaspoon plus ⅛ teaspoon table salt, divided

½ teaspoon sugar

2 tablespoons extra-virgin olive oil

2 tablespoons lemon juice

¼ teaspoon pepper

4 Persian cucumbers, quartered lengthwise and chopped

1 red bell pepper, stemmed, seeded, and chopped

4 radishes, trimmed and chopped

¼ cup minced fresh mint

¼ cup minced fresh parsley

1 shallot, minced

2 teaspoons ground sumac

WHY THIS RECIPE WORKS Nearly every cuisine of the eastern Mediterranean serves a refreshing, crunchy, raw chopped vegetable salad with most meals. Whether called shepherd's salad (çoban salatası), as in Turkey; country salad (salata baladi), as in Egypt; Arab salad (salat aravi), as in Israel; or one of many other names, this essential salad consists of finely chopped cucumbers, tomatoes, and parsley, dressed with lemon juice and olive oil. Some renditions add peppers, radishes, red onions and/or scallions, along with herbs or finishing spices. This version changes the sweet-tart axis of the salad, taking a cue from a version made at the eastern Mediterranean–inspired restaurant Sarma, in Somerville, Massachusetts, where stone fruit is substituted for the tomatoes. The sweet, juicy, somewhat meaty fruit interplays with the mildly spicy radishes and pepper and cooling cucumber to enliven any dish they accompany like rich roasted salmon fillets or lamb kebabs. Generous amounts of parsley, mint, and puckery sumac vivify the contrasts. Salting and lightly sugaring the fruit first helps intensify its flavor while also extracting some of the juice that would otherwise create a watery salad.

1 Toss plums with ½ teaspoon salt and sugar in bowl. Transfer to fine-mesh strainer and let drain for 15 minutes, tossing occasionally.

2 Whisk oil, lemon juice, pepper, and remaining ⅛ teaspoon salt together in large bowl. Add drained plums, cucumbers, bell pepper, radishes, mint, parsley, shallot, and sumac and gently toss to combine. Season with salt and pepper to taste, and serve immediately.

*Cals 110 | Total Fat 5g | Sat Fat 0.5g
Chol 0mg | Sodium 250mg
Total Carb 15g | Dietary Fiber 3g
Total Sugars 11g | Protein 2g*

PARSLEY-CUCUMBER SALAD WITH FETA, POMEGRANATE, AND WALNUTS

1 tablespoon pomegranate molasses

1 tablespoon red wine vinegar

¼ teaspoon table salt

⅛ teaspoon pepper

Pinch cayenne pepper

3 tablespoons extra-virgin olive oil

3 cups fresh parsley leaves

1 English cucumber, halved lengthwise and sliced thin

1 cup walnuts, toasted and chopped coarse, divided

1 cup pomegranate seeds, divided

4 ounces feta cheese, sliced thin

WHY THIS RECIPE WORKS There are many salads of the Mediterranean that rightfully treat herbs like other leafy greens, not just simple stir-ins or a flavorful garnish. In this pretty salad, a welcome generous quantity—3 cups—of parsley pairs well with sweet, crisp, nearly seedless English cucumber in terms of both flavor and texture. The salad is a refreshing accompaniment to rich grilled meats. A bracing vinaigrette, made from olive oil, sweet-tart pomegranate molasses, and red wine vinegar, brings layers of flavor, while adding a pinch of cayenne pepper to the dressing gives it a bit of heat. For a beautiful finishing touch and some richness, we top the salad with thinly sliced feta cheese, chopped toasted walnuts, and juicy, jewel-like pomegranate seeds.

Whisk pomegranate molasses, vinegar, salt, pepper, and cayenne together in large bowl. Whisking constantly, slowly drizzle in oil until emulsified. Add parsley, cucumber, ½ cup walnuts, and ½ cup pomegranate seeds and toss to coat. Season with salt and pepper to taste. Transfer to serving platter and top with feta, remaining ½ cup walnuts, and remaining ½ cup pomegranate seeds. Serve.

Cals 156 | Total Fat 12g | Sat Fat 4g
Chol 17mg | Sodium 296mg
Total Carb 10g | Dietary Fiber 2g
Total Sugars 6g | Protein 4g

CHOPPED VEGETABLE
VEGETABLE
AND # STONE
FRUIT SALAD

TRIPLE PEA SALAD

4 ounces sugar snap peas, strings removed, cut on bias into ½-inch pieces

½ teaspoon plus pinch table salt, divided, plus salt for blanching

9 ounces shell-on English peas, shelled (¾ cup)

5 tablespoons extra-virgin olive oil, divided

¼ cup plain Greek yogurt

2 tablespoons plus 1 teaspoon lemon juice, divided

1 garlic clove, minced

2 teaspoons Dijon mustard

¼ teaspoon pepper

2 ounces (2 cups) baby arugula

4 ounces snow peas, strings removed, sliced thin on bias

4 radishes, trimmed, halved, and sliced thin

⅓ cup fresh mint leaves, torn if large

WHY THIS RECIPE WORKS When peas, long a staple pulse of the Mediterranean, are in season, we avoid cooking them beyond the briefest blanch. They're perfect. This salad showcases three peas in a knockout salad. English peas add pops of earthy-sweet flavor, snap peas contribute lots of crunch, and snow peas provide a more delicate crispness and mineral-y notes. Other ingredients break up the legumes: Bright-red radishes contribute color and crunch, peppery baby arugula provides fluff and bulk, and lots of fresh mint leaves serve as a secondary salad green. We spread the dressing onto a dish and then place the salad on top. Constructed this way, the salad keeps its arresting appearance and can be tossed together at the table just before serving. This salad can be substantial on its own; great topped with a poached egg; or, with the peas and mint, it's a natural pairing for lamb chops. If you can't find fresh English peas, you can substitute ¾ cup of thawed frozen peas (there is no need to blanch them).

1 Fill large bowl halfway with ice and water. Nestle colander into ice bath. Bring 1 quart water to boil in medium saucepan over high heat. Add snap peas and 1 tablespoon salt and cook until snap peas are bright green and crisp-tender, about 1 minute. Using spider skimmer or slotted spoon, transfer snap peas to colander set in ice bath. Add English peas to boiling water and cook until bright green and tender, about 1½ minutes. Transfer to colander with snap peas and let sit until chilled, about 5 minutes. Lift colander from ice bath and transfer peas to plate lined with triple layer paper towels and dry well; set aside.

2 Whisk ¼ cup oil, yogurt, 2 tablespoons lemon juice, garlic, mustard, pepper, and ½ teaspoon salt together in bowl. Spread yogurt mixture over serving platter.

3 Toss arugula, snow peas, radishes, mint, and chilled peas with remaining 1 teaspoon lemon juice, remaining pinch salt, and remaining 1 tablespoon oil in separate large bowl. Arrange salad on top of yogurt mixture. Serve immediately, combining salad with yogurt mixture as you serve.

Cals 150 | Total Fat 12g | Sat Fat 2g
Chol 2mg | Sodium 256mg
Total Carb 8g | Dietary Fiber 3g
Total Sugars 3g | Protein 4g

SWEET POTATO SALAD WITH CUMIN, SMOKED PAPRIKA, AND ALMONDS

SERVES
6

1¼ HRS

- 3 pounds sweet potatoes, peeled and cut into ¾-inch pieces
- 6 tablespoons extra-virgin olive oil, divided
- 2 teaspoons table salt
- 3 scallions, sliced thin
- 3 tablespoons lime juice (2 limes)
- 1 jalapeño chile, stemmed, seeded, and minced
- 1 teaspoon ground cumin
- 1 teaspoon smoked paprika
- 1 teaspoon pepper
- 1 garlic clove, minced
- ½ teaspoon ground allspice
- ½ cup fresh cilantro leaves and stems, chopped coarse
- ½ cup whole almonds, toasted and chopped

WHY THIS RECIPE WORKS This vibrant potato salad stands out from the rest, boasting surprising yet harmonious contrasts at every turn. Here, we roast earthy sweet potatoes at a high temperature so their caramel flavor becomes concentrated and they develop browned exteriors and fluffy interiors. We let the roasted potatoes cool down (to protect their structural integrity) before dressing them confidently, in a vinaigrette with explicitly strong flavors to contrast the sweetness: sharp scallions, punchy lime juice, spicy minced jalapeño, ground cumin to amplify the earthiness, smoked paprika, black pepper, pungent minced garlic, ground allspice for unbeatable complexity, and, of course, olive oil. For texture, some toasted, chopped almonds also enter the dressing as does a wealth of coarsely chopped fresh cilantro. Serve this salad for a light meal, paired with another salad like our Crispy Lentil and Herb Salad (page 204), or as a hearty dinner side.

1 Adjust oven rack to middle position and heat oven to 450 degrees. Toss potatoes with 2 tablespoons oil and salt, then transfer to rimmed baking sheet and spread into even layer. Roast until potatoes are tender and just beginning to brown, 30 to 40 minutes, stirring halfway through roasting. Let potatoes cool for 30 minutes.

2 Meanwhile, combine scallions, lime juice, jalapeño, cumin, paprika, pepper, garlic, allspice, and remaining ¼ cup oil in large bowl. Add cilantro, almonds, and potatoes and toss to combine. Serve.

Cals 309 | Total Fat 15g | Sat Fat 2g
Chol 0mg | Sodium 473mg
Total Carb 38g | Dietary Fiber 7g
Total Sugars 8g | Protein 5g

HORIATIKI SALATA

1¾ pounds ripe tomatoes, cored

1¼ teaspoons table salt, divided

½ red onion, sliced thin

2 tablespoons red wine vinegar

1 teaspoon dried oregano, plus extra for seasoning

½ teaspoon pepper

1 English cucumber, quartered lengthwise and cut into ¾-inch pieces

1 green bell pepper, stemmed, seeded, and cut into 2 by ½-inch strips

1 cup pitted kalamata olives

2 tablespoons capers, rinsed

¼ cup extra-virgin olive oil, plus extra for drizzling

1 (8-ounce) block feta cheese, sliced into ½-inch-thick triangles

WHY THIS RECIPE WORKS Bites of sweet tomatoes, briny olives, savory onion, crunchy cucumber, and tangy slabs of feta make this classic Greek salad—the real Greek salad. As with any ingredient-driven dish, sourcing high-quality components is important: Ripe, sweet tomatoes are essential. We toss halved tomato wedges with salt and set them in a colander to drain for 30 minutes. Soaking the onion slices in ice water lessens their hot bite. A creamy Greek feta brings richness to the lean vegetables. Dried oregano is the traditional choice: Its delicate flavor complements the vegetables and doesn't upstage them like fresh oregano could. It is customary to dress horiatiki salata with drizzles of oil and vinegar, but we did tweak the custom by tossing the vegetables with vinegar before drizzling with oil for even dressing. Use only large, round tomatoes here, not Roma or cherry tomatoes.

1 Cut tomatoes into ½-inch-thick wedges. Cut wedges in half crosswise. Toss tomatoes and ½ teaspoon salt together in colander set in large bowl. Let drain for 30 minutes. Place onion in small bowl, cover with ice water, and let sit for 15 minutes. Whisk vinegar, oregano, pepper, and remaining ¾ teaspoon salt together in second small bowl.

2 Discard tomato juice and transfer tomatoes to now-empty bowl. Drain onion and add to bowl with tomatoes. Add vinegar mixture, cucumber, bell pepper, olives, and capers and toss to combine. Drizzle with oil and toss gently to coat. Season with salt and pepper to taste. Transfer to serving platter and top with feta. Season each slice of feta with extra oregano to taste, and drizzle with extra oil. Serve.

*Cals 240 | Total Fat 19g | Sat Fat 7g
Chol 35mg | Sodium 980mg
Total Carb 10g | Dietary Fiber 3g
Total Sugars 6g | Protein 7g*

Greek Feta

What makes Greek feta so good? First, the milk itself is rich and complex: At least 70 percent of it must be sheep's milk, which contains twice as much fat as cow's milk; any remainder must be goat's milk. Because Greek sheep and goats eat uniquely diverse diets, their milks contain fatty acids that impart distinctively gamy, savory flavors to the feta. Second, Greek feta is produced via a slower, more methodical process that encourages the development of exceptionally complex flavors.

FETA, JICAMA, AND TOMATO SALAD

SERVES 4 TO 6

50 MINS

1¾ pounds ripe tomatoes, cored

¼ teaspoon table salt, plus salt for salting vegetables

½ red onion, sliced thin

3 tablespoons lime juice (2 limes)

1¼ teaspoons dried oregano, divided

¾ cup chopped fresh cilantro, divided

½ teaspoon pepper

12 ounces jicama, peeled and cut into ¼-inch pieces

6 radishes, trimmed and cut into ¼-inch pieces

1 cup pitted kalamata olives

¼ cup extra-virgin olive oil, plus extra for drizzling

1 (8-ounce) block feta cheese, sliced into ½-inch-thick triangles

WHY THIS RECIPE WORKS In Greece, traditional salad, Horiatiki Salata (page 40) is a simple presentation that celebrates abundant produce—and, of course, the banner feta cheese—and is always a welcome addition to the table. To change things up a bit, we created a version bringing in different crunchy elements. This salad pairs juicy tomatoes with another New World vegetable: jicama, a Central American root vegetable that is as crisp and cool as a cucumber, with a pleasant addition of subtle sweetness. Cubes of radish provide a contrasting bite and the whole thing is dressed with punchy lime juice and herbs to freshen up any meal it's shared with. Use only large, round tomatoes here, not Roma or cherry tomatoes.

1 Cut tomatoes into ½-inch-thick wedges. Cut wedges in half crosswise. Toss tomatoes and ½ teaspoon salt together in colander set in large bowl. Let drain for 30 minutes. Place onion in small bowl, cover with ice water, and let sit for 15 minutes. Whisk lime juice, 1 teaspoon oregano, ½ cup cilantro, pepper, and remaining ¼ teaspoon salt together in second small bowl.

2 Discard tomato juice and transfer tomatoes to now-empty bowl. Drain onion and add to bowl with tomatoes. Add lime mixture, jicama, radishes, and olives and toss to combine. Drizzle with oil and toss gently to coat. Season with salt and pepper to taste. Transfer to serving platter and top with feta. Sprinkle feta evenly with remaining ¼ teaspoon oregano and remaining ¼ cup cilantro. Serve, drizzling with extra oil.

Cals 250 | Total Fat 19g | Sat Fat 7g
Chol 35mg | Sodium 530mg
Total Carb 13g | Dietary Fiber 6g
Total Sugars 4g | Protein 7g

ROASTED PATTYPAN SQUASH SALAD WITH DANDELION GREEN PESTO

SERVES
4 TO 6

1 HR

Pesto

- 1 ounce dandelion greens, trimmed and torn into bite-size pieces (1 cup)
- 3 tablespoons roasted sunflower seeds
- 3 tablespoons water
- 1 tablespoon maple syrup
- 1 tablespoon cider vinegar
- 1 garlic clove, minced
- ¼ teaspoon table salt
- ⅛ teaspoon red pepper flakes
- ¼ cup extra-virgin olive oil

Salad

- 2 tablespoons extra-virgin olive oil
- 2 teaspoons maple syrup
- ½ teaspoon table salt
- ⅛ teaspoon pepper
- 1½ pounds baby pattypan squash, halved horizontally
- 4 ears corn, kernels cut from cob
- 1 pound ripe tomatoes, cored, cut into ½-inch-thick wedges, and wedges halved crosswise
- 1 ounce dandelion greens, trimmed and torn into bite-size pieces (1 cup)
- 2 tablespoons roasted sunflower seeds

WHY THIS RECIPE WORKS Pattypan squash tastes like zucchini but its unique shape gives it an advantage when it comes to providing texture. Pattypans come in different sizes; for this salad, we use baby green and yellow ones for their tender skin and vibrant flavor (some say the squash loses flavor as it matures). Before roasting the diminutive squashes, we cut them horizontally to make flower-shaped slabs, which we toss with just-off-the-cob corn in oil and maple syrup. We counter these fresh ingredients with an earthy-tasting pesto made from dandelion greens and roasted sunflower seeds. You can use baby arugula or watercress instead of dandelion greens. Use baby pattypan squashes that measure between 1½ and 2 inches in diameter. If you can't find baby pattypan squash, you can use zucchini or summer squash cut crosswise into 1-inch-thick rounds.

1 For the pesto Adjust oven rack to lowest position, place rimmed baking sheet on rack, and heat oven to 500 degrees. Process dandelion greens, sunflower seeds, water, maple syrup, vinegar, garlic, salt, and pepper flakes in food processor until finely ground, about 1 minute, scraping down sides of bowl as needed. With processor running, slowly drizzle in oil until incorporated. (Pesto can be refrigerated for up to 2 days.)

2 For the salad Whisk oil, maple syrup, salt, and pepper together in large bowl. Add squash and corn and toss to coat. Working quickly, spread vegetables in single layer on hot sheet, arranging squash cut side down. Roast until cut side of squash is browned and tender, 15 to 18 minutes. Transfer pan to wire rack and let cool slightly, about 15 minutes.

3 Combine roasted squash and corn, half of pesto, tomatoes, and dandelion greens in large bowl and toss gently to combine. Drizzle with remaining pesto and sprinkle with sunflower seeds. Serve.

Cals 270 | Total Fat 20g | Sat Fat 2.5g | Chol 0mg | Sodium 310mg Total Carb 24g | Dietary Fiber 4g | Total Sugars 12g | Protein 6g

HARISSA CARROT NOODLES

**SERVES
4**

15 MINS

¼ cup Harissa (page 17)

3 tablespoons lemon juice

2 tablespoons water

4 teaspoons honey

¼ teaspoon table salt

¼ teaspoon pepper

1½ pounds carrot noodles, cut into 6-inch lengths

4 cups (4 ounces) baby arugula

¼ cup chopped fresh mint, divided

4 ounces goat cheese, crumbled (1 cup)

¼ cup dried apricots, sliced thin

¼ cup pistachios, toasted and chopped

WHY THIS RECIPE WORKS Carrots work well with harissa. The naturally sweet vegetable can take the spice well and pairs with it in such recipes as Tunisian ommek hourria, a carrot caviar salad, or even our Carrot and Beet Salad with Rose Harissa (page 56). For this salad, we cut the carrots into noodles and give them a bright, fiery, and slightly sweet coating of harissa vinaigrette. Pairing the noodles with peppery arugula creates a boldly flavored salad with smoky heat and earthiness as well as transforms them into a light meal. Chopped mint provides contrasting freshness, while jammy bites of dried apricots echo the carrots' sweetness and provide chewy texture. Topping our jewel-colored bowl with crumbled goat cheese adds creaminess and tang that's the perfect contrast to the smoky carrot noodle base. You will need 2 pounds of carrots to get 1½ pounds of noodles; we prefer to make our own using a spiralizer, but in a pinch you can use store-bought. For the best results, use carrots that are at least ¾ inch wide at the thinnest end and 1½ inches wide at the thickest end.

Whisk harissa, lemon juice, water, honey, salt, and pepper together in large bowl. Add carrot noodles, arugula, and 3 tablespoons mint and toss to coat; season with salt and pepper to taste. Divide among individual serving bowls, then top with goat cheese, apricots, and pistachios and sprinkle with remaining 1 tablespoon mint. Serve.

*Cals 320 | Total Fat 18g | Sat Fat 6g
Chol 15mg | Sodium 550mg
Total Carb 34g | Dietary Fiber 8g
Total Sugars 21g | Protein 9g*

ROASTED VEGETABLE AND KALE SALAD WITH POMEGRANATE VINAIGRETTE

**SERVES
4 TO 6**

45 MINS

1½ pounds butternut squash, peeled, seeded, and cut into ¾-inch pieces (4½ cups)

1 fennel bulb, stalks discarded, bulb halved, cored, and cut into ¾-inch pieces

3 tablespoons extra-virgin olive oil, divided

¼ teaspoon table salt, divided

⅛ teaspoon ground cardamom

⅛ teaspoon ground cinnamon

⅛ teaspoon pepper, divided

1 pound sweet turkey sausage

8 ounces curly kale, stemmed and sliced crosswise into ½-inch-wide strips

2 tablespoons pomegranate molasses

1 tablespoon red wine vinegar

1 teaspoon honey

1 small shallot, minced

WHY THIS RECIPE WORKS We think salad can be comfort food even in winter if it's filled with roasted, rather than raw, robust winter vegetables and warm flavors. Here, butternut squash's sweet, creamy interior and fennel's satisfying crunch make the perfect duo, and we roast them with sweet, warm spices. Turkey sausage provides just a little richness to the salad. For a green, we use kale, which we soften quickly in warm water for tenderness. A sweet-tart pomegranate-honey vinaigrette accents the flavor of the squash and sausage. It's important to use very hot water (110 to 115 degrees) when soaking the kale or the leaves will be tough.

1 Adjust oven racks to upper-middle and lower-middle positions, place aluminum foil–lined rimmed baking sheet on each rack, and heat oven to 450 degrees. Toss squash, fennel, 1 tablespoon oil, ⅛ teaspoon salt, cardamom, cinnamon, and pinch pepper together in bowl. Working quickly, spread butternut squash mixture evenly over 1 hot sheet and place sausages on second hot sheet. Place sheet with sausage on lower rack and sheet with squash mixture on upper rack. Roast until sausage is spotty brown and registers 160 degrees, 10 to 15 minutes. Transfer sausage to cutting board.

2 Stir squash mixture on sheet and continue to roast until tender and spotty brown, 5 to 10 minutes. Once sausage has cooled slightly, slice ½ inch thick on bias.

3 Meanwhile, place kale in bowl, cover with very hot tap water, and let sit for 10 minutes. Swish kale around to remove grit, then drain and spin dry in salad spinner. Pat leaves dry with paper towels if still wet.

4 Whisk pomegranate molasses, vinegar, honey, shallot, remaining ⅛ teaspoon salt, and remaining pinch pepper together in bowl. Whisking constantly, slowly drizzle in remaining 2 tablespoons oil until emulsified. Toss kale with half of vinaigrette, then season with salt and pepper to taste. Divide among individual serving bowls, then top with roasted squash mixture and sliced sausage. Drizzle with remaining dressing. Serve.

*Cals 420 | Total Fat 20g | Sat Fat 4g
Chol 85mg | Sodium 870mg
Total Carb 37g | Dietary Fiber 7g
Total Sugars 16g | Protein 26g*

ROASTED CIPOLLINI AND ESCAROLE SALAD

SERVES 4 TO 6

1¼ HRS

1½ pounds cipollini onions

6 tablespoons extra-virgin olive oil, divided

¼ teaspoon table salt

⅛ teaspoon pepper

4 ounces thinly sliced prosciutto

2 tablespoons apple cider vinegar

2 teaspoons Dijon mustard

1½ teaspoons caraway seeds, toasted and cracked

1 teaspoon honey

1 head escarole (1 pound), trimmed and cut into 1-inch pieces

½ head frisée (3 ounces), trimmed and cut into 1-inch pieces

2 ounces blue cheese, crumbled (½ cup)

WHY THIS RECIPE WORKS In the world of onions, Italian cipollini are truly stellar. They're gentler and sweeter in flavor and aroma than regular yellow, white, or red onions, making them perfect for use in salads. With more residual sugars, they caramelize easily during roasting, creating a melt-in-your-mouth texture that contrasts beautifully with the crunch of crisp, slightly bitter escarole and frisée in this salad. Crispy prosciutto and creamy blue cheese add saltiness and make the salad a textured meal. A tangy dressing with cracked caraway seeds (a common pairing with cipollini) balances all the flavors. You can use prepeeled cipollini onions in this recipe; simply halve them through the root end and proceed with step 2.

1 Adjust oven rack to middle position and heat oven to 400 degrees. Bring 2 quarts water to boil in large saucepan. Add onions and cook for 30 seconds. Drain in colander and rinse with cold water until onions are cool enough to handle, about 1 minute. Transfer onions to paper towel–lined plate and pat dry. Trim root and stem ends, then peel and discard onion skins. Halve onions through root end and transfer to bowl.

2 Add 3 tablespoons oil, salt, and pepper to bowl with onions and toss to coat. Arrange onions, cut side down, on parchment paper–lined rimmed baking sheet and roast until well browned and softened, 35 to 40 minutes, rotating sheet halfway through roasting. Let cool slightly, about 10 minutes.

3 Place prosciutto in single layer between 2 layers of paper towels on plate and microwave until rendered and beginning to crisp, 2 to 4 minutes. Let cool slightly, then crumble into bite-size pieces.

4 Whisk vinegar, mustard, caraway seeds, and honey together in large bowl. Whisking constantly, slowly drizzle in remaining 3 tablespoons oil until emulsified. Add escarole, frisée, roasted onions, and prosciutto and toss to combine. Season with salt and pepper to taste. Transfer to serving platter and sprinkle with blue cheese. Serve.

Cals 290 | Total Fat 19g | Sat Fat 4.5g
Chol 20mg | Sodium 790mg
Total Carb 21g | Dietary Fiber 3g
Total Sugars 5g | Protein 10g

CANTALOUPE SALAD WITH OLIVES AND RED ONION

SERVES
4

20 MINS

½ red onion, halved and sliced thin

⅓ cup lemon juice (2 lemons)

1–3 teaspoons honey (optional)

1 teaspoon ground dried Aleppo pepper

½ teaspoon table salt

1 cantaloupe, peeled, halved, seeded, and cut into 1½-inch pieces (6 cups)

5 tablespoons chopped fresh parsley, divided

5 tablespoons chopped fresh mint, divided

¼ cup finely chopped pitted oil-cured olives, divided

WHY THIS RECIPE WORKS There's a reason that honey-like juicy melon benefits from pungent pairings, like watermelon and feta in Greece or cantaloupe wrapped in prosciutto in Italy. The sweetness of the fruit balances the saltiness of the rich ingredients, and the saltiness makes the fruit seem even sweeter and more explosively juicy. Here cantaloupe is the rightful star of the salad, with other components there to brighten the spotlight—pickled red onion for zing, chopped oil-cured olives to balance the melon's leanness, liberal parsley and mint for grassy freshness, and a lemony dressing with heat from Aleppo pepper. While it can be a refreshing summer snack, imagine this salad brightening your plate next to a pristine piece of white fish. If your melon is very sweet, omit the honey from the dressing.

Combine onion and lemon juice in large bowl and let sit for 5 minutes. Stir in honey, if using; Aleppo pepper; and salt. Add cantaloupe, ¼ cup parsley, ¼ cup mint, and 3 tablespoons olives and stir to combine. Sprinkle with remaining 1 tablespoon parsley, remaining 1 tablespoon mint, and remaining 1 tablespoon olives. Serve.

Pepper Flakes of the Middle East

We call for Aleppo pepper, also known as pul biber in Turkey ("pul" means "flake" and "biber" means "pepper"), quite often. The pepper flakes dried and crushed from Halaby chiles (the name meaning "from Aleppo") have slow-to-build heat, but just as profound is their raisin-like sweetness and tang. A good kitchen substitute is a combination of 3 parts paprika and 1 part cayenne pepper. A pepper flake close in heat and flavor if Aleppo is unavailable is Turkish Maras biberi (find it as Marash pepper as well). Urfa biber, also from Turkey, is a flake with more fire. Coming in at 30 to 50 thousand Scoville units (as opposed to around 10 thousand units for the aforementioned peppers) it's about as hot as cayenne. But its complexity in this heat range is hard to match; the dark brown-red flakes are extra smoky but also have hints of that raisiny sweetness.

Cals 54 | Total Fat 1g | Sat Fat 0g
Chol 0mg | Sodium 266mg
Total Carb 12g | Dietary Fiber 2g
Total Sugars 10g | Protein 1g

GRILLED PEACH AND TOMATO SALAD WITH BURRATA AND BASIL

**SERVES
4 TO 6**

1 HR

Peaches

1½ pounds ripe but slightly
    firm peaches, nectarines,
    or plums, halved and pitted

2   tablespoons extra-virgin
    olive oil

Salad

12 ounces ripe tomatoes, cored
    and cut into ½-inch pieces

¾   teaspoon table salt, divided

1   tablespoon white wine
    vinegar

5   tablespoons extra-virgin
    olive oil, divided

8   ounces burrata cheese,
    room temperature

⅓   cup chopped fresh basil

WHY THIS RECIPE WORKS When you're going to eat cheese, creamy, dreamy burrata is a particularly good choice that interweaves beautifully with vibrant vegetable and fruit dishes. The dairy-forward cheese nicely balances punchy, acidic ingredients and we like it here with peaches and tomatoes. Grilling the peaches softens their skin, caramelizes their sugars, and gives them a smoky flavor that elevates this summer salad. A simple vinaigrette of white wine vinegar and extra-virgin olive oil, along with a handful of fresh basil, naturally complements all of the other ingredients. Placing the burrata on top of the salad makes a beautiful presentation, with the stark white contrasting the colorful produce; breaking up the burrata with a spoon to serve allows the creamy liquid to meld with the dressing. This recipe can also be made with nectarines or plums.

1 For the peaches Brush cut side of peaches with oil.

2A For a charcoal grill Open bottom vent completely. Light large chimney starter three-quarters filled with charcoal briquettes (4½ quarts). When top coals are partially covered with ash, pour evenly over half of grill. Set cooking grate in place, cover, and open lid vent completely. Heat grill until hot, about 5 minutes.

2B For a gas grill Turn all burners to high; cover; and heat grill until hot, about 15 minutes. Leave primary burner on high and turn off other burner(s).

3 Clean and oil cooking grate. Arrange peaches cut side down on hotter side of grill and cook (covered if using gas) until grill marks have formed, 5 to 7 minutes, moving peaches as needed to ensure even cooking.

4 Transfer peaches cut side up to 13 by 9-inch baking pan and cover loosely with aluminum foil. Place pan on cooler side of grill. If using gas, turn primary burner to medium. Cover and cook until peaches are very tender and paring knife slips in and out with little resistance, 10 to 15 minutes. When peaches are cool enough to handle, discard skins, then let cool completely.

*Cals 342 | Total Fat 28g | Sat Fat 11g
Chol 49mg | Sodium 530mg
Total Carb 14g | Dietary Fiber 2g
Total Sugars 11g | Protein 11g*

5 For the salad While peaches cool, toss tomatoes with ¼ teaspoon salt and let drain in colander for 30 minutes. Cut each peach half into 4 wedges and cut each wedge in half crosswise.

6 Whisk vinegar and remaining ½ teaspoon salt together in large bowl. Whisking constantly, slowly drizzle in ¼ cup oil. Add peaches and tomatoes and toss gently to combine; transfer to shallow serving bowl. Place burrata on top of salad and drizzle with remaining 1 tablespoon oil. Season with pepper to taste, and sprinkle with basil. Serve, breaking up burrata with spoon.

Burrata

Imagine slicing open a tender ball of fresh mozzarella to find luscious, thick cream teeming with plush bits of curd. A mozzarella offshoot, burrata is made in much the same way, but before the ball is twisted and sealed, it's stuffed with a mixture of curd and cream. Cheesemakers in the Puglia region of Italy began making burrata in the early 20th century as a way to use up leftovers from the production of fresh mozzarella—the best kind of leftovers.

The Queen of Fruits

Figs trees are one of the most revered plants across the Mediterranean, a symbol of good health and good luck. One of the earliest fruits cultivated in the Mediterranean, figs thrive in this climate. Planting is easy: Planting a fig branch produces an identical tree. They're good for you too, nutrient-dense and packed with soluble fiber. They're commonly dried—their flavor desired all year and all around the world. There are more than 700 fig varieties. Among the figs you're most likely to find in an American supermarket are jammy, ultrasweet Black Mission figs (the Spanish fig that's one of the most valued); large, velvety Brown Turkey figs; and green, globe-like, deliciously sticky-sweet Turkish Calimyrna figs.

BITTER GREENS AND FIG SALAD WITH WARM SHALLOT DRESSING

SERVES
4

1 HR

Vinaigrette

- ¼ cup sherry vinegar
- 1 tablespoon Dijon mustard
- 1 tablespoon minced shallot
- 1 teaspoon minced fresh thyme
- ¼ teaspoon table salt
- ¼ teaspoon pepper
- 2 tablespoons extra-virgin olive oil

Salad

- 3 ounces thinly sliced prosciutto
- 2 tablespoons extra-virgin olive oil
- 8 shallots, peeled and quartered lengthwise

  Pinch table salt
- 8 fresh figs, halved and sliced thin
- ⅓ cup pine nuts
- 12 ounces (10–12 cups) bitter greens, such as escarole, chicory, and/or frisée, trimmed and cut into 1-inch pieces
- 1½ ounces Parmesan cheese, shaved

WHY THIS RECIPE WORKS Fresh figs thrive in the Mediterranean, their ultrasweet, perfumed honey flavor making them one of the most revered fruits—they're really something special. And while a plate of sun-soaked figs served with salty prosciutto and some cheese is a stellar snack, we wanted to make figs the focus of a fulfilling mealworthy salad. To match the strong flavors of figs and prosciutto, we created a wilted frisée and escarole salad with a rich warm dressing. Quartered shallots, sautéed until caramelized, play just as much a role as the figs here: They complement the sweet profile, as well as add a little allium bite. We crisp the prosciutto for textural contrast and create more crunch by adding rich pine nuts. The volume measurement of the greens may vary depending on the variety or combination used.

1 For the vinaigrette Whisk vinegar, mustard, shallot, thyme, salt, and pepper together in bowl. Whisking constantly, slowly drizzle in oil until emulsified.

2 For the salad Place prosciutto in single layer between 2 layers of paper towels on plate and microwave until rendered and beginning to crisp, 2 to 4 minutes. Let cool slightly, then crumble into bite-size pieces; set aside.

3 Heat oil in Dutch oven over medium heat until shimmering. Add shallots and salt and cook, stirring frequently, until browned and softened, 12 to 15 minutes. Add figs and pine nuts and continue to cook, stirring occasionally, until pine nuts are golden, 3 to 4 minutes longer. Remove pot from heat and let cool for 5 minutes.

4 Add half of vinaigrette to pot, then add half of greens and toss for 1 minute to warm and wilt. Add remaining greens followed by remaining vinaigrette and continue to toss until greens are evenly coated and warmed through, about 2 minutes longer. Season with salt and pepper to taste. Transfer greens to serving platter, top with prosciutto and Parmesan, and serve.

Cals 431 | Total Fat 26g | Sat Fat 5g | Chol 22mg | Sodium 817mg
Total Carb 37g | Dietary Fiber 10g | Total Sugars 19g | Protein 16g

CARROT AND BEET SALAD WITH ROSE HARISSA

SERVES
4 TO 6

50 MINS

1 pound beets, peeled and cut into ½-inch wedges

1 pound carrots, peeled and cut ¼ inch thick on bias

6 shallots, peeled and halved lengthwise

3 tablespoons Rose Harissa (page 18), divided

2 tablespoons extra-virgin olive oil

1 tablespoon grated lemon zest plus 2 tablespoons juice

½ teaspoon table salt

¼ teaspoon pepper

2 large eggs

¼ cup pitted oil-cured olives, halved

3 tablespoons chopped fresh parsley

¼ cup whole almonds, toasted and chopped

3 tablespoons crumbled rose petals

WHY THIS RECIPE WORKS Sometimes the Tunisian spicy red pepper paste harissa (see page 17) gets the floral treatment. Rose harissa is also a staple of the cuisine, and it's served with everything from grilled meats and couscous to roasted vegetables. Dried rosebuds and rosewater add delicate floral aroma and sweetness to counterbalance the chiles' heat and the spices' warmth. Rose harissa shows off in this colorful salad of roasted beets, carrots, and shallots. Roasting harissa-coated vegetables coaxes out their natural sweetness while deepening the harissa's complementary sweet heat. Tossing the still-warm vegetables with lemon zest and juice, parsley, and a fresh hit of harissa results in a beautifully balanced salad. Hard-cooked eggs and olives are traditional additions to Tunisian dishes and they make this salad substantial enough to be a light meal. Toasted almonds add textural contrast, and a scattering of dried rose petals gives the salad a fresh floral finish.

1 Adjust oven racks to upper-middle and lower-middle positions and heat oven to 450 degrees. Toss beets, carrots, and shallots with 1 tablespoon rose harissa, oil, lemon zest, salt, and pepper in large bowl. Spread in single layer over 2 rimmed baking sheets. (Do not wash bowl.) Roast until vegetables are tender and well browned on one side, 20 to 25 minutes (do not stir during roasting).

2 Meanwhile, bring 1 inch water to rolling boil in medium saucepan over high heat. Place eggs in steamer basket and transfer basket to saucepan. Cover, reduce heat to medium-low, and cook eggs for 13 minutes. When eggs are almost finished cooking, combine 2 cups ice cubes and 2 cups cold water in second bowl. Using tongs or slotted spoon, transfer eggs to ice bath and let sit for 15 minutes. Peel and quarter eggs. (Hard-cooked eggs can be refrigerated, peeled or unpeeled, for up to 3 days.)

3 Whisk lemon juice and remaining 2 tablespoons rose harissa in now-empty bowl. Transfer roasted vegetables to bowl with rose harissa mixture and toss to combine. Stir in olives and parsley and season with salt and pepper to taste. Transfer vegetables to serving platter, sprinkle with almonds and rose petals and arrange egg quarters over top. Serve.

Cals 250 | Total Fat 15g | Sat Fat 2g
Chol 60mg | Sodium 410mg
Total Carb 22g | Dietary Fiber 7g
Total Sugars 11g | Protein 6g

PERSIMMON AND BURRATA SALAD WITH PROSCIUTTO

SERVES 4 TO 6

30 MINS

- 2 ounces thinly sliced prosciutto, divided
- 2 tablespoons extra-virgin olive oil, divided
- 2 teaspoons lemon juice
- ⅛ teaspoon table salt

  Pinch pepper
- 1 pound ripe but firm Fuyu persimmons, stemmed, peeled if desired, and sliced ¼ inch thick
- 8 ounces burrata cheese, room temperature
- ½ cup fresh basil leaves, torn
- ¼ cup pomegranate seeds
- 2 teaspoons pomegranate molasses

  Flake sea salt

WHY THIS RECIPE WORKS Caprese salad is at its peak in late summer when juicy sweet-tart tomatoes still warm from the sun are paired with aromatic basil and slices of soft, creamy fresh mozzarella. This simple salad from Capri, Italy, is a classic for a reason, and we loved the idea of being able to enjoy this interplay of flavors and textures in the fall and winter with seasonal ingredients. We achieve the sweet-tart balance with juicy honey-scented persimmons and punchy pomegranate seeds. While pomegranates have been cultivated in the Mediterranean for millennia, persimmons are a newer arrival from Asia, but are popular in Italy, Israel, and parts of Turkey. To add richness to this cooler-season salad, we use chunks of creamy burrata instead of mozzarella and add pieces of prosciutto, some crisped up in the microwave, for meaty saltiness. A drizzle of pomegranate molasses balances the sweetness and acidity of the salad. The skins of Fuyu persimmons can be tough; if yours are particularly tough we recommend peeling them before slicing.

1 Place half of prosciutto in single layer between 2 layers of paper towels on plate and microwave until rendered and beginning to crisp, 2 to 4 minutes. Let cool slightly, then crumble into bite-size pieces.

2 Whisk 1 tablespoon oil, lemon juice, salt, and pepper together in large bowl. Add persimmons and gently toss to coat.

3 Arrange persimmons on serving platter, then drizzle any remaining dressing from bowl over top. Tear remaining half of prosciutto into bite-size pieces and arrange on top of persimmons. Cut burrata into 1-inch pieces, collecting creamy liquid, and arrange with liquid on top of persimmons and prosciutto. Sprinkle with basil, pomegranate seeds, and crispy prosciutto. Drizzle with pomegranate molasses and remaining 1 tablespoon oil. Season with sea salt and pepper to taste. Serve.

Cals 360 | Total Fat 23g | Sat Fat 10g
Chol 55mg | Sodium 640mg
Total Carb 27g | Dietary Fiber 1g
Total Sugars 1g | Protein 16g

CARROT AND BEET SALAD WITH ROSE HARISSA

ROASTED CAULIFLOWER AND GRAPE SALAD WITH CHERMOULA

SERVES 4

50 MINS

Salad

- 1 head cauliflower (2 pounds), core chopped coarse, florets cut into 1-inch pieces (6 cups)
- 1 cup seedless red grapes
- ½ small red onion, sliced thin
- 2 tablespoons extra-virgin olive oil
- ½ teaspoon table salt
- ¼ teaspoon pepper
- 2 tablespoons fresh cilantro or parsley leaves
- 2 tablespoons coarsely chopped toasted walnuts or sliced almonds

Chermoula

- 1 cup fresh cilantro or parsley leaves
- 5 tablespoons extra-virgin olive oil
- 2 tablespoons lemon juice
- 4 garlic cloves, minced
- ½ teaspoon ground cumin
- ½ teaspoon paprika
- ¼ teaspoon table salt
- ⅛ teaspoon cayenne pepper

WHY THIS RECIPE WORKS Heady with cilantro, brightened with lots of lemon juice, and deepened with warm spices, the North African herb sauce chermoula is most often a marinade for meat and fish but here it paints a cauliflower canvas with tremendous flavor. We start by roasting cauliflower until it's caramelized. Instead of discarding the core, we blitz it in the food processor and add it to the salad for a contrasting rice-like texture. Then we make the chermoula in the empty food processor. We balance its flavor in the salad with sweetness, roasting red onion and plenty of grapes as well. Fresh cilantro leaves and crunchy walnuts are the finishing touches to this substantial roasted vegetable salad. This salad is satisfying enough to be a meal but also lovely doled out as a side to hearty grains or rich meat.

1 For the salad Adjust oven rack to lowest position and heat oven to 475 degrees. Toss cauliflower florets, grapes, onion, oil, salt, and pepper together in bowl. Transfer to rimmed baking sheet and roast until vegetables are tender, florets are deep golden, and onion slices are charred at edges, 12 to 15 minutes, stirring halfway through roasting. Let cool slightly, about 15 minutes.

2 Meanwhile, pulse cauliflower core in food processor until finely ground into ⅛-inch pieces, 6 to 8 pulses, scraping down sides of bowl as needed; transfer to large bowl.

3 For the chermoula Process all ingredients in now-empty processor until smooth, about 1 minute, scraping down sides of bowl as needed. (Chermoula can be refrigerated for up to 2 days.) Transfer to bowl with cauliflower core.

4 Add roasted cauliflower mixture to chermoula mixture in bowl and toss to combine. Season with salt and pepper to taste. Sprinkle with cilantro and walnuts. Serve.

Cals 340 | Total Fat 28g | Sat Fat 4g | Chol 0mg | Sodium 510mg
Total Carb 22g | Dietary Fiber 6g | Total Sugars 11g | Protein 6g

SEARED HALLOUMI AND VEGETABLE SALAD BOWL

**SERVES
4**

45 MINS

¼ cup extra-virgin olive oil, divided

1 pound eggplant, cut into ½-inch pieces

1 head radicchio (10 ounces), cored and cut into 1-inch pieces

1 red bell pepper, stemmed, seeded, and cut into ½-inch pieces

1 zucchini, trimmed and sliced lengthwise into ribbons

6 ounces halloumi cheese, sliced into ½-inch-thick slabs

2 tablespoons honey

1 teaspoon minced fresh thyme

1 garlic clove, minced

½ teaspoon grated lemon zest plus 2 tablespoons juice

¼ teaspoon table salt

⅛ teaspoon pepper

1 cup jarred whole artichoke hearts packed in water, halved, rinsed, and patted dry

WHY THIS RECIPE WORKS This salad incorporates some flavors and ingredients you might find on a Greek meze spread into a filling meal bowl. Eggplant, radicchio, and red peppers (all browned); zucchini (sliced into attractive ribbons and left raw); and jarred artichokes fill our bowl. After searing halloumi in slabs, we cut it into ½-inch pieces so its flavor is distributed through our bowl. An herbaceous honey-thyme vinaigrette contrasts the salty cheese and bitter radicchio. To slice zucchini, use a vegetable peeler to shave the length of the squash, rotating the squash 90 degrees after each slice.

1 Heat 1 tablespoon oil in 12-inch nonstick skillet over medium-high heat until shimmering. Add eggplant and cook, stirring frequently, until tender and browned, 8 to 10 minutes; transfer to large bowl. Heat 1 tablespoon oil in now-empty skillet over medium-high heat until shimmering. Add radicchio and bell pepper and cook until wilted and beginning to char, 4 to 6 minutes. Transfer to bowl with eggplant; stir in zucchini and set aside.

2 Heat 1 tablespoon oil in again-empty skillet over medium heat until shimmering. Add halloumi in single layer and cook until golden brown, 2 to 4 minutes per side. Transfer cheese to cutting board and cut into ½-inch pieces.

3 Whisk honey, thyme, garlic, lemon zest and juice, salt, and pepper together in bowl. While whisking constantly, slowly drizzle in remaining 1 tablespoon oil until combined. Toss vegetable mixture with half of vinaigrette to coat, then season with salt and pepper to taste. Divide among individual serving bowls, then top with halloumi and artichokes. Drizzle with remaining vinaigrette. Serve.

Greek Frying Cheese
Halloumi is a firm, brined cheese popular in Cyprus (where it originated), Greece, and Turkey. It's made from goat's or sheep's milk (or a combination of both). Because of how it's made, it has a solid consistency and a very strong protein network, which means when it's heated, it softens but doesn't melt. That makes it perfect for pan searing into salty, creamy, chewy charred slabs.

*Cals 380 | Total Fat 26g | Sat Fat 10g
Chol 30mg | Sodium 690mg
Total Carb 24g | Dietary Fiber 5g
Total Sugars 15g | Protein 13g*

SALMON, AVOCADO, GRAPEFRUIT, AND WATERCRESS SALAD

1 pound skin-on salmon, 1 inch thick

1 teaspoon plus 3 tablespoons extra-virgin olive oil, divided

¾ teaspoon table salt

¼ teaspoon pepper

2 red grapefruits

1 tablespoon minced shallot

1 teaspoon white wine vinegar

1 teaspoon Dijon mustard

4 ounces (4 cups) watercress, torn into bite-size pieces

1 ripe avocado, halved, pitted, and sliced ¼ inch thick

¼ cup fresh mint leaves, torn

¼ cup blanched hazelnuts, toasted and chopped

WHY THIS RECIPE WORKS This colorful salad of contrasting flavors and textures is dinner-worthy thanks to some of the most nutrient-dense, filling ingredients on the planet. Sturdy watercress, with its slight, pleasant bitterness and peppery punch, acts as the perfect bed for the rich toppings. We roast the salmon just until it's medium-rare before flaking it into substantial chunks. The slices of buttery avocado contribute creaminess. For a bright, light contrast, we cut up two sweet-tart red grapefruits and reserve some of the grapefruit juice to whisk up a simple vinaigrette brought into focus with a little white wine vinegar and Dijon mustard. Finally, we add a sprinkling of crunchy toasted hazelnuts and torn mint leaves for crunch and complexity.

1 Adjust oven rack to lowest position, place foil-lined rimmed baking sheet on rack, and heat oven to 500 degrees. Pat salmon dry with paper towels, rub with 1 teaspoon oil, and sprinkle with ¼ teaspoon salt and pepper. Reduce oven to 275 degrees. Carefully place salmon skin side down on prepared sheet. Roast until center is still translucent when checked with tip of paring knife and registers 125 degrees (for medium-rare), 6 to 8 minutes. Let salmon cool to room temperature, about 20 minutes. Flake salmon into large 2-inch pieces.

2 Meanwhile, cut away peel and pith from grapefruits. Holding fruit over bowl, use paring knife to slice between membranes to release segments. Measure out 2 tablespoons grapefruit juice and transfer to separate bowl.

3 Whisk shallot, vinegar, mustard, and remaining ½ teaspoon salt into grapefruit juice. Whisking constantly, slowly drizzle in remaining 3 tablespoons oil. Arrange watercress in even layer on platter. Arrange salmon pieces, grapefruit segments, and avocado on top of watercress. Drizzle dressing over top, then sprinkle with mint and hazelnuts. Serve.

Cals 360 | Total Fat 26g | Sat Fat 4.5g
Chol 40mg | Sodium 370mg
Total Carb 15g | Dietary Fiber 7g
Total Sugars 7g | Protein 18g

GRILLED TOMATO GAZPACHO

SERVES
4

50 MINS
plus 2 hrs chilling

2 pounds ripe but firm tomatoes, cored and halved along equator

6 tablespoons extra-virgin olive oil, divided

1 teaspoon table salt, divided

¼ teaspoon pepper

1 small cucumber, peeled and cut into 1-inch pieces

1 slice hearty white sandwich bread, crust removed, torn into 1-inch pieces

1 small shallot, peeled and halved

1 small serrano chile, stemmed and halved lengthwise

1 garlic clove, chopped

2 tablespoons minced fresh parsley

1 teaspoon sherry vinegar, plus extra for seasoning

WHY THIS RECIPE WORKS Aside from the bread base, glugs of golden olive oil, and a good sherry vinegar, ripe tomatoes, naturally, shine in traditional creamy Andalusian gazpacho, a most refreshing summertime soup. So we concentrate on the tomatoes—literally—by grilling them for extra sweetness plus smoky char. Salting the tomatoes before grilling draws out their moisture—a good thing, as drier tomatoes caramelize more. Don't throw away those juices, though; adding them to the soup base helps it retain bright flavor. Use in-season round tomatoes so they will hold their shape on the grill. Refrigerating the gazpacho overnight melds the flavors. We suggest topping this soup with chopped or sliced cucumber, shallot, and black pepper, if desired.

1 Toss tomatoes with 1 tablespoon oil, ½ teaspoon salt, and pepper in bowl. Let sit for at least 15 minutes or up to 1 hour.

2A For a charcoal grill Open bottom vent completely. Light large chimney starter filled with charcoal briquettes (6 quarts). When top coals are partially covered with ash, pour evenly over grill. Set cooking grate in place, cover, and open lid vent completely. Heat grill until hot, about 5 minutes.

2B For a gas grill Turn all burners to high, cover, and heat grill until hot, about 15 minutes. Leave all burners on high.

3 Clean and oil cooking grate. Place tomatoes cut sides down on grill (reserve any juice left behind in bowl) and cook (covered if using gas) until tomatoes are charred and beginning to soften, 4 to 6 minutes. Carefully flip tomatoes and continue to cook (covered if using gas) until skin sides are charred and juice bubbles, 4 to 6 minutes longer. Transfer tomatoes to bowl and let cool completely.

4 Process tomatoes, reserved tomato juice, cucumber, bread, shallot, serrano, garlic, and remaining ½ teaspoon salt in blender for 30 seconds. With blender running, slowly drizzle in remaining 5 tablespoons oil; continue to process until completely smooth, about 2 minutes. Strain soup through fine-mesh strainer set over large bowl, using back of ladle or rubber spatula to press soup through strainer; discard solids. Stir parsley and vinegar into strained soup, then add enough water to yield 4 cups of soup. Cover and refrigerate for at least 2 hours to chill and develop flavors. Season with salt, pepper, and sherry vinegar to taste. Serve.

Cals 270 | Total Fat 22g | Sat Fat 3g
Chol 0mg | Sodium 630mg
Total Carb 17g | Dietary Fiber 3g
Total Sugars 8g | Protein 3g

New World Favorite

The ubiquity of tomatoes across the Mediterranean is noted. They grow well in warm parts of the region and are largely considered a key ingredient of the Mediterranean diet. But tomatoes originated in the Americas and weren't introduced to Europe from the New World by explorers until the 16th century—and they weren't even eaten at that point. They served only as ornament, as it was believed they might be poisonous. But once they took off, they really took off. Tomatoes are beloved raw in salads that celebrate them, cooked into sauces, stuffed with flavorful ingredients, and used in countless other applications.

Hawaij Blends

Spice blends of any origin are rarely a set formula. Some span cuisines and differ from country to country, state to state, town to town, or even household to household. Some are interpreted differently by different families, the blend at the hands of the cook of the household. The Yemeni spice blend hawaij, which means "mixture" in Arabic, is no exception. This warm, almost pungent, spice blend used for soup almost always contains cumin, black pepper, turmeric, and cardamom in differing amounts. Other spices such as caraway, ground cloves, coriander, fenugreek, nutmeg, ground onion, and saffron may make an appearance, each contributing significantly to the blend's profile and potency. Hawaij is popular among Yemenite Jewish cooks and so is common in Israeli cuisine. Don't confuse this savory blend with hawaij made for coffee and dessert, which is a blend of sweeter spices.

CREAMY HAWAIJ
CAULIFLOWER SOUP
WITH ZHOUG

SERVES
4 TO 6

1½ HRS

1 head cauliflower (2 pounds)

¼ cup extra-virgin olive oil, divided, plus extra for serving

1 leek, white and light green parts only, halved lengthwise, sliced thin, and washed thoroughly

1 small onion, halved and sliced thin

1½ teaspoons table salt

1 tablespoon Hawaij (page 15)

4½ cups water

1 recipe Green Zhoug (page 19), divided

1 teaspoon white wine vinegar

WHY THIS RECIPE WORKS A creamy cauliflower soup is a marvelous way to not only nourish yourself with all of the cruciferous vegetable's nutrients and fiber but also unlock its range of flavors—from bright and cabbage-like to nutty and even sweet. To enhance these multiple personalities further, we opened the spice cabinet. Hawaij is a Yemeni spice blend also common to Israeli cuisine that's used for soup and boasts its own impressive range of flavors—earthy, sweet, and distinctly savory. Some well-cooked cauliflower quickly whips into a velvety soup—no flavor-diluting dairy required. We add the cauliflower to simmering water in two stages to bring out the grassy flavor of just-cooked cauliflower and the nutty flavor of longer-cooked cauliflower in our soup. The hawaij blooms with the aromatics so its flavors flourish from the beginning. In addition to a countering topping of the grassy-hot cilantro-chile sauce zhoug and browned cauliflower florets, we also like to serve the soup with chopped Pink Pickled Turnips (page 18).

1 Pull off outer leaves of cauliflower and trim stem. Using paring knife, cut around core to remove; slice core thin and reserve. Cut heaping 1 cup of ½-inch florets from head of cauliflower; set aside. Cut remaining cauliflower crosswise into ½-inch-thick slices.

2 Heat 3 tablespoons oil in large saucepan over medium-low heat until shimmering. Add leek, onion, and salt and cook, stirring often, until leek and onion are softened but not browned, about 7 minutes. Stir in hawaij and cook until fragrant, about 30 seconds. Stir in water, reserved sliced core, and half of sliced cauliflower. Increase heat to medium-high and bring to simmer. Reduce heat to medium-low and simmer gently for 15 minutes. Add remaining sliced cauliflower and simmer until cauliflower is tender and crumbles easily, 15 to 20 minutes.

3 Meanwhile, heat remaining 1 tablespoon oil in 8-inch skillet over medium heat until shimmering. Add reserved florets and cook, stirring often, until golden brown, 6 to 8 minutes. Transfer to bowl, add ¼ cup zhoug, and toss until well coated. Working in batches, process soup in blendor until smooth, about 45 seconds. Return pureed soup to clean pot and bring to brief simmer over medium heat. Off heat, stir in vinegar and season with salt to taste. Spoon browned florets and remaining zhoug over individual serving bowls. Serve.

Cals 270 | Total Fat 24g | Sat Fat 3.5g
Chol 0mg | Sodium 740mg
Total Carb 12g | Dietary Fiber 4g
Total Sugars 4g | Protein 4g

PUREED BUTTERNUT SQUASH SOUP WITH FENNEL

SERVES
4 TO 6

1½ HRS

¼ cup extra-virgin olive oil, divided

1 large shallot, chopped

2 pounds butternut squash, quartered and seeded, with fibers and seeds reserved

1 teaspoon fennel seeds

6 cups water

1 teaspoon table salt

1 large fennel bulb, stalks discarded, bulb halved, cored, and cut into 1-inch-thick strips

½ cup plain whole-milk yogurt

1 teaspoon packed brown sugar

Pinch ground nutmeg

WHY THIS RECIPE WORKS Pumpkins or squash are often pureed, so they make a natural choice for a smooth warming autumn soup. This squash soup has lots of intrigue, flavored not by copious warm spices but by fresh-tasting, anise-y fennel, which gives it a seductive perfume. To first get the most flavor out of the squash, we sauté a shallot with the reserved squash seeds and fibers, simmer the mixture in water, and then use the flavorful liquid to steam the squash flesh that we puree with the cooking liquid. A bonus: There's no need to peel the squash. Some yogurt adds richness and tang and fortifies the creamy texture, and a little brown sugar and nutmeg balance the squash's earthy flavor, bringing out its sweetness further.

1 Heat 2 tablespoons oil in Dutch oven over medium heat until shimmering. Add shallot and cook until softened, 2 to 3 minutes. Stir in squash seeds and fibers and fennel seeds and cook until mixture turns orange, about 4 minutes.

2 Stir in water and salt and bring to boil. Reduce heat as needed to maintain simmer, place squash cut side down in steamer basket along with fennel, and lower basket into pot. Cover and steam vegetables until completely tender, 30 to 40 minutes.

3 Using tongs, transfer cooked squash and fennel to rimmed baking sheet. Let squash cool slightly, then scrape cooked squash from skin using spoon; discard skin.

4 Strain cooking liquid through fine-mesh strainer set over large bowl. Working in batches, process cooked squash, fennel, 3 cups strained cooking liquid, and yogurt in blender until smooth, 1 to 2 minutes. Return pureed soup to now-empty pot and stir in sugar, nutmeg, and remaining 2 tablespoons oil. Return to gentle simmer, adjusting soup consistency with extra cooking liquid as needed. Season with salt and pepper to taste. Serve.

Cals 220 | Total Fat 17g | Sat Fat 6g
Chol 25mg | Sodium 430mg
Total Carb 19g | Dietary Fiber 4g
Total Sugars 6g | Protein 2g

HEARTY SPRING VEGETABLE SOUP

SERVES
4

45 MINS

1 tablespoon extra-virgin olive oil

1 pound asparagus, trimmed and cut into ½-inch lengths

12 ounces zucchini, cut into ½-inch pieces

2 cups chopped green cabbage

⅛ teaspoon table salt

¼ teaspoon pepper

2 garlic cloves, minced

2½ cups chicken or vegetable broth

1 cup water

2 ounces snap peas, strings removed, sliced thin on bias

2 radishes, trimmed, halved, and sliced thin

¼ cup Basil Pesto (page 17)

WHY THIS RECIPE WORKS Everything green—from all the vegetables to the savory basil pesto topping—goes into this hearty soup. We sauté the mix of asparagus, zucchini, and cabbage to build flavor and bring out their seasonal sweetness. The vegetables maintain their integrity (and a little crunch) with just a brief 3- to 5-minute cook time in broth. A swirl of basil pesto just before serving releases the aromas of basil and garlic into the soup and provides buttery goodness by way of the pine nuts and Parmesan. You simply can't forget how fresh this soup is: It's also topped with thinly sliced snap peas and radishes.

1 Heat oil in Dutch oven over medium-high heat until just smoking. Add asparagus, zucchini, cabbage, salt, and pepper and cook until vegetables are softened, about 3 minutes. Stir in garlic and cook until fragrant, about 30 seconds.

2 Stir in broth and water, bring to simmer, and cook until vegetables are tender and bright green, 3 to 5 minutes. Season with salt and pepper to taste. Sprinkle individual portions with snap peas and radishes and dollop with pesto. Serve.

Cals 300 | Total Fat 25g | Sat Fat 4.5g
Chol 5mg | Sodium 740mg
Total Carb 12g | Dietary Fiber 4g
Total Sugars 6g | Protein 8g

Chestnuts Roasting

You can purchase peeled and cooked chestnuts jarred or vacuum-packed, which makes easy work of using chestnuts in this recipe that purees the soft fruit. If you can't find them precooked, or if you're attracted to the baskets of raw chestnuts at the store in the winter months, you can prepare them at home. When purchasing, be sure to look for nuts with glossy shells, and avoid those that rattle when shaken, as this indicates that they have dried out. For this recipe, cut 20 ounces of whole chestnuts in half crosswise, then blanch for 8 minutes in 8 cups of boiling water. Remove the pot from the heat, leaving the nuts in the water. One at a time, hold the chestnuts with a dish towel and squeeze the shell to extract the meat. Using a paring knife, trim any bits of husk.

CHESTNUT SOUP WITH MUSHROOMS AND BAHARAT

SERVES
4 TO 6

1¼ HRS

- 2 cups water, divided
- ¼ ounce dried porcini mushrooms, rinsed
- 2 tablespoons extra-virgin olive oil, divided, plus extra for drizzling
- 1 pound shallots, quartered
- 1 teaspoon table salt, divided
- ¾ teaspoon Baharat (page 14)
- 14 ounces (3 cups) peeled and cooked chestnuts, chopped
- 2 cups chicken or vegetable broth
- 10 ounces shiitake mushrooms, stemmed and sliced thin
- ¼ teaspoon pepper
- ¾ cup plain whole-milk yogurt
- ½ cup plus 2 tablespoons minced fresh parsley, divided

Cals 290 | Total Fat 8g | Sat Fat 1.5g
Chol 5mg | Sodium 590mg
Total Carb 49g | Dietary Fiber 6g
Total Sugars 15g | Protein 8g

WHY THIS RECIPE WORKS The appeal of chestnuts goes beyond roasting plain, and in Turkey, the third-largest producer of chestnuts in the world, they're used in myriad ways. Here, we were inspired by kestane çorbasi, a pureed chestnut soup that can lean sweet or savory depending on who is at the stovetop. Along with the woodsy, rich chestnuts, our soup achieves an appealing sweet-savory balance from shallots and mushrooms (both classic ingredients). The addition of baharat in our version, which we saw in some recipes, manages to augment all the distinct flavors in the soup with its complex spice. For a strong mushroom backbone, we use dried porcini mushrooms, incorporating their soaking liquid, too, to add depth. We stir in nutty browned sautéed shiitakes after pureeing the soup, and they add welcome texture. Versions of this soup smooth things out with crème fraîche or yogurt, and we enjoy the mellow tanginess of creamy whole-milk yogurt.

1 Microwave ½ cup water and porcini mushrooms in covered bowl until steaming, about 1 minute. Let sit until softened, about 5 minutes. Drain mushrooms in fine-mesh strainer lined with coffee filter, reserving soaking liquid, and chop mushrooms fine.

2 Heat 1 tablespoon oil in Dutch oven over medium-low heat until shimmering. Add shallots and ½ teaspoon salt, cover, and cook until shallots are softened and beginning to brown, 12 to 15 minutes, stirring occasionally. Stir in minced porcini and baharat and cook until fragrant, about 30 seconds. Stir in chestnuts, broth, reserved porcini soaking liquid, and remaining 1½ cups water and bring to boil. Reduce heat to medium-low, cover, and simmer until chestnuts are very tender, about 20 minutes.

3 Meanwhile, heat remaining 1 tablespoon oil in 12-inch nonstick skillet over medium heat until shimmering. Add shiitake mushrooms, remaining ½ teaspoon salt, and pepper, cover, and cook until mushrooms are softened, about 5 minutes. Uncover and continue to cook, stirring occasionally, until liquid has evaporated and mushrooms begin to brown, 8 to 10 minutes longer; set aside.

4 Working in batches, process soup and yogurt in blender until smooth, about 1 minute. Return pureed soup to now-empty pot. Stir in all but ¼ cup reserved browned shiitakes and bring to gentle simmer over medium heat, adjusting consistency with hot water if desired. Stir in ½ cup parsley and season with salt and pepper to taste. Serve, sprinkling with reserved shiitakes and remaining 2 tablespoons parsley and drizzling with extra oil.

SPICED EGGPLANT AND KALE SOUP

SERVES
4

1¼ HRS

6 tablespoons extra-virgin olive oil, divided

1¼ pounds eggplant, cut into ½-inch pieces

2 garlic cloves, minced

1½ teaspoons ground coriander

1½ teaspoons ground cumin

1 teaspoon grated fresh ginger

¾ teaspoon ground dried Aleppo pepper, divided

¼ teaspoon ground cinnamon

¼ teaspoon table salt

¼ teaspoon pepper

3 cups chicken or vegetable broth

1½ cups water

2 ounces (2 cups) baby kale, chopped coarse

½ cup plain Greek yogurt

2 tablespoons sliced almonds, toasted

2 tablespoons minced fresh cilantro

WHY THIS RECIPE WORKS Eggplant, kale, and ample spices combine in this quick vegetarian soup with a distinct meatiness. Cumin, coriander, ginger, garlic, and Aleppo pepper, which we bloom in oil to fully awaken them, flavor the recipe. Toppings heighten the dish: Sliced almonds add a pleasant crunch, cilantro lends freshness, and a dollop of yogurt provides rich tang. Finally, an additional sprinkle of Aleppo pepper finishes the soup with a striking pop of rich red color against the milky-white yogurt.

1 Heat ¼ cup oil in Dutch oven over medium-high heat until just smoking. Add eggplant and cook, stirring occasionally, until tender and deeply browned, 6 to 8 minutes; transfer to bowl.

2 Heat remaining 2 tablespoons oil in now-empty Dutch oven over medium heat until shimmering. Stir in garlic, coriander, cumin, ginger, ½ teaspoon Aleppo pepper, cinnamon, salt, and pepper and cook until fragrant, about 30 seconds. Stir in broth and water, scraping up any browned bits, and bring to simmer. Reduce heat to medium-low, cover partially, and cook until flavors meld, about 15 minutes.

3 Off heat, stir in kale and eggplant, along with any accumulated juices. Let sit until kale is wilted and warmed through, about 2 minutes. Season with salt and pepper to taste. Dollop individual portions with yogurt and sprinkle with almonds, cilantro, and remaining ¼ teaspoon Aleppo pepper before serving.

Cals 310 | Total Fat 27g | Sat Fat 6g
Chol 5mg | Sodium 730mg
Total Carb 14g | Dietary Fiber 6g
Total Sugars 6g | Protein 5g

PATATAS A LA RIOJANA

- 1 tablespoon extra-virgin olive oil, plus extra for drizzling
- 1 leek, white and light green parts only, halved lengthwise, sliced thin, and washed thoroughly
- 1 red bell pepper, stemmed, seeded, and cut into ½-inch pieces
- ⅛ teaspoon table salt
- 8 ounces Spanish-style chorizo sausage, halved lengthwise and sliced ½ inch thick
- 4 garlic cloves, minced
- 1 teaspoon smoked paprika
- ¼ teaspoon red pepper flakes, plus extra for seasoning
- 1½ pounds Yukon Gold potatoes, peeled and cut into ¾-inch pieces
- 1 cup dry white wine
- 2 cups water
- 1¼ cups frozen peas, thawed
- 2 tablespoons chopped fresh parsley

WHY THIS RECIPE WORKS This stew-like Spanish potato dish in a smoky paprika broth is a prime example of an omnivore's recipe that's still all about the vegetables, the modest amount of meat acting as a flavoring that imbues the potatoes. Ample potatoes and peas form the bulk of this dish from La Rioja, the wine region of northern Spain (a cup of wine is a key flavor in the braise). The stew broth gets thickness from the potatoes, their starch coaxed out through vigorous simmering. And to amplify the supporting flavor of the chorizo in the dish, we use a healthy amount of garlic, pepper flakes, and colorful paprika. Serve with crusty bread.

1 Heat oil in Dutch oven over medium heat until shimmering. Add leek, bell pepper, and salt. Cover, reduce heat to medium-low, and cook, stirring occasionally, until vegetables are softened, 5 to 7 minutes.

2 Stir in chorizo, garlic, paprika, and pepper flakes and cook, until chorizo is softened, about 2 minutes. Stir in potatoes and cook over medium heat until edges are translucent, 2 to 4 minutes.

3 Stir in wine and cook until reduced by half, about 2 minutes. Stir in water and bring to simmer over high heat. Reduce heat to medium-low, cover, and simmer vigorously until potatoes are tender, about 20 minutes, stirring occasionally. Stir in peas and parsley and season with salt and pepper flakes to taste. Serve, drizzling individual portions with extra oil.

Cals 540 | Total Fat 25g | Sat Fat 9g
Chol 50mg | Sodium 800mg
Total Carb 45g | Dietary Fiber 3g
Total Sugars 4g | Protein 21g

EGGS IN SWISS CHARD AND HERB SAUCE

SERVES
4

40 MINS

2 pounds Swiss chard, stems removed and reserved, leaves chopped

¼ cup extra-virgin olive oil, divided

1 large onion, chopped fine

¼ teaspoon table salt

4 garlic cloves, minced

2 teaspoons ground coriander

11 ounces (11 cups) baby spinach, chopped

½ cup chicken or vegetable broth

1 cup frozen peas

1½ tablespoons lemon juice

8 large eggs

½ teaspoon ground dried Aleppo pepper

2 ounces feta cheese, crumbled (½ cup) (optional)

2 tablespoons chopped fresh dill

2 tablespoons chopped fresh mint

WHY THIS RECIPE WORKS Good-for-you greens pack this verdant spin on the classic North African egg dish shakshuka. Traditionally, eggs are cooked in a long-simmered, spiced tomato and pepper sauce. This serves as a template for a version that swaps out the red sauce for a fresh mix of good-for-you greens. Sautéed savory Swiss chard and easy-to-prep baby spinach form much of the sauce and we complement them with coriander and mild Aleppo pepper rather than the traditional strong flavors of cumin and paprika. We blend a cup of the greens mixture with broth to give the sauce a creamy, cohesive texture and then add frozen peas for contrasting pops of sweetness. The eggs poach inside this mix, and feta cheese tops everything with welcome salty richness. The Dutch oven will seem crowded when you first add the greens, but they will quickly wilt down. Avoid removing the lid during the first 5 minutes of cooking the eggs, as it will increase their cooking time. Serve with toasted pita or crusty bread.

1 Slice chard stems thin to yield 1 cup; discard remaining stems or reserve for another use. Heat 2 tablespoons oil in Dutch oven over medium heat until shimmering. Add chard stems, onion, and salt and cook until vegetables are softened and lightly browned, 5 to 7 minutes. Stir in garlic and coriander and cook until fragrant, about 1 minute.

2 Add chard leaves and spinach. Increase heat to medium-high, cover, and cook, stirring occasionally, until wilted but still bright green, 3 to 5 minutes. Off heat, transfer 1 cup chard mixture to blender. Add broth and process until smooth, about 45 seconds, scraping down sides of blender jar as needed. Stir chard mixture, peas, and lemon juice into pot.

3 Make 4 shallow indentations (about 2 inches wide) in surface of greens using back of spoon. Crack 2 eggs into each indentation, then sprinkle with Aleppo pepper. Cover and cook over medium-low heat until edges of egg whites are just set, 5 to 10 minutes. Off heat, let sit, covered, until whites are fully set and yolks are still runny, 2 to 4 minutes. Season with salt and pepper to taste. Sprinkle with feta, if using; dill; and mint and drizzle with remaining 2 tablespoons oil. Serve immediately.

Cals 310 | Total Fat 18g | Sat Fat 4g
Chol 15mg | Sodium 990mg
Total Carb 21g | Dietary Fiber 8g
Total Sugars 7g | Protein 18g

CABBAGE, KOHLRABI, AND LAMB TAGINE WITH PRUNES

SERVES 4 TO 6

3¼ HRS

1 pound bone-in lamb shoulder chops, trimmed

1¼ teaspoons table salt, divided

¼ teaspoon pepper, divided

3 tablespoons extra-virgin olive oil, divided

2 onions, chopped

4 garlic cloves, minced

1 teaspoon ground cumin

½ teaspoon ground ginger

½ teaspoon ground cinnamon

¼ teaspoon cayenne pepper

1½ cups water

2 tablespoons honey

½ head (1 pound) red cabbage, halved, cored, and cut into 2-inch pieces (6 cups)

1 pound Yukon gold potatoes, peeled and cut into 1-inch pieces

1 pound kohlrabi, peeled, halved, and cut into 1-inch-thick wedges

¾ cup prunes

½ teaspoon orange blossom water (optional)

2 tablespoons sliced almonds, toasted

Cals 440 | Total Fat 21g | Sat Fat 7g
Chol 45mg | Sodium 610mg
Total Carb 47g | Dietary Fiber 6g
Total Sugars 21g | Protein 17g

WHY THIS RECIPE WORKS North African tagines are most commonly generously spiced, assertively flavored stews slow-cooked in earthenware vessels of the same name. They can include all manner of meats, vegetables, and fruit. For this tagine, we were inspired by the flavors of a popular sweet dish eaten throughout Algeria during Ramadan known as lham lahlou, Arabic for "sweet meat." During the month of Ramadan, when the daylong fast is broken with a bountiful meal, bites of this unctuous, fragrant, syrupy tagine of tender lamb simmered with sweet fruits are seen as nourishing and reviving. Often, the dish is delicately perfumed by aromatics like cinnamon and orange blossom water. We created a vegetable-forward, more savory-leaning tagine with this complex and satisfying flavor profile, using hearty red cabbage, kohlrabi, and potatoes—vegetables that pack their own sort of meatiness. Our tagine isn't meat-free, however: The addition of a modest amount of lamb acts as a secondary seasoning, providing the vegetables with more savor and succulence.

1 Adjust oven rack to lower-middle position and heat oven to 325 degrees. Pat lamb dry with paper towels and sprinkle with ¼ teaspoon salt and pepper. Heat 1 tablespoon oil in Dutch oven over medium-high heat until just smoking. Brown lamb on both sides, 7 to 10 minutes; transfer to plate.

2 Heat remaining 2 tablespoons oil in now-empty Dutch oven over medium heat until shimmering. Add onions and ½ teaspoon salt and cook until onions are softened and browned, 8 to 10 minutes. Stir in garlic, cumin, ginger, cinnamon, and cayenne and cook until fragrant, about 30 seconds.

3 Stir in water, scraping up any browned bits. Stir in honey, cabbage, potatoes, kohlrabi, and remaining ½ teaspoon salt. Nestle browned lamb and any accumulated juices into pot and bring to simmer. Cover pot, transfer to oven, and cook for 1 hour.

4 Stir in prunes and continue to cook, covered, until lamb and vegetables are tender, about 1 hour.

5 Remove pot from oven. Transfer lamb to cutting board, let cool slightly, then shred into bite-size pieces using 2 forks; discard fat and bones. Stir lamb and orange blossom water, if using, into vegetables in pot. Season with salt and pepper to taste. Sprinkle with almonds. Serve.

WHOLE ROMANESCO WITH BERBERE AND YOGURT-TAHINI SAUCE

SERVES
4

50 MINS

Yogurt-Tahini Sauce

- ½ cup plain whole-milk yogurt
- 2 tablespoons tahini
- 1 garlic clove, minced
- ½ teaspoon grated lemon zest plus 1 tablespoon juice

Romanesco

- 1 head romanesco or cauliflower (2 pounds), outer leaves removed, stem trimmed flush with bottom florets
- 1 teaspoon plus 3 tablespoons extra-virgin olive oil, divided
- ¼ teaspoon table salt
- ½ teaspoon paprika
- ¼ teaspoon cayenne pepper
- ¼ teaspoon ground coriander
- ⅛ teaspoon ground allspice
- ⅛ teaspoon ground cardamom
- ⅛ teaspoon ground cumin
- ⅛ teaspoon ground black pepper
- 2 tablespoons pine nuts, toasted and chopped
- 1 tablespoon minced fresh cilantro

WHY THIS RECIPE WORKS Named for its appearance first in Italy, this dramatically beautiful, fractal-looking vegetable, which is a pale green relative of cauliflower, is a showstopper when cooked and presented whole. Like other brassica, romanesco has plenty of earthy flavor, so strong seasoning and deep browning are valuable additional touches of drama. We use the broiler to provide the head of romanesco with a nicely charred exterior, but because this large, dense vegetable can burn under the intense heat before it's cooked through all the way, we first parcook it in the microwave. We then brush olive oil over it and transfer it to the broiler to brown. We baste the broiled romanesco with a mixture of more oil and berbere, a warmly aromatic and highly flavorful Ethiopian spice blend. A bright, cooling yogurt sauce with some nutty depth from tahini pleasantly offsets the warm spice coating, and pine nuts provide crunch against the just-perfectly-tender romanesco. Serve with a grain for a hearty meal.

1 For the Yogurt-Tahini Sauce Whisk all ingredients together in bowl and season with salt and pepper to taste. Set aside.

2 For the Romanesco Adjust oven rack 6 inches from broiler element and heat broiler. Microwave romanesco in covered bowl until paring knife slips easily in and out of core, 8 to 12 minutes.

3 Transfer romanesco stem side down to 12-inch ovensafe skillet. Drizzle romanesco evenly with 1 teaspoon oil and sprinkle with salt. Transfer skillet to oven and broil until top of romanesco is spotty brown, 8 to 10 minutes. Meanwhile, microwave paprika, cayenne, coriander, allspice, cardamom, cumin, pepper, and remaining 3 tablespoons oil in now-empty bowl, stirring occasionally, until fragrant and bubbling, 1 to 2 minutes.

4 Remove skillet from oven, transfer to wire rack, and pour oil mixture over romanesco. Being careful of hot skillet handle, gently tilt skillet so oil pools to 1 side. Using spoon, baste romanesco until oil is absorbed, about 30 seconds.

5 Cut romanesco into wedges and transfer to serving platter. Sprinkle pine nuts and cilantro over top. Serve with yogurt-tahini sauce.

Cals 260 | Total Fat 20g | Sat Fat 3.5g | Chol 5mg | Sodium 230mg Total Carb 16g | Dietary Fiber 5g | Total Sugars 6g | Protein 7g

Vegetable Mathematics

The cruciferous vegetable romanesco goes by many names, including romanesco broccoli (a nod to its green color) and Roman cauliflower (a nod to its more cauliflower-like flavor). It has a striking fractal geography with spiraling cones of florets reaching from its core. Each bud consists of six smaller buds. And the total number of buds on a head represents a Fibonacci number. No matter the pattern, romanesco is a striking, delicious vegetable that deserves to be displayed like it is here—whole.

WHOLE POT-ROASTED CAULIFLOWER WITH TOMATOES AND OLIVES

- 2 (28-ounce) cans whole peeled tomatoes
- 2 tablespoons extra-virgin olive oil, plus extra for drizzling
- 6 garlic cloves, minced
- 2 anchovy fillets, rinsed and minced
- ¼ teaspoon red pepper flakes
- ¼ cup golden raisins
- ¼ cup pitted kalamata olives, chopped coarse
- 2 tablespoons capers, rinsed
- 1 head cauliflower (2 pounds), outer leaves removed, stem trimmed flush with bottom florets
- 1 ounce Parmesan cheese, grated (½ cup)
- ¼ cup minced fresh parsley

WHY THIS RECIPE WORKS Like romanesco (see page 84), cauliflower is lovely served whole—especially when coated in a piquant sauce of chunky tomatoes, golden raisins, and salty capers and olives. With a sauce so flavorful, this cauliflower doesn't need browning, so we pot-roast it. To ensure that all of the rich flavors penetrate the dense vegetable, we start by cooking it upside down and spooning some of the sauce into the crevices between the stalk and florets. Then we flip it right side up, spoon more sauce over the top, and leave the pot uncovered to finish cooking. The sauce thickens but remains plentiful and the flavors intensify as the cauliflower becomes fork-tender. Serve the cauliflower with a grain or bread; both are nice with the chunky sauce.

1 Adjust oven rack to middle position and heat oven to 450 degrees. Pulse tomatoes and their juice in food processor until coarsely chopped, 6 to 8 pulses.

2 Cook oil, garlic, anchovies, and pepper flakes in Dutch oven over medium heat, stirring constantly, until fragrant, about 2 minutes. Stir in processed tomatoes, bring to simmer, and cook until slightly thickened, about 10 minutes. Stir in raisins, olives, and capers, then nestle cauliflower head, stem side up, into sauce. Spoon some of sauce over top, cover, transfer pot to oven, and roast until cauliflower is just tender (paring knife slips in and out of core with some resistance), 30 to 35 minutes.

3 Uncover pot and, using tongs, flip cauliflower stem side down. Spoon some of sauce over cauliflower, then scrape down sides of pot. Continue to roast, uncovered, until cauliflower is tender, 10 to 15 minutes.

4 Remove pot from oven. Sprinkle cauliflower with Parmesan and parsley and drizzle with extra oil. Cut cauliflower into wedges and serve, spooning sauce over individual portions.

Cals 280 | Total Fat 28g | Sat Fat 2.5g
Chol 5mg | Sodium 1250mg
Total Carb 37g | Dietary Fiber 8g
Total Sugars 21g | Protein 12g

BUTTERNUT SQUASH STEAKS WITH HONEY-NUT TOPPING

SERVES 4

1 HR

¼ cup extra-virgin olive oil, divided

2 teaspoons sugar

2 teaspoons ground cumin

1 teaspoon garlic powder

1 teaspoon table salt

½ teaspoon ground dried Aleppo pepper

½ teaspoon ground coriander

½ teaspoon ground cinnamon

½ teaspoon pepper

2 (3-pound) butternut squashes

2 tablespoons chopped toasted pistachios

1 tablespoon sesame seeds, toasted

2 tablespoons honey

1 tablespoon torn fresh mint

1 recipe Garlic Yogurt Sauce (page 16)

Lime wedges

WHY THIS RECIPE WORKS The emphasis on the benefits of plants in the Mediterranean diet allows us to reimagine what we put in the center of our plate (see page 4). Case in point: butternut squash steaks. The squash's dense texture gives it a meaty bite, and its sweet, mild flavor can handle a liberal coating of bold seasonings (think cinnamon, coriander, and Aleppo pepper), much like a beef steak. Also, as we do with meat, we use a reverse-searing method, first cooking slabs from the necks of butternut squash through in the oven and then browning and crisping them in a skillet. To serve, we sprinkle toasted pistachios and sesame seeds on the steaks for nuttiness and crunch and dollop them with tangy garlic yogurt. A drizzle of honey brings all the flavors together, ensuring that every forkful has a balance of sweet, spicy, and savory. These squash steaks pair nicely with a number of steak accompaniments, though we particularly like them with a simple side of couscous.

1 Adjust oven rack to middle position and heat oven to 450 degrees. Combine 3 tablespoons oil, sugar, cumin, garlic powder, salt, Aleppo pepper, coriander, cinnamon, and pepper; set aside.

2 Working with 1 squash at a time, cut crosswise into 2 pieces at base of neck; reserve bulb for another use. Peel away skin and fibrous threads just below skin (squash should be completely orange, with no white flesh), then carefully cut each piece in half lengthwise. Cut one ¾-inch-thick slab lengthwise from each half. Repeat with remaining squash. (You should have 4 steaks; reserve remaining squash for another use.)

3 Place steaks on wire rack set in rimmed baking sheet and brush evenly with spice mixture. Flip steaks and brush second side with spice mixture. Roast until nearly tender and knife inserted into steaks meets with some resistance, 15 to 20 minutes; remove from oven.

4 Heat remaining 1 tablespoon oil in 12-inch nonstick skillet over medium-high heat until just smoking. Carefully place steaks in skillet and cook, without moving, until well browned and crisp on first side, about 3 minutes. Flip steaks and continue to cook until well browned and crisp on second side, about 3 minutes. Transfer steaks to serving platter

5 Sprinkle steaks with pistachios and sesame seeds. Microwave honey until fluid, about 10 seconds, then drizzle evenly over steaks. Sprinkle with mint and serve with yogurt sauce and lime wedges.

Cals 400 | Total Fat 20g | Sat Fat 5g Chol 5mg | Sodium 610mg Total Carb 55g | Dietary Fiber 8g Total Sugars 19g | Protein 7g

SEARED SHRIMP AND ZUCCHINI NOODLES WITH TOMATO-ARTICHOKE SAUCE

- 1 pound extra-large shrimp (21 to 25 per pound), peeled, deveined, and tails removed
- 5 tablespoons extra-virgin olive oil, divided
- 2 shallots, minced
- 2 garlic cloves, minced
- 12 ounces cherry tomatoes, halved
- 2 cups jarred whole artichoke hearts packed in water, rinsed, patted dry, and halved
- 1 teaspoon grated lemon zest, plus lemon wedges for serving
- ½ teaspoon table salt, divided
- ¼ teaspoon pepper, divided
- 2 tablespoons chopped fresh dill
- 1½ pounds zucchini noodles, cut into 6-inch lengths, divided
- 2 ounces feta cheese, crumbled (½ cup)
- 2 tablespoons pitted kalamata olives, chopped

WHY THIS RECIPE WORKS If you need any proof that seafood and cheese work together, turn your attention to saganaki. The word is Greek for a frying pan with two handles in which any of a category of appetizers of the same name is cooked. Fried cheese is most common but a shrimp variety, in which shrimp is cooked in a spicy tomato sauce and baked with feta cheese, is also beloved: The ocean essence of the shrimp echoes the brininess of the feta, the sweet-tart tomato sauce complements the sweetness of the shrimp, and the feta gives the sauce a rich creaminess. In this perfectly constructed (compositionally and nutritionally) dish, we combine that concept with a bed of satisfying strands of zucchini noodles to create a full meal. You will need 1 pound of zucchini to get 12 ounces of noodles; we prefer to make our own using a spiralizer, but in a pinch you can use store-bought. Cook the zucchini to your desired level of doneness but be careful not to overcook.

1 Pat shrimp dry with paper towels. Heat 1 tablespoon oil in 12-inch nonstick skillet over medium-high heat until just smoking. Add shrimp in single layer and cook, without stirring, until spotty brown and edges turn pink on bottom side, about 1 minute. Flip shrimp and continue to cook until all but very center is opaque, about 30 seconds; transfer shrimp to plate.

2 Heat 1 tablespoon oil in now-empty skillet over medium heat until shimmering. Add shallot and garlic and cook until fragrant, about 30 seconds. Stir in tomatoes, artichoke hearts, lemon zest, ¼ teaspoon salt, and ⅛ teaspoon pepper and cook, stirring frequently, until tomatoes have softened, 3 to 5 minutes. Transfer to bowl and stir in dill and 1 tablespoon oil. Cover with aluminum foil to keep warm and set aside until ready to serve.

3 Wipe out skillet with paper towels. Heat 1 tablespoon oil in now-empty skillet over medium-high heat until shimmering. Add half of zucchini noodles, ⅛ teaspoon salt, and pinch pepper and cook, tossing frequently, until crisp-tender, about 1 minute. Transfer to individual serving bowl and repeat with remaining 1 tablespoon oil, remaining zucchini noodles, remaining ⅛ salt, and remaining pinch pepper. Top zucchini noodles with tomato-artichoke mixture, shrimp, feta, and olives. Serve with lemon wedges.

Cals 350 | Total Fat 23g | Sat Fat 5g
Chol 15mg | Sodium 810mg
Total Carb 15g | Dietary Fiber 4g
Total Sugars 6g | Protein 21g

CORN AND LAMB HASH

SERVES
4

50 MINS

1½ pounds russet potatoes, peeled and cut into ½-inch pieces

2 tablespoons extra-virgin olive oil, divided

1 teaspoon table salt, divided

¼ teaspoon pepper

3 ears corn, kernels cut from cobs (2 cups)

8 ounces ground lamb

1 small onion, chopped fine

1–2 serrano chiles, stemmed, seeded, and chopped fine

3 garlic cloves, minced

2 teaspoons Ras el Hanout (page 15)

¾ teaspoon dried mint

3 radishes, trimmed, quartered, and sliced thin

1 tablespoon chopped fresh mint

WHY THIS RECIPE WORKS A hash is the perfect any-time-of-day recipe for fitting lots of good-for-you ingredients into one simple, balanced dish. Potatoes are standard but this recipe takes a fun turn, packing in an ingredient not typically seen in hash: corn, which provides a unique sweetness when charred. A modest amount of ground lamb serves as a flavoring, its deep savor contrasting the sweet corn. We wanted some spice to bring the elements together and North African ras el hanout, a common flavoring for lamb, also accentuates the corn. Serrano chiles add surprising heat to keep the dish interesting. Each element of this hash cooks at a different rate so we first cook them separately; then we mix them together and pack them into the skillet to get good browning; finally, we portion and flip the hash. Mint and another surprising ingredient, raw radishes, make the dish pop, the latter with their crunchy bite emphasizing the textures of the hash below. You can use thawed, frozen corn if you can't find fresh.

1 Toss potatoes with 1 tablespoon oil, ½ teaspoon salt, and pepper in bowl. Cover and microwave until potatoes are translucent around edges, 7 to 9 minutes, stirring halfway through microwaving; drain well.

2 Heat 1 tablespoon oil in 12-inch nonstick skillet over medium-high heat until shimmering. Add corn and ¼ teaspoon salt, cover, and cook, without stirring, until corn is charred, 3 to 5 minutes. Remove skillet from heat and let sit, covered, until any popping subsides, about 1 minute. Transfer corn to bowl with potatoes.

3 Cook lamb in now-empty skillet over medium-high heat, breaking up meat with wooden spoon, until no pink remains, about 5 minutes. Stir in onion and remaining ¼ teaspoon salt and cook until softened, about 5 minutes. Stir in serrano, garlic, ras el hanout, and dried mint and cook until fragrant, about 1 minute.

4 Stir in potato-corn mixture. Using back of spatula, gently pack potato mixture into skillet and cook, without stirring, for 2 minutes. Flip hash, 1 portion at a time, and lightly repack into skillet. Repeat flipping process every few minutes until potatoes are well browned, 6 to 8 minutes. Sprinkle with radishes and fresh mint. Serve.

Cals 460 | Total Fat 24g | Sat Fat 7g
Chol 40mg | Sodium 640mg
Total Carb 48g | Dietary Fiber 5g
Total Sugars 6g | Protein 17g

MUSHROOM BOURGUIGNON

**SERVES
4 TO 6**

3 HRS

½ cup extra-virgin olive oil, divided

5 pounds portobello mushroom caps, quartered, divided

1½ cups frozen pearl onions, thawed, divided

½ teaspoon table salt, divided

¼ teaspoon pepper, divided

⅓ cup all-purpose flour

4 cups chicken or vegetable broth

1 (750-ml) bottle red wine, divided

2 tablespoons unflavored gelatin

2 tablespoons tomato paste

1 tablespoon anchovy paste

2 onions, chopped coarse

2 carrots, peeled and chopped

1 garlic head, cloves separated (unpeeled), and smashed

1 ounce dried porcini mushrooms, rinsed

10 sprigs fresh parsley, plus 3 tablespoons minced

6 sprigs fresh thyme

2 bay leaves

½ teaspoon black peppercorns

*Cals 420 | Total Fat 21g | Sat Fat 3g
Chol 0mg | Sodium 840mg
Total Carb 27g | Dietary Fiber 5g
Total Sugars 13g | Protein 13g*

WHY THIS RECIPE WORKS Chunks of portobello mushrooms napped with a silky, luscious sauce with pearl onions, carrots, garlic, and red wine will make you forget that traditional French bourguignon has beef. Dried porcini mushrooms and anchovy paste beef up the flavor in this stew with their umami qualities. To achieve the body that would normally come from the collagen in the meat breaking down, we stir in a bit of powdered gelatin, which gives us a smooth, unctuous sauce and cuts the cooking time to boot. You can substitute agar agar flakes for the gelatin and omit the anchovies to make this recipe vegetarian. Use a good-quality medium-bodied red wine, such as a Burgundy or Pinot Noir. If the pearl onions have a papery outer coating, remove it by rinsing the onions in warm water and gently squeezing individual onions between your fingertips. Serve the stew over pasta, grains, or polenta.

1 Heat 3 tablespoons oil in Dutch oven over medium-high heat until shimmering. Add half of portobello mushrooms, half of pearl onions, ¼ teaspoon salt, and ⅛ teaspoon pepper, cover, and cook, stirring occasionally, until mushrooms have released their moisture, 8 to 10 minutes. Uncover and continue to cook, stirring occasionally and scraping bottom of pot, until mushrooms are tender and pan is dry, 12 to 15 minutes. Transfer vegetables to bowl, cover, and set aside. Repeat with 3 tablespoons oil, remaining portobello mushrooms, remaining pearl onions, and remaining ¼ teaspoon salt and ⅛ teaspoon pepper.

2 Add remaining 2 tablespoons oil and flour to now-empty pot and whisk until no dry flour remains. Whisk in broth, 2 cups wine, gelatin, tomato paste, and anchovy paste until combined and no lumps remain, scraping up any browned bits. Stir in chopped onions, carrots, garlic, porcini mushrooms, parsley sprigs, thyme sprigs, bay leaves, and peppercorns. Bring to boil and cook, stirring occasionally, until liquid is slightly thickened and onions are translucent and softened, about 15 minutes.

3 Strain liquid through fine-mesh strainer set over large bowl, pressing on solids to extract as much liquid as possible; discard solids. Return liquid to now-empty pot and stir in remaining wine. Bring mixture to boil over medium-high heat. Cook, stirring occasionally, until sauce has thickened to consistency of heavy cream, 5 to 7 minutes. Reduce heat to medium-low, stir in reserved portobello-onion mixture, and cook until just heated through, 3 to 5 minutes. Stir in minced parsley and serve.

BAHARAT CAULIFLOWER AND EGGPLANT WITH CHICKPEAS

SERVES
4

1¼ HRS

- 1½ pounds eggplant, cut into 1½-inch pieces
- 1 teaspoon table salt, divided
- ⅓ cup tahini
- 3 tablespoons water
- 5 tablespoons lemon juice, divided, plus lemon wedges for serving
- 1 small garlic clove, grated
- ½ teaspoon honey
- ⅛ teaspoon cayenne (optional)
- 1 small head cauliflower (1½ pounds), cored and cut into 1½-inch florets
- 1 (15-ounce) can chickpeas, rinsed and patted dry
- ¼ cup extra-virgin olive oil
- 1 tablespoon Baharat (page 14)
- ¾ cup chopped fresh cilantro, divided

  Quick-Pickled Onions (page 19)

  Plain yogurt

  Pita bread, warmed

WHY THIS RECIPE WORKS Warm spice and cauliflower are a smart pairing (in fact, you'll find them in other recipes in this chapter), and here Baharat brings out the nuttiness and subtle sweetness of this cruciferous vegetable. We roast the cauliflower with eggplant that's also spiced up for a sheet-pan recipe with contrasting textures and flavors all from vegetables. Stirring chickpeas into the mix turns roasted vegetables into dinner, and the beans highlight the nuttiness of the dish further. Serving the mix with a lemony tahini sauce that's a little sweet and a little spicy and pickled red onions enlivens the warm-spiced dish. Served with yogurt, this warm meal is made for scooping up with soft warm pita bread.

1 Adjust oven rack to lower middle position and heat oven to 450 degrees. Line rimmed baking sheet with aluminum foil and spray with vegetable oil spray. Toss eggplant with ½ teaspoon salt in colander and let drain for 30 minutes, tossing occasionally. Whisk together tahini, water, 3 tablespoons lemon juice, garlic, honey, and cayenne, if using, until smooth; season with salt and pepper to taste and set aside until ready to serve. (If needed, add more water 1 teaspoon at a time until sauce is thick but pourable.)

2 Pat eggplant dry with paper towels. Toss eggplant, cauliflower, chickpeas, oil, baharat, and remaining ½ teaspoon salt together in large bowl, then spread in even layer on prepared sheet. Roast until vegetables are very tender and beginning to brown in spots, 30 to 40 minutes, stirring occasionally.

3 Gently toss vegetables with ½ cup cilantro and remaining 2 tablespoons lemon juice and season with salt and pepper to taste. Sprinkle with remaining ¼ cup cilantro and serve with reserved tahini sauce, pickled red onion, yogurt, and pita.

Cals 570 | Total Fat 28g | Sat Fat 3.5
Chol 0mg | Sodium 1220mg
Total Carb 70g | Dietary Fiber 13g
Total Sugars 10g | Protein 20g

HERB VEGETABLE AND LENTIL BAKE WITH FETA

SERVES
4

1 HR

Herb Oil

½ cup fresh parsley leaves

¼ cup fresh dill

¼ cup fresh mint leaves

¼ cup extra-virgin olive oil

2 tablespoons lemon juice

1 garlic clove, minced

Roasted Vegetables

8 ounces small Yukon gold or red potatoes, quartered

1 large fennel bulb, stalk discarded, bulb halved, core left intact, and cut through core into ½-inch-thick wedges

2 tablespoons extra-virgin olive oil, divided

¾ teaspoon ground cumin

¾ teaspoon table salt, divided

½ teaspoon pepper, divided

2 zucchini, cut ½-inch-thick on bias

8 ounces cherry tomatoes

2 shallots, sliced thin

1 (15-ounce) can lentils, rinsed and drained well

4 ounces feta cheese, crumbled (1 cup)

WHY THIS RECIPE WORKS A garden's worth of vegetables star in this summery meal splashed with timeless flavors. When in season, the fennel, potatoes, zucchini, and tomatoes in this vegetable bake all have a fresh sweetness that benefits from the savor of a cumin rub. Leaving the core in the fennel (it softens nicely) ensures the pretty wedges stay intact and are easy to flip. Lentils round out the roasted vegetables, providing filling protein and a complementary earthy flavor—using canned lentils makes stirring them into the dish easy. Near the end of roasting, we sprinkle the vegetables with feta for a salty, briny flavor; it softens and browns appealingly over the dish. The finishing touch is a drizzle of an herbaceous—a whole lot of parsley, dill, and mint—oil. Dinner doesn't get much fresher than this. Use small potatoes measuring 1 to 2 inches in diameter.

1 For the herb oil Pulse all ingredients in food processor until coarsely chopped, about 10 pulses, scraping down sides of bowl as needed. Transfer to bowl and season with salt to taste; set aside until ready to serve.

2 For the roasted vegetables Adjust oven rack to upper-middle position and heat oven to 475 degrees. Toss potatoes, fennel, 1 tablespoon oil, cumin, ½ teaspoon salt, and ¼ teaspoon pepper together in bowl. Arrange vegetables cut side down on rimmed baking sheet and cover tightly with aluminum foil. Roast until vegetables are beginning to brown and are nearly tender, 15 to 20 minutes.

3 Remove foil and flip fennel wedges. Toss zucchini, tomatoes, shallots, lentils, shallots remaining 1 tablespoon oil, remaining ¼ teaspoon salt, and remaining ¼ teaspoon pepper together in bowl. Scatter evenly over top of vegetables on sheet then sprinkle with feta. Roast until tomatoes blister, feta starts to soften and brown slightly, and vegetables are tender, about 15 minutes. Drizzle with reserved herb oil and serve.

Cals 460 | Total Fat 28g | Sat Fat 7g | Chol 25mg | Sodium 850mg Total Carb 41g | Dietary Fiber 11g | Total Sugars 13g | Protein 14g

HASSELBACK EGGPLANT WITH MUHAMMARA

2 large eggplants (1½ pounds each)

1 teaspoon table salt, divided

1 cup jarred roasted red bell peppers, patted dry and chopped

¾ cup walnuts, toasted

10 tablespoons panko bread crumbs, divided

6 scallions, cut into 1-inch pieces

3 tablespoons pomegranate molasses

2 tablespoons ground dried Aleppo pepper

1 tablespoon lemon juice

1 teaspoon ground cumin

3 tablespoons extra-virgin olive oil

2 tablespoons chopped fresh mint

1 recipe Garlic Yogurt Sauce (page 16)

WHY THIS RECIPE WORKS Roasty, smoky eggplant typically has a creamy texture from edge to edge. It's delicious but we also wanted to experience eggplant with textural variety for a substantive main dish. To achieve a creamy interior and crispy edges, we borrowed the technique used for Hasselback potatoes. By making slices every ¼ inch crosswise down the length of the eggplant, stopping just short of slicing through, we create a setup that allows steam to escape during cooking so the eggplant gets tender without bursting and turning to mush. Just as important, we're able to pack the spaces between the slices with flavorful, robust muhammara. The sweet-spicy flavor awakens the earthy meatiness and slight bitterness of the eggplant. A creamy yogurt sauce rounds out the richness and is an attractive finishing touch. The eggplants are substantial on their own but you can also serve them with rice or grains, or a simple side of green beans.

1 Adjust oven rack to upper-middle position and heat oven to 400 degrees. Line rimmed baking sheet with aluminum foil and place wire rack in sheet.

2 Trim stem and bottom ¼ inch of eggplants, then halve lengthwise. Working with 1 half at a time, place eggplant cut side down on cutting board and slice crosswise at ¼-inch intervals, leaving bottom ¼ inch intact. Sprinkle eggplant fans evenly with ½ teaspoon salt, making sure to get salt in between slices. Transfer eggplant fanned side up to prepared rack and let sit for 15 minutes.

3 Process red peppers, walnuts, 6 tablespoons panko, scallions, pomegranate molasses, Aleppo pepper, lemon juice, cumin, and remaining ½ teaspoon salt in food processor to coarse paste, about 30 seconds, scraping down sides of bowl as needed. With processor running, slowly add oil until incorporated.

4 Pat eggplant dry with paper towels. Spread 1½ cups muhammara over eggplant, making sure to spread paste in between slices. Roast until eggplant is tender and easily pierced with tip of paring knife and edges are crispy and golden brown, 1 hour to 1 hour 20 minutes.

5 Remove eggplant from oven and heat broiler. Combine remaining 4 tablespoons panko and remaining muhammara in bowl. Spread panko mixture evenly over top of eggplant and broil until topping is crisp and golden brown, 1 to 3 minutes. Sprinkle with mint. Serve with yogurt sauce.

Cals 440 | Total Fat 25g | Sat Fat 3.5g
Chol 5mg | Sodium 800mg
Total Carb 51g | Dietary Fiber 12g
Total Sugars 26g | Protein 10g

LOADED SWEET POTATO WEDGES WITH TEMPEH

SERVES
4 TO 6

45 MINS

2 pounds sweet potatoes, unpeeled, cut lengthwise into 2-inch-wide wedges

5 tablespoons extra-virgin olive oil, divided

¾ teaspoon table salt, divided

8 ounces tempeh, crumbled into pea-size pieces

1 teaspoon ground cumin

1 teaspoon ground coriander

1 teaspoon smoked paprika

⅛ teaspoon ground cinnamon

4 ounces cherry tomatoes, halved

4 radishes, trimmed, halved, and sliced thin

1 jalapeño, sliced into thin rings

¾ cup chopped fresh cilantro

3 scallions, sliced thin

Plain yogurt

Lime wedges

WHY THIS RECIPE WORKS Sturdy caramelized wedges of sweet potatoes are excellent as a side dish, but they're an incredible base for a layered (and fun!) plant-based meal. Browning ground tempeh with generous spices gives this excellent source of plant-based protein a flavor that complements the sweet tubers as well as contrasting texture. But the toppings don't end there: Sweet cherry tomatoes, crisp radishes, spicy jalapeño, and generous fresh cilantro add more vegetables, lots of flavor, and color to boot. Some yogurt brings all the components together. You can plate this dish however you like but we think it's a great opportunity to eat dinner with your hands. This dish is great served simply with yogurt and lime wedges, but we also like this served with Quick-Pickled Onions (page 19) and Avocado-Yogurt Sauce (page 16).

1 Adjust oven rack to middle position and heat oven to 450 degrees. Line rimmed baking sheet with aluminum foil and spray with vegetable oil spray. Toss potatoes, 1 tablespoon oil, and ½ teaspoon salt together in bowl, then arrange potato wedges, cut sides down, in single layer on prepared sheet. Roast until tender and sides in contact with sheet are well browned, about 30 minutes.

2 Meanwhile, heat remaining ¼ cup oil in 12-inch skillet over medium heat until shimmering. Add tempeh, cumin, coriander, paprika, cinnamon, and remaining ¼ teaspoon salt and cook until well browned, 8 to 12 minutes, stirring often; set aside until ready to serve.

3 Transfer sweet potatoes to platter or individual serving plates and top with crispy tempeh, cherry tomatoes, radishes, jalapeño, cilantro, and scallion. Serve with yogurt and lime wedges.

*Cals 440 | Total Fat 20g | Sat Fat 3g
Chol 0mg | Sodium 630mg
Total Carb 54g | Dietary Fiber 9g
Total Sugars 14g | Protein 12g*

STUFFED PORTOBELLO MUSHROOMS WITH SPINACH AND GORGONZOLA

SERVES
4
—
1 HR

- 3 tablespoons extra-virgin olive oil, divided
- 10 large portobello mushroom caps (8 whole, 2 chopped fine)
- ½ teaspoon table salt, divided
- ¼ teaspoon pepper
- 12 ounces (12 cups) baby spinach
- 2 tablespoons water
- 1 onion, chopped fine
- 4 garlic cloves, minced
- ½ cup dry sherry
- 3 ounces Gorgonzola cheese, crumbled (1 cup)
- ½ cup walnuts, toasted and chopped
- ¾ cup panko bread crumbs

WHY THIS RECIPE WORKS Portobello mushrooms have a wide surface and naturally concave shape that make them ideal for achieving browning and holding robust ingredients. Roasting them gill side down allows any moisture released during cooking to drain away, and it protects the delicate underside of the mushrooms from burning. While the mushrooms roast, we make an easy stuffing with baby spinach, flavorful Gorgonzola cheese, and toasted walnuts that we top with panko bread crumbs. A quick run under the broiler heats everything through and crisps up the crown of bread crumbs. You can substitute cream sherry with a squeeze of lemon juice for the dry sherry.

1 Adjust oven rack to upper-middle position and heat oven to 500 degrees. Brush rimmed baking sheet with 1 tablespoon oil. Lay whole mushroom caps, gill side down, on baking sheet and brush tops with 1 tablespoon oil. Roast until tender, 10 to 12 minutes. Remove baking sheet from oven, flip mushrooms gill side up, and sprinkle with ¼ teaspoon salt and pepper.

2 Meanwhile, microwave spinach, water, and remaining ¼ teaspoon salt in covered bowl until spinach is wilted, about 2 minutes. Drain spinach in colander, let cool slightly, then place in clean dish towel and squeeze out excess liquid. Transfer spinach to cutting board and chop coarse.

3 Cook onion and remaining 1 tablespoon oil in 12-inch skillet over medium-high heat until softened, about 3 minutes. Stir in chopped mushrooms and cook until they begin to release their liquid, about 4 minutes. Stir in garlic and cook until fragrant, about 30 seconds. Stir in sherry and cook until evaporated, about 2 minutes. Stir in chopped spinach, Gorgonzola, and walnuts and cook until heated through, about 1 minute. Season with salt and pepper to taste.

4 Spoon filling into roasted mushroom caps, press filling flat with back of spoon, then sprinkle with panko. Bake until panko is golden and filling is warmed through, 5 to 10 minutes. Serve.

Cals 420 | Total Fat 28g | Sat Fat 7g
Chol 20mg | Sodium 700mg
Total Carb 29g | Dietary Fiber 6g
Total Sugars 7g | Protein 15g

LOADED SWEET POTATO WEDGES WITH TEMPEH

COUSCOUS-STUFFED ACORN SQUASH

2 acorn squashes (1½ pounds each), halved pole to pole and seeded

2 tablespoons extra-virgin olive oil, divided

¾ teaspoon table salt, divided

½ teaspoon pepper

1 shallot, minced

½ cup pine nuts or chopped walnuts

2 garlic cloves, minced

2 teaspoons Ras el Hanout (page 15)

½ cup couscous

1 cup water

¼ cup raisins

½ cup coarsely chopped fresh parsley, divided

¼ cup frozen peas, thawed

2 tablespoons pomegranate molasses

2 tablespoons pomegranate seeds

Cals 440 | Total Fat 22g | Sat Fat 2g
Chol 0mg | Sodium 450mg
Total Carb 59g | Dietary Fiber 6g
Total Sugars 18g | Protein 8g

WHY THIS RECIPE WORKS Stuffing vegetables of any shape, size, or texture is beloved across the Mediterranean, an activity that brings families together to make some fine comfort food. From boats of eggplant to small and hardy potatoes, if it's a vegetable it can serve as a vessel for stretching a meal. Acorn squash is a particularly tidy package for a complete meal. Here, we dress up a couscous filling with fragrant ras el hanout, aromatics, rich pine nuts, and hearty peas. After roasting the squash we scoop out the amber flesh and gently fold it into the couscous; this binds the mixture and gives it an earthy sweetness. We mound this filling into the squash shells and, since everything's cooked, all they need is a quick broil—and a drizzle of tart pomegranate molasses that knits the savory and sweet elements together, creating a satiating vegetarian weeknight dinner.

1 Adjust oven rack to upper-middle position and heat oven to 400 degrees. Line rimmed baking sheet with aluminum foil. Brush cut sides of squash halves with 1 tablespoon oil and sprinkle with ½ teaspoon salt and pepper. Place squash cut side down on prepared sheet and roast until tender and squash offers no resistance when pierced with paring knife, 35 to 45 minutes. Flip squash cut side up and let cool slightly, about 10 minutes.

2 Meanwhile, heat remaining 1 tablespoon oil in medium saucepan over medium heat until shimmering. Add shallot and remaining ¼ teaspoon salt and cook until softened and beginning to brown, about 5 minutes. Stir in pine nuts, garlic, and ras el hanout and cook until fragrant, about 30 seconds. Add couscous and cook, stirring constantly, until grains begin to brown, about 5 minutes. Stir in water and raisins. Cover and let sit until water is absorbed and couscous is tender, about 7 minutes. Fluff with fork and set aside.

3 Heat broiler. Using spoon, scoop flesh from each squash half into large bowl, leaving about ⅛-inch thickness of flesh. Fold couscous, ¼ cup parsley and peas into cooked squash. Gently mound squash-couscous mixture into squash shells.

4 Broil squash until beginning to brown, about 5 minutes. Drizzle with pomegranate molasses and sprinkle with pomegranate seeds and remaining ¼ cup parsley. Serve.

SPICED STUFFED PEPPERS WITH YOGURT-TAHINI SAUCE

½ cup extra-virgin olive oil

6 shallots (3 sliced thin, 3 chopped)

½ cup plain whole-milk yogurt

2 tablespoons tahini

2 tablespoons plus 3 cups water, divided

6 garlic cloves, minced, divided

1 tablespoon lemon juice

4 red bell peppers, halved lengthwise through stem and seeded

1 teaspoon table salt, divided

12 ounces 90 percent lean ground beef

3 tablespoons dried mint, divided

1½ tablespoons ground sumac, plus extra for sprinkling

1 tablespoon ground fenugreek

2 teaspoons ground cumin

2 teaspoons mustard seeds

¾ cup medium-grind bulgur, rinsed

1 (15-ounce) can lentils, rinsed

½ cup dried apricots, chopped

WHY THIS RECIPE WORKS Stuffed peppers are a crowd-pleaser, and the filling of our version is inspired by kibbeh, a Middle Eastern croquette-like dish made from bulgur, beef or lamb, onions, and aromatic spices. Browning beef and shallots with dried mint, sumac, fenugreek, cumin, and mustard seeds develops flavorful bits on the bottom of the pot, creating a savory base for steaming the bulgur. Adding meaty lentils and dried apricots allows us to use less beef; plus, the earthiness of the lentils and sweetness of the apricots round out the flavor. We halve the peppers through the stem for stability, and we char (rather than blanch) the peppers under the broiler before stuffing them for deeper flavor. A topping of fried shallots brings out the onion flavor and adds crispy contrast, while a generous sprinkle of dried mint gives the whole dish a vibrant accent. These posh peppers are dressed up further with a drizzle of yogurt-tahini sauce. Look for bell peppers that weigh at least 8 ounces each.

1 Microwave oil and sliced shallots in medium bowl for 5 minutes. Stir and continue to microwave in 2-minute increments until beginning to brown, 2 to 6 minutes. Stir and microwave in 30-second increments until golden brown, 30 seconds to 2 minutes. Using slotted spoon, transfer shallots to paper towel–lined plate and season shallots with salt to taste. Set shallots aside and reserve shallot oil. (Shallots can be stored in airtight container at room temperature for up to 1 month; shallot oil can be refrigerated for up to 1 month.) Whisk yogurt, tahini, 2 tablespoons water, one-third of garlic, and lemon juice together in bowl, then season with salt and pepper to taste; set aside until ready to serve.

2 Adjust oven rack 6 inches from broiler element and heat broiler. Line rimmed baking sheet with aluminum foil and place bell peppers on sheet. Drizzle bell peppers with 2 tablespoons reserved shallot oil and sprinkle with ½ teaspoon salt, then rub all over to coat. Arrange bell peppers skin side up and broil until spotty brown, 9 to 11 minutes. Set aside to cool while making filling.

3 Heat oven to 350 degrees. Cook beef and chopped shallots in large saucepan over medium-high heat, breaking up meat with wooden spoon, until beef is cooked through and shallots are softened and beginning to brown, 8 to 10 minutes. Stir in 1½ tablespoons mint, sumac, fenugreek, cumin, mustard seeds, remaining two-thirds of garlic, and remaining ½ teaspoon salt and cook until fragrant, about 1 minute.

4 Stir in remaining 3 cups water and bulgur, scraping up any browned bits, and bring to simmer. Reduce heat to low, cover, and simmer gently until bulgur is just tender and no liquid remains, about 10 minutes. Off heat, stir in lentils and apricots, lay clean dish towel underneath lid, and let mixture sit for 10 minutes. Season with salt and pepper to taste.

5 Arrange cooled bell pepper halves cut side up on sheet and divide beef-bulgur mixture evenly among halves, packing mixture and mounding as needed. Bake until warmed through, 20 to 25 minutes. Transfer to serving platter, drizzle with reserved yogurt-tahini sauce, and sprinkle with reserved crispy shallots, remaining 1½ tablespoons mint, and extra sumac. Serve.

Cals 520 | Total Fat 29g | Sat Fat 6g
Chol 40mg | Sodium 510mg
Total Carb 46g | Dietary Fiber 10g
Total Sugars 16g | Protein 21g

STUFFED TOMATOES WITH COUSCOUS AND ZUCCHINI

SERVES 4

1¼ HRS

8 large tomatoes (8 ounces each)

⅛ teaspoon table salt

3 tablespoons extra-virgin olive oil, divided

1 fennel bulb, stalks discarded, bulb halved, cored, and chopped fine

2 shallots, minced

1 zucchini (8 ounces), cut into ¼-inch pieces

4 garlic cloves, minced

⅔ cup couscous

¾ cup chicken or vegetable broth

2 ounces Parmesan cheese, grated (1 cup), divided

2 ounces goat cheese, crumbled (½ cup)

¼ cup chopped fresh basil

WHY THIS RECIPE WORKS Round tomatoes look like they're made for stuffing. The problem is that the fruit's watery nature can result in drab stuffed tomatoes with soggy fillings. We core and seed the tomatoes, salt their interiors, and let them drain, drawing out their excess liquid. After 30 minutes, the tomatoes give up most of their liquid so we can pack them with filling without it becoming soggy. The world of stuffed tomato options across the Mediterranean is more vast than just the rice, orzo, or bread crumb landscape you might find stateside. We use nutty-tasting couscous and pair it with sautéed zucchini and fennel. Goat cheese and Parmesan add richness and keep the filling cohesive. We sprinkle the stuffed tomatoes with Parmesan before baking them until the cheese is browned and the tomatoes are tender. Two tomatoes make a nice meal. Look for tomatoes of equal size with flat, sturdy bottoms that can sit upright on their own.

1 Adjust oven rack to upper-middle position and heat oven to 375 degrees. Slice top ⅛ inch off each tomato and carefully remove core and seeds. Sprinkle inside of each tomato with salt. Place upside down on large paper towel–lined plate and let drain for 30 minutes.

2 Meanwhile, heat 2 tablespoons oil in large saucepan over medium heat until shimmering. Add fennel and shallots and cook until softened and lightly browned, 10 to 12 minutes.

3 Stir in zucchini and cook until tender, about 5 minutes. Stir in garlic and cook until fragrant, about 30 seconds. Stir in couscous and cook until lightly toasted, 1 to 2 minutes. Stir in broth and bring to brief simmer. Remove saucepan from heat, cover, and let sit for 5 minutes. Using fork, gently fluff couscous, then stir in ½ cup Parmesan, goat cheese, and basil. Season with salt and pepper to taste.

4 Pat inside of each tomato dry with paper towels. Arrange tomatoes, cut side up, in 13 by 9-inch baking dish lined with aluminum foil. Brush cut edges of tomatoes with remaining 1 tablespoon oil. Mound couscous filling into tomatoes and pack lightly with back of spoon. Sprinkle with remaining ½ cup Parmesan. Bake until cheese is lightly browned and tomatoes are tender, about 15 minutes. Serve.

*Cals 420 | Total Fat 19g | Sat Fat 6g
Chol 15mg | Sodium 560mg
Total Carb 48g | Dietary Fiber 9g
Total Sugars 16g | Protein 18g*

SIMPLE VEGETABLE SIDES

The bounty of plants captured in the colorful dishes in this chapter is vast: There are multicomponent, substantial salads, vegetable-centric steaks and centerpieces, and one-pan vegetable dishes that can be paired with a number of grain side dishes, finished with a marvelous sauce or topping. The Mediterranean way rejects vegetables as just side dishes— they're stars. But stars needs sides too. A simple vegetable side you can prepare, often on the stovetop, while your main dish is cooking is a valuable way to get green next to your protein or grain main, or to bolster a plant-based meal. Eat an abundant diversity of vegetables for good health. Here are some foolproof recipes that would pair well with the Mediterranean flavors in this book— and still have personality of their own.

BOILED CARROTS WITH FENNEL AND CITRUS

SERVES: 4   TOTAL TIME: 30 MINS

Carrots are available year-round, making them a great go-to vegetable. Boiling them simply in very salty water is super-easy and has several benefits: It seasons them as they cook, it helps them retain more of their own natural sugars for flavor, and it helps them cook faster. Finishing touches of fat (olive oil) for richness, acid (lemon juice) for brightness, and fresh herbs (parsley) and spices (fennel seed) for flavor make this simple side dish a complement to any meal. We particularly like the sweet pieces as a contrast to cruciferous main dishes like Whole Romanesco with Berbere and Tahini-Yogurt Sauce (page 16); wheaty Bulgur Salad with Spinach, Chickpeas, and Apples (page 187); or warm-spiced Cumin-Coriander Roasted Cornish Game Hens (page 376). Crush the fennel seeds with a mortar and pestle or spice grinder.

1   pound carrots, peeled
2   teaspoons table salt
1   tablespoon extra-virgin olive oil
1   teaspoon lemon juice, plus extra for serving
½   teaspoon grated orange zest
½   teaspoon fennel seeds, crushed
1   tablespoon chopped fresh parsley

1 Cut carrots into 1½- to 2-inch lengths. Leave thin pieces whole, halve medium pieces lengthwise, and quarter thick pieces lengthwise.

2 Bring 2 cups water to boil in medium saucepan over high heat. Add carrots and salt, cover, and cook until tender throughout, about 6 minutes (start timer as soon as carrots go into water).

3 Drain carrots and return them to saucepan. Add olive oil, lemon juice, orange zest, and fennel seeds and stir until combined. Stir in parsley. Season with extra lemon juice to taste, and serve.

PAN-ROASTED BRUSSELS SPROUTS WITH LEMON AND PECORINO ROMANO

SERVES: 4   TOTAL TIME: 15 MINS

To create stovetop brussels sprouts that we'd jump to eat—deeply browned on the cut sides while still bright green on the uncut sides and crisp-tender within—we start these nutritional powerhouses in a cold skillet with plenty of oil and cook them covered. This gently heats the sprouts and creates a steamy environment that cooks them through. We then remove the lid and continue to cook the sprouts cut sides down so they develop a substantial, caramelized crust. Serve as a side to Barley with Fennel and Dried Apricots (page 188) or a number of simple proteins.

1   pound brussels sprouts, trimmed and halved
5   tablespoons extra-virgin olive oil
1   tablespoon lemon juice
    Salt and pepper
¼   cup shredded Pecorino Romano cheese

1 Arrange brussels sprouts in single layer, cut sides down, in 12-inch nonstick skillet. Drizzle oil evenly over sprouts. Cover skillet, place over medium-high heat, and cook until sprouts are bright green and cut sides have started to brown, about 5 minutes.

2 Uncover and continue to cook until cut sides of sprouts are deeply and evenly browned and paring knife meets little to no resistance, 2 to 3 minutes, adjusting heat and moving sprouts as needed to prevent them from over-browning. While sprouts cook, combine lemon juice and ¼ teaspoon salt in small bowl.

3 Off heat, add lemon juice mixture to skillet and stir to evenly coat sprouts. Season with salt and pepper to taste. Transfer to serving platter, sprinkle with Pecorino, and serve.

SPINACH WITH GARLIC AND LEMON

SERVES: 4   TOTAL TIME: 15 MINS

Tender sautéed spinach leaves seasoned with a perfect balance of garlic and lemon are a 5-minute avenue to adding a healthful side to any meal. We prefer the hearty flavor and texture of curly-leaf spinach over baby spinach, which wilts into mush, and we cook it in extra-virgin olive oil and then use tongs to squeeze the cooked spinach in a colander to get rid of the excess moisture. Lightly toasted minced garlic, cooked after the spinach, adds sweet nuttiness. Leave some water clinging to the spinach leaves after rinsing to help encourage steam when cooking. Let your spinach saddle up next to Pesto Farro Salad with Cherry Tomatoes and Artichokes (page 182) or perfectly cooked lentils (see page 200). Cook it as a bed for Halibut Puttanesca (page 339) or Arrosticini (page 409).

- 3 tablespoons extra-virgin olive oil, divided
- 20 ounces curly-leaf spinach, stemmed
- 2 garlic cloves, minced
  Lemon juice

1 Heat 1 tablespoon oil in Dutch oven over high heat until shimmering. Add spinach 1 handful at a time, stirring and tossing each handful to wilt slightly before adding more. Cook spinach, stirring constantly, until uniformly wilted, about 1 minute. Transfer spinach to colander and squeeze between tongs to release excess liquid. Wipe pot dry with paper towels.

2 Add garlic and remaining 2 tablespoons oil to now-empty pot and cook over medium heat until fragrant, about 30 seconds. Add squeezed spinach and toss to coat. Off heat, season with salt and lemon juice to taste. Serve.

PAN-ROASTED CAULIFLOWER WITH GARLIC AND LEMON

SERVES: 4 TO 6   TOTAL TIME: 40 MINS

Cauliflower is hearty but this fast stovetop method caramelizes its sugars and transforms the mild vegetable into something sweet and nutty-tasting, fast. Starting the oil and cauliflower together in a cold pan, cooking it first covered, then uncovered, results in both tender and caramelized florets. A combination of sautéed capers and lemon zest, plus fresh minced chives, perks up the flavors. And a sprinkle of crunchy toasted pine nuts makes it a complete and interesting side for Eggplant and Tomato Phyllo Pie (page 143), Tabil Couscous with Sardines (page 239), or Seared Tempeh with Tomato Jam (page 312).

- ¼ cup extra-virgin olive oil
- 1 head cauliflower (2 pounds), cut into 1½-inch florets
- 1 teaspoon table salt
- ½ teaspoon pepper
- 2 tablespoons capers, rinsed and minced
- 1 teaspoon grated lemon zest, plus lemon wedges for serving
- ¼ cup pine nuts, toasted
- 2 tablespoons minced fresh chives

1 Combine 2 tablespoons oil and cauliflower florets in 12-inch nonstick skilled and sprinkle with salt and pepper. Cover skillet and cook over medium-high heat until florets start to brown and edges just start to become translucent (do not lift lid during this time), about 5 minutes.

2 Uncover and continue to cook, stirring occasionally, until golden, about 12 minutes. Push florets to edges of skillet. Add remaining 2 tablespoons oil, capers, and lemon zest to center and cook, stirring with rubber spatula, until fragrant, about 30 seconds. Stir capers mixture into florets and continue to cook, stirring occasionally, until florets are tender but still firm, about 3 minutes.

3 Remove skillet from heat and stir in pine nuts and chives. Transfer florets to serving platter and serve, passing lemon wedges separately.

ROASTED ASPARAGUS WITH CILANTRO-LIME GREMOLATA

SERVES: 4 TO 6   TOTAL TIME: 20 MINS

We roast relatively thick asparagus spears on a preheated baking sheet in a 500-degree oven, which ensures that they brown deeply and quickly—no mush. Not moving the spears during cooking allows them to get a rich sear on one side and remain vibrant green on the other so they retain their freshness and tender snap. A topping of a freshened gremolata makes the simple spears special to coexist with (but not detract from) dishes like Brown Rice Pilaf with Dates and Pistachios (page 190), White Bean and Tuna Salad (page 199), or Tofu and Chickpea Flour Frittata with Mushrooms (page 308). To avoid harsh garlic flavor, don't mince the garlic until you're ready to mix the gremolata. This recipe works best with thick asparagus spears that are between ½ and ¾ inch in diameter.

Gremolata

- 4 tablespoons minced fresh cilantro
- 2 teaspoons grated lime zest
- 1 garlic clove, minced

Asparagus

- 2 pounds thick asparagus
- 2 tablespoons plus 2 teaspoons extra-virgin olive oil
- ½ teaspoon salt
- ¼ teaspoon pepper

1 For the gremolata Combine all ingredients in bowl; set aside.

2 For the asparagus Adjust oven rack to lowest position, place rimmed baking sheet on rack, and heat oven to 500 degrees.

3 Trim bottom inch of asparagus spears and discard. Peel bottom halves of spears until white flesh is exposed. Place asparagus in large baking pan and toss with 2 tablespoons oil, salt, and pepper.

4 Transfer asparagus to preheated sheet and spread into even layer. Roast, without moving asparagus, until undersides of spears are browned, tops are vibrant green, and tip of paring knife inserted at base of largest spear meets little resistance, 8 to 10 minutes. Transfer asparagus to serving platter, drizzle with remaining 2 teaspoons oil, sprinkle with gremolata, and serve immediately.

SAUTÉED RADISHES

SERVES: 4 TO 6   TOTAL TIME: 20 MINS

When sautéed, radishes are mellow and sweet: Heat concentrates the natural sugars in radishes while downplaying compounds responsible for radishes' pungent, peppery flavors. Since radishes contain relatively little water, within 10 minutes they become golden brown all over and perfectly tender, with a slight bite. To provide some textural variety and color, we cook the greens at the end, so that they retain a slight crispness that complements the heartier radish pieces. These are surprisingly versatile; try them with Riced Cauliflower with Preserved Lemon (page 123), Spelt Salad with Pickled Fennel, Pea Greens, and Mint (page 162), or Pork Tenderloin with White Beans and Mustard Greens (page 397). If you can't find radishes with their greens, you can substitute baby arugula or watercress, or skip step 2.

- 3   tablespoons extra-virgin olive oil
- 1½ pounds radishes with their greens, radishes trimmed and quartered, 8 cups greens reserved
-     Salt and pepper
- 1   garlic clove, minced
-     Lemon wedges

1 Heat 2 tablespoons oil in 12-inch skillet over medium-high heat until shimmering. Add radishes, ¼ teaspoon salt, and ⅛ teaspoon pepper and cook, stirring occasionally, until radishes are lightly browned and crisp-tender, 10 to 12 minutes. Stir in garlic and cook until fragrant, about 30 seconds; transfer to bowl.

2 Heat remaining 1 tablespoon oil in now-empty skillet over medium heat. Add radish greens, ⅛ teaspoon salt, and ⅛ teaspoon pepper and cook, stirring frequently, until wilted, about 1 minute. Off heat, stir in radishes and season with salt and pepper to taste. Serve with lemon wedges.

BROILED BROCCOLI RABE

SERVES: 4   TOTAL TIME: 20 MINS

Recipes tend to wash out broccoli rabe's spicy, distinctive flavor. Broiling broccoli rabe is a simple, superfast way to create deep caramelization, adding just a touch of contrasting sweetness to this bitter green vegetable. And it takes mere minutes. To keep things streamlined, we skip the usual blanching step and simply cut the tops (the leaves and florets) from the stalks, but do no further chopping. Toss the pieces with the garlicky oil and they're ready for the oven. The broccoli rabe is a great side dish but it's also tops—try using as a topping for Sweet Potato Hummus (page 295) or letting it share the bowl with Mushroom Farrotto (page 224).

- 3   tablespoons extra-virgin olive oil
- 1   pound broccoli rabe, trimmed
- 1   garlic clove, minced
- ¾   teaspoon kosher salt
- ¼   teaspoon red pepper flakes
-     Lemon wedges

1 Adjust oven rack 4 inches from broiler element and heat broiler. Brush rimmed baking sheet with 1 tablespoon oil.

2 Cut tops (leaves and florets) of broccoli rabe from stalks, keeping tops whole, then cut stalks into 1-inch pieces. Transfer to prepared sheet.

3 Combine remaining 2 tablespoons oil, garlic, salt, and pepper flakes in small bowl. Pour oil mixture over broccoli rabe and toss to combine.

4 Broil until exposed half of leaves are well browned, 2 to 2½ minutes. Using tongs, toss to expose unbrowned leaves. Return sheet to oven and continue to broil until most leaves are lightly charred and stalks are crisp-tender, 2 to 2½ minutes. Serve with lemon wedges.

PAN-ROASTED PARSNIPS

SERVES: 4   TOTAL TIME: 25 MINS

Uniquely floral, candy-sweet, and fully filling parsnips give us a lot of reasons to love them. In this convenient recipe, we replicate the sweet caramelized flavor of oven-roasted parsnips on the stovetop. After browning the parsnips in oil, we add water to the pan before covering—this creates a gentle steaming effect that guarantees perfectly cooked interiors. Cutting the parsnips into ½-inch-thick pieces on the bias assures even and plentiful browning. A sprinkling of fresh herbs and a squeeze of citrus does a delicious job of balancing the earthy vegetable and cutting through its sweetness. Look for parsnips no wider than 1 inch at their base, or you may need to discard their fibrous cores. Poultry is a favorite parsnip pairing as are super-savory legume dishes, like Lentils with Roasted Broccoli and Lemony Bread Crumbs (page 251), that can take the sweetness.

1	tablespoon extra-virgin olive oil
1¼	pounds parsnips, peeled and cut ½ inch thick on bias
½	cup water
¼	teaspoon table salt
1	teaspoon minced fresh parsley

1 Heat oil in 12-inch skillet over medium-high heat until shimmering. Add parsnips and cook, stirring occasionally, until golden, 8 to 10 minutes.

2 Add water and salt and bring to simmer. Cover, reduce heat to medium-low, and cook, stirring occasionally, until parsnips are tender and liquid has evaporated, 8 to 10 minutes. Off heat, stir in parsley and season with salt and pepper to taste. Serve.

CAULIFLOWER PUREE WITH BLISTERED TOMATOES AND 'NDUJA

SERVES
4

45 MINS

¼ cup extra-virgin olive oil, divided

4 garlic cloves, sliced thin

1 teaspoon table salt, divided

1 large head cauliflower (3 pounds), florets cut into 1-inch pieces, core peeled and sliced ¼ inch thick

1 pound cherry tomatoes, halved

⅓ cup balsamic vinegar

2 ounces 'nduja sausage, casing removed

2 tablespoons pine nuts, toasted

WHY THIS RECIPE WORKS Creamy polenta is a versatile dish that can stand as a meal on its own, especially when served with a topping (see page 228). We adapt that concept from grain to nutrient-packed vegetable: Cauliflower puree is equally silky and also has a mild, almost sweet, flavor that ably serves as a blank canvas for a simple but inspired topping that's hearty enough to make cauliflower the main event. We combine blistered cherry tomatoes with balsamic vinegar and tangy-spicy 'nduja, a fermented sausage consisting of fatty cuts of pork and spices. As these potent ingredients cook, the vinegar reduces into a sweet lacquering glaze. A sprinkling of pine nuts and garlic chips adds crunch and depth to this layered vegetable-centric dish.

1 Heat 3 tablespoons oil and garlic in 12-inch nonstick skillet over medium-low heat, stirring constantly once garlic starts to sizzle. Cook until garlic is light golden brown and crisp, 3 to 5 minutes. Off heat, using slotted spoon, transfer garlic to paper towel–lined plate and sprinkle with ⅛ teaspoon salt; set aside for serving. Transfer garlic oil to small bowl and set aside.

2 Meanwhile, bring 2½ cups water to boil in Dutch oven over high heat. Add cauliflower, cover, and cook until cauliflower is tender, stirring once halfway through, 14 to 16 minutes.

3 Drain cauliflower and transfer to food processor. Add 2 tablespoons water and ¾ teaspoon salt and process cauliflower until mostly smooth, 3 to 4 minutes, scraping down sides of bowl as needed. With processor running, drizzle in reserved garlic oil and process until completely smooth, about 30 seconds. (If puree is too thick, add extra hot water, 1 tablespoon at a time, until desired consistency is reached.) Season with salt to taste, set aside, and cover to keep warm.

4 Heat remaining 1 tablespoon oil in now-empty skillet over medium-high heat until just smoking. Add tomatoes and remaining ⅛ teaspoon salt and cook until skins blister and begin to release their juices, about 2 minutes. Stir in vinegar, scraping up any browned bits, and cook until thickened and syrupy, about 1 minute. Stir in 'nduja, breaking up meat with wooden spoon, and cook until fully incorporated and warmed through, about 30 seconds. Season with salt and pepper to taste. Top individual portions of cauliflower puree with tomato mixture and sprinkle with pine nuts and reserved garlic chips. Serve.

Cals 280 | Total Fat 22g | Sat Fat 3.5g
Chol 10mg | Sodium 790mg
Total Carb 17g | Dietary Fiber 4g
Total Sugars 9g | Protein 7g

Spreadable Sausage

So soft it's spreadable, 'nduja—a kind of salumi that traces to the small town of Spilinga in the Italian region Calabria—may be thrifty in its composition but represents an indulgence of the highest order. Named for its resemblance to French andouille, it's often made from a mix of pork shoulder, belly, and fatback as well as various less valuable cuts; liberally spiced to a fiery brick red; and slow-fermented so it takes on a notable tangy funk. What brings 'nduja's heat? Hot Calabrian peppers. Traditionally served at room temperature and spread on slices of bread or served with cheese, 'nduja is also added to tomato sauce; the meat effectively melts into the sauce, making it piquant and supersavory. You can find 'nduja in most Italian markets.

PATATE ALLA LUCANA

SERVES
4

2¼ HRS

1 tablespoon minced fresh oregano, divided

1 teaspoon table salt, divided

¾ teaspoon pepper, divided

¼ cup extra-virgin olive oil, divided

2 onions, halved and sliced thin

2 pounds russet potatoes

3 pounds plum tomatoes, cored and sliced ¼ inch thick

3 ounces Pecorino Romano cheese, grated (1½ cups), divided

¼ cup panko bread crumbs

WHY THIS RECIPE WORKS Lucania is an area of Italy settled by the Lucani in ancient times. It is now known as Basilicata, but even today, residents refer to themselves as Lucani. In keeping with much of the local cuisine, this rustic potato-tomato gratin is simple and intended to showcase the humble fruits of the region's rich soil—it's so full of vegetables, you don't need much besides a salad to eat the dish as a meal. To prevent a wet casserole, we make the dish with plum tomatoes and slowly sauté the onions until golden brown, which drives away water and adds a layer of complexity. Starchy russet potatoes help soak up the remaining juices. We like to serve the casserole with a simple braised green or salad. It is important not to slice the potatoes any earlier than the beginning of step 2 or they will begin to brown (do not store them in water; this will make the gratin bland and watery). Use a mandoline, a V-slicer, or a food processor fitted with an ⅛-inch-thick slicing blade to make quick work of slicing the potatoes.

1 Adjust oven rack to upper-middle position and heat oven to 400 degrees. Grease 13 by 9-inch baking dish. Combine 2 teaspoons oregano, ½ teaspoon salt, and ½ teaspoon pepper in bowl; set aside. Heat 2 tablespoons oil in 12-inch skillet over medium heat until shimmering. Add onions, remaining 1 teaspoon oregano, remaining ½ teaspoon salt, and remaining ¼ teaspoon pepper and cook, stirring frequently, until soft and golden brown, 15 to 20 minutes; set aside.

2 Peel and slice potatoes ⅛ inch thick. Shingle half of tomatoes evenly in prepared dish, then sprinkle with ½ cup Pecorino. Shingle half of potatoes on top, then sprinkle with half of reserved oregano mixture. Spread reserved onions over potatoes, then shingle remaining potatoes over top, followed by remaining tomatoes. Sprinkle with remaining reserved oregano mixture and drizzle with remaining 2 tablespoons oil.

3 Bake, uncovered, for 1 hour. Sprinkle with remaining 1 cup Pecorino and panko and bake until well browned and potatoes are tender (paring knife can be slipped in and out of potatoes with little resistance), about 20 minutes. Let cool for 30 minutes before serving.

Cals 480 | Total Fat 21g | Sat Fat 6g
Chol 15mg | Sodium 910mg
Total Carb 64g | Dietary Fiber 8g
Total Sugars 13g | Protein 15g

SPIRALIZED SWEET POTATOES WITH CRISPY SHALLOTS, PISTACHIOS, AND URFA

SERVES
4 TO 6

50 MINS

⅓ cup extra-virgin olive oil

2 shallots, sliced thin

2 pounds sweet potatoes, peeled

¾ teaspoon table salt, divided

2 teaspoons Urfa pepper, divided

1 teaspoon grated lemon zest plus 2 tablespoons juice

1 teaspoon honey

¼ cup shelled pistachios, toasted and chopped coarse

2 tablespoons chopped fresh tarragon

WHY THIS RECIPE WORKS The kick that spicy, smoky, slightly sweet Urfa pepper gives earthy sweet potatoes makes this swirly salad a star that's as delightful to eat as it is to look at. Urfa pepper (or Urfa biber) is a Turkish chile pepper named for the Urfa region where it's grown ("biber" means "pepper" in Turkish), and its notes of coffee, chocolate, and molasses add lots of depth to the dish, which we expand on by incorporating crispy shallots and brighten with a lemon vinaigrette. Spiralizing the sweet potatoes creates a beautiful-looking salad and enables this meal to come together quickly. Tossing the sweet potatoes in shallot oil from the crispy shallots before roasting stretches the ingredient and adds still more flavor to the potatoes. Finishing the sweet potatoes with tarragon and toasted pistachios contributes delicate fresh licorice flavor and sweet crunch, respectively. A larger serving is an intriguing meal; or you can pair it with a fried egg (see page 358) or a contrasting vegetable like brussels sprouts (see page 111). Look for sweet potatoes that are at least 2 inches in diameter at their widest point.

1 Adjust oven racks to upper-middle and lower-middle positions and heat oven to 450 degrees. Microwave oil and shallots in bowl for 5 minutes. Stir and continue to microwave in 2-minute increments until beginning to brown, 2 to 6 minutes. Stir and microwave in 30-second increments until golden brown, 30 seconds to 2 minutes. Using slotted spoon, transfer shallots to paper towel–lined plate and season shallots with salt to taste. Reserve shallot oil and let shallots drain for at least 5 minutes; set aside. (Shallots can be stored in airtight container at room temperature for up to 1 month; shallot oil can be refrigerated for up to 1 month.)

2 Square off potatoes by cutting ¼-inch-thick slices from each of their 2 short sides. Using spiralizer, cut sweet potatoes into ¼-inch-thick noodles, then cut noodles into 12-inch lengths. Toss potato noodles with 2 tablespoons reserved shallot oil and ½ teaspoon salt and spread in single layer over 2 rimmed baking sheets. Roast until potatoes are just tender, 12 to 14 minutes, switching and rotating sheets halfway through baking. Transfer potatoes to serving platter.

3 Whisk 1 teaspoon urfa, lemon zest and juice, honey, and remaining ¼ teaspoon salt together in bowl. Whisking constantly, slowly drizzle in 1 tablespoon reserved shallot oil until emulsified, then drizzle vinaigrette over potatoes. Sprinkle with reserved crispy shallots, pistachios, tarragon, and remaining 1 teaspoon urfa. Serve.

*Cals 240 | Total Fat 9g | Sat Fat 2g
Chol 5mg | Sodium 320mg
Total Carb 35g | Dietary Fiber 6g
Total Sugars 11g | Protein 5g*

RICED CAULIFLOWER WITH PRESERVED LEMON

SERVES
4

40 MINS

1 head cauliflower (2 pounds), cored and cut into 1-inch florets (6 cups)

1 tablespoon extra-virgin olive oil

1 shallot, minced

2 teaspoons paprika

1 teaspoon ground coriander

¾ teaspoon ground cumin

¾ teaspoon caraway seeds

½ cup chicken or vegetable broth

½ teaspoon table salt

¾ cup pitted green olives, chopped

1 tablespoon rinsed and minced Preserved Lemons (page 18)

½ cup chopped fresh parsley

WHY THIS RECIPE WORKS Wheat is a staple in Morocco, and the cuisine is known for many flavorful grain dishes—from wheat berries to, of course, its couscous—some of which are prepared to stand alone and some of which ably soak up the sumptuous flavors of famed stews and tagines. Cauliflower is another Moroccan standard that's become popular stateside "riced" in the food processor so its texture resembles that of couscous. We like that you can pack extra vegetables into your meal by serving cauliflower this way, and here we use the cruciferous vegetable to make a grainless "grain" dish that embodies the spirit of Moroccan couscous to surprising effect. Our steaming method allows the riced cauliflower to absorb flavors (paprika, coriander, cumin, and caraway) and cook up light and fluffy, with a tender chew. We finish with briny green olives, potent preserved lemon, and a sprinkle of parsley for a dish that could complement a full-flavored tagine or meat dish—just like couscous.

1 Working in 2 batches, pulse cauliflower in food processor until finely ground into ¼- to ⅛-inch pieces, 6 to 8 pulses, scraping down sides of bowl as needed; transfer to bowl.

2 Heat oil in large saucepan over medium-low heat until shimmering. Add shallot and cook until softened, about 3 minutes. Stir in paprika, coriander, cumin, and caraway seeds and cook until fragrant, about 30 seconds. Stir in processed cauliflower, broth, and salt. Cover and cook, stirring occasionally, until cauliflower is tender, 12 to 15 minutes.

3 Stir in olives and preserved lemon and cook uncovered, stirring occasionally, until cauliflower rice is almost completely dry, about 3 minutes. Off heat, stir in parsley and season with salt and pepper to taste. Serve.

Cals 100 | Total Fat 4g | Sat Fat 1g
Chol 0mg | Sodium 540mg
Total Carb 13g | Dietary Fiber 5g
Total Sugars 5g | Protein 5g

BRAISED EGGPLANT WITH PAPRIKA, CORIANDER, AND YOGURT

SERVES 4

1¼ HRS

- 2 (8- to 10-ounce) globe or Italian eggplants
- 3 tablespoons extra-virgin olive oil
- 2 garlic cloves, minced
- 1 tablespoon tomato paste
- 2 teaspoons paprika
- 1 teaspoon table salt
- 1 teaspoon ground coriander
- ½ teaspoon sugar
- ½ teaspoon ground cumin
- ½ teaspoon ground cinnamon
- ½ teaspoon ground nutmeg
- ½ teaspoon ground ginger
- 2¾ cups water
- ⅓ cup plain whole-milk yogurt
- 2 tablespoons minced fresh cilantro

WHY THIS RECIPE WORKS Name a cooking method, and it's probably used in the Mediterranean to cook the much-beloved eggplant. Sautéing, roasting, stewing, grilling, pureeing—each technique highlights eggplant's meaty-creamy texture and flavor in different ways. Braising—a method used for eggplant the world over—in a tomato-y warm-spiced liquid that reduces to a sauce produces meltingly tender, creamy-textured eggplant that's perfect for a vegetable-centric meal. Paired with a simple grain, this saucy dish satisfies big appetites. Cutting the eggplant into slim wedges means each has some skin attached to keep it from falling apart during cooking. A drizzle of tangy yogurt on top adds welcome richness. Large globe and Italian eggplants disintegrate when braised, so do not substitute a single 1- to 1¼-pound eggplant here. You can substitute 1 to 1¼ pounds of long, slim Chinese or Japanese eggplants if they are available.

1 Trim ½ inch from top and bottom of 1 eggplant. Halve eggplant crosswise. Cut each half lengthwise into 2 pieces. Cut each piece into ¾-inch-thick wedges. Repeat with remaining eggplant; set aside.

2 Heat oil in 12-inch nonstick skillet over medium heat until shimmering. Add garlic and cook until fragrant, about 30 seconds. Add tomato paste, paprika, salt, coriander, sugar, cumin, cinnamon, nutmeg, and ginger and cook, stirring constantly, until mixture starts to darken, 1 to 2 minutes. Spread eggplant evenly in skillet (pieces will not form single layer). Add water and bring to boil over high heat. Reduce heat as needed to maintain gentle boil. Cover and cook until eggplant is soft and has decreased in volume enough to form single layer on bottom of skillet, about 15 minutes, gently shaking skillet to settle eggplant halfway through cooking (some pieces will remain opaque).

3 Uncover and continue to cook, swirling skillet occasionally, until liquid is thickened and reduced to a few tablespoons, 12 to 14 minutes longer. Off heat, season with salt and pepper to taste. Transfer to platter, dollop with yogurt, sprinkle with cilantro, and serve.

Cals 150 | Total Fat 12g | Sat Fat 3g
Chol 0mg | Sodium 630mg
Total Carb 11g | Dietary Fiber 4g
Total Sugars 6g | Protein 2g

ROASTED FENNEL WITH CRUNCHY OIL-CURED OLIVES

Fennel

- 2   fennel bulbs, bases lightly trimmed, 2 tablespoons fronds chopped coarse, stalks discarded
- 2   tablespoons water
- ½   teaspoon table salt
- 3   tablespoons extra-virgin olive oil
- ¼   teaspoon pepper

Topping

- 2   tablespoons coarsely chopped pitted oil-cured olives
- ¼   teaspoon grated lemon zest

WHY THIS RECIPE WORKS Fragrant fennel is delicious—and high heat turns the vegetable into an even better version of itself. Roasting coaxes out hidden flavors, turning fennel into a nutty, savory-sweet vegetable that's the perfect accompaniment to light white fish dishes or more robust roast chicken. Layered fennel stays intact in the oven when cut into wedges and has lots of surface area for caramelization. Tossing the wedges with salted water gets seasoning between the layers and gives them some moisture for steaming to the right tender texture during roasting. Just as amazing? The sprinkle of salty, crunchy olives we top the fennel with, made by quickly microwaving oil-cured olives. Look for fennel bulbs that measure 3½ to 4 inches in diameter and weigh around 1 pound with the stalks (12 to 14 ounces without). The olives for the topping will crisp as they cool.

1 For the fennel Adjust oven rack to lower-middle position and heat oven to 450 degrees. Spray rimmed baking sheet with vegetable oil spray.

2 Cut each fennel bulb lengthwise through core into 8 wedges (do not remove core). Whisk water and salt in large bowl until salt is dissolved. Add fennel wedges to bowl and toss gently to coat. Drizzle with oil, sprinkle with pepper, and toss gently to coat. Arrange fennel wedges cut side down along 2 longer sides of prepared sheet. Drizzle any water in bowl evenly over fennel wedges. Cover sheet tightly with aluminum foil and roast for 20 minutes.

3 For the topping While fennel roasts, line plate with double layer of paper towels. Spread olives on towels. Microwave, stirring every 30 seconds, until olives start to dry and no longer clump together, 2½ to 3 minutes. Let cool for 10 minutes. Transfer olives to cutting board, sprinkle with lemon zest, and chop fine.

4 Remove foil from baking sheet and continue to roast fennel until side of each wedge touching sheet is browned, 5 to 8 minutes longer, rotating sheet halfway through roasting. Flip each fennel wedge to second cut side. Continue to roast until second side is browned, 3 to 5 minutes longer. Transfer to large plate. Sprinkle with olive mixture and fennel fronds and serve.

Cals 90 | Total Fat 7g | Sat Fat 1g
Chol 0mg | Sodium 216mg
Total Carb 6g | Dietary Fiber 3g
Total Sugars 3g | Protein 1g

HORTA

2 pounds dandelion greens, trimmed and cut into 2-inch lengths

Table salt for blanching

¼ cup extra-virgin olive oil

Flake sea salt

Lemon wedges

WHY THIS RECIPE WORKS In Greece, where this recipe hails from, horta simply means any wild greens, and they are prepared simply: either boiled or steamed and then drizzled with plenty of good olive oil, sprinkled with salt, and served with lemon. Dandelion greens—nutritious, easily accessible, and unabashedly bitter—are especially popular prepared in this manner. After boiling the greens, we lavish them with the traditional undistracting accompaniments that really bring the best out of the greens. Served with various starters and small plates or as a side to salmon, horta, as simple as it is, can surprise as the standout of a meal. This dish can be served warm, at room temperature, or chilled. Use mature dandelion greens for this recipe; do not use baby dandelion greens.

1 Bring 4 quarts water to boil in large pot over high heat. Add dandelion greens and 1 tablespoon salt and cook until thickest stems are just tender, 4 to 7 minutes. Drain greens in colander and, using rubber spatula, gently press greens to release excess liquid.

2 Transfer greens to serving platter, drizzle with oil, and season with sea salt to taste. Serve with lemon wedges.

A Foraged Green

While you may never forage in the wild for your food, there's an undeniable romance to the tradition. If you prefer to do your foraging at farmers' markets, you're in luck. Many wild greens are now available at farmers' markets and supermarkets. Some have even been transformed from foraged to cultivated status, like dandelions. Dandelions are, in fact, the most commonly seen foraged green (others include purslane, fiddleheads, ramps, nettles, and sorrel). Their culinary history in the Mediterranean is long and rich. When shopping for dandelion greens, avoid any bunches with yellow or wilted leaves or woody stems. Wrap them in paper towels inside a plastic produce bag and refrigerate for up to several days.

Cals 110 | Total Fat 8g | Sat Fat 1g Chol 0mg | Sodium 160mg Total Carb 10g | Dietary Fiber 4g Total Sugars 1g | Protein 3g

CHARRED GREEN BEANS WITH CORIANDER, SESAME, AND NIGELLA SEEDS

SERVES 4 TO 6

30 MINS

- 3 tablespoons tahini
- ¼ cup water, divided, plus extra as needed
- ½ teaspoon grated lemon zest plus 1 tablespoon juice
- ¼ cup extra-virgin olive oil, divided
- 1 garlic clove, minced
- 1 tablespoon sesame seeds, toasted
- 2 teaspoons coriander seeds, toasted and cracked
- 2 teaspoons nigella seeds
- 1½ pounds green beans, trimmed
- ½ teaspoon table salt
- ½ teaspoon pepper

WHY THIS RECIPE WORKS Green beans hold a special place on the celebration table at Rosh Hashanah, the Jewish New Year holiday, symbolizing prosperity. These green beans are appropriately celebratory and feature flavors found in Israeli cuisine. The cooking method, a hybrid covered-uncovered skillet method, turns out transcendently tender green beans with lots of charring. Tossing them off the heat with an aromatic blend of toasted coriander seeds, sesame seeds, and nigella seeds elevates the green beans with savory, citrusy, and nutty flavors and unique crunch. A final drizzle of creamy tahini sauce makes these beans memorable. While the dish is an impressive side, these beans wouldn't feel out of place as a resting place for poached or hard-cooked eggs as a light meal.

1 Whisk tahini, 2 tablespoons water, lemon juice, 1 tablespoon oil, and garlic together in bowl. Season with salt and pepper to taste, and adjust consistency with extra water as needed until sauce slowly drips from spoon; set aside. Combine lemon zest, sesame seeds, coriander seeds and nigella seeds in bowl; set aside.

2 Combine green beans, salt, pepper, remaining 2 tablespoons water, and remaining 3 tablespoons oil in 12-inch nonstick skillet. Cover and cook over medium-high heat until beans are bright green and nearly tender, 8 to 10 minutes, shaking skillet occasionally to redistribute beans.

3 Stir and continue to cook, uncovered, until water has evaporated and beans are spotty brown and fully tender, 7 to 12 minutes.

4 Off heat, stir in reserved seed mixture and season with salt and pepper to taste. Drizzle with reserved tahini sauce. Serve.

Cals 170 | Total Fat 14g | Sat Fat 2g
Chol 0mg | Sodium 210mg
Total Carb 10g | Dietary Fiber 4g
Total Sugars 3g | Protein 4g

Nigella Seeds

Not to be confused with black sesame seeds, nigella seeds have amazing taste and aroma, almost like that of onion and cumin and pine. That means a dish finished with these beautiful seeds gets more than just crunch. The seeds are common in the cuisines of India and the Middle East, baked into bread, seasoning meat, and sprinkled on salads. The allium kick they provide atop this simple dish of green beans is largely responsible for its superstar status.

SKILLET-ROASTED CARROTS WITH ZA'ATAR BREAD CRUMBS AND CILANTRO

SERVES
4

45 MINS

2 tablespoons panko bread crumbs

1 tablespoon Za'atar (page 15)

2 teaspoons plus 2 tablespoons extra-virgin olive oil, divided

⅛ teaspoon plus ½ teaspoon table salt, divided

½ cup water

1½ pounds large carrots, peeled and cut cross-wise into 3-inch-long by ¾-inch-wide pieces

1 tablespoon minced fresh cilantro

WHY THIS RECIPE WORKS Layers of textures and flavors help turn a humble side dish into something you can build your plate around. These carrots feature a trio of flavors—sweet, herbal, and tart—that appear often in Mediterranean cooking. Pan-steaming the carrots with a bit of water softens them and lets them shrink a bit to fit the size of the pan. We then cook off the moisture over medium-high heat, which gives the carrots great browning with streaks of char, a tender bite, and a concentrated flavor. Piles of these burnished carrots have plenty of texture and flavor notes on their own, but we elevate them further with a topping of panko bread crumbs that have been toasted with savory-tart za'atar and flecked with herbal cilantro. We prefer large carrots from the bulk bin for this recipe. Leave whole any carrots that are narrower than ¾ inch.

1 Combine panko, za'atar, 2 teaspoons oil, and ⅛ teaspoon salt in 12-inch nonstick skillet. Cook over medium-high heat, stirring constantly, until panko is deep golden brown and fragrant, 1 to 3 minutes. Transfer to small bowl and set aside to cool completely, about 10 minutes. Wipe skillet clean with paper towels.

2 Stir water and remaining ½ teaspoon salt in now-empty skillet until salt is dissolved. Place carrots in skillet, arranging as many carrots flat side down as possible (carrots will not fit in single layer). Drizzle remaining 2 tablespoons oil over carrots. Bring to boil over medium-high heat. Cover and cook, without moving carrots, until carrots are crisp-tender and water has almost evaporated, 8 to 10 minutes.

3 Uncover and gently shake skillet until carrots settle into even layer. Continue to cook, not moving carrots but occasionally pressing them gently against skillet with spatula, until undersides of carrots are deeply browned, 3 to 5 minutes longer. Stir carrots and flip pale side down. Cook until second side is lightly browned, about 2 minutes. Transfer to serving dish. Stir cilantro into panko mixture, then sprinkle carrots with panko mixture. Serve.

Cals 162 | Total Fat 10g | Sat Fat 1g
Chol 0mg | Sodium 489mg
Total Carb 18g | Dietary Fiber 5g
Total Sugars 8g | Protein 2g

The Beauty of Za'atar

In Arabic, za'atar can refer to a specific herb (*Thymbra spicata*); to several herbs that are related to thyme, savory, and oregano; or to a blend of spices (as we use it) that contains these herbs along with sesame seeds, salt, and sumac. This pleasantly pungent blend is a multipurpose ingredient used in the Mediterranean and Middle East. Za'atar (the blend) can be incorporated at the start or end of cooking. As a finisher, it's traditionally sprinkled on such dishes as kebabs, vegetables, and labneh to enliven them and add a little crunch. It's also incorporated into pastries, borek fillings, and salads. Mixed with oil it can lavish bread before baking, as is typical, or even a roast chicken.

PAN-STEAMED KALE
WITH BAHARAT

SERVES
4

35 MINS

1 cup chicken or vegetable broth

3 tablespoons extra-virgin olive oil, divided

1¼ pounds curly kale, stemmed and cut into 2-inch pieces (14 cups)

¼ cup golden or regular raisins

½ teaspoon Baharat (page 14)

1 teaspoon lemon juice, plus extra for seasoning

2 tablespoons slivered almonds, toasted

WHY THIS RECIPE WORKS In many cuisines, the touches of bitterness characteristic of dark, leafy greens are commonly countered with adornments. Rich olive oil, garlic, spices, dried fruits, or nuts transform braised or sautéed greens into thrilling, more complex dishes. Kale cooks quickly, retains its bite and viridity when tender, and its moderate bitterness is balanced by earthy sweetness. Our countering adornments here? Chiefly, baharat, a blend of more sweet and more savory spices that both brings out kale's sweet side and stands up to its pleasant bitterness. We bring a small amount of broth to a boil and steam the kale in it to a bright green while plumping golden raisins into juicy, sweet bites. The quick-to-make side is elevated with a sprinkle of crunchy slivered almonds.

1 Bring broth and 2 tablespoons oil to boil in Dutch oven over high heat. Add kale and raisins, cover, and reduce heat to medium-high. Cook until kale is tender with some resilience, about 7 minutes, stirring halfway through cooking. Combine baharat and remaining 1 tablespoon oil in bowl; set aside.

2 Uncover, increase heat to high, and cook, stirring frequently, until liquid has evaporated and kale starts to sizzle, 2 to 3 minutes. Push kale to 1 side of pot, add reserved baharat mixture, and cook until fragrant, about 30 seconds. Stir baharat mixture into kale. Off heat, stir in lemon juice. Season with salt and extra lemon juice to taste. Sprinkle with almonds and serve.

> ### The Spice's Spice
> Baharat is a spice blend used all over the Middle East, and the word is actually Arabic for "spice." The spices that make up the blend can vary from cuisine to cuisine, with most versions commonly including cumin, black pepper, and cinnamon, and often cardamom and clove. Regional additions include mint, rosebuds, allspice, saffron, ginger, and paprika. The intense profile befits meat dishes but also the heartier flavors of other ingredients like legumes or this kale. The blends work well as both a fundamental recipe ingredient and a finishing spice. Find our recipe on page 14.

Cals 200 | Total Fat 13g | Sat Fat 1.5g
Chol 0mg | Sodium 180mg
Total Carb 18g | Dietary Fiber 4g
Total Sugars 10g | Protein 6g

ROASTED OKRA WITH FENNEL AND OREGANO

1½ pounds okra, stemmed

3 tablespoons extra-virgin olive oil

2 teaspoons dried oregano

2 teaspoons fennel seeds, cracked

¼ teaspoon table salt

Lemon wedges

WHY THIS RECIPE WORKS Stewed okra is classic in many cuisines including those across the Eastern Mediterranean, where the vegetable is popular, but high-heat applications also bring out the best qualities of okra while being remarkably simple. We roast whole okra pods in a very hot oven; its dry environment keeps the okra from becoming too gelatinous and beautifully browns the outside. To speed things along, we preheat the baking sheet on the lowest rack. We season the okra with cracked fennel and dried oregano; a fair amount of oil gives the okra a good sear and helps these spices toast and bloom. Beyond this aromatic spice, all that the okra needs is a squeeze of lemon juice to add brightness. While they're a crispy-good snack, the pods make a great partner for other dishes; we particularly like pairing them with grain dishes. Do not substitute frozen okra here.

1 Adjust oven rack to lowest position, place rimmed baking sheet on rack, and heat oven to 500 degrees. Toss okra with oil, oregano, fennel, and salt in bowl.

2 Working quickly, carefully transfer okra to hot sheet and spread into single layer. Roast until okra is crisp-tender and well browned on most sides, 20 to 25 minutes, stirring occasionally to ensure even browning. Season with salt and pepper to taste. Serve with lemon wedges.

Understanding Okra

Okra contains a substance called mucilage. It's made up of chains of sugar molecules secreted outside the okra pod's cells and glycoproteins. Just like other food gels we're more familiar with, like gelatin or cornstarch slurry, okra's starches need both heat and water to fully form a gel. The molecules are loosened by the heat, and they then form a microscopic network that retains the water. This is why okra's mucilage viscosity increases with exposure to heat and water (this means slimy). Dry heat above 190°F damages the sugar-molecule chains so that they're less able to turn viscous. For this reason, our roasted okra stays as crisp as possible with minimal sliminess.

Cals 100 | Total Fat 7g | Sat Fat 1g
Chol 0mg | Sodium 105mg
Total Carb 8g | Dietary Fiber 4g
Total Sugars 1g | Protein 2g

WHOLE-WHEAT PIZZA WITH KALE AND SUNFLOWER SEED PESTO

SERVES 6 TO 8
makes 2 pizzas

1¼ HRS

2 garlic cloves, unpeeled

½ cup raw sunflower seeds

9½ ounces curly kale, stemmed and cut into 1½-inch pieces (5½ cups), divided

1 cup fresh basil leaves

1 teaspoon red pepper flakes (optional)

½ cup plus 1 tablespoon extra-virgin olive oil, divided, plus extra for drizzling

2½ ounces Parmesan cheese, 1½ ounces grated (¾ cup) and 1 ounce shaved, divided

¼ teaspoon table salt

6 ounces cherry tomatoes, quartered, divided

1 recipe Whole-Wheat Pizza Dough (page 147), room temperature

WHY THIS RECIPE WORKS Pizza has a rightful place in a healthful Mediterranean diet. Loaded with healthy kale, this is a nutritional powerhouse of a pizza that's also delicious. We top a hearty whole-wheat crust with a generous layer of kale and sunflower seed pesto. Cherry tomatoes provide bursts of sweetness and acidity to balance the earthy pesto underneath. We top the pizza with even more kale, which crisps in the oven. A few shavings of Parmesan complete the picture. We like the flavor of whole-wheat pizza dough in this recipe, but you can use any kind of pizza dough. Shape the second dough ball while the first pizza bakes, but don't top the pizza until right before you bake it. For more information on pizza dough, see page 147.

1 Adjust oven rack to middle position, set pizza stone on rack, and heat oven to 500 degrees. Toast garlic in 8-inch skillet over medium heat, shaking skillet occasionally, until softened and spotty brown, about 8 minutes. When garlic is cool enough to handle, remove and discard skins and chop coarse. Meanwhile, toast sunflower seeds in now-empty skillet over medium heat, stirring often, until golden and fragrant, 4 to 5 minutes.

2 Place 2 cups kale and basil in 1-gallon zipper-lock bag. Pound bag with flat side of meat pounder or with rolling pin until all leaves are bruised. Process garlic; sunflower seeds; bruised kale-basil mixture; and pepper flakes, if using, in food processor until finely chopped, about 1 minute, scraping down sides of bowl as needed. With processor running, slowly add ½ cup oil until incorporated. Transfer pesto to bowl, stir in grated Parmesan, and season with salt and pepper to taste. (Pesto can be refrigerated for up to 3 days or frozen for up to 3 months. To prevent browning, press plastic wrap flush to surface or top with thin layer of olive oil. Bring to room temperature before using.)

Cals 430 | Total Fat 25g | Sat Fat 4g
Chol 5mg | Sodium 790mg
Total Carb 41g | Dietary Fiber 5g
Total Sugars 3g | Protein 12g

3 Combine salt, remaining 3½ cups kale, and remaining 1 tablespoon oil, in bowl and massage lightly to coat leaves evenly; set aside. Heat broiler for 10 minutes. Working with 1 dough ball at a time, press, stretch, and roll dough into 12-inch round on lightly floured counter. Transfer dough to well-floured pizza peel and stretch into 13-inch round.

4 Spread half of pesto over surface of dough, leaving ½-inch border around edge. Scatter half of tomatoes and half of reserved kale mixture over pizza. Slide pizza carefully onto stone, return oven to 500 degrees, and bake until crust is well browned and edges of kale leaves are crisp and brown, 8 to 10 minutes. Remove pizza, place on wire rack, and let pizza rest for 5 minutes. Drizzle with extra oil and sprinkle with half of shaved Parmesan. Slice and serve.

5 Heat broiler for 10 minutes. Repeat process of stretching, topping, and baking with remaining dough ball and toppings, returning oven to 500 degrees when pizza is placed on stone.

ARUGULA PESTO AND POTATO PIZZA

SERVES
4 TO 6
makes 1 pizza

50 MINS

6 tablespoons extra-virgin olive oil, divided

1 pound small red potatoes, unpeeled, sliced ⅛ inch thick

2 ounces (2 cups) baby arugula

¼ cup pine nuts, toasted

1 garlic clove, minced

3½ ounces Parmesan cheese, 1½ ounces grated (¾ cup) and 2 ounces shaved

1 (1-pound) ball Thin-Crust Pizza Dough (page 147), room temperature

WHY THIS RECIPE WORKS Mild, creamy potato slices are the perfect taming partner to the peppery arugula that forms and flavors the pesto sauce on this pizza. We top the potatoes with shaved Parmesan to complement our pesto and add the requisite cheese component. We parcook the potatoes in the microwave; this ensures that they not only brown but also cook through in the short time the pizza is in the oven. Use a mandoline, V-slicer, or a food processor fitted with a slicing disk to make quick work of slicing the potatoes. Use small red potatoes that measure 1 to 2 inches in diameter. This recipe calls for one ball of dough; reserve and store the other dough ball for another use. For more information on pizza dough, see page 147.

1 Adjust oven rack to upper-middle position and heat oven to 500 degrees. Brush rimmed baking sheet with 1 tablespoon oil; set aside. Toss potatoes with 1 tablespoon oil in bowl. Cover bowl and microwave until potatoes are just tender, 3 to 7 minutes.

2 Process arugula, pine nuts, and garlic in food processor until smooth, 30 to 60 seconds. With processor running, slowly add remaining ¼ cup oil until incorporated, about 30 seconds. Transfer to bowl, stir in grated Parmesan, and season with salt and pepper to taste.

3 Press, stretch, and roll dough into 16 by 9-inch oval on lightly floured counter. Transfer to prepared sheet. Spread pesto over dough, leaving ½-inch border around edge. Shingle potatoes over pesto and top potatoes with shaved Parmesan. Bake until crust is well browned, 10 to 15 minutes. Let pizza rest on wire rack for 5 minutes. Slice and serve.

Cals 480 | Total Fat 25g | Sat Fat 5g
Chol 10mg | Sodium 750mg
Total Carb 49g | Dietary Fiber 2g
Total Sugars 6g | Protein 15g

LAVASH PIZZA WITH CAULIFLOWER, FENNEL, AND CORIANDER

¼ cup extra-virgin olive oil, divided

2 cups chopped cauliflower florets

1 fennel bulb, stalks discarded, bulb halved, cored, and chopped

3 garlic cloves, minced

3 tablespoons water

1 teaspoon ground coriander

½ teaspoon table salt

4 ounces whole-milk mozzarella cheese, shredded (1 cup)

¼ teaspoon red pepper flakes

2 (12 by 9-inch) lavash breads

2 ounces goat cheese, crumbled (½ cup)

1 scallion, sliced thin

WHY THIS RECIPE WORKS The Middle Eastern flatbread known as lavash has a crisp, cracker-like texture that makes a great base for a quick and easy dinner—maybe the easiest pizza you've ever made. To make sure the flatbreads are crisp enough to support the toppings, we brush them with oil and toast them quickly in the oven. A combination of cauliflower, fennel, and fragrant coriander makes for a simple yet flavorful topping. Two types of cheese, mild, milky mozzarella and tangy goat cheese, complement the vegetables and give our lavash more complex flavor. You will need a 12-inch skillet with a tight-fitting lid for this recipe.

1 Adjust oven racks to upper-middle and lower-middle positions and heat oven to 475 degrees. Heat 2 tablespoons oil in 12-inch skillet over medium heat until shimmering. Add cauliflower florets, fennel, garlic, water, coriander, and salt. Cover and cook, stirring occasionally, until tender, 6 to 8 minutes. Transfer to large bowl and let cool slightly, about 10 minutes. Stir in mozzarella and pepper flakes.

2 Brush both sides of lavash with remaining 2 tablespoons oil, lay on 2 baking sheets, and bake until golden brown, about 4 minutes, flipping lavash halfway through baking. Spread cauliflower mixture evenly over each lavash and sprinkle with goat cheese. Bake until cheese is melted and spotty brown, 6 to 8 minutes, switching and rotating sheets halfway through baking. Sprinkle with scallion. Slice and serve.

*Cals 400 | Total Fat 24g | Sat Fat 8g
Chol 25mg | Sodium 610mg
Total Carb 31g | Dietary Fiber 4g
Total Sugars 6g | Protein 15g*

HORTOPITA

SERVES
4 TO 6

2¼ HRS

1¼ pounds kale, Swiss chard, and/or dandelion greens, stemmed

¼ teaspoon plus ⅛ teaspoon table salt, divided, plus salt for blanching greens

7 tablespoons extra-virgin olive oil, divided

2 leeks, white and light green parts only, halved lengthwise, sliced thin, and washed thoroughly

3 garlic cloves, minced

¼ teaspoon pepper, divided

6 ounces feta cheese, crumbled (1½ cups)

2 large eggs, lightly beaten

⅓ cup minced fresh dill

3 tablespoons minced fresh mint

14 sheets (14 by 9-inch) phyllo, thawed, room temperature

2 teaspoons sesame seeds and/or nigella seeds (optional)

Cals 430 | Total Fat 27g | Sat Fat 8g
Chol 85mg | Sodium 770mg
Total Carb 36g | Dietary Fiber 3g
Total Sugars 4g | Protein 13g

WHY THIS RECIPE WORKS Savory pies are among the most iconic of Greek foods: Made with crispy, flaky phyllo layers enveloping herbs, greens, or other vegetables; eggs or meat; and cheese, they're as texturally interesting as they are rich and deeply flavorful. While spanakopita is one of the best-known pies, its wilder ancestor—hortopita—relies on a variety of wild greens (horta; see page 127), including dandelion, mustard, chicory, and sorrel, as well as wild fennel and dill fronds that were traditionally foraged by Greek cooks. While we encourage you to experiment with your favorites (foraged or not), we developed our recipe using kale, Swiss chard, and dandelion greens, a pleasing combination of both hearty and tender greens that provides a balance of mild and assertive flavors. Supplemented with a generous dose of dill and mint, a base of sweet leeks, and a sprinkling of briny feta, the filling is complex and aromatic, perfect for encasing in tissue-thin sheets of phyllo that crisp up into flaky layers. Serve with a salad and you're sure to get your greens. Thaw phyllo in the refrigerator overnight or on the counter for 4 to 5 hours; don't thaw it in the microwave. Allow phyllo to come to room temperature before using. For more information on phyllo dough, see page 149.

1 Adjust oven rack to upper-middle position and heat oven to 400 degrees. Line rimmed baking sheet with parchment paper. Bring 4 quarts water to boil in large pot over high heat. Add greens and 1 tablespoon salt and cook until tender and bright green, 2 minutes for Swiss chard and dandelion greens and 4 minutes for kale. Drain in colander and run under cold water until cool enough to handle, about 1 minute. Using your hands, firmly press cooled greens to release as much liquid as possible. Chop greens fine, then transfer to large bowl and set aside.

2 Heat 3 tablespoons oil in now-empty pot over medium heat until shimmering. Add leeks, garlic, ⅛ teaspoon pepper, and ¼ teaspoon salt and cook until leeks are softened, 5 to 7 minutes. Transfer leeks to bowl with chopped greens and set aside to cool slightly, about 10 minutes. Stir in feta, eggs, dill, mint, remaining ⅛ teaspoon salt, and remaining ⅛ teaspoon pepper; set aside.

3 Place remaining ¼ cup oil in small bowl. Place 16 by 12-inch sheet of parchment paper on counter with long side parallel to edge of counter. Place 1 phyllo sheet on parchment with long side parallel to edge of counter. Lightly brush sheet with oil. Repeat with 6 more phyllo sheets and oil, stacking sheets as you go.

4 Arrange half of greens mixture in 2½ by 10-inch rectangle 2 inches from bottom edge of phyllo and about 2 inches from each side. Using parchment, fold sides of phyllo over filling, then fold bottom edge of phyllo over filling. Brush folded portions of phyllo with oil. Fold top edge over filling, making sure top and bottom edges overlap by about 1 inch. (If they do not overlap, unfold, rearrange filling into slightly narrower strip, and refold.) Press firmly to seal. Using thin metal spatula, carefully transfer to prepared sheet. Repeat process with remaining phyllo, oil, and remaining greens mixture, evenly spacing hortopita on prepared sheet. Lightly brush top and sides with oil. Using sharp knife, make 6 evenly spaced ¼-inch deep slashes, 2 inches long, on top of each hortopita. Sprinkle with sesame and nigella seeds, if using.

5 Bake hortopita until golden brown, 35 to 40 minutes, rotating sheet halfway through baking. Let cool for 15 minutes before slicing. Serve.

EGGPLANT AND TOMATO PHYLLO PIE

SERVES 4 TO 6

2¾ HRS

1 pound tomatoes, cored and sliced ¼ inch thick

1¼ teaspoons table salt, divided

1 pound eggplant, sliced into ¼-inch-thick rounds

½ cup extra-virgin olive oil, divided

12 sheets (14 by 9-inch) phyllo, thawed, room temperature

3 garlic cloves, minced

2 teaspoons minced fresh oregano

¼ teaspoon pepper

6 ounces mozzarella cheese, shredded (1½ cups)

2 tablespoons grated Parmesan cheese

1 tablespoon chopped fresh basil

Cals 410 | Total Fat 28g | Sat Fat 8g
Chol 20mg | Sodium 800mg
Total Carb 28g | Dietary Fiber 3g
Total Sugars 4g | Protein 10g

WHY THIS RECIPE WORKS Eggplants and tomatoes live together famously in a number of satisfying dishes across the Mediterranean. We combine the two with cheese, garlic, and fresh herbs and bake them in a shatteringly crisp phyllo crust. To bring out the best in the tomatoes' flavor, capture their juiciness, and avoid a soggy tart, we salt the slices and let them sit in a colander to draw out excess moisture before building the tart. Broiling the eggplant first gives it deeper flavor and a delightful char. Shredded fresh mozzarella melts beautifully into the crust for a satisfying cheesy layer that keeps the bottom from getting soggy. Thaw phyllo in the refrigerator overnight or on the counter for 4 to 5 hours; don't thaw it in the microwave. Allow phyllo to come to room temperature before using. For more information on phyllo dough, see page 150.

1 Adjust oven rack 6 inches from broiler element and heat broiler. Line rimmed baking sheet with aluminum foil. Toss tomatoes and ¾ teaspoon salt together in colander and set aside to drain for 30 minutes.

2 Meanwhile, arrange eggplant in single layer on prepared sheet and brush both sides with 2 tablespoons oil. Broil eggplant until softened and beginning to brown, 10 to 12 minutes, flipping eggplant halfway through broiling. Set aside to cool slightly, about 10 minutes.

3 Heat oven to 375 degrees. Line second rimmed baking sheet with parchment paper. Place ¼ cup oil in small bowl. Place 1 phyllo sheet on prepared sheet then lightly brush phyllo with prepared oil. Turn baking sheet 30 degrees and place second phyllo sheet on first phyllo sheet, leaving any overhanging phyllo in place. Brush second phyllo sheet with oil. Repeat turning baking sheet and layering remaining 10 phyllo sheets in pinwheel pattern, brushing each with oil (you should have 12 total layers of phyllo).

4 Shake colander to rid tomatoes of excess juice. Combine tomatoes, garlic, oregano, pepper, 1 tablespoon oil, and remaining ½ teaspoon salt in bowl. Sprinkle mozzarella evenly in center of phyllo in 9-inch circle. Shingle tomatoes and eggplant on top of mozzarella in concentric circles, alternating tomatoes and eggplant as you go. Sprinkle Parmesan cheese over top.

5 Gently fold edges of phyllo over vegetable mixture, pleating every 2 to 3 inches as needed, and lightly brush edges with remaining 1 tablespoon oil. Bake until phyllo is crisp and golden brown, about 30 to 35 minutes. Let galette cool for 15 minutes then sprinkle with basil. Slice and serve.

KATAIFI-WRAPPED FETA WITH TOMATOES AND ARTICHOKES

SERVES
4 TO 6

55 MINS

1 (8-ounce) block feta cheese, cut into eight 3-inch-long by ¾-inch-thick fingers

7 tablespoons extra-virgin olive oil, divided

½ teaspoon dried oregano

¼ teaspoon red pepper flakes

6 ounces kataifi, thawed, unwrapped, and covered with damp towel

1½ pounds grape tomatoes, halved

1½ cups jarred whole artichoke hearts packed in water, rinsed, patted dry, and quartered

3 garlic cloves, minced

¼ teaspoon table salt

¼ teaspoon pepper

1 cup fresh parsley, dill, or mint leaves, torn

WHY THIS RECIPE WORKS Watching the creation of thin strands of kataifi pastry is mesmerizing: A batter drips out of tiny holes onto a huge spinning hot metal plate. The concentric circles of batter briefly cook before being swept up by hand into a bundle of thin, delicate strands. (While the dough is known as kataifi in Greece, it is also known as knafeh or kunafa in Arab countries, and kadayif in Turkey.) The dough is most frequently used for baklava-style desserts, wrapped tightly around nut fillings, or broken into pieces and pressed into layers to encase a sweet cheese filling in the eponymous sugar syrup–soaked dessert knafeh. Here we use kataifi in a savory application, showcasing the unique crispy quality of the pastry by wrapping it around soft baked feta. We serve the bundles nestled in a barely-cooked tomato and artichoke sauce, which stands in juicy contrast to the pastry and rounds out the plate. Thaw kataifi in the refrigerator overnight or on the counter for 4 to 5 hours; don't thaw it in the microwave. Allow kataifi to come to room temperature before using for easiest handling. For more information, see page 151.

1 Adjust oven rack to upper-middle position and heat oven to 400 degrees. Line rimmed baking sheet with parchment paper. Brush feta with 1 tablespoon oil and sprinkle with oregano and red pepper flakes. Set aside.

2 Unspool kataifi so that strands lay flat in straight line, then cut into 8-inch lengths, discarding excess. Divide strands of kataifi into eight 8-inch-long by 3-inch-wide rectangles with short side parallel to edge of counter. Gently dab and brush rectangles with 3 tablespoons oil.

3 Place 1 feta finger at narrow end of kataifi rectangle, parallel to edge of counter, and roll kataifi around feta into tidy bundle. Place on prepared sheet. Repeat with remaining feta and kataifi rectangles, spacing feta bundles evenly apart on prepared sheet. Bake until pastry is golden brown, about 25 minutes.

4 Meanwhile, heat remaining 3 tablespoons oil in 12-inch nonstick skillet over medium-high heat until shimmering. Add tomatoes, artichokes, garlic, salt, and pepper and cook until tomatoes release their juices and just begin to break down, about 5 minutes. Off heat, stir in parsley. Serve kataifi-wrapped feta with tomato-artichoke mixture.

Cals 380 | Total Fat 26g | Sat Fat 8g Chol 35mg | Sodium 630mg Total Carb 27g | Dietary Fiber 2g Total Sugars 5g | Protein 10g

DOUGHS FOR MEDITERRANEAN RECIPES

Pizzas with chewy, wheaty crusts and savory pastries enveloped in what seems like countless layers of crispy phyllo dough are a go on a Mediterranean diet—they serve as a base or wrapper for plant-forward, good-for-you fillings. Once you master working with the staple doughs we've shared, dinner is a breeze—just shape, top, and bake.

Pizza Doughs

Use these pizza dough recipes for the pizzas in this book or for your own creations. You can make the doughs up to 2 days ahead and proceed with step 3 when you're ready to bake. Be sure to bring the dough to room temperature before rolling. If you're making one pizza and want to freeze the rest of the dough, allow the dough to proof in the refrigerator for 24 hours in step 2. Place one dough ball on a plate lined with parchment paper. Cover with plastic wrap and freeze until firm, about 3 hours. Wrap dough ball in plastic and store in zipper-lock bag in freezer for up to 2 weeks. To thaw, unwrap ball, place in lightly oiled bowl, cover with plastic, and refrigerate for 12 to 24 hours.

WHOLE-WHEAT PIZZA DOUGH

MAKES ENOUGH FOR TWO 13-INCH PIZZAS
TOTAL TIME: 25 MINS, PLUS 19 HOURS RESTING

- 1½ cups (8¼ ounces) whole-wheat flour
- 1 cup (5½ ounces) bread flour
- 2 teaspoons sugar
- ¾ teaspoon instant or rapid-rise yeast
- 1¼ cups ice water
- 2 tablespoons extra-virgin olive oil
- 1¾ teaspoons table salt

1 Process whole-wheat flour, bread flour, sugar, and yeast in food processor until combined, about 2 seconds. With processor running, slowly add ice water and process until dough is just combined and no dry flour remains, about 10 seconds. Let dough rest for 10 minutes.

2 Add oil and salt to dough and process until dough forms satiny, sticky ball that clears sides of bowl, 45 to 60 seconds. Transfer dough to lightly oiled counter and knead by hand to form smooth, round ball, about 1 minute. Place dough seam side down in lightly greased large bowl, cover tightly with plastic wrap, and refrigerate for at least 18 hours or up to 2 days.

3 Remove dough from refrigerator and divide in half. Shape each half into smooth, tight ball. Space dough balls 3 inches apart on lightly oiled rimmed baking sheet, cover loosely with greased plastic wrap, and let rest for 1 hour.

THIN-CRUST PIZZA DOUGH

MAKES ENOUGH FOR TWO 13-INCH PIZZAS
TOTAL TIME: 25 MINUTES, PLUS 25 HOURS RESTING

- 3 cups (16½ ounces) bread flour
- 2 tablespoons sugar
- ½ teaspoon instant or rapid-rise yeast
- 1⅓ cups ice water
- 1 tablespoon vegetable oil
- 1½ teaspoons table salt

1 Process flour, sugar, and yeast in food processor until combined, about 2 seconds. With processor running, slowly add ice water and process until dough is just combined and no dry flour remains, about 10 seconds. Let dough rest for 10 minutes.

2 Add oil and salt to dough and process until dough forms satiny, sticky ball that clears sides of bowl, 30 to 60 seconds. Transfer dough to lightly oiled counter and knead by hand to form smooth, round ball, about 1 minute. Place dough seam side down in lightly greased large bowl, cover tightly with plastic wrap, and refrigerate for at least 24 hours or up to 3 days.

3 Remove dough from refrigerator and divide in half. Shape each half into smooth, tight ball. Space dough balls 3 inches apart on lightly oiled rimmed baking sheet, cover loosely with greased plastic wrap, and let rest for 1 hour.

Forming Pizza Dough

1 Press, stretch, and roll dough into 12-inch round on lightly floured counter.

2 Transfer dough to well-floured pizza peel and stretch into 13-inch round.

Phyllo Dough

Phyllo dough, tissue-thin layers of pastry dough used for sweet and savory pastries in Greece and the Middle East (and in this book), is available in two sizes: full-size sheets that are 18 by 14 inches (about 20 per box) and half-size sheets that are 14 by 9 inches (about 40 per box). The smaller sheets are more common, so we use those in our recipes. If you buy the large sheets, simply cut them in half. Below are some other pointers that make working with this delicate dough easier, followed by instruction on forming the recipes in this book using it.

■ **Thaw the phyllo dough completely before using.** Frozen phyllo must be thawed before using. This is best achieved by placing the phyllo in the refrigerator for at least 12 hours.

■ **Keep the phyllo covered when using.** Phyllo dries out very quickly. As soon as the phyllo is removed from its plastic sleeve, unfold the dough and carefully flatten it with your hands. Cover with plastic wrap, then a damp dish towel.

■ **Throw out badly torn sheets of dough.** Usually each box has one or two badly torn sheets of phyllo that can't be salvaged. But if the sheets have just small cuts or tears, you can still work with them—put them in the middle of the pastry, where imperfections will go unnoticed. If all of the sheets have the exact same tear, alternate the orientation of each sheet when assembling the pastry.

■ **Don't refreeze leftover dough.** Leftover sheets cannot be refrozen, but they can be rerolled, wrapped in plastic wrap, and stored in the refrigerator for up to five days.

Making Hortopita (page 140) with Phyllo

1 Place 16 by 12-inch sheet of parchment paper on counter with long side parallel to edge of counter. Place 1 phyllo sheet on parchment with long side parallel to edge of counter.

2 Lightly brush phyllo sheet with oil.

3 Repeat with 6 more phyllo sheets and oil, stacking sheets as you go.

4 Arrange half of greens mixture in 2½ by 10-inch rectangle 2 inches from bottom edge of phyllo and about 2 inches from each side. Using parchment, fold sides of phyllo over filling, then fold bottom edge of phyllo over filling.

5 Fold bottom edge of phyllo over filling.

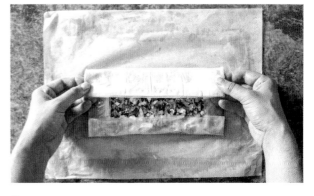

6 Brush folded portions of phyllo with oil. Fold top edge over filling, making sure top and bottom edges overlap by about 1 inch. Press firmly to seal.

Making Eggplant and Tomato Phyllo Pie (page 143) with Phyllo

1 Line rimmed baking sheet with parchment paper. Place 1 phyllo sheet on prepared sheet then lightly brush phyllo with prepared oil.

2 Turn baking sheet 30 degrees and place second phyllo sheet on first phyllo sheet, leaving any overhanging phyllo in place. Brush second phyllo sheet with oil.

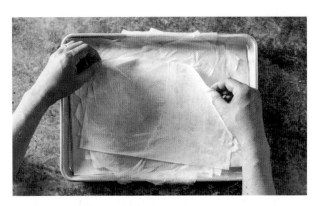

3 Repeat turning baking sheet and layering remaining 10 phyllo sheets in pinwheel pattern, brushing each with oil (you should have 12 total layers of phyllo).

4 Gently fold edges of phyllo over vegetable mixture, pleating every 2 to 3 inches as needed, and lightly brush edges with remaining 1 tablespoon oil.

Kataifi Dough

Kataifi is essentially shreds of phyllo dough, made by dripping the batter in circles on a hot metal plate. Oftentimes the dough wraps around sticky-sweet nut fillings like baklava; other times the pastries are savory. In this book it forms a crispy, crunchy nest around fingers of briny feta, slightly softened from the oven's heat.

Like phyllo, the dough needs to stay moist; be sure to mist the kataifi if it becomes dry while using and keep it covered with damp towel. Similarly you should thaw the kataifi dough completely before using. This is best achieved by placing the kataifi in the refrigerator overnight or on the counter for 4 to 5 hours. (Be sure not to use the microwave.) And it should be at room temperature for easiest handling. Unused thawed kataifi can be stored in the refrigerator for 2 weeks.

Making Kataifi-Wrapped Feta with Tomatoes and Artichokes (page 144)

1 Unspool kataifi so that strands lay flat in straight line, then cut into 8-inch lengths, discarding excess.

2 Divide strands of kataifi into eight 8-inch-long by 3-inch-wide rectangles with short side parallel to edge of counter.

3 Gently dab and brush rectangles with 3 tablespoons oil.

4 Place 1 feta finger at narrow end of kataifi rectangle, parallel to edge of counter, and roll kataifi around feta into tidy bundle.

Fresh Turmeric

Turmeric, the rhizome (underground stem) of a plant in the ginger family, might be more familiar to you as the ground spice with a bright yellow color; earthy, slightly bitter flavor; and touch of gingery heat. Fresh turmeric has its own beautiful qualities, however, bringing brightness and complexity. It's most perceptible in raw foods; in cooked applications, it can be hard to tell fresh turmeric from dried. You can buy just a small amount of fresh turmeric (which makes it inexpensive) and refrigerate any extra for up to four weeks in an airtight container or zipper-lock bag to keep it fresh. A spoon makes quick work of removing turmeric's thin skin, and a rasp-style grater breaks it down in a flash.

SPICED CAULIFLOWER FRITTERS

**SERVES
4**

45 MINS

Yogurt

- ½ cup whole-milk Greek yogurt
- 1 tablespoon minced fresh tarragon
- 1½ teaspoons grated fresh turmeric
- ½ teaspoon grated lemon or lime zest plus 2 teaspoons juice
- 1 small garlic clove, minced to paste

Fritters

- 1 head cauliflower (2 pounds), cored and cut into 1-inch florets
- ¼ cup water
- 1 teaspoon table salt
- ½ cup all-purpose flour
- 2 large eggs
- 4 scallions, sliced thin
- 1½ teaspoons ground cumin
- ½ teaspoon ground allspice
- ½ teaspoon pepper
- ½ cup extra-virgin olive oil for frying

Cals 300 | Total Fat 20g | Sat Fat 6g
Chol 100mg | Sodium 660mg
Total Carb 21g | Dietary Fiber 3g
Total Sugars 3g | Protein 10g

WHY THIS RECIPE WORKS Cooked cauliflower, bound with flour and eggs and then fried into golden fritters, can be found in various parts of the Mediterranean. This recipe, lightly crisp and delectable, takes inspiration from Middle Eastern spiced versions. We start by steaming the cauliflower rather than boiling it to preserve its sweet, nutty, vegetal flavor. We mash it, purposefully leaving a few small chunks for contrasting texture. We use the bare minimum amount of flour so that the fritters hold together but are still delicate. Shallow frying is easier to manage—and clean up after—than deep frying. Dipping the hot fritters into our fresh turmeric-dyed cool and creamy yogurt sauce after cooking is a delight. And they're versatile: Make them the vegetable side to your dinner or give them star status next to a beautiful vegetable salad or grain dish like Kamut with Carrots and Pomegranate (page 178). The fritters can also be enjoyed at room temperature, stuffed into sandwiches. When taking the temperature of the frying oil, tilt the skillet so the oil pools on one side. Use two spatulas to flip the fritters to prevent splattering.

1 For the yogurt Combine all ingredients in bowl. Let sit for 30 minutes for flavors to meld, then season with salt and pepper to taste. Set aside.

2 For the fritters Combine cauliflower, water, and salt in large saucepan. Cover and cook over medium-low heat, stirring occasionally, until just tender, 15 to 20 minutes. Remove from heat. Using potato masher, mash cauliflower until mostly smooth with some small chunks remaining. Transfer to large bowl and let cool slightly, about 10 minutes.

3 Set wire rack in rimmed baking sheet and line half of rack with triple layer of paper towels. Stir flour, eggs, scallions, cumin, allspice, and pepper into cooled cauliflower mixture until fully combined.

4 Heat oil in 12-inch nonstick skillet over medium heat to 350 degrees. Using greased ¼-cup dry measuring cup, place 6 portions of cauliflower mixture in skillet, evenly spaced. Gently press and spread portions into approximate 3-inch disks with back of spoon. Cook fritters until well browned, 3 to 5 minutes per side, using 2 spatulas to carefully flip.

5 Transfer fritters to paper towel–lined side of prepared rack to drain for 15 seconds on each side, then move to unlined side of rack. Return oil to 350 degrees and repeat with remaining cauliflower mixture. Serve warm or at room temperature with yogurt.

SPICY ROASTED RED PEPPER WHIPPED FETA

SERVES
6 TO 8

30 MINS

1 red bell pepper, stemmed, halved from pole to pole, and seeded

1 poblano chile, stemmed, halved from pole to pole, and seeded

8 ounces feta cheese, crumbled (2 cups)

2 tablespoons extra-virgin olive oil, plus extra for drizzling

1½ teaspoons lemon juice

¼ teaspoon smoked paprika, plus extra for sprinkling

⅛ teaspoon cayenne pepper (optional)

WHY THIS RECIPE WORKS Whipped feta dips make regular appearances on meze platters across Greece. Perhaps the most recognizable is htipiti, a strikingly salmon-colored, spicy feta dip. The name means "whipped," but we can now rely on the food processor to achieve this consistency in about a minute. Most recipes have roasted spicy peppers, feta, olive oil, and lemon juice as their only ingredients. There are often a variety of different types of peppers, and we love the combination of sweet and easy-to-find roasted red bell peppers and contrasting smoky and spicy blistered poblano peppers, with their touch of green bitterness, for our version. We stir bits of the latter into the already-whipped concoction to prevent the beautiful salmon from being painted with gray. This adds little intense smoky pockets of the charred green pepper as well. The spiciness of poblanos can vary; if yours is spicy, omit the cayenne. If your dip is very loose after whipping, refrigerate the dip for about 90 minutes to stiffen.

1 Adjust oven rack 3 to 4 inches from broiler element and heat broiler. Line rimmed baking sheet with aluminum foil. Arrange bell pepper and poblano skin side up on prepared sheet, flattening peppers with your hand. Broil until skin is puffed and most of surface is well charred, 7 to 15 minutes, rotating sheet halfway through broiling.

2 Using tongs, gather peppers in center of foil, then crimp foil around peppers to form closed pouch; let steam for 10 minutes. Open foil packet carefully and spread out peppers. Once cool enough to handle, peel and discard pepper skins. Finely chop poblano and set aside.

3 Process feta; oil; lemon juice; paprika; cayenne, if using; and roasted bell pepper in food processor until mostly smooth, about 1 minute, scraping down sides of bowl. (Feta dip and roasted poblano can be refrigerated separately for up to 2 days; bring to room temperature before serving.) Transfer feta dip to serving bowl and sprinkle with reserved chopped poblano and extra smoked paprika. Drizzle with extra oil and serve.

Cals 110 | Total Fat 10g | Sat Fat 4.5g
Chol 25mg | Sodium 260mg
Total Carb 3g | Dietary Fiber 0g
Total Sugars 2g | Protein 4g

SHISHITO PEPPERS WITH MINT, POPPY SEEDS, AND ORANGE

1 teaspoon ground dried mint

1 teaspoon poppy seeds

½ teaspoon flake sea salt

¼ teaspoon grated orange zest, plus orange wedges for serving

2 tablespoons extra-virgin olive oil

8 ounces shishito peppers

WHY THIS RECIPE WORKS Mild little chile peppers, fried until blistered, that you pick up by the stems and pop into your mouth whole fly out of the kitchen wherever trendy bar snacks are sold. Shishitos are what you usually find at Asian restaurants; they are the Japanese cousin to Spain's Padrón chiles, which are common at tapas restaurants. But here, the bright-tasting, citrusy, mild green chiles serve as a crisp-textured vehicle for robust Mediterranean flavors. Restaurants often deep-fry the whole shishitos, but we've found that cooking them in a small amount of oil works just as well. A combination of dried mint, orange zest, and poppy seeds enlivens the peppers and adds more crunch. Offering orange wedges on the side cleanses the palate and brightens the dish. The skillet will look full.

Combine mint, poppy seeds, salt, and orange zest in small bowl; set aside. Heat oil in 12-inch skillet over medium-high heat until just smoking. Add shishitos and cook, without moving, until skins are blistered, about 3 minutes. Using tongs, flip shishitos and continue to cook until blistered on second side, about 3 minutes. Transfer to serving platter and sprinkle with spice mixture. Serve with orange wedges.

Cals 80 | Total Fat 7g | Sat Fat 0.5g
Chol 0mg | Sodium 140mg
Total Carb 3g | Dietary Fiber 1g
Total Sugars 1g | Protein 1g

BEET MUHAMMARA

SERVES
8

30 MINS

8 ounces beets, trimmed, peeled, and shredded

1 cup jarred roasted red peppers, rinsed and patted dry

1 cup walnuts, toasted

1 scallion, sliced thin

2 tablespoons extra-virgin olive oil, plus extra for drizzling

2 tablespoons pomegranate molasses

2 teaspoons lemon juice

¾ teaspoon table salt

½ teaspoon ground cumin

⅛ teaspoon cayenne pepper

2 tablespoons minced fresh parsley

WHY THIS RECIPE WORKS Beets are a beautiful (to behold and taste) addition to muhammara, a smoky red pepper dip from Syria that's eaten throughout the Middle East. The multidimensional beets bring out the best qualities in all the traditional ingredients, heightening the sweetness of the red peppers and pomegranate molasses, bolstering the earthiness of the walnuts—and making the color all the more vibrant. Microwaving grated beets softens them enough to blend into the creamy mixture and keeps the recipe time short. Muhammara makes a delicious dip for crudités or pita, a spread for sandwiches, or a sauce for meat and fish. You can use the large holes of a box grater or a food processor fitted with a shredding disk to shred the beets.

1 Microwave beets in covered bowl, stirring often, until beets are tender, about 4 minutes. Transfer beets to fine-mesh strainer set over bowl and let drain for 10 minutes.

2 Process drained beets, peppers, walnuts, scallion, oil, pomegranate molasses, lemon juice, salt, cumin, and cayenne in food processor until smooth, about 1 minute, scraping down sides of bowl as needed.

3 Transfer mixture to serving bowl. Season with salt to taste. (Muhammara can be refrigerated for up to 3 days; bring to room temperature before serving.) Drizzle with extra oil and sprinkle with parsley before serving.

Cals 150 | Total Fat 12g | Sat Fat 1.5g
Chol 0mg | Sodium 330mg
Total Carb 9g | Dietary Fiber 2g
Total Sugars 6g | Protein 2g

BUTTERNUT SQUASH TARTLETS WITH ALMONDS, POMEGRANATE, AND MINT

MAKES
15

40 MINS

2   tablespoons sliced almonds, toasted

2   tablespoons pomegranate seeds

1   tablespoon chopped fresh mint

1   pound butternut squash, peeled, seeded, and cut into 1-inch pieces (3½ cups)

1   tablespoon extra-virgin olive oil, plus extra for drizzling

½   teaspoon table salt

¼   teaspoon smoked paprika

15   frozen mini phyllo cups

Pomegranate molasses

WHY THIS RECIPE WORKS Small bites are as versatile as they are fun because one bite can be an hors d'oeuvre but a few paired with a side can make an exciting light meal. These elegant tartlets are a cinch to make with crispy, flaky store-bought mini phyllo cups. We fill the cups with a delicately sweet and smoky butternut squash puree, steamed in the microwave and processed to an ultravelvety texture that complements the crunch of the phyllo. The topping is a combination of bright, juicy pomegranate seeds, toasty sliced almonds, and fresh mint, as well as a drizzle of tangy, bittersweet pomegranate molasses and smooth, rich olive oil. A standard (2.1-ounce) box of frozen mini phyllo cups contains 15 pieces. Use two teaspoons to distribute the filling among the phyllo cups.

1 Adjust oven rack to middle position and heat oven to 350 degrees. Combine almonds, pomegranate seeds, and mint in bowl; season with salt and pepper to taste and set aside.

2 Microwave squash in covered bowl, stirring occasionally, until tender, 10 to 12 minutes; drain well. Process squash, oil, salt, and paprika in food processor until smooth, about 30 seconds, scraping down sides of bowl as needed; season with salt and pepper to taste and set aside to cool slightly.

3 Arrange phyllo cups on rimmed baking sheet and bake until golden and crisp, 3 to 5 minutes; transfer to wire rack to cool slightly. Divide squash mixture evenly among phyllo cups then top with almond mixture. Drizzle with pomegranate molasses and extra oil. Serve warm or at room temperature.

Crown Jewels
The hundreds of small, sparkling crimson kernels inside a pomegranate are tart and slightly crunchy and make a jewel-like topping we turn to often. To release the kernels with less mess (the juice stains), halve the pomegranate and submerge it in a bowl of water. As you gently pull it apart, the seeds will sink, separating from the bitter pith and membrane that hold them.

Cals 110 | Total Fat 4.5g | Sat Fat 0g
Chol 0mg | Sodium 220mg
Total Carb 16g | Dietary Fiber 2g
Total Sugars 2g | Protein 2g

Mainly Grains &Beans

SPELT SALAD WITH PICKLED FENNEL, PEA GREENS, AND MINT

SERVES
4 TO 6

1½ HRS

1 cup spelt

½ teaspoon table salt, divided, plus salt for cooking spelt

⅓ cup cider vinegar

2 tablespoons sugar

1 small fennel bulb, 1 tablespoon fronds minced, stalks discarded, bulb halved, cored, and sliced thin

3 tablespoons extra-virgin olive oil

2 tablespoons lemon juice

1 small shallot, minced

¼ teaspoon pepper

2 ounces pea tendrils, torn into bite-size pieces (2 cups)

¼ cup torn fresh mint

1 ounce feta cheese, crumbled (¼ cup)

WHY THIS RECIPE WORKS A little sweet, a little nutty, and a lot flavorful, spelt is a whole grain that more than deserves a frequent place on your supper plate. The sweetness of this ancient species of wheat is brought out in full effect in this lively grain salad with other sweet mix-ins: pea greens, fresh mint, and sliced fennel that we pickle quickly in vinegar and sugar. Feta cheese is a creamy, salty, briny contrast to the chewy grains and a lemony vinaigrette awakens all the flavors. To cook the spelt, we use one of our favorite methods for whole grains, the pasta method. With a full 2 quarts of boiling salted water in the pot, the liquid penetrates the grains evenly from all sides, softening them uniformly. Pea tendrils are also called pea greens or pea shoots. Watercress can be used in place of the pea tendrils. Pickle the fennel while cooking the spelt. This salad pairs nicely with seared flank steak but it's hearty enough to make your meal with a vegetable like roasted carrots.

1 Bring 2 quarts water to boil in large saucepan. Stir in spelt and 2 teaspoons salt and return to boil. Reduce heat to maintain gentle boil and cook until tender, 50 minutes to 1 hour 5 minutes. Drain spelt, spread onto rimmed baking sheet, and let cool for about 20 minutes.

2 Microwave vinegar, sugar, and ¼ teaspoon salt in bowl until steaming, about 2 minutes. Stir in sliced fennel bulb until completely submerged and let cool completely, about 30 minutes. Drain and discard liquid. (Drained pickled fennel can be refrigerated for up to 3 days.)

3 Whisk oil, lemon juice, shallot, pepper, and remaining ¼ teaspoon salt together in large bowl. Add spelt, pea tendrils, mint, fennel fronds, and ½ cup pickled fennel (reserve remaining pickled fennel for another use) to dressing and toss to combine. Season with salt and pepper to taste, and sprinkle with feta. Serve.

Cals 190 | Total Fat 9g | Sat Fat 1.5g
Chol 5mg | Sodium 210mg
Total Carb 26g | Dietary Fiber 4g
Total Sugars 4g | Protein 5g

Spelt

Before modern wheat came spelt, a species that was domesticated around 5000 BCE. It was a staple crop and now is valued for its nutritional benefits. The ancient grain is noted for being easier than conventional wheat for many to digest. It's not only an excellent source of fiber and protein, it's rich in beneficial B vitamins as well as minerals like iron. Also called dinkel, hulled, or German wheat, spelt is sweet and nutty and here featured as nice chewy berries. Spelt flour has also gained popularity as a substitute for all-purpose or other whole-wheat flours for baked goods.

Big and Little Bulgur

Bulgur has been a source of nutrition across the Mediterranean for roughly 4,000 years. It's made from parboiled or steamed wheat kernels/berries that are then dried, partially stripped of their outer bran layer, and ground. The result is a fast-cooking, highly nutritious grain. Chewy-firm coarse-grind bulgur, which requires simmering, is our choice for pilaf; we like medium-grind bulgur best in salads in which it's merely soaked and it becomes tender; fine-grind bulgur rehydrates into a seamless binder for dishes like baked kibbeh. Fine granules are similar in size to raw sugar, medium granules are similar to mustard seeds, and coarse granules are similar to sesame seeds. Cracked wheat, sold alongside bulgur, is not precooked and cannot be substituted. Rinse bulgur to remove excess starches that can turn the grain gluey.

TABBOULEH WITH GARLICKY TOFU

3 tomatoes, cored and cut into ½-inch pieces

1 teaspoon table salt, divided

½ cup medium-grind bulgur, rinsed

¼ cup lemon juice (2 lemons), divided

14 ounces extra-firm tofu, cut into 2-inch pieces

¼ teaspoon pepper

¼ cup extra-virgin olive oil, divided

3 garlic cloves, minced

⅛ teaspoon cayenne pepper

1½ cups minced fresh parsley

½ cup minced fresh mint

2 scallions, sliced thin

WHY THIS RECIPE WORKS Tabbouleh is a Lebanese herb and grain salad in which heaps of fresh herbs are interspersed with bulgur wheat (less the other way around) and tomatoes, and dressed in a bracing lemon dressing. Here we shake up the ratios with the addition of garlicky, savory sautéed tofu, which transforms the light dish into a meal with plenty of lean protein. Rather than using large cubes of tofu, we pulse it in the food processor to create a texture remarkably similar to that of the bulgur; the extra surface area means it can absorb more flavor from the dressing, too, just like the bulgur. We start by salting our tomatoes to rid them of excess liquid, and we use their juice (rather than water) to soak the bulgur. Meanwhile, we sauté our tofu with a hefty dose of toasted garlic. When shopping, don't confuse bulgur with cracked wheat, which has a much longer cooking time and will not work in this recipe. You can substitute firm tofu for the extra-firm.

1 Toss tomatoes with ¼ teaspoon salt in fine-mesh strainer set over bowl and let drain, tossing occasionally, for 30 minutes; reserve 2 tablespoons drained tomato juice. Toss bulgur with 2 tablespoons lemon juice and reserved tomato juice in bowl and let sit until grains begin to soften, 30 to 40 minutes.

2 Meanwhile, spread tofu on paper towel–lined baking sheet and let drain for 20 minutes. Gently press dry with paper towels and sprinkle with ¼ teaspoon salt and pepper. Pulse tofu in food processor until coarsely chopped, 3 or 4 pulses. Line now-empty sheet with clean paper towels. Spread processed tofu over prepared sheet and press gently with paper towels to dry.

3 Heat 2 teaspoons oil in 12-inch nonstick skillet over medium-high heat until shimmering. Add tofu and cook, stirring occasionally, until tofu is lightly browned, 10 to 12 minutes. (Tofu should start to sizzle after about 1½ minutes; adjust heat as needed.) Push tofu to sides of skillet. Add 1 teaspoon oil and garlic to center and cook, mashing garlic into skillet, until fragrant, about 1 minute. Stir mixture into tofu. Transfer to bowl and let cool for 10 minutes.

4 Whisk remaining 2 tablespoons lemon juice, remaining 3 tablespoons oil, cayenne, and remaining ½ teaspoon salt together in large bowl. Add drained tomatoes, soaked bulgur, cooled tofu, parsley, mint, and scallions and toss to combine. Cover and let sit until bulgur is tender, about 1 hour. Toss to recombine and season with salt and pepper to taste before serving.

Cals 160 | Total Fat 10g | Sat Fat 1.5g
Chol 0mg | Sodium 300mg
Total Carb 12g | Dietary Fiber 2g
Total Sugars 2g | Protein 7g

FARRO SALAD WITH BUTTERNUT SQUASH AND RADICCHIO

SERVES 4

45 MINS

- 2 pounds butternut squash, peeled, seeded, and cut into ½-inch pieces (3⅓ cups)
- ¼ cup extra-virgin olive oil, divided
- ¾ teaspoon table salt, divided, plus salt for cooking farro
- 1½ cups whole farro
- 2 tablespoons cider vinegar, plus extra for seasoning
- 2 tablespoons minced shallot
- 1 teaspoon Dijon mustard
  Pinch cayenne pepper
- 1 cup chopped radicchio
- ½ cup chopped fresh parsley
- 2 ounces blue cheese, crumbled (½ cup)

WHY THIS RECIPE WORKS Farro has been an Italian food staple for centuries, and the ancient whole wheat–grain wheat, originating in the Fertile Crescent, is as texturally interesting and flavorful in salads as it is highly nutritious. For this appealing dinner salad, we turn to ingredients that hold their own among those chewy-tender, warmly flavored grains. Sweet roasted butternut squash, assertive chopped radicchio, and tangy blue cheese carry enough boldness to mingle with the farro. To cook the farro, we bypass the traditional step of soaking the grains overnight and then cooking them slowly for more than an hour in favor of a simpler, quicker method. After testing out a few cooking techniques, we learned that boiling the grains in plenty of salted water and then draining them yields nicely firm but tender farro—no soaking necessary. While the farro cooks, we roast butternut squash and assemble the dressing.

1 Adjust oven rack to lowest position and heat oven to 500 degrees. Toss squash with 1 tablespoon oil and ½ teaspoon salt. Spread squash in even layer on rimmed baking sheet and roast until tender, 20 to 22 minutes. Push squash to 1 side of sheet and transfer to wire rack to cool.

2 While squash roasts, bring 4 quarts water to boil in large pot. Stir in farro and 1 tablespoon salt, return to boil, and cook until grains are tender with slight chew, 15 to 30 minutes. Drain farro, spread onto empty side of sheet with squash and let cool for about 20 minutes.

3 Whisk remaining 3 tablespoons oil, vinegar, shallot, mustard, cayenne, and remaining ¼ teaspoon salt together in large bowl. Add cooled farro and squash, radicchio, parsley, and blue cheese and toss to combine. Season with salt, pepper, and extra vinegar to taste. Serve.

Cals 530 | Total Fat 21g | Sat Fat 4.5g
Chol 10mg | Sodium 680mg
Total Carb 78g | Dietary Fiber 10g
Total Sugars 8g | Protein 14g

QUINOA LETTUCE WRAPS WITH FETA AND OLIVES

SERVES
4 TO 6

1 HR
plus 20 mins
cooling

1½ cups prewashed white quinoa

2¼ cups water

1 teaspoon table salt, divided

4 ounces feta cheese, crumbled (1 cup)

½ cup plain yogurt

¼ cup minced fresh mint

3 tablespoons red wine vinegar

2 tablespoons minced fresh oregano or 1½ teaspoons dried

¼ teaspoon pepper

½ cup extra-virgin olive oil

2 tomatoes, cored, seeded, and cut into ¼-inch pieces

1 cucumber, peeled, halved lengthwise, seeded, and cut into ¼-inch pieces

1 shallot, minced

¼ cup pitted kalamata olives, chopped

2 heads Bibb lettuce (8 ounces each), leaves separated

WHY THIS RECIPE WORKS Whatever the filling, lettuce wraps almost always present a meal in a fun, fresh—and refreshing—way. These wraps are filled with an easy grain salad with bright flavor. Quinoa may have famously originated in the Peruvian Andes, but the vitamin- and protein-packed grain (seed, actually) happens to pair well with salty feta, briny olives, and fresh mint and oregano—they all counterbalance its deep nuttiness. Rather than crumbling the feta into the salad, we blend it with some yogurt and vinegar to make a flavorful vinaigrette. Once the quinoa is cool, we toss it with our refreshing mix-ins and some of the vinaigrette, reserving the rest for drizzling after we scoop the salad into the lettuce leaves. Large, crisp leaves of Boston or Bibb lettuce are the perfect size for wrapping.

1 Toast quinoa in medium saucepan over medium-high heat, stirring frequently, until quinoa is very fragrant and makes continuous popping sound, 5 to 7 minutes. Stir in water and ½ teaspoon salt and bring to simmer. Cover, reduce heat to low, and simmer gently until grains are just tender and liquid is absorbed, 18 to 20 minutes. Spread quinoa onto rimmed baking sheet and let cool for about 20 minutes.

2 Meanwhile, process feta, yogurt, mint, vinegar, oregano, pepper, and remaining ½ teaspoon salt in blender until smooth, about 15 seconds. With blender running, slowly add oil until incorporated, about 30 seconds.

3 Combine tomatoes, cucumber, shallot, olives, cooled quinoa, and ⅔ cup feta dressing in bowl and toss to combine. Season with salt and pepper to taste. Spoon quinoa mixture into lettuce leaves (about ⅓ cup each), drizzle with remaining dressing, and serve.

Cals 420 | Total Fat 27g | Sat Fat 6g
Chol 20mg | Sodium 600mg
Total Carb 35g | Dietary Fiber 5g
Total Sugars 6g | Protein 11g

PEARL COUSCOUS WITH CHORIZO AND CHICKPEAS

SERVES
6

45 MINS

- 2 cups pearl couscous
- 8 ounces Spanish-style chorizo, cut into ½-inch pieces
- 4 carrots, peeled and chopped
- 2 tablespoons extra-virgin olive oil, divided
- ½ teaspoon table salt
- 2⅔ cups chicken or vegetable broth
- 2 teaspoons smoked paprika
- 2 teaspoons ground cumin
- 2 (15-ounce) cans chickpeas, rinsed and patted dry
- ½ cup chopped fresh parsley
- ½ cup raisins
- 2 tablespoons lemon juice, plus lemon wedges for serving

WHY THIS RECIPE WORKS Pasta salad doesn't have to taste like it came from a deli container or refrigerator case. In this bright-yet-smoky, sweet-yet-tart warm pasta salad, we use quick-cooking pearl couscous and toast it with chorizo and carrots, and then stir in broth with some smoked paprika and cumin and let the couscous cook through absorption. Creamy canned chickpeas contrast with the chewy pasta and add heft, and parsley freshens up this warm, spicy dish. Dried fruit provides even more textural contrast as well as sweetness, and a squeeze of lemon juice brightens all these beautiful flavors.

1 Combine couscous, chorizo, carrots, 1 tablespoon oil, and salt in large saucepan. Cook over medium heat, stirring frequently, until half of pearl couscous grains are golden, about 5 minutes. Stir in broth, paprika, and cumin and bring to simmer. Cover, reduce heat to low, and simmer, stirring occasionally, until broth is absorbed, 10 to 15 minutes. Let sit off heat, covered, for 3 minutes.

2 Stir in chickpeas, parsley, raisins, lemon juice, and remaining 1 tablespoon oil. Season with salt and pepper to taste. Serve with lemon wedges.

Cals 600 | Total Fat 21g | Sat Fat 6g
Chol 35mg | Sodium 1190mg
Total Carb 78g | Dietary Fiber 6g
Total Sugars 14g | Protein 23g

QUINOA LETTUCE WRAPS WITH FETA AND OLIVES

WHEAT BERRY SALAD WITH CHICKPEAS, SPINACH, AND ORANGE

SERVES
6 TO 8

1¾ HRS

1½ cups wheat berries

½ teaspoon table salt, plus salt for cooking wheat berries

3 oranges

4 teaspoons sherry vinegar

2 teaspoons Dijon mustard

1 garlic clove, minced

¾ teaspoon sweet smoked paprika

¼ teaspoon pepper

3 tablespoons extra-virgin olive oil

1 (15-ounce) can chickpeas, rinsed

3 ounces (3 cups) baby spinach, chopped

1 small red onion, sliced thin

¼ cup minced fresh mint

WHY THIS RECIPE WORKS Beyond their nutrition and incomparable taste, the beauty of whole-grain dishes is that they're so simple to make from items on hand in the kitchen. In this one we showcase a classic pair of ingredients from Spanish cuisine—chickpeas and spinach. The fresh ingredients: spinach (when don't you have a wilting bag to use?) and red onion (part of our storage vegetable arsenal) plus segments of juicy orange (always in our fruit bowl). Canned chickpeas have a creamy texture that's a foil against the chewy wheat berries. Big flavor comes from an aromatic vinaigrette made with sherry vinegar, Dijon mustard, garlic, sweet smoked paprika, and extra-virgin olive oil. Minced fresh mint rounds out the dish with verdant brightness.

1 Bring 4 quarts water to boil in large pot. Add wheat berries and 1½ teaspoons salt, return to boil, and cook until tender but still chewy, 1 hour to 1 hour 20 minutes. Drain wheat berries, spread onto rimmed baking sheet, and let cool for about 20 minutes.

2 Meanwhile, cut away peel and pith from oranges. Cut each fruit into quarters, then slice each quarter into ¼-inch-thick pieces. Transfer oranges to bowl.

3 Whisk vinegar, mustard, garlic, paprika, pepper, and salt together in large bowl. Whisking constantly, slowly drizzle in oil. Add wheat berries, chickpeas, spinach, onion, oranges, and mint and toss gently to combine. Season with salt and pepper to taste, and serve.

Cals 230 | Total Fat 6g | Sat Fat 0.5g
Chol 0mg | Sodium 340mg
Total Carb 38g | Dietary Fiber 7g
Total Sugars 6g | Protein 7g

MARINATED EGGPLANT AND BARLEY SALAD

SERVES 4 TO 6

1¼ HRS
plus 1 hr cooling

12 ounces Italian eggplant, sliced into 1-inch-thick rounds

1 teaspoon table salt, divided, plus salt for cooking barley

1½ cups pearl barley

6 tablespoons extra-virgin olive oil, divided

1 tablespoon minced fresh mint

2 teaspoons red wine vinegar

1 teaspoon capers, rinsed and minced

1 small garlic clove, minced

¼ teaspoon grated lemon zest

¼ teaspoon minced fresh oregano

⅛ teaspoon plus ½ teaspoon pepper, divided

2 tablespoons pomegranate molasses

½ teaspoon ground cinnamon

¼ teaspoon ground cumin

½ cup chopped fresh cilantro

¼ cup golden raisins

2 ounces feta cheese, crumbled (½ cup)

½ cup pomegranate seeds

6 scallions, green parts only, sliced thin

¼ cup chopped toasted pistachios

WHY THIS RECIPE WORKS This satisfying salad is a true celebration of all plants, in which vegetables (eggplant) and grains (pearl barley) have equal prominence, complemented by just the right aromatics, nuts, and seeds. Eggplant's absorbency means the vegetable holds on to amazing flavor in a grain salad that lets it shine. Cooked eggplant rounds drink up a bright vinaigrette full of capers and mint. We broil the eggplant to caramelize it nicely before letting it soak. The pearl barley base boasts warm spices and sweetness in every grain. A pomegranate seed and pistachio topping finishes this thoughtful salad with crunch and color, and crumbles of feta are a briny treat to complement the meal. We like this dish served warm or at room temperature.

1 Spread eggplant on paper towel–lined rimmed baking sheet, sprinkle both sides with ¼ teaspoon salt, and let sit for 30 minutes. Meanwhile, bring 4 quarts water to boil in large pot. Stir in barley and 1 tablespoon salt, return to boil, and cook until grains are tender, 20 to 40 minutes. Drain barley and set aside to cool. Adjust oven rack 4 inches from broiler element and heat broiler.

2 Thoroughly pat eggplant dry with paper towels, arrange in single layer on aluminum foil–lined rimmed baking sheet, and lightly brush both sides of eggplant with 1½ teaspoons oil. Broil eggplant until mahogany brown and lightly charred, 4 to 8 minutes per side. Let cool to room temperature, about 1 hour, then chop coarse.

3 Whisk 1½ tablespoons oil, mint, vinegar, capers, garlic, lemon zest, oregano, and ⅛ pepper together in large bowl. Add eggplant and gently toss to combine.

4 Whisk pomegranate molasses, cinnamon, cumin, remaining ½ teaspoon salt, remaining ¼ cup oil, and remaining ½ teaspoon pepper together in bowl. Toss barley, cilantro, and raisins with 1 tablespoon vinaigrette to coat, then season with salt and pepper to taste. Divide among individual bowls, then top with eggplant, feta, pomegranate seeds, and scallion greens. Drizzle with remaining vinaigrette and sprinkle with pistachios. Serve.

Cals 430 | Total Fat 20g | Sat Fat 3.5g | Chol 10mg | Sodium 520mg Total Carb 57g | Dietary Fiber 11g | Total Sugars 12g | Protein 9g

BROWN RICE SALAD WITH FENNEL, MUSHROOMS, AND WALNUTS

SERVES
4

1¼ HRS

1½ cups long-grain brown rice

1¼ teaspoons table salt, divided, plus salt for cooking rice

3 tablespoons white wine vinegar, divided

¼ cup extra-virgin olive oil, divided

1 pound white mushrooms, trimmed and quartered

1 large fennel bulb, stalks discarded, bulb halved, cored, and sliced thin

1 shallot, minced

½ teaspoon pepper

⅔ cup walnuts, toasted and chopped coarse, divided

2 tablespoons minced fresh tarragon

2 tablespoons minced fresh parsley, divided

WHY THIS RECIPE WORKS Rice salads are a great way to enliven the flavor of hearty, earthy brown rice—you can dress them brightly and fill the salad with fresh vegetables and crunch. For warm brown rice side dishes, we prefer to bake the brown rice. But once cooled and drizzled with dressing, as you need to do for salads, the baked rice turns gummy. So instead, we cook the rice much like other grains for salad, pasta-style, by boiling it in a large pot of water, a method that washes away the rice's excess starches. Then we spread the rice on a baking sheet to cool rapidly, preventing it from overcooking as it sits. To give every grain bright flavor, we drizzle it with white wine vinegar while it's still warm. After dressing the rice, abundant sautéed mushrooms, and browned fennel, we let the dressing's flavors permeate the salad. With a sprinkling of toasted walnuts and parsley, our salad is loaded with fresh, vibrant flavors and contrasting textures. Cremini mushrooms can be substituted for the white mushrooms.

1 Bring 4 quarts water to boil in large pot. Stir in rice and 2 teaspoons salt and cook until rice is tender, 22 to 25 minutes. Drain rice, spread onto rimmed baking sheet, and drizzle with 1 tablespoon vinegar. Let rice cool completely, about 10 minutes; transfer to large bowl.

2 Heat 1 tablespoon oil in 12-inch skillet over medium-high heat until shimmering. Add mushrooms and ½ teaspoon salt and cook, stirring occasionally, until pan is dry and mushrooms are browned, 6 to 8 minutes; transfer to plate and let cool.

3 Heat 1 tablespoon oil in now-empty skillet over medium-high heat until shimmering. Add fennel and ¼ teaspoon salt and cook, stirring occasionally, until just browned and crisp-tender, 3 to 4 minutes; transfer to plate with mushrooms and let cool.

4 Whisk shallot, pepper, remaining ½ teaspoon salt, remaining 2 tablespoons vinegar, and remaining 2 tablespoons oil together in small bowl, then drizzle over cooled rice. Add mushroom-fennel mixture and toss to combine. Let sit for 10 minutes.

5 Add ½ cup walnuts, tarragon, and 1 tablespoon parsley and toss to combine. Season with salt and pepper to taste. Sprinkle with remaining walnuts and remaining 1 tablespoon parsley and serve.

Cals 560 | Total Fat 29g | Sat Fat 3.5g
Chol 0mg | Sodium 920mg
Total Carb 65g | Dietary Fiber 6g
Total Sugars 7g | Protein 11g

KAMUT WITH CARROTS AND POMEGRANATE

**SERVES
4 TO 6**

1¾ HRS

- 1 cup kamut
- ¼ teaspoon table salt, plus salt for cooking kamut
- 2 tablespoons extra-virgin olive oil
- 2 carrots, peeled and cut into ¼-inch pieces
- 2 garlic cloves, minced
- ¾ teaspoon garam masala
- ¼ cup shelled pistachios, lightly toasted and chopped coarse, divided
- 3 tablespoons chopped fresh cilantro, divided
- 1 teaspoon lemon juice
- ¼ cup pomegranate seeds

WHY THIS RECIPE WORKS Bright, spiced, and looking like a platter of jewels, this lively grain salad features nutty, ultrarich kamut. Kamut's relatively large grains (larger than modern-day wheat) make it really stand out in this salad, even with all of the stunning selections accompanying it. Garam masala warms the whole dish, and pops of flavor from sweet carrots, crunchy pistachios, pleasantly grassy cilantro, and tart pomegranate seeds perk the salad up. Just a teaspoon of lemon juice is enough to awaken this warm and warm-spiced satisfying whole grain dish. Kamut is also sold as Khorasan wheat.

1 Bring 2 quarts water to boil in large saucepan. Stir in kamut and 2 teaspoons salt and return to boil. Reduce heat to maintain gentle boil and cook until tender, 55 to 75 minutes. Drain well, spread onto rimmed baking sheet, and let cool for about 20 minutes.

2 Heat oil in 12-inch skillet over medium heat until shimmering. Add carrots and salt and cook, stirring frequently, until carrots are softened and lightly browned, 4 to 6 minutes. Stir in garlic and garam masala and cook until fragrant, about 1 minute. Add kamut and cook until warmed through, 2 to 5 minutes.

3 Off heat, stir in half of pistachios, 2 tablespoons cilantro, and lemon juice. Season with salt and pepper to taste and sprinkle with pomegranate seeds, remaining pistachios, and remaining 1 tablespoon cilantro. Serve.

What to Do with Kamut?
Almost anything. Kamut is known as Khorasan wheat as that refers to the region of Afghanistan and Iran in which the ancient grain historically grew. Beyond being plumper than standard wheat, kamut is extra delightful in any wheat berry application—soups, salads, pilafs, gratins—as it has a deep buttery flavor and a smooth texture that costars nicely with vibrant ingredients.

*Cals 190 | Total Fat 8g | Sat Fat 1g
Chol 0mg | Sodium 160mg
Total Carb 27g | Dietary Fiber 5g
Total Sugars 5g | Protein 6g*

RED RICE AND QUINOA SALAD WITH BLOOD ORANGES

SERVES
6 TO 8

1¼ HRS

¾   cup red rice

    Table salt for cooking grains

¾   cup prewashed white quinoa

3   tablespoons lime juice
    (2 limes), divided

2   blood oranges

¼   cup extra-virgin olive oil

1   small shallot, minced

1   tablespoon minced fresh
    cilantro plus 1 cup leaves

¼   teaspoon red pepper flakes

6   ounces pitted dates, chopped
    (1 cup)

WHY THIS RECIPE WORKS White rice of all grain sizes; aromatic basmati; chewy, healthful brown rice; and even rustic wild rice are common pantry items. But there's one rice variety that doesn't get enough play: red rice. Red rice sports—surprise—a red color (from the pigment anthocyanin), and it has a nutty flavor and is highly nutritious. For a rice and grain salad that's colorful and hearty, we mix this healthful rice with nutty protein-providing quinoa, cooking both in the same pot using the pasta method, starting with the rice and then adding the quinoa. Then we drain them, drizzle them while warm with lime juice to add bright flavor, and let them cool. Next the salad needs freshness and some pleasing sweetness. Dates and ruby-bright blood oranges do a sweet job. Cilantro and red pepper flakes add fresh bite and spiciness to round things out. This salad pairs beautifully with a white fish fillet. We like the convenience of prewashed quinoa; rinsing removes the quinoa's bitter protective coating (called saponin). If you buy unwashed quinoa (or if you are unsure whether it's washed), rinse it before cooking.

1 Bring 4 quarts water to boil in large pot over high heat. Add rice and 1 tablespoon salt and cook, stirring occasionally, for 15 minutes. Add quinoa to pot and continue to cook until grains are tender, 12 to 14 minutes. Drain rice-quinoa mixture, spread onto rimmed baking sheet, and drizzle with 2 tablespoons lime juice; let cool for about 20 minutes.

2 Meanwhile, cut away peel and pith from blood oranges. Holding fruit over bowl, use paring knife to slice between membranes to release segments. Cut segments in half crosswise. If needed, squeeze orange membranes to equal 2 tablespoons juice in bowl.

3 Whisk oil, shallot, minced cilantro, pepper flakes, 2 tablespoons orange juice, and remaining 1 tablespoon lime juice together in large bowl. Add rice-quinoa mixture, dates, orange segments, and remaining 1 cup cilantro leaves and toss to combine. Season with salt and pepper to taste, and serve.

Cals 260 | Total Fat 8g | Sat Fat 1g
Chol 0mg | Sodium 75mg
Total Carb 44g | Dietary Fiber 3g
Total Sugars 18g | Protein 4g

PESTO FARRO SALAD WITH CHERRY TOMATOES AND ARTICHOKES

SERVES 4 TO 6

40 MINS
plus 20 mins cooling

- 1½ cups whole farro
- ½ teaspoon table salt, plus salt for cooking farro
- 2 cups fresh basil leaves
- 1½ ounces (1½ cups) baby spinach
- ½ cup roasted sunflower seeds
- 1 ounce Parmesan cheese, grated (½ cup)
- 2 garlic cloves, minced
- ¼ teaspoon pepper
- ½ cup extra-virgin olive oil
- ⅓ cup plain yogurt
- 12 ounces cherry tomatoes, halved
- 2 cups jarred whole baby artichoke hearts packed in water, rinsed, patted dry, and quartered

WHY THIS RECIPE WORKS Pesto can paint more than pasta. Farro's distinct, chewy-tender texture (thanks to a pasta cooking method) and complex flavor make it perfect for a nourishing update on pesto pasta salad, one that's hearty enough to be a meal. While updating the pasta, we also updated the pesto, supercharging it by combining basil with spinach; the latter adds nutrients and helps retain the sauce's vibrant color. We use sunflower seeds and cut the oil with yogurt, which further lightens the pesto's color and gives it a nice creamy texture. Halved cherry tomatoes pair as well as ever with the basil and brighten the salad. Jarred artichoke hearts are a meaty flavor addition with plenty of nutrition, to boot.

1 Bring 4 quarts water to boil in large pot. Stir in farro and 1 tablespoon salt, return to boil, and cook until grains are tender with slight chew, 15 to 30 minutes. Drain farro, spread onto rimmed baking sheet, and let cool for about 20 minutes.

2 Meanwhile, pulse basil, spinach, sunflower seeds, Parmesan, garlic, pepper, and salt in food processor until finely ground, 20 to 30 pulses, scraping down sides of bowl as needed. With processor running, slowly add oil until incorporated. Add yogurt and pulse to incorporate, about 5 pulses; transfer pesto to large bowl.

3 Toss cooled farro with pesto until combined. Gently stir in tomatoes and artichoke hearts and season with salt and pepper to taste. Stir in warm water as needed, 1 tablespoon at a time, to adjust consistency. Serve.

Cals 460 | Total Fat 27g | Sat Fat 4g
Chol 5mg | Sodium 460mg
Total Carb 46g | Dietary Fiber 7g
Total Sugars 5g | Protein 13g

WHEAT BERRY SALAD WITH RADICCHIO, DRIED CHERRIES, AND PECANS

SERVES 6 TO 8

1¾ HRS

1 cup wheat berries

½ teaspoon table salt, plus salt for cooking wheat berries

3 tablespoons extra-virgin olive oil

2 tablespoons red wine vinegar

1 small shallot, minced

½ teaspoon pepper

1 cup chopped radicchio

1 cup loosely packed fresh parsley leaves

½ cup pecans, toasted and chopped coarse, divided

¼ cup dried cherries

1 ounce blue cheese, crumbled (¼ cup)

WHY THIS RECIPE WORKS Wheat berries get bold in this gutsy and satisfying salad in which no ingredient goes unnoticed. Chopped radicchio is a nice change from a baby green in the salad, and it carries a pleasant bitterness and crunch that the wheat berries ably stand up to. For rich notes, a modest amount of crumbled blue cheese pairs well with sweet-tart, almost wine-y dried cherries. Pecans, with their buttery sweetness, are the right nut, and an extra-generous handful of parsley (leaves left whole for salad-green-like appeal) works to freshen up all these intense flavors. A bracing red wine vinaigrette brings this exciting salad together.

1 Bring 2 quarts water to boil in large saucepan. Stir in wheat berries and 2 teaspoons salt and return to boil. Reduce heat to maintain gentle boil and cook until tender, 1 hour to 1 hour 20 minutes. Drain wheat berries, spread onto rimmed baking sheet, and let cool for about 20 minutes.

2 Whisk oil, vinegar, shallot, pepper, and salt together in large bowl. Add wheat berries, radicchio, parsley, half of pecans, and cherries to dressing and toss to combine. Season with salt and pepper to taste, and sprinkle with blue cheese and remaining pecans. Serve.

Cals 200 | Total Fat 11g | Sat Fat 2g
Chol 5mg | Sodium 190mg
Total Carb 22g | Dietary Fiber 4g
Total Sugars 3g | Protein 5g

BULGUR SALAD WITH SPINACH, CHICKPEAS, AND APPLES

SERVES
4

25 MINS
plus 15 mins cooling

1½ cups medium-grind bulgur, rinsed

½ teaspoon table salt, plus salt for cooking bulgur

5 tablespoons extra-virgin olive oil

1 shallot, minced

1 teaspoon smoked paprika

½ teaspoon grated lemon zest, plus ¼ cup juice (2 lemons)

1 tablespoon honey

1 (15-ounce) can chickpeas, rinsed

5 ounces (5 cups) baby spinach, chopped

2 apples, cored and cut into ½-inch pieces

½ cup walnuts, toasted and chopped

WHY THIS RECIPE WORKS Tabbouleh (see page 165) is an iconic bulgur dish, but bulgur's appearance in salads shouldn't end there. You'll love the combinations in this inspired salad. Spinach and chickpeas, a pairing that's always a winner (see pages 173 and 246), add more plant-powered heft to the bulgur salad, and plenty of chopped apples interrupt the earthiness with some sweetness. All the components are dressed in a lemony, smoked paprika–spiced, honey-sweetened vinaigrette; the honey rounds out the smokiness of the peppery paprika. We briefly microwave the mix to bloom the flavor of the smoked paprika.

1 Bring 4 quarts water to boil in large pot. Stir in bulgur and 1 teaspoon salt and cook until tender, about 5 minutes. Drain well, spread over rimmed baking sheet, and set aside to cool, about 15 minutes.

2 Meanwhile, whisk oil, shallot, paprika, and lemon zest together in large bowl, then microwave until bubbling and fragrant, about 30 seconds. Whisk in lemon juice, honey, and salt.

3 Add cooled bulgur, chickpeas, spinach, and apples to vinaigrette and toss to combine. Season with salt and pepper to taste, and sprinkle with walnuts. Serve.

Cals 580 | Total Fat 29g | Sat Fat 3.5g
Chol 0mg | Sodium 530mg
Total Carb 72g | Dietary Fiber 14g
Total Sugars 15g | Protein 14g

BARLEY WITH FENNEL AND DRIED APRICOTS

SERVES
6 TO 8

1 HR

1½ cups pearl barley

½ teaspoon table salt, plus salt for cooking pearl barley

3 tablespoons red wine vinegar

2 tablespoons extra-virgin olive oil

2 tablespoons minced shallot

1 garlic clove, minced

½ teaspoon grated orange zest plus 2 tablespoons juice

¼ teaspoon pepper

20 dried apricots, chopped

1 small fennel bulb, 2 tablespoons fronds minced, stalks discarded, bulb halved, cored, and chopped fine

¼ cup minced fresh parsley

WHY THIS RECIPE WORKS Sweetness is often an important element of the cuisines of the Mediterranean, sometimes coming from fresh native fruits or, more often, from those that are dried. There's a reason for that: Since so many fruits thrive in the region, drying is a way to preserve the abundance (and share it with the world). Here that sun-soaked sweetness comes in the form of floral, almost citrusy, dried apricots, which work well in this earthy, nutty barley salad. Complementary orange zest and juice brighten the red wine vinaigrette that graces the grains. And some finely chopped fennel has a fresh crispness and licorice-like aroma that scents the whole dish. This salad is just as welcome next to nutty roasted cauliflower as it is next to a fillet of pan-seared white fish. Sweeter Turkish apricots can be substituted for the apricots, but use 12 instead of 20.

1 Bring 4 quarts water to boil in large pot. Stir in barley and 1 tablespoon salt and return to boil. Reduce heat to maintain gentle boil and cook until tender with slight chew, 25 to 45 minutes.

2 Drain barley, spread onto rimmed baking sheet, and let cool until no longer steaming, 5 to 7 minutes. Whisk vinegar, oil, shallot, garlic, orange zest and juice, pepper, and salt together in large bowl. Add barley, apricots, fennel fronds and bulb, and parsley and toss to combine. Season with salt and pepper to taste, and serve.

Cals 230 | Total Fat 4g | Sat Fat 0.5g
Chol 0mg | Sodium 190mg
Total Carb 44g | Dietary Fiber 9g
Total Sugars 11g | Protein 5g

BROWN RICE PILAF WITH DATES AND PISTACHIOS

SERVES
6 TO 8

2 HRS

1 tablespoon extra-virgin olive oil

1 onion, chopped fine

½ teaspoon table salt

3¼ cups chicken or vegetable broth

1½ cups long-grain brown rice, rinsed

1 bay leaf

1½ ounces pitted dates, chopped (¼ cup)

⅓ cup shelled pistachios, toasted and coarsely chopped

¼ cup minced fresh mint

WHY THIS RECIPE WORKS Brown rice likes to get baked. Unlike wheat-related whole grains, brown rice can become mushy on the stovetop while the rice on the bottom of the pot dries out. Baking brown rice guarantees an even and appealing texture. We sauté a base of onions, stir in broth, rice, and a bay leaf, and bake it all, covered, for about an hour. When the rice is tender, we remove it from the oven, sprinkle chopped dates over the top, cover the pot again, and let it sit for 5 minutes, just enough time for the dates to become plump and tender. After a quick fluff with a fork to incorporate a sprinkling of pistachios and mint, the pilaf is good to go with perhaps some warm spiced chicken thighs or braised eggplant. Medium-grain or short-grain brown rice can be substituted for the long-grain rice.

1 Adjust oven rack to middle position and heat oven to 375 degrees. Heat oil in Dutch oven over medium heat until shimmering. Add onion and salt and cook until softened and beginning to brown, 5 to 7 minutes.

2 Stir in broth, cover, and bring to boil. Off heat, stir in rice and bay leaf. Cover, transfer pot to oven, and bake until liquid is absorbed and rice is tender, 55 minutes to 1 hour 5 minutes.

3 Remove pot from oven. Sprinkle dates over rice and let sit, covered, for 10 minutes. Discard bay leaf. Fluff rice with fork, stir in pistachios and mint, and season with salt and pepper to taste. Serve.

Cals 200 | Total Fat 5g | Sat Fat 1g
Chol 0mg | Sodium 380mg
Total Carb 34g | Dietary Fiber 3g
Total Sugars 5g | Protein 4g

QUINOA PILAF WITH OLIVES, RAISINS, AND CILANTRO

SERVES
6 TO 8

1 HR

1½ cups prewashed white quinoa

2 tablespoons extra-virgin olive oil

1 small onion, chopped fine

¾ teaspoon table salt

¼ teaspoon ground cumin

¼ teaspoon dried oregano

⅛ teaspoon ground cinnamon

1¾ cups water

¼ cup golden raisins

⅓ cup pitted green olives, coarsely chopped

3 tablespoons chopped fresh cilantro

4 teaspoons red wine vinegar

WHY THIS RECIPE WORKS You might not think of warm or sweet spices when you think of quinoa, but they perfectly complement its nutty flavor and somewhat crunchy texture. Here the spices are cumin and cinnamon. Warm-spiced foods benefit from contrasting flavor elements for liveliness, and fruity golden raisins, briny green olives, and grassy cilantro do the job. Serve alongside a seared protein or a bean dish like Espinacas con Garbanzos (page 246).

1 Toast quinoa in medium saucepan over medium-high heat, stirring frequently, until quinoa is very fragrant and makes continuous popping sound, 5 to 7 minutes; transfer to bowl.

2 Heat oil in now-empty saucepan over medium-low heat until shimmering. Add onion, salt, cumin, oregano, and cinnamon and cook until onion is softened and light golden, 5 to 7 minutes. Stir in water and toasted quinoa, increase heat to medium-high, and bring to simmer. Cover, reduce heat to low, and simmer until grains are just tender and liquid is absorbed, 18 to 20 minutes, stirring in golden raisins halfway through cooking. Remove saucepan from heat and let sit, covered, for 10 minutes. Fluff quinoa with fork and stir in olives, cilantro, and vinegar. Serve.

The Colors of Quinoa

White quinoa is the most commonly found variety of these tiny seeds native to South America, but red and black varieties are increasingly available. White quinoa, the largest seed of the three, has a slightly nutty, vegetal flavor with a hint of bitterness; it also has the softest texture. The medium-size red seeds offer nuttier flavor and a heartier crunch, thanks to their additional seed coat. Black quinoa seeds, the smallest of the three, have the thickest seed coat. They are notably crunchy in pilaf and retain their shape but have a sandy texture. These seeds have the mildest flavor, with a hint of molasses-like sweetness. You can use white and red quinoa interchangeably, but black quinoa is better in recipes specifically tailored to its distinctive texture and flavor.

Cals 180 | Total Fat 6g | Sat Fat 0.5g
Chol 0mg | Sodium 300mg
Total Carb 26g | Dietary Fiber 3g
Total Sugars 5g | Protein 5g

COOKING GRAINS OF ALL KINDS

While many grains originated in the Mediterranean, we embrace all good-for-you grains as a key dietary component of this book—there's no need to exclude any healthful (and delicious) ingredients. Here is a guide to cooking and shopping tips for all the grains we use in the recipes in this book.

Barley

This high-fiber grain has a nutty, subtly sweet flavor. Both hulled and pearl barley (the most widely available varieties) are stripped of their tough outer covering, but we prefer quicker-cooking pearl barley, which has been polished to remove the bran layer as well. The cooking time for pearl barley will vary from product to product, so start checking it for doneness early. We often cook barley in a large pot of salted boiling water like with pasta (the pasta method) as you see in Barley with Fennel and Dried Apricots (page 188). Pearl barley is also starchy enough to make an alternative risotto like Beet Barley Risotto (page 227).

Bulgur

Bulgur is made from parboiled or steamed wheat kernels/berries that are then dried, partially stripped of their outer bran layer, and coarsely ground. We most often cook medium-grind bulgur either by the pasta method as in Bulgur Salad with Spinach, Chickpeas, and Apples (page 187) or merely by soaking it in liquid as in Tabbouleh with Garlicky Tofu (page 165). When shopping, don't confuse bulgur with cracked wheat, which has a much longer cooking time (and cannot merely soak) and will not work in our recipes. When it's done cooking, the grains will be somewhat tender but still firm.

Couscous

Calling couscous a variety of pasta wouldn't be far off the mark. Like great pasta, it's made from semolina flour and—in its best form—very little else. To "cook" it, really, is just to rehydrate it with a hot liquid such as water, broth (as in our Tabil Couscous with Sardines on page 239), or sauce. Couscous found at the grocery store has very small grains and takes just a few minutes to soften and warm through.

Pearl Couscous

Sometimes called "Israeli" couscous, this pasta has rounded grains that are larger than regular couscous and take a few more minutes to cook through. The result is chubby and chewier, providing a nice bite and a satisfying result as in our recipe for Pearl Couscous with Chorizo and Chickpeas (page 169).

Wheat Berries

These are whole, husked wheat kernels with a rich, earthy flavor and firm chew. Because they're unprocessed, they remain firm, smooth, and distinct when cooked, which makes them great for salads. When they're done cooking, through boiling, the grains will be softened but still quite chewy, smooth, and separate. Try our Spelt Salad with Pickled Fennel, Pea Greens, and Mint (page 162).

Farro

A favorite ingredient in Tuscan cuisine, these hulled whole-wheat kernels boast a sweet, nutty flavor and a chewy bite. In Italy, the grain is available in three sizes—farro piccolo, farro medio, and farro grande—but the midsize type is most common in the United States. When the grains are done cooking, they'll be tender but have a slight chew, similar to al dente pasta. Farro takes best to the pasta cooking method because the abundance of water cooks the grains more evenly. We prefer the flavor and texture of whole farro; pearled farro can be used, but the texture may be softer. Do not use quick-cooking or presteamed farro. The cooking time for farro can vary greatly among brands, so we recommend beginning to check for doneness after 10 minutes. Try it in Pesto Farro Salad with Cherry Tomatoes and Artichokes (page 182).

Freekeh

Freekeh, a traditional Middle Eastern grain, is made from roasted durum wheat that's been harvested while the grains are still young and green. The grains are polished ("freekeh" is a colloquialization of "farik," which means "rubbed" in Arabic) and sold whole as well as cracked into smaller pieces. We simmer cracked freekeh in our recipe for Chorba Frik (page 208); whole freekeh requires a different, longer cooking time.

Fregula

Fregula (or fregola Sarda) is a round Sardinian pasta made from semolina flour—the shape of pearl couscous but more rustic in flavor and texture. It simmers until al dente in stewy pasta dishes like Fregula with Chickpeas, Tomatoes, and Fennel (page 270).

Kamut

Kamut is also sold as Khorasan wheat because it comes from that region of Afghanistan and Iran. Kamut is a delicious, plumper substitute for wheat berries in recipes with a deep, rich flavor and smooth texture. For a kamut recipe, try Kamut with Carrots and Pomegranate (page 178).

Maftoul

Ultra nutty-tasting maftoul is another Middle Eastern hand-rolled pasta from Palestine made from bulgur wheat. Maftoul is available at well-stocked Middle Eastern grocery stores, or online. If you are unable to find maftoul, you can substitute an equal amount (by weight) of fregula, or moghrabieh. Because the size of maftoul grains can vary considerably, we provide a wide range of cook times in our eponymous Maftoul with Carrots and Chickpeas (page 264); cook until just tender.

Polenta

Polenta (and cornmeal) is simply dried corn that is ground into grains of varying coarseness. To make the Italian porridge polenta (see page 233), we use coarse-ground degerminated cornmeal such as yellow grits (with grains the size of couscous). Avoid instant and quick-cooking products, as well as whole-grain, stone-ground, and regular cornmeal.

Quinoa

Though actually a seed, quinoa is often referred to as a "supergrain" because it's a nutritionally complete protein. We love the pinhead-size seeds (which can be white, red, black, or purple) for their faint crunch and mineral taste. When the grains are done cooking they will unfurl and expand to about three times their size. Toast quinoa in a dry (no oil or butter) pot before adding water to simmer; we've found that toasting it in fat gives the grain a slightly bitter flavor. We like the convenience of prewashed quinoa; rinsing removes the quinoa's bitter protective coating (called saponin). If you buy unwashed quinoa (or if you are unsure whether it's washed), rinse it and then spread it out over a clean dish towel to dry for 15 minutes before cooking.

Basmati Rice

True basmati rice comes from India or Pakistan but is used throughout the Middle East and greater Mediterranean. The rice is aged for a minimum of a year (and often much longer) before packaging. Aging dehydrates the rice, which translates into cooked grains that expand greatly in length—more so than any other long-grain rice. This creates a gorgeous distinctive texture in go-with-anything Basmati Rice Pilaf (page 231). It's helpful (and traditional in many cuisines) to rinse raw grains to remove surface starch that otherwise absorbs water during cooking, causing grains to stick. Once the rice is cooked, covering the pan with a clean dish towel under the lid and allowing the rice to sit off heat for 10 minutes soaks up steam to further prevent stickiness.

Brown Rice

For warm brown rice sides, we like the even cooking produced by baking the rice (see page 231). For salads, you can cook brown rice according to the pasta method, which washes away excess starches for a good salad texture (see page 176). You can find basmati, short-grain, long-grain, and jasmine brown rice, and all will work (with a similar cooking time) in our recipes but will have textural differences mimicking those parent rice varieties.

Red Rice

There are different varieties of red rice cultivated all over the world. The rice gets its hue from the pigment anthocyanin. This rice is nutty and super-nutritious, as the germ is intact—a great addition to your pantry. We use red rice in our Red Rice and Quinoa Salad with Blood Oranges (page 180).

Wild Rice

Wild rice isn't rice exactly but an aquatic grass (and most wild rice is in fact cultivated). This largely American rice has a shiny black coat—and because of that chewy outer husk it takes time to get tender on the stovetop. For that reason we bake it like we do brown rice (see page 232). Do not use quick-cooking or presteamed wild rice; you may need to read the ingredient list on the package carefully to determine if the wild rice is presteamed.

Arborio Rice

This short-grain rice has a high proportion of amylopectin, that is, the starch that makes risotto (see pages 221 and 222) creamy. It's named for a town in Piedmont; for this Italian dish, you can also use Carnaroli rice cultivated in Piedmont as well as Lombardy. It is a stellar option.

Spelt

This sweet, nutty ancient grain predates modern wheat and is good for you and good to digest. It's also called dinkel, hulled, or German wheat. Berries of it, boiled until tender-chewy (they take a fair deal of time), are delicious in our Spelt Salad with Pickled Fennel, Pea Greens, and Mint (page 162).

RED LENTIL KIBBEH

**SERVES
4**

1¼ HRS

3   tablespoons extra-virgin olive oil, divided

1   onion, chopped fine

1   red bell pepper, stemmed, seeded, and chopped fine

1   teaspoon table salt

2   tablespoons Harissa (page 17)

2   tablespoons tomato paste

½   teaspoon cayenne pepper (optional)

4   cups water

1   cup medium-grind bulgur, rinsed

¾   cup dried red lentils, picked over and rinsed

½   cup chopped fresh parsley

2   tablespoons lemon juice

1   head Bibb lettuce (8 ounces), leaves separated

½   cup plain yogurt

Lemon wedges

WHY THIS RECIPE WORKS Kibbeh is a popular Middle Eastern dish made from bulgur, minced onions, varying spices, and (traditionally) ground meat. During Lent, those who observe often prepare this common meal with lentils in lieu of meat, as the texture of the two is similar. Here, both the color and flavor of the red lentils are enhanced with two red pastes. Tomato paste brings sweetness and an umami quality, and harissa adds complexity. We give the bulgur a head start before adding the quicker-cooking lentils to the same pan, which allows both components to finish cooking at the same time. Lemon juice and parsley brighten the kibbeh. The spoonable mixture can be served on its own with some Bibb lettuce and yogurt, and it makes a showstopping addition to a larger spread, on a platter alongside dips like Beet Muhammara (page 158) and Sweet Potato Hummus (page 295) or with nuts, pickled radishes, and pita. You can use our Harissa or store-bought harissa, though spiciness can vary greatly by brand. If your harissa is spicy, omit the cayenne.

1 Heat 1 tablespoon oil in large saucepan over medium heat until shimmering. Add onion, bell pepper, and salt and cook until softened, about 5 minutes. Stir in harissa; tomato paste; and cayenne, if using, and cook, stirring frequently, until fragrant, about 1 minute.

2 Stir in water and bulgur and bring to simmer. Reduce heat to low, cover, and simmer gently until bulgur is barely tender, about 8 minutes. Stir in lentils, cover, and continue to cook, stirring occasionally, until lentils and bulgur are tender, 8 to 10 minutes.

3 Off heat, lay clean dish towel underneath lid and let mixture sit for 10 minutes. Stir in 1 tablespoon oil, parsley, and lemon juice and stir vigorously until mixture is cohesive. Season with salt and pepper to taste. Transfer to platter and drizzle with remaining 1 tablespoon oil. Spoon kibbeh into lettuce leaves and drizzle with yogurt. Serve with lemon wedges.

*Cals 450 | Total Fat 19g | Sat Fat 3g
Chol 5mg | Sodium 760mg
Total Carb 60g | Dietary Fiber 13g
Total Sugars 6g | Protein 16g*

WHITE BEAN AND TUNA SALAD

- 1 (6-ounce) container olive oil-packed tuna
- 2 (15-ounce) cans cannellini beans, rinsed
- ¼ cup extra-virgin olive oil
- ¼ cup very coarsely chopped fresh parsley
- 1 shallot, sliced thin
- 4 teaspoons sherry vinegar
- ¼ teaspoon table salt
- ¼ teaspoon red pepper flakes

WHY THIS RECIPE WORKS Preserved tuna has a remarkable presence across the Mediterranean, from nourishing garnish for North African dishes to salad and sandwich star in Western Europe. And olive oil–packed tuna is a delicious tinned fish for this role, its moist, silky texture and rich, meaty taste enhanced by its oil preservation. This tuna and white bean salad celebrates the product with simplicity, so good ingredients are key. A good-quality olive oil contributes fresh, fruity flavor and cannellini beans have an extra-creamy texture here. Sherry vinegar adds a pop of brightness while parsley provides freshness. This is a most satisfying lunch; you won't regret eating it with some baguette or rustic bread.

Remove tuna from container and discard packing oil. Coarsely flake tuna into medium bowl. Add beans, oil, parsley, shallot, vinegar, salt, and pepper flakes and toss to combine. Serve.

*Cals 190 | Total Fat 10g | Sat Fat 1.5g
Chol 10mg | Sodium 440mg
Total Carb 16g | Dietary Fiber 5g
Total Sugars 2g | Protein 12g*

LENTIL SALAD WITH ORANGES, CELERY, AND FETA

SERVES 4 TO 6

1 HR
plus 1 hr soaking

- 1 cup dried brown lentils, picked over and rinsed
- 1 teaspoon table salt for brining
- ¼ teaspoon table salt, plus salt for cooking lentils
- 2 tablespoons cider vinegar
- 1 shallot, minced
- 1 tablespoon honey
- ½ teaspoon dried mint
- ¼ cup extra-virgin olive oil
- 1 orange, peel and pith cut away, fruit cut into 8 wedges, then sliced crosswise ¼ inch thick
- 2 celery ribs, sliced thin on bias, plus ¼ cup celery leaves
- ¼ cup pecans, toasted and chopped coarse, divided
- 1 ounce feta cheese, crumbled (¼ cup)

WHY THIS RECIPE WORKS It sounds so simple but a great lentil salad comes down first and foremost to perfectly cooked lentils. Tender-firm with intact skins, perfect lentils remain distinct in salad, with no sticking, no stodginess, and, conversely, no underdone legumes. Our path to lentil perfection? We first brine the lentils in warm salt water, which softens their skins and leads to fewer blowouts and seasons them nicely throughout. Then we cook the lentils in the oven, which heats them gently and uniformly rather than by the direct heat from the stovetop. The remaining elements of this perfect protein- and fiber-packed lentil salad are a tart vinaigrette and boldly flavored mix-ins to brighten the earthy legumes, here a fruity combination of cider vinaigrette and oranges, tangy feta, enlivening mint, and sweet, crunchy pecans and celery. Serve as a stand-alone salad or alongside roasted vegetables or a simply prepared piece of fish or chicken. You can use lentilles du Puy (French green lentils) in place of the brown lentils if you prefer.

1 Place lentils and 1 teaspoon salt in bowl. Cover with 4 cups warm water (about 110 degrees) and soak for at least 1 hour or up to 1 day. Drain well.

2 Adjust oven rack to middle position and heat oven to 325 degrees. Combine drained lentils, 4 cups water, and ½ teaspoon salt in medium ovensafe saucepan. Cover, transfer to oven, and bake until lentils are tender, 40 minutes to 1 hour. Drain lentils well.

3 Whisk vinegar, shallot, honey, mint, and salt together in large bowl. While whisking constantly, slowly drizzle in oil until combined. Add drained lentils, orange slices, celery and celery leaves, and 2 tablespoons pecans and toss to combine. Season with salt and pepper to taste.

4 Sprinkle with feta and remaining 2 tablespoons pecans. Serve warm or at room temperature.

Cals 260 | Total Fat 14g | Sat Fat 2.5g
Chol 5mg | Sodium 350mg
Total Carb 26g | Dietary Fiber 6g
Total Sugars 6g | Protein 8g

MODERN SUCCOTASH WITH FENNEL AND SCALLIONS

SERVES
4 TO 6

25 MINS

1 (15-ounce) can cannellini beans, 2 tablespoons liquid reserved, beans rinsed

2 teaspoons lemon juice

3 tablespoons extra-virgin olive oil

1 fennel bulb, stalks discarded, bulb halved, cored, and cut into ¼-inch pieces

4 scallions, white and green parts separated and sliced thin on bias

½ teaspoon table salt

2 garlic cloves, minced

¼ teaspoon ground fennel

4 ears corn, kernels cut from cobs (3 cups)

WHY THIS RECIPE WORKS When you think of succotash, a mix of frozen corn and lima beans in abundant cream sauce might come to mind—not a Mediterranean diet dish. This version is different, made with crisp, sweet fresh corn and creamy beans. For the corn, crisp kernels fresh from the cob are the only option for this dish. Sautéed fennel and scallions are surprising additions to the corn that give it complementary sweet anise flavor and a clarifying allium bite. For the beans, we use canned cannellini beans instead of limas as they're superquick and have a creamy consistency and pleasant, mild flavor. Some of the canning liquid from the beans creates a "sauce" that binds the succotash's ingredients together, creating a dish with a cohesive texture. The result doesn't weigh down anything its paired with; we quite like topping the succotash with a piece of simple pan-seared halibut or sautéed catfish, but it can also live with other simple warm vegetable salads. Do not use frozen or canned corn in this dish.

1 Stir reserved bean liquid and lemon juice together in small bowl; set aside. Heat oil in 12-inch nonstick skillet over medium-high heat until shimmering. Add fennel, scallion whites, and salt and cook, stirring frequently, until softened and beginning to brown, 4 to 5 minutes. Stir in garlic and ground fennel and cook until fragrant, about 30 seconds.

2 Reduce heat to medium and add corn and beans. Cook, stirring occasionally, until corn and beans are warmed through, about 4 minutes. Add bean liquid mixture and cook, stirring constantly, for 1 minute. Remove skillet from heat, stir in scallion greens, and season with salt and pepper to taste. Serve.

Cals 209 | Total Fat 7g | Sat Fat 4g
Chol 15mg | Sodium 461mg
Total Carb 32g | Dietary Fiber 6g
Total Sugars 6g | Protein 8g

LENTIL SALAD WITH ORANGES, CELERY, AND FETA

CRISPY LENTIL AND HERB SALAD

SERVES
4 TO 6

40 MINS
plus 1 hr
brining

1 teaspoon table salt for brining

½ cup dried lentilles du Puy, picked over and rinsed

⅓ cup extra-virgin olive oil for frying

½ teaspoon ground cumin

¼ teaspoon plus pinch table salt, divided

1 cup plain Greek yogurt

3 tablespoons extra-virgin olive oil, divided

1 teaspoon grated lemon zest plus 1 teaspoon juice

1 garlic clove, minced

½ cup fresh parsley leaves

½ cup torn fresh dill

½ cup fresh cilantro leaves

¼ cup dried cherries, chopped

Pomegranate molasses

Pita, warmed

WHY THIS RECIPE WORKS Many lentil salads use simmered lentils (see page 200), but we decided to fry ours in this salad inspired by lentil preparations in the Middle East. The result is a crispy, craveable treat (it's tough not to snack on the lentils before making the salad). Salt-soaking the lentils before frying softens them enough to ensure that they turn tender and lightly crispy—not burnt and hard. The firm texture of lentilles du Puy holds up well to quickly frying in a saucepan. We use thick (and filling) yogurt as an anchor for the other ingredients, spreading it on a platter and topping it with a lightly dressed blend of fresh herbs tossed with the crunchy lentils and sweet bits of dried cherries. We think pita is a must for scooping up everything in this surprisingly filling salad. You can use brown lentils instead of the lentilles du Puy. Be sure to use a large saucepan to fry the lentils, as the oil mixture will bubble and steam.

1 Dissolve 1 teaspoon salt in 1 quart water in large bowl. Add lentils and let sit at room temperature for at least 1 hour or up to 24 hours. Drain well and pat dry with paper towels.

2 Heat ⅓ cup oil in large saucepan over medium heat until shimmering. Add lentils and cook, stirring constantly, until crispy and golden in spots, 8 to 12 minutes (oil should bubble vigorously throughout; adjust heat as needed). Carefully drain lentils in fine-mesh strainer set over bowl, then transfer lentils to paper towel–lined plate. Discard oil. Sprinkle lentils with cumin and ¼ teaspoon salt and toss to combine; set aside. (Cooled lentils can be stored in airtight container at room temperature for up to 24 hours.)

3 Whisk yogurt, 2 tablespoons oil, lemon zest and juice, and garlic together in bowl and season with salt and pepper to taste. Spread yogurt mixture over serving platter. Toss parsley, dill, cilantro, remaining pinch salt, and remaining 1 tablespoon oil together in bowl, then gently stir in lentils and cherries and arrange on top of yogurt mixture, leaving 1-inch border. Drizzle with pomegranate molasses. Serve with pita.

Cals 240 | Total Fat 17g | Sat Fat 5g
Chol 10mg | Sodium 220mg
Total Carb 16g | Dietary Fiber 3g
Total Sugars 5g | Protein 7g

CANNELLINI BEANS WITH ROASTED RED PEPPERS AND KALE

SERVES 4 TO 6

50 MINS

¼ cup extra-virgin olive oil, plus extra for drizzling

4 garlic cloves, minced

¼ teaspoon red pepper flakes

1 small red onion, halved and sliced thin

¼ teaspoon table salt

1 cup jarred roasted red peppers, sliced thin

1 pound kale, stemmed and sliced thin crosswise

2 (15-ounce) cans cannellini beans, rinsed

½ cup dry white wine

½ cup water

Lemon wedges

WHY THIS RECIPE WORKS A pantry bean dish gets a shot of freshness and ultranutritious heartiness with kale. Many delicious beans-and-greens dishes come from Italy, so for this full-flavored one-pot take on the combination, we use Italian flavors. We sauté garlic and onion with some hot red pepper flakes; the subtle spiciness balances the sweetness of the beans and roasted peppers. Slicing the kale into thin ribbons and adding it to the skillet a handful at a time allows it to wilt evenly. For the cooking liquid, we use equal parts water and white wine to add light body and acidity to the dish. We serve it all with lemon wedges for squeezing over the top and a drizzle of extra-virgin olive oil. Swiss chard can be substituted for the kale, if you prefer.

1 Cook oil, garlic, and pepper flakes in 12-inch skillet over medium-high heat until garlic turns golden brown, about 2 minutes. Stir in onion and salt, reduce heat to medium, and cook until onion is softened, about 5 minutes. Stir in red peppers and cook until softened and glossy, about 3 minutes.

2 Stir in kale, 1 handful at a time, and cook until wilted, about 3 minutes. Stir in beans, wine, and water and bring to simmer. Reduce heat to medium-low, cover, and cook until flavors meld and kale is tender, 15 to 20 minutes. Season with salt and pepper to taste, and drizzle with oil. Serve with lemon wedges.

Cals 220 | Total Fat 10g | Sat Fat 1.5g
Chol 0mg | Sodium 480mg
Total Carb 24g | Dietary Fiber 7g
Total Sugars 5g | Protein 8g

CHORBA FRIK

**SERVES
4 TO 6**

1½ HRS

1   (14.5 ounce) can whole peeled tomatoes, drained with juice reserved

2   (5- to 7-ounce) bone-in chicken thighs

1¼   teaspoon table salt, divided

2   tablespoons extra-virgin olive oil

1   onion, chopped fine

1   celery rib, minced

1   cup minced fresh cilantro, plus ¼ cup leaves for serving

2   tablespoons tomato paste

3   garlic cloves, minced

1   tablespoon ground coriander

1   tablespoon paprika

2   teaspoons ground cumin

½   teaspoon pepper

¼   teaspoon ground cinnamon

¼   teaspoon cayenne pepper

6   cups water

1   (15-ounce) can chickpeas, undrained

½   cup cracked freekeh, rinsed

1   teaspoon dried mint

    Lemon wedges

WHY THIS RECIPE WORKS Soup is a universal starter on Ramadan Iftar dinner tables worldwide, as the warm dish hydrates and prepares digestion after a day of fasting. Chorba, meaning soup, with its many variations, is widely consumed in Algeria, Tunisia, Morocco, and Libya. Carbohydrate-rich foods are common in Algeria and, especially in the western part, chorba frik, a freekeh-filled soup, is a high favorite and a culinary tradition. "It is a wonderful bowl of nourishing comfort," points out Algerian culinary expert Radia SiYoucef, who offered her tutelage for us to develop this recipe. She prepares a superlative version of the savory soup for her family every Ramadan. And she acknlowedges that chorba frik may vary with nuance from household to household, and even night to night of Ramadan, but its foundation is consistent: A nourishing bowl of an aromatic, well-spiced tomato-based broth simmered with lots of fresh cilantro, plentiful freekeh, morsels of meat (sheep and lamb are most common, but poultry is also used), and sometimes chickpeas too. The focal ingredient is the flavorful freekeh celebrated in the soup. Consumed throughout the Mediterranean for thousands of years, freekeh is made from roasted durum wheat that has been harvested while the grains are still young and green. The grains are polished, and in Algeria, used cracked. Through simmering, the grain retains its pleasantly chewy texture and imparts a beautiful subtle smoky, nutty flavor to the soup—the soup's signature flavor. Our recipe uses two bone-in chicken thighs, making the soup even more filling without detracting from the freekeh. The rich meat is shredded into bite-size pieces. A combination of canned tomatoes pulsed to puree and tomato paste imparts acidity, vibrant color, and a satisfying body that are trademarks of this soup. Whole freekeh requires a different cooking method and will not work in this recipe.

*Cals 270 | Total Fat 13g | Sat Fat 2.5g | Chol 40mg | Sodium 850mg
Total Carb 25g | Dietary Fiber 7g | Total Sugars 3g | Protein 13g*

1 Pulse tomatoes and their juice in food processor until pureed, about 30 seconds. Pat chicken dry with paper towels and sprinkle with ¼ teaspoon salt. Heat oil in Dutch oven over medium-high heat until just smoking. Cook chicken skin side down until well browned, about 5 minutes; transfer chicken to plate. Pour off all but 2 tablespoons fat from pot.

2 Add onion, celery, and remaining 1 teaspoon salt to fat in pot and cook over medium heat until softened, about 5 minutes. Stir in minced cilantro, tomato paste, garlic, coriander, paprika, cumin, pepper, cinnamon, and cayenne and cook until fragrant, about 1 minute. Stir in pureed tomatoes, water, chickpeas and their liquid, and freekeh, scraping up any browned bits. Nestle chicken and any accumulated juices into pot and bring to simmer. Adjust heat as needed to maintain simmer and cook until freekeh is tender and chicken registers 195 degrees and easily shreds with fork, 35 to 45 minutes.

3 Transfer chicken to clean plate and let cool slightly. Once chicken is cool enough to handle, using two forks, shred chicken into bite-size pieces and discard skin and bones. Stir shredded chicken and any accumulated juices back into pot and season with salt and pepper to taste. Serve with cilantro leaves, dried mint, and lemon wedges.

GARLICKY WILD RICE SOUP WITH ARTICHOKES

SERVES 4

1½ HRS

3 tablespoons extra-virgin olive oil, divided

3 cups jarred whole baby artichoke hearts packed in water, quartered, rinsed, and patted dry

1 leek, white and light green parts only, halved lengthwise, sliced ¼ inch thick, and washed thoroughly

8 garlic cloves, minced, divided

4 anchovy fillets, rinsed, patted dry, and minced

1 teaspoon minced fresh thyme or ¼ teaspoon dried

¼ cup dry white wine

6 cups chicken or vegetable broth

1 cup wild rice, rinsed

2 bay leaves

1 pound asparagus, trimmed and cut into 1-inch pieces

2 tablespoons minced fresh tarragon

1 teaspoon grated lemon zest plus 1 tablespoon juice

WHY THIS RECIPE WORKS Wild rice shines in soups, the substantial, chewy grains adding hearty texture and filling fiber without making them stodgy. Though the rice is a North American ingredient, this soup's profile takes inspiration from spring flavors of the South of France. An abundant amount of aromatics gets this soup off to a flavorful start; leeks, garlic, anchovies, wine, and thyme all contribute to a pleasantly potent backbone. We cook the rice until it's almost done, and then stir in asparagus and artichokes (which we've sautéed to achieve browning), so everything—from hearty rice to light asparagus—finishes cooking at the same time. Stirring in a fresh combination of tarragon, lemon, and additional garlic off the heat ensures that their flavors have presence.

1 Heat 2 tablespoons oil in Dutch oven over medium heat until shimmering. Add artichokes and cook until browned, 8 to 10 minutes. Transfer to bowl and set aside.

2 Heat remaining 1 tablespoon oil in now-empty pot over medium heat until shimmering. Stir in leek and cook until leek is softened and beginning to brown, 5 to 7 minutes. Stir in half of garlic, anchovies, and thyme and cook until fragrant, about 30 seconds. Stir in wine, scraping up any browned bits, and cook until nearly evaporated, about 1 minute.

3 Stir in broth, rice, and bay leaves and bring to simmer. Cover, reduce heat to medium-low, and simmer gently for 35 minutes. Stir in reserved artichokes and asparagus and cook, covered, until rice and vegetables are tender, about 10 minutes.

4 Remove pot from heat and discard bay leaves. Stir tarragon, lemon zest and juice, and remaining garlic into soup and season with salt and pepper to taste. Serve.

Cals 420 | Total Fat 12g | Sat Fat 1.5g
Chol 5mg | Sodium 1220mg
Total Carb 58g | Dietary Fiber 7g
Total Sugars 7g | Protein 20g

HARIRA

⅓ cup extra-virgin olive oil

1 large onion, chopped fine

2 celery ribs, chopped fine

5 garlic cloves, minced

1 tablespoon grated
fresh ginger

2 teaspoons ground coriander

2 teaspoons smoked paprika

1 teaspoon ground cumin

½ teaspoon ground cinnamon

⅛ teaspoon red pepper flakes

¾ cup minced fresh cilantro,
divided

½ cup minced fresh parsley,
divided

4 cups chicken or vegetable
broth

4 cups water

1 (15-ounce) can chickpeas,
rinsed

1 cup brown lentils, picked
over and rinsed

1 (28-ounce) can crushed
tomatoes

½ cup orzo

4 ounces Swiss chard, stemmed
and cut into ½-inch pieces

2 tablespoons lemon juice

Lemon wedges

WHY THIS RECIPE WORKS There are countless adaptations of the traditional Moroccan soup harira, depending on the region or even the family. They share the use of tomatoes, legumes, dried spices, and fresh herbs. Often lamb or chicken is included; this version is vegetarian. Many include fresh greens, and we stir in a generous amount of tender, earthy-sweet Swiss chard at the end of cooking. Canned chickpeas work well here, and coriander, paprika, cumin, cinnamon, and red pepper flakes bring the dish warmth. Finishing the harira with lemon juice focuses all the flavors. We prefer brown or green lentils for this recipe, but it will work with any type of lentil except red or yellow (note that cooking times will vary depending on the type used). For extra heat, garnish the soup with Harissa (page 17).

1 Heat oil in Dutch oven over medium-high heat until shimmering. Add onion and celery and cook, stirring frequently, until translucent and starting to brown, 7 to 8 minutes. Reduce heat to medium, add garlic and ginger, and cook until fragrant, about 1 minute. Stir in coriander, paprika, cumin, cinnamon, and pepper flakes and cook for 1 minute. Stir in ½ cup cilantro and ¼ cup parsley and cook for 1 minute.

2 Stir in broth, water, chickpeas, and lentils, increase heat to high, and bring to simmer. Reduce heat to medium-low, partially cover, and gently simmer until lentils are just tender, about 20 minutes.

3 Stir in tomatoes and pasta and simmer, partially covered, for 7 minutes, stirring occasionally. Stir in chard and continue to cook, partially covered, until pasta is tender, about 5 minutes longer. Off heat, stir in lemon juice, remaining ¼ cup cilantro, and remaining ¼ cup parsley. Season with salt and pepper to taste. Serve, passing lemon wedges separately.

Cals 390 | Total Fat 15g | Sat Fat 2g | Chol 0mg | Sodium 780mg
Total Carb 51g | Dietary Fiber 11g | Total Sugars 9g | Protein 17g

PASTA E CECI

**SERVES
4 TO 6**

1 HR

- 2 ounces pancetta, cut into ½-inch pieces
- 1 small carrot, peeled and cut into ½-inch pieces
- 1 small celery rib, cut into ½-inch pieces
- 4 garlic cloves, peeled
- 1 onion, halved and cut into 1-inch pieces
- 1 (14-ounce) can whole peeled tomatoes, drained
- ¼ cup extra-virgin olive oil, plus extra for drizzling
- 1 anchovy fillet, rinsed, patted dry, and minced
- ¼ teaspoon red pepper flakes
- 2 teaspoon minced fresh rosemary or ¾ teaspoon dried
- 2 (15-ounce) cans chickpeas, undrained
- 2 cups water
- 1 teaspoon table salt
- 8 ounces (1½ cups) ditalini
- 1 tablespoon lemon juice
- 1 tablespoon minced fresh parsley

  Grated Parmesan cheese

WHY THIS RECIPE WORKS Pasta e ceci, pasta and chickpeas, have been paired up in Italian cuisine for centuries. The combination is inexpensive, simple, and pantry-ready, and the dish itself—a sibling of pasta e fagioli—is hearty, flavorful, and fast to make. It's a one-pot meal that home cooks turn to over and over again. And every home cook has a version, from brothy soups to hearty stews and even lightly sauced pastas. This one's a loose stew that's thick with creamy beans and stubby pasta but also savory enough to balance the starchy components. We cook chickpeas and ditalini in the same pot to blend the dish, using the starch released by the pasta to create a silky, stick-to-your-ribs texture. Flavor (without a distracting texture) comes from a finely minced soffritto of onions, garlic, carrot, celery, and pancetta, a small addition that manages to gives the dish a great meaty backbone. Depth comes from anchovies, tomatoes, and Parmesan cheese. Another short pasta, such as orzo, can be substituted for the ditalini, but make sure to substitute by weight and not by volume.

1 Process pancetta in food processor until ground to paste, about 30 seconds, scraping down sides of bowl as needed. Add carrot, celery, and garlic and pulse until finely chopped, 8 to 10 pulses. Add onion and pulse until onion is cut into ⅛- to ¼-inch pieces, 8 to 10 pulses. Transfer pancetta mixture to Dutch oven. Pulse tomatoes in now-empty food processor until coarsely chopped, 8 to 10 pulses. Set aside.

2 Add oil to pancetta mixture in Dutch oven and cook over medium heat, stirring frequently, until fond begins to form on bottom of pot, about 5 minutes. Add anchovy, pepper flakes, and rosemary and cook until fragrant, about 1 minute. Stir in tomatoes, chickpeas and their liquid, water, and salt and bring to boil, scraping up any browned bits. Reduce heat to medium-low and simmer for 10 minutes.

3 Add pasta and cook, stirring frequently, until tender, 10 to 12 minutes. Stir in lemon juice and parsley and season with salt and pepper to taste. Serve, drizzling individual portions with extra oil, and passing Parmesan separately.

*Cals 506 | Total Fat 19g | Sat Fat 4g | Chol 10mg | Sodium 905mg
Total Carb 67g | Dietary Fiber 13g | Total Sugars 10g | Protein 19g*

BUTTERNUT SQUASH AND WHITE BEAN SOUP WITH SAGE PESTO

Pesto

⅓ cup walnuts, toasted

1 garlic clove, minced

½ cup fresh parsley leaves

½ cup fresh sage leaves

½ cup extra-virgin olive oil

1 ounce Parmesan cheese, grated (½ cup)

Soup

1 (2- to 2½-pound) butternut squash, peeled, seeded, bulb cut into 8 wedges, and neck cut into ½-inch pieces

4 cups chicken or vegetable broth

3 cups water

1 tablespoon soy sauce

1 tablespoon extra-virgin olive oil

1 pound leeks, white and light green parts only, halved lengthwise, sliced thin, and washed thoroughly

1 tablespoon tomato paste

2 garlic cloves, minced

¼ teaspoon pepper

3 (15-ounce) cans cannellini beans, undrained

1 teaspoon white wine vinegar

Grated Parmesan cheese

WHY THIS RECIPE WORKS While we love creamy, pureed butternut squash soups (see page 70), we also like the idea of enlisting the vegetable to make a hearty-textured soup that can serve as a meal. Here we opt to feature chunks of squash paired with creamy cannellini beans in an aromatic broth. The bulb portion of the squash is difficult to cut into cubes that will cook evenly and naturally cooks faster than the dense neck portion, so we cut the bulb into wedges, cook them in the broth until they're soft, and then mash them to make a "squash stock" that gives the soup base body and flavor. We then cook the neck portion, cut into distinct chunks, in this stock. A swirl of sage pesto, which we make quickly in the food processor, lends the right bright, herbal finish and welcome richness.

1 For the pesto Pulse walnuts and garlic in food processor until coarsely chopped, about 5 pulses. Add parsley and sage; with processor running, slowly add oil and process until smooth, about 1 minute. Transfer to bowl, stir in Parmesan, and season with salt and pepper to taste; set aside.

2 For the soup Bring squash wedges, broth, water, and soy sauce to boil in large saucepan over high heat. Reduce heat to medium, partially cover, and simmer vigorously until squash is very tender and starting to fall apart, about 20 minutes. Off heat, use potato masher to mash squash, still in broth, until completely broken down. Cover to keep warm; set aside.

3 Heat oil in Dutch oven over medium heat until shimmering. Add leeks and tomato paste and cook, stirring occasionally, until leeks are softened and tomato paste is darkened, about 5 minutes. Stir in garlic and cook until fragrant, about 30 seconds. Add squash pieces and pepper and cook, stirring occasionally, for 5 minutes. Add squash broth and bring to simmer. Partially cover and cook for 10 minutes.

4 Add beans and their liquid, partially cover, and cook, stirring occasionally, until squash is just tender, 15 to 20 minutes. Stir in vinegar and season with salt and pepper to taste. Serve, passing pesto and Parmesan separately.

Cals 520 | Total Fat 27g | Sat Fat 4g | Chol 5mg | Sodium 1210mg
Total Carb 55g | Dietary Fiber 14g | Total Sugars 9g | Protein 19g

LABLABI

Soup

1 pound (2¾ cups) dried chickpeas, picked over and rinsed

1 onion, chopped fine

½ cup Harissa (page 17), divided

4 garlic cloves, minced

2 teaspoons ground cumin

1 teaspoon table salt

2 tablespoons lemon juice, plus lemon wedges for serving

¼ cup chopped fresh cilantro

Toppings

Crusty bread

Extra-virgin olive oil

Canned tuna

Capers, rinsed

Pitted green olives

Lemon wedges

Hard-cooked eggs

Greek yogurt

WHY THIS RECIPE WORKS Dinner—or lunch, or breakfast—is served with this simple but superlatively satisfying Tunisian chickpea soup. And it's really all about the chickpeas: They're simmered in only water until they're just tender and their flavor becomes omnipresent, giving the soup meatiness (rather than broth doing that job). Traditional aromatics (garlic, cumin, and harissa paste) are added in the final minutes of simmering for an invigorating brew. This soup is traditionally enhanced with extras for a meal; crusty bread, one of the most common, is highly recommended to help soak up all the delectable broth. A squeeze of lemon and a dollop of additional harissa are also traditional and add freshness. From there, there are myriad other toppings that can make the dish as filling as you wish, from hard-cooked eggs to canned tuna. Don't be afraid to try several different combinations.

1 For the soup Combine chickpeas and 2 quarts water in large container. Let soak at room temperature for at least 8 hours or up to 24 hours. Drain and rinse well.

2 Bring chickpeas and 10 cups water to boil in Dutch oven. Reduce heat and simmer, stirring occasionally until chickpeas are just tender, 30 to 45 minutes. (Skim any loose bean skins or foam from surface of liquid as beans cook.)

3 Stir in onion, ¼ cup harissa, garlic, cumin, and salt and cook until vegetables are softened and chickpeas are tender, 10 to 15 minutes. Off heat, stir in lemon juice and season with salt to taste. Divide soup among individual bowls and top with cilantro and remaining ¼ cup harissa.

4 For the toppings Serve with your preferred toppings.

Cals 420 | Total Fat 19g | Sat Fat 2.5g
Chol 0mg | Sodium 610mg
Total Carb 49g | Dietary Fiber 14g
Total Sugars 9g | Protein 15g

SHRIMP, TOMATO, AND WHITE BEAN STEW

SERVES
4 TO 6

1 HR

2 tablespoons sugar

1 tablespoon table salt for brining

1 pound large shell-on shrimp (26 to 30 per pound), peeled, deveined, and tails removed, shells reserved

¼ cup extra-virgin olive oil, divided

1 onion, chopped fine

4 garlic cloves sliced thin

2 anchovy fillets, rinsed, patted dry, and minced

¼ teaspoon red pepper flakes

¼ teaspoon table salt

⅛ teaspoon pepper

2 (15-ounce) cans cannellini beans (1 can drained and rinsed, 1 can undrained)

1 (14.5-ounce) can diced tomatoes, drained

¼ cup shredded fresh basil

½ teaspoon grated lemon zest plus 1 tablespoon juice

WHY THIS RECIPE WORKS Brothy white bean dishes are commonplace in Tuscany, and we love a version with shrimp included—the tender bite of the shrimp is a nice foil to the creamy beans. These beans are typically quite fragrant with aromatics, but to give them fuller seafood flavor, we make a quick concentrated shrimp-shell stock and use it to simmer the beans. We also cook the shrimp with the beans rather than separately (we add the shrimp late in the cooking process and reduce the heat so they cook gently) and sauté minced anchovies with the aromatics. Canned beans and canned tomatoes make this dish fast and doable at any time of year; plus, the liquid from one of the cans of beans lends the dish nice body. Plenty of fresh basil plus lemon juice and zest provide freshness and nice acidity. You will need a 12-inch skillet with a tight-fitting lid for this recipe. Serve with crusty bread. We prefer untreated shrimp, but if your shrimp are treated with added salt or preservatives like sodium tripolyphosphate, skip brining in step 1 and increase the salt to ½ teaspoon in step 3.

1 Dissolve sugar and 1 tablespoon salt in 1 quart cold water in large bowl. Submerge shrimp in brine, cover, and refrigerate for 15 minutes. Remove shrimp from brine and pat dry with paper towels.

2 Heat 1 tablespoon oil in 12-inch skillet over medium heat until shimmering. Add shrimp shells and cook, stirring frequently, until they begin to turn spotty brown and skillet starts to brown, 5 to 6 minutes. Remove skillet from heat and carefully add 1 cup water. When bubbling subsides, return skillet to medium heat and simmer gently, stirring occasionally, for 5 minutes. Strain mixture through colander set over large bowl. Discard shells and reserve liquid (you should have about ¼ cup). Wipe skillet clean with paper towels.

3 Heat 2 tablespoons oil, onion, garlic, anchovies, pepper flakes, salt, and pepper in now-empty skillet over medium-low heat. Cook, stirring occasionally, until onion is softened, about 5 minutes. Add beans, tomatoes, and shrimp stock and bring to simmer. Simmer, stirring occasionally, for 15 minutes.

4 Reduce heat to low, add shrimp, cover, and cook, stirring once during cooking, until shrimp are just opaque, 5 to 7 minutes. Remove skillet from heat and stir in basil and lemon zest and juice. Season with salt and pepper to taste. Transfer to serving dish, drizzle with remaining 1 tablespoon oil, and serve.

Cals 260 | Total Fat 10g | Sat Fat 1.5g
Chol 95mg | Sodium 660mg
Total Carb 24g | Dietary Fiber 6g
Total Sugars 8g | Protein 17g

CREAMY WHITE BEAN SOUP WITH PICKLED CELERY

Pickled Celery

- ½ cup rice vinegar
- 1 tablespoon sugar
- ½ teaspoon table salt
- 1 celery rib, chopped fine

Soup

- ¼ cup extra-virgin olive oil, divided, plus extra for drizzling
- ½ cup chopped onion
- 1 small celery rib, chopped fine
- 3 sprigs fresh thyme
- 2 garlic cloves, sliced thin
  Pinch cayenne pepper
- 2 (15-ounce) cans great Northern beans, undrained
- 2 tablespoons grated Parmesan cheese
- 2 cups chicken or vegetable broth, divided
- ½ teaspoon lemon juice, plus extra for seasoning

Cals 220 | Total Fat 11g | Sat Fat 2g
Chol 0mg | Sodium 640mg
Total Carb 23g | Dietary Fiber 5g
Total Sugars 3g | Protein 9g

WHY THIS RECIPE WORKS As proven in our cornerstone hummus recipe (see page 294), sophistication can come from a can, as it does in this super-creamy white bean soup with a special celery topping. To keep the creamy, smooth promise, and do it quickly, we start by briefly simmering canned great Northern beans and their seasoned canning liquid with softened aromatic vegetables and herbs. Heating the beans causes their starches to hydrate, which makes the soup especially creamy. Blending the beans with a small amount of liquid helps their skins break down, making for an ultrasmooth puree. Broth plus a little Parmesan cheese boosts the soup's flavor and richness. Extra-virgin olive oil and quick-pickled celery make an easy but impressive garnish that complements the neutral soup base with vibrant color, flavor, and contrasting crunchy texture. Use a conventional blender here; an immersion blender will not produce as smooth a soup.

1 For the pickled celery Combine vinegar, sugar, and salt in medium bowl and microwave until simmering, 1 to 2 minutes. Stir in celery and let sit for 15 minutes. Drain celery, discarding liquid, and set aside until ready to serve.

2 For the soup Heat 2 tablespoons oil in large saucepan over medium heat until shimmering. Add onion and celery and cook, stirring frequently, until softened but not browned, 6 to 8 minutes. Add thyme sprigs, garlic, and cayenne and cook, stirring constantly, until fragrant, about 1 minute. Add beans and their liquid and stir to combine. Reduce heat to medium-low, cover, and cook, stirring occasionally, until beans are heated through and just starting to break down, 6 to 8 minutes. Remove saucepan from heat and discard thyme sprigs.

3 Process bean mixture and Parmesan in blender on low speed until thick, smooth puree forms, about 2 minutes. With blender running, add 1 cup broth and remaining 2 tablespoons oil. Increase speed to high and continue to process until oil is incorporated and mixture is pourable, about 1 minute longer.

4 Return soup to clean saucepan and whisk in remaining 1 cup broth. Cover and bring to simmer over medium heat, adjusting consistency with up to 1 cup hot water as needed. Off heat, stir in lemon juice. Season with salt and extra lemon juice to taste. Drizzle each portion of soup with extra oil and sprinkle with reserved quick-pickled celery.

MISO MUSHROOM RISOTTO

**SERVES
4**

1¼ HRS

4 cups chicken or vegetable broth

3 cups water

⅓ cup white miso

¼ cup extra-virgin olive oil, divided

1 pound cremini mushrooms, trimmed and sliced ¼ inch thick

1 onion, chopped fine

4 garlic cloves, minced

1 ounce dried porcini mushrooms, rinsed and minced

2 cups arborio rice

½ cup dry white wine

¼ cup chopped fresh parsley

WHY THIS RECIPE WORKS The ideal risotto is beloved for its plush creaminess, often derived in part from copious amounts of butter and Parmesan. We wanted to have an option that was fully plant-based. Many plant-based risottos include cashew cheese, extra olive oil, or even chia seeds for richness and body but we found these options heavy and gluey. Miso is the breakthrough ingredient. It not only gives the risotto savor; it acts as a thickener, dressing the risotto in a satiny gloss. This more hands-off method requires precise timing, so we highly recommend using a timer.

1 Bring broth, water, and miso to boil in large saucepan over high heat; reduce heat to medium-low and simmer, whisking occasionally, until miso is dissolved, about 5 minutes. Reduce heat to lowest setting and cover to keep warm.

2 Meanwhile, heat 1 tablespoon oil in Dutch oven over medium heat until shimmering. Add cremini mushrooms, cover, and cook until mushrooms have released their liquid, about 5 minutes. Uncover and continue to cook until well browned, 10 to 12 minutes longer; transfer to bowl.

3 Heat 2 tablespoons oil in now-empty pot over medium heat until shimmering. Stir in onion and cook until softened, about 5 minutes. Add garlic and porcini mushrooms and cook until fragrant, about 30 seconds. Add rice and cook, stirring frequently, until grains are translucent around edges, about 3 minutes.

4 Add wine and cook, stirring constantly, until fully absorbed, 2 to 3 minutes. Stir in 5 cups hot broth mixture, then reduce heat to medium-low, cover, and simmer until almost all liquid has been absorbed and rice is just al dente, 16 to 18 minutes, stirring twice during simmering. Add ¾ cup hot broth mixture and browned cremini mushrooms to risotto and stir gently and constantly until risotto becomes creamy, about 3 minutes. Cover pot and let sit off heat for 5 minutes.

5 Stir in parsley and remaining 1 tablespoon oil and season with salt and pepper to taste. Before serving, adjust consistency with additional broth mixture as needed.

*Cals 600 | Total Fat 17g | Sat Fat 2g
Chol 0mg | Sodium 1090mg
Total Carb 90g | Dietary Fiber 4g
Total Sugars 9g | Protein 20g*

SHRIMP RISOTTO

SERVES
4

1¾ HRS

1 pound extra-large shrimp (21 to 25 per pound), peeled, deveined, and tails removed, shells reserved

1 teaspoon table salt, divided

5 tablespoons extra-virgin olive oil, divided

7 cups water

15 black peppercorns

2 bay leaves

1 onion, chopped fine

1 fennel bulb, stalks discarded, bulb halved, cored, and chopped fine

⅛ teaspoon baking soda

2 garlic cloves, minced

1½ cups arborio rice

¾ cup dry white wine

1 ounce Parmesan cheese, grated (½ cup), plus extra for serving

¼ cup minced fresh chives

½ teaspoon grated lemon zest plus 1 tablespoon juice, plus lemon wedges for serving

Cals 560 | Total Fat 22g | Sat Fat 3.5g
Chol 110mg | Sodium 920mg
Total Carb 62g | Dietary Fiber 4g
Total Sugars 4g | Protein 23g

WHY THIS RECIPE WORKS Risotto can contain any number of shellfish, but here we focus on shrimp, cut small for easier eating—the sweet bites are a nice relief from the richness of the surrounding creamy rice. We sear shrimp shells to extract their flavorful compounds, add water and seasonings, and simmer for just 5 minutes to make a seafood broth. Meanwhile, we salt the shrimp to ensure that they remain juicy through cooking. We simmer the risotto covered to trap and distribute heat uniformly and release starches from the grains for evenly cooked, creamy risotto without frequent stirring or sore wrists. Adding the shrimp off the heat allows them to cook very gently. This more hands-off method requires precise timing, so we highly recommend using a timer.

1 Cut each shrimp crosswise into thirds, then toss with ¼ teaspoon salt; set aside. Heat 1 tablespoon oil in Dutch oven over high heat until shimmering. Add reserved shrimp shells and cook, stirring frequently, until shells begin to turn spotty brown, 2 to 4 minutes. Add water, peppercorns, bay leaves, and ½ teaspoon salt and bring to boil. Reduce heat to low and simmer for 5 minutes. Strain stock through fine-mesh strainer set over large bowl, pressing on solids to extract as much liquid as possible; discard solids.

2 Heat 2 tablespoons oil in now-empty pot over medium heat until shimmering. Add onion, fennel, baking soda, and remaining ¼ teaspoon salt. Cook, stirring frequently, until vegetables are softened but not browned, 8 to 10 minutes (volume will be largely reduced and onion will be disintegrating). Add garlic; stir until fragrant, about 30 seconds. Add rice and cook, stirring frequently, until grains are translucent around edges, about 3 minutes.

3 Add wine and cook, stirring constantly, until fully absorbed, 2 to 3 minutes. Stir in 4 cups stock, then reduce heat to medium-low, cover, and simmer until almost all liquid has been absorbed and rice is just al dente, 16 to 18 minutes, stirring twice during simmering. Add ¾ cup stock to risotto and stir gently and constantly until risotto becomes creamy, about 3 minutes. Stir in Parmesan and shrimp. Cover pot and let sit off heat for 5 minutes.

4 Gently stir chives, lemon zest and juice, and remaining 2 tablespoons oil into risotto. Season with salt and pepper to taste. Stir in additional stock to loosen texture of risotto, if desired. Serve, passing lemon wedges and extra Parmesan separately.

MUSHROOM FARROTTO

SERVES
4

1½ HRS

1½   cups whole farro

¾   ounce dried porcini mushrooms, rinsed

6   cups water, divided

¼   cup extra-virgin olive oil, divided

12   ounces cremini mushrooms, trimmed and sliced thin

1   teaspoon table salt, divided

½   onion, chopped fine

1   garlic clove, minced

2   teaspoons minced fresh thyme

¾   teaspoon pepper

1½   ounces Parmesan cheese, grated (¾ cup)

2   tablespoons minced fresh chives

2   teaspoons sherry vinegar

WHY THIS RECIPE WORKS Farrotto is a robust risotto-style dish that swaps in farro for the traditional arborio rice; the results are just as rich but even more nourishing. The translation is foolproof in this recipe: Because farro is a less-starchy grain, we crack about half the farro grains in a blender, which frees enough starch to create a creamy, risotto-like consistency through cooking. Farro works well with other hearty ingredients, and here deeply savory mushrooms make this simple dish an incredibly satisfying main course. We prefer the flavor and texture of whole farro. Do not use quick-cooking or pearled farro. The consistency of farrotto is largely a matter of personal taste; if you prefer a looser texture, add more of the hot water in step 4.

1 Pulse farro in blender until about half of grains are broken into smaller pieces, about 6 pulses.

2 Microwave porcini mushrooms and 1 cup water in covered bowl until steaming, about 1 minute. Let sit until softened, about 5 minutes. Drain mushrooms in fine-mesh strainer lined with coffee filter. Transfer liquid to medium saucepan and finely chop porcini mushrooms. Add remaining 5 cups water to saucepan with porcini liquid and bring to boil over high heat. Reduce heat to lowest setting and cover to keep warm.

3 Heat 2 tablespoons oil in Dutch oven over medium-low heat until shimmering. Add cremini mushrooms and ½ teaspoon salt and cook, stirring frequently, until moisture released by mushrooms evaporates and pan is dry, 4 to 5 minutes. Add onion and chopped porcini mushrooms and continue to cook until onion has softened, 3 to 4 minutes. Stir in garlic and cook until fragrant, about 30 seconds. Add farro and cook, stirring frequently, until grains are lightly toasted, about 3 minutes.

4 Stir 5 cups hot water into farro, reduce heat to low, cover, and cook until almost all liquid has been absorbed and farro is just al dente, about 25 minutes, stirring twice during cooking. Add thyme, pepper, and remaining ½ teaspoon salt and continue to cook, stirring constantly, until farro becomes creamy, about 5 minutes. Remove pot from heat. Stir in Parmesan, chives, vinegar, and remaining 2 tablespoons oil. Season with salt and pepper to taste. Adjust consistency with remaining hot water as needed. Serve immediately.

Cals 430 | Total Fat 17g | Sat Fat 3.5g
Chol 10mg | Sodium 930mg
Total Carb 53g | Dietary Fiber 6g
Total Sugars 2g | Protein 18g

Risotto Grains

While this Italian dish has rice in the root of its name, we've had great success making the dish with other grains. Why mess with a good thing? We love traditional risottos and have recipes for them in this book (see pages 221, and 222), but whole grains can offer different flavor dimensions or nutritional boosts. Traditional risotto is made with short-grain rices like arborio, carnaroli, and Vialone Nano. But if a grain has enough starch that can slough off during cooking, it can similarly come together into a porridge-like dish of grains suspended in a creamy (albeit creamless) sauce. We make risotto-style dishes with farro and barley in this book. Pearl couscous and orzo (both pastas) also work.

BEET BARLEY RISOTTO

3 cups chicken or vegetable broth

3 cups water

2 tablespoons extra-virgin olive oil

1 pound beets with greens attached, beets trimmed, peeled, and shredded, divided, greens stemmed and cut into 1-inch pieces (2 cups)

1 onion, chopped

½ teaspoon table salt

1½ cups pearl barley, rinsed

4 garlic cloves, minced

1 teaspoon minced fresh thyme or ¼ teaspoon dried

1 cup dry white wine

1 ounce Parmesan cheese, grated (½ cup)

2 tablespoons chopped fresh parsley

WHY THIS RECIPE WORKS Hearty pearl barley holds its own against the sweet earthiness of beets and their sturdy greens in this creamy, vegetable-forward, purple-hued risotto. Pearl barley has had its outer husk removed, exposing the starchy interior, which helps create the velvety sauce when simmered. We stir raw grated beets into the barley—half at the beginning for a base of flavor, and half at the end for freshness and color. Do not substitute hulled, hull-less, quick-cooking, or presteamed barley for the pearl barley. You can use the large holes of a box grater or a food processor fitted with a shredding disk to shred the beets.

1 Bring broth and water to simmer in medium saucepan. Reduce heat to lowest setting and cover to keep warm.

2 Heat oil in large saucepan over medium heat until shimmering. Add half of grated beets, onion, and salt and cook until vegetables are softened, 5 to 7 minutes. Stir in barley and cook, stirring often, until fragrant, about 4 minutes. Stir in garlic and thyme and cook until fragrant, about 30 seconds. Stir in wine and cook until fully absorbed, about 2 minutes.

3 Stir in 3 cups warm broth. Simmer, stirring occasionally, until liquid is absorbed and bottom of pan is dry, 22 to 25 minutes. Stir in 2 cups warm broth and simmer, stirring occasionally, until liquid is absorbed and bottom of pan is dry, 15 to 18 minutes.

4 Add beet greens and continue to cook, stirring often and adding remaining broth as needed to prevent bottom of pan from becoming dry, until greens are softened and barley is cooked through but still somewhat firm in center, 5 to 10 minutes. Off heat, stir in remaining grated beets and Parmesan. Season with salt and pepper to taste, and sprinkle with parsley. Serve.

Cals 500 | Total Fat 11g | Sat Fat 2g
Chol 5mg | Sodium 1000mg
Total Carb 77g | Dietary Fiber 17g
Total Sugars 10g | Protein 17g

CREAMY POLENTA WITH RADICCHIO AGRODOLCE

SERVES 4

1 HR

5   cups water

½   teaspoon table salt, divided

    Pinch baking soda

1   cup coarse-ground cornmeal

¼   cup extra-virgin olive oil, divided, plus extra for drizzling

1   ounce Parmesan cheese, grated (1 cup), plus extra for serving

3   celery ribs, cut into ½-inch pieces, plus ½ cup celery leaves

2   shallots, sliced thin

1   teaspoon minced fresh thyme or ¼ teaspoon dried

1   cup red wine vinegar

3   tablespoons sugar

3   ounces seedless red grapes, halved (½ cup)

1   head radicchio (10 ounces), halved, cored, and cut into ½-inch pieces

¼   cup whole almonds, toasted and chopped coarse

Cals 370 | Total Fat 25g | Sat Fat 6g
Chol 20mg | Sodium 860mg
Total Carb 20g | Dietary Fiber 2g
Total Sugars 15g | Protein 15g

WHY THIS RECIPE WORKS Agrodolce is a boldly flavored Italian sauce that's both sweet and sour, with an eye-catching luster. Made by reducing vinegar and sugar, its tangy sweetness is ideal for livening up a rich meal. In this plant-foward application, we combine agrodolce sauce with celery and radicchio and top a bed of nourishing creamy polenta with it. We sauté the celery and shallots until they're softened; add fresh thyme for slightly peppery notes; and reduce red wine vinegar and sugar in the same pan. The vinegar and sugar thicken into the signature coating glaze. Grapes provide pops of appropriately wine-y sweetness. Charring the radicchio counterbalances the sweetness from the grapes with smoky bitterness, and adds heft to the dish. Richness, sweetness, sourness, and bitterness join forces for a meal to remember. You can use parsley if your celery doesn't come with leaves.

1 Bring water to boil in large saucepan over medium-high heat. Stir in ¼ teaspoon salt and baking soda. Slowly add cornmeal in steady stream, stirring constantly. Bring mixture to boil, stirring constantly, about 1 minute. Reduce heat to lowest possible setting, cover, and cook for 5 minutes.

2 Whisk cornmeal to smooth out any lumps, making sure to scrape down sides and bottom of saucepan. Cover and continue to cook, without stirring, until cornmeal is tender but slightly al dente, about 25 minutes. (Polenta should be loose and barely hold its shape but will continue to thicken as it cools.) Off heat, stir in 2 tablespoons oil and Parmesan and season with salt and pepper to taste. Cover and keep warm.

3 Meanwhile, heat 1 tablespoon oil in 12-inch nonstick skillet over medium heat until shimmering. Add celery ribs, shallots, and remaining ¼ teaspoon salt and cook, stirring occasionally, until softened and lightly browned, 7 to 9 minutes. Stir in thyme and cook until fragrant, about 30 seconds. Stir in vinegar and sugar, bring to simmer, and cook until liquid is thickened to syrupy glaze, about 10 minutes. Transfer to large bowl and stir in grapes. Cover with aluminum foil to keep warm.

4 Heat remaining 1 tablespoon oil in now-empty skillet over medium-high heat until shimmering. Add radicchio and cook until browned, about 5 minutes. Transfer to bowl with celery mixture and toss to combine. Serve polenta with radicchio mixture, sprinkling with almonds, extra Parmesan, and celery leaves and drizzling with extra oil.

SIMPLE GRAIN AND BEAN SIDES

The vibrant grain and bean dishes in this chapter—jeweled with dried fruit and nuts, studded with fresh produce, dressed with bright vinaigrettes, and shaped into satisfying burgers—can make a meal. But as grains, particularly whole, and legumes are staples of a healthful Mediterranean meal plan, it's helpful to have some quick grain sides to serve with other dishes, like the hearty vegetable meals in the first chapter of this book, or the more protein-forward dishes in the third, when you need to fill out your plate. Serve a braised dish over one of the simple grains. Or set a scoop of one of the bean salads next to your dinner—they're easy because they start with opening a can.

BASMATI RICE PILAF

SERVES 4 TO 6   TOTAL TIME: 50 MINS

Sometimes there's nothing more comforting than some perfectly cooked white rice, and fragrant basmati is a choice throughout the Middle East. Rinsing the rice before cooking removes excess starch and produces the fluffy, rather than clumpy, grains that we were after, and toasting it for a few minutes in the pan deepens its flavor. This pilaf is the perfect partner to Whole Romanesco with Berbere and Yogurt-Tahini Sauce (page 84), Pan-Seared Shrimp with Pistachio, Cumin, and Parsley (page 354), or even right to round out Carrot and Beet Salad with Rose Harissa (page 56). Placing a dish towel under the lid while the rice finished steaming off the heat absorbed excess moisture and guaranteed perfectly fluffy rice. Long-grain white, jasmine, or Texmati rice can be substituted for the basmati. A nonstick saucepan works best here, although a traditional saucepan will also work.

    1   tablespoon extra-virgin olive oil
    1   small onion, chopped fine
    ¼   teaspoon table salt
    1½ cups basmati rice, rinsed
    2¼ cups water

1 Heat oil in large saucepan over medium heat until shimmering. Add onion and salt and cook until softened, about 5 minutes. Stir in rice and cook, stirring often, until rice edges begin to turn translucent, about 3 minutes.

2 Stir in water and bring to simmer. Reduce heat to low, cover, and continue to simmer until rice is tender and water is absorbed, 16 to 18 minutes. Remove pot from heat and lay clean folded dish towel underneath lid. Let sit for 10 minutes. Fluff rice with fork, season with salt and pepper to taste, and serve.

Basmati Rice Pilaf with Currants and Cinnamon

Add 1 minced garlic clove, ½ teaspoon ground turmeric, and ¼ teaspoon ground cinnamon to pot after cooking onion in step 1. Cook until fragrant, about 30 seconds. Sprinkle ¼ cup dried currants over cooked rice before letting rice sit in step 3.

BAKED BROWN RICE WITH PARMESAN, LEMON, AND HERBS

SERVES 4 TO 6   TOTAL TIME: 1 HR 40 MINS

Brown rice has a nutty, gutsy flavor and textural personality that's slightly sticky and just a bit chewy. It also takes a lot longer to cook than white rice. Cranking up the stovetop in an effort to hurry along these slow-cooking grains leads to a burnt pot and crunchy, scorched rice. Instead, we bake the rice in the oven for about an hour and let it rest before serving. It's great to bake while Mushroom Bourguignon (page 93) simmers on the stove or alongside Halibut Puttanesca (page 339). You can use long-, medium-, or short-grain brown rice for this recipe. Be sure to cover the pot when bringing the broth to a boil in step 2; any water loss due to evaporation will affect how the rice cooks.

    1½ cups brown rice, rinsed and drained
    2   tablespoons extra-virgin olive oil
    1   small onion, chopped fine
    2⅓ cups chicken broth
    ⅛   teaspoon table salt
    ½   cup grated Parmesan cheese
    ¼   cup minced fresh parsley
    ¼   cup chopped fresh basil
    1   teaspoon grated lemon zest plus
        ½ teaspoon juice
    ⅛   teaspoon pepper

1 Adjust oven rack to middle position and heat oven to 375 degrees. Spread rice in 8-inch square baking dish.

2 Heat oil in 10-inch skillet over medium heat until shimmering. Add onion and cook until translucent, about 3 minutes. Bring broth to boil, covered, in medium saucepan. Once boiling, stir in salt and pour over rice in dish. Stir in onion and oil. Cover dish tightly with 2 layers of aluminum foil. Bake until liquid is absorbed and rice is tender, about 1 hour.

3 Remove dish from oven and uncover. Add Parmesan, parsley, basil, lemon zest and juice, and pepper. Fluff rice with fork, then re-cover dish with foil and let rice sit for 5 minutes. Uncover and let rice sit for 5 minutes longer. Serve immediately.

BAKED WILD RICE

SERVES 4 TO 6   TOTAL TIME: 1 HR 50 MINS

Wild rice has a delectably chewy outer husk and a nutty, savory flavor and thus, like brown rice, it takes quite some time to become tender on the stovetop. Again we use the oven to serve up this healthful grain. Wild rice's hearty texture makes it a nice side for Skillet-Roasted Chicken Breasts with Harissa-Mint Carrots (page 371) or Butternut Squash Steaks with Honey-Nut Topping (page 88). Be sure to cover the pot when bringing the water to a boil in step 2; any water loss due to evaporation will affect how the rice cooks. Do not use quick-cooking or presteamed wild rice in this recipe; you may need to read the ingredient list on the package carefully to determine if the wild rice is presteamed.

- 1½   cups wild rice, rinsed
- 3   cups water
- 2   teaspoons extra-virgin olive oil
- ¾   teaspoon table salt

1 Adjust oven rack to middle position and heat oven to 375 degrees. Spread rice into 8-inch square glass baking dish.

2 Bring water, oil, and salt to boil in covered medium saucepan over high heat. Once boiling, stir to combine, then pour immediately over rice. Cover baking dish tightly with aluminum foil and bake until liquid is absorbed and rice is tender, 1 hour 10 minutes to 1 hour 20 minutes.

3 Remove baking dish from oven, uncover, and fluff rice with fork. Re-cover dish with foil and let rice sit for 10 minutes before serving.

CREAMY PARMESAN POLENTA

SERVES 6 TO 8   TOTAL TIME: 1¼ HRS

You see polenta cooked as the base in our dish Creamy Polenta with Radicchio Agrodolce (page 228) but prepare it separately and it can serve as a landing pad for a simple topping like Broiled Broccoli Rabe (page 114), or as an accompaniment to a saucy vegetable dish like Whole Pot-Roasted Cauliflower with Tomatoes and Olives (page 87) or a braise like Salmon en Cocotte with Roasted Garlic and Cherry Tomatoes (page 348). Coarse-ground degerminated cornmeal gives us a soft but hearty texture and nutty flavor. A pinch of baking soda in the pot cuts cooking time in half and eliminates the need for stirring, making the recipe quick and arm-saving. Coarse-ground degerminated cornmeal such as yellow grits (with grains the size of couscous) works best in this recipe. Avoid instant and quick-cooking products, as well as whole-grain, stone-ground, and regular cornmeal. The polenta should do little more than emit wisps of steam. If it bubbles or sputters even slightly after the first 10 minutes, the heat is too high and you may need a flame tamer. A flame tamer can be found at most kitchen supply stores, or you can make your own by fashioning aluminum foil into a ring.

- 7½   cups water
-    Salt and pepper
-    Pinch baking soda
- 1½   cups coarse-ground cornmeal
- 4   ounces Parmesan cheese, grated (2 cups), plus extra for serving
- 2   tablespoons extra-virgin olive oil

1 Bring water to boil in large saucepan over medium-high heat. Stir in 1½ teaspoons salt and baking soda. Slowly pour cornmeal into water in steady stream while stirring back and forth with wooden spoon or rubber spatula. Bring mixture to boil and cook, stirring constantly, for about 1 minute. Reduce heat to lowest setting and cover.

2 After 5 minutes, whisk polenta, smoothing out any lumps that have formed, for about 15 seconds. (Make sure to scrape down sides and bottom of saucepan.) Cover and continue to cook, without stirring, until grains of polenta are tender but slightly al dente, about 25 minutes longer. (Polenta should be loose and barely hold its shape but will continue to thicken as it cools.) Off heat, stir in Parmesan and oil and season with pepper to taste. Let stand, covered, for 5 minutes. Serve, passing extra Parmesan separately.

QUINOA PILAF WITH LEMON AND HERBS

SERVES 4 TO 6   TOTAL TIME: 1 HR

For quinoa as it should be—with an appealingly nutty flavor and a satisfying, crunchy texture—we start by toasting the quinoa in a dry saucepan to bring out that flavor before simmering in a modest amount of water. We flavor our pilaf simply so the quinoa can pair with a variety of dishes, with some sautéed onion, herbs, and a squeeze of lemon juice. We like the convenience of prewashed quinoa; rinsing removes the quinoa's bitter protective coating (called saponin). If you buy unwashed quinoa (or if you are unsure whether it's washed), rinse it and then spread it out over a clean dish towel to dry for 15 minutes before cooking. Any soft herbs, such as cilantro, parsley, chives, mint, and tarragon, can be used.

1½	cups prewashed quinoa
2	tablespoons extra-virgin olive oil
1	small onion, chopped fine
¾	teaspoon salt
1¾	cups water
3	tablespoons chopped fresh herbs
1	tablespoon lemon juice

1 Toast quinoa in medium saucepan over medium-high heat, stirring frequently, until quinoa is very fragrant and makes continuous popping sound, 5 to 7 minutes. Transfer quinoa to bowl and set aside.

2 Return now-empty pan to medium-low heat and heat oil until shimmering. Add onion and salt; cook, stirring frequently, until onion is softened and light golden, 5 to 7 minutes.

3 Increase heat to medium-high, stir in water and quinoa, and bring to simmer. Cover, reduce heat to low, and simmer until grains are just tender and liquid is absorbed, 18 to 20 minutes, stirring once halfway through cooking. Remove pan from heat and let sit, covered, for 10 minutes. Fluff quinoa with fork, stir in herbs and lemon juice, and serve.

SIMPLE COUSCOUS

SERVES 4 TO 6   TOTAL TIME: 20 MINS

You'll find absorbent couscous, with its great texture and quick cooking time, is excellent served under stews and braises, especially those of the North African variety (like Cabbage, Kohlrabi, and Lamb Tagine with Prunes on page 83 or Fish Tagine on page 338). It can also work equally well as a lighter, quicker alternative to everyday side dishes like rice pilaf. So you need a simple couscous recipe in your arsenal. Toasting the couscous grains deepens their flavor and helps them cook up fluffy and separate. And to bump up the flavor even further, we replace half of the water with chicken broth.

- 2 tablespoons extra-virgin olive oil
- 2 cups couscous
- 1 cup water
- 1 cup chicken or vegetable broth
- 1 teaspoon table salt

Heat oil in medium saucepan over medium-high heat until shimmering. Add couscous and cook, stirring frequently, until grains are just beginning to brown, 3 to 5 minutes. Stir in water, broth, and salt. Cover, remove saucepan from heat, and let sit until couscous is tender, about 7 minutes. Gently fluff couscous with fork and season with pepper to taste. Serve.

WARM FARRO WITH ORANGE AND HERBS

SERVES 4 TO 6   TOTAL TIME: 50 MINS

Chewy, nutty farro is a great base for a unique and flavorful side dish. A few tests proved that the best way to achieve evenly cooked, tender farro was to cook it using the pasta method, in plenty of water. Garlic and onion together make an aromatic base for the simple side, bringing out some of the farro's natural sweetness. A splash of fresh orange juice provides subtle acidity, which helps enhance the nuttiness of the grains. A healthy sprinkling of chopped fresh parsley and mint gives the dish a nice pop of color and brightness.

- 1½ cups whole farro
- Salt and pepper
- 3 tablespoons extra-virgin olive oil
- 1 onion, chopped
- 1 garlic clove, minced
- ¼ cup chopped fresh parsley
- ¼ cup chopped fresh mint
- 1 tablespoon orange juice

1 Bring 4 quarts water to boil in Dutch oven. Stir in farro and 1 tablespoon salt, return to boil, and cook until grains are tender with slight chew, 15 to 30 minutes. Drain farro, return it to now-empty pot, and cover to keep warm.

2 Heat 2 tablespoons oil 12-inch skillet over medium heat until shimmering. Add onion and ¼ teaspoon salt and cook until softened, about 5 minutes. Stir in garlic and cook until fragrant, about 30 seconds. Add remaining 1 tablespoon oil and farro and cook, stirring frequently, until heated through, about 2 minutes.

3 Off heat, stir in parsley, mint, and orange juice. Season with salt and pepper to taste. Serve.

CHICKPEA SALAD WITH CARROTS, RAISINS, AND ALMONDS

SERVES 6
TOTAL TIME: 20 MINS plus 30 mins resting

A simple bean salad is even simpler when it comes from a can. Microwaving the canned chickpeas to get them hot helps them absorb any flavorings applied, and letting them sit allows that flavor to shine. Bright mix-ins make the salad a welcome side dish to liven up a number of dishes from Charred Green Beans with Coriander, Sesame, and Nigella Seeds (page 128) to a simple piece of seared fish. Shred the carrots on the large holes of a box grater or use a food processor fitted with the shredding disk.

- 2   (15-ounce) cans chickpeas, rinsed
- ¼   cup extra-virgin olive oil
- 2   tablespoons lime juice
-     Salt and pepper
-     Pinch cayenne pepper
- 3   carrots, peeled and shredded
- ½   cup golden raisins
- ¼   cup chopped fresh mint
- ¼   cup sliced almonds, toasted

Microwave chickpeas in bowl until hot, about 1 minute 30 seconds. Stir in oil, lime juice, ¾ teaspoon salt, ½ teaspoon pepper, and cayenne and let sit for 30 minutes. Add carrots, raisins, mint, and almonds and toss to combine. Season with salt and pepper to taste. Serve.

LENTIL SALAD WITH POMEGRANATES AND WALNUTS

SERVES 6   TOTAL TIME: 20 MINS

If you're used to dried lentils, we want you to get to know the canned variety, too. They're a super-fast way to a fresh side that's not the norm. This impressive salad pairs the firm-on-the-outside, creamy-on-the-inside canned legume with a tart vinaigrette, pomegranate seeds for juicy pops of sweetness, and some crunchy walnuts. Sliced radishes and liberal chopped parsley bring welcome freshness to a complexly flavored, beautifully textured, good-for-you salad that might just steal the show from main meals like Hasselback Eggplant with Muhammara (page 99) and Arrosticini (page 409).

- 3   tablespoons extra-virgin olive oil
- 1½ tablespoons lemon juice
- ¼   teaspoon table salt
- ¼   teaspoon pepper
- 2   (15-ounce) cans lentils, rinsed
- ¼   cup chopped fresh parsley
- 6   radishes, trimmed, halved, and sliced thin
- ¼   cup walnuts, toasted and chopped coarse, divided
- ½   cup pomegranate seeds, divided

Whisk oil, lemon juice, salt, and pepper together in large bowl. Add lentils, parsley, radishes, half of walnuts, and half of pomegranate seeds to dressing and toss to combine. Season with salt and pepper to taste. Transfer to serving dish and sprinkle with remaining walnuts and pomegranate seeds. Serve.

SHAKSHUKA WITH CHICKPEAS

2 tablespoons extra-virgin olive oil, plus extra for drizzling

1 onion, chopped fine

1 cup jarred roasted red peppers, rinsed, patted dry, and chopped coarse

1 teaspoon table salt

½ teaspoon pepper

1 (15-ounce) can chickpeas, rinsed

1½ teaspoons smoked paprika

1 teaspoon ground cumin

1 (28-ounce) can crushed tomatoes

8 large eggs

2 ounces goat cheese, crumbled (½ cup)

2 tablespoons chopped fresh parsley

WHY THIS RECIPE WORKS The beloved dish of eggs poached in spicy tomato sauce enjoyed throughout the Mediterranean, Middle East, and North Africa gets a filling boost with the untraditional addition of chickpeas. Incorporating canned chickpeas into the sauce maintains the ease that convenience products (canned tomatoes and jarred roasted red peppers) lend many versions of shakshuka. And in addition to substance, the chickpeas add nutty depth to the dish. Eggs poached in the tomato-chickpea sauce and a sprinkle of goat cheese on top finish the hearty dish with richness. Spooning sauce over the whites of the eggs as they cook ensures that the eggs cook evenly. We like serving this for breakfast but it's filling and robust enough to be a great eggs-for-dinner option. Serve the shakshuka with toasted bread to scoop up the sauce.

1 Heat oil in 12-inch nonstick skillet over medium-high heat until shimmering. Add onion, red peppers, salt, and pepper and cook until onion is softened, about 5 minutes. Add chickpeas, paprika, and cumin and cook until fragrant, about 1 minute. Stir in tomatoes and bring to simmer. Cover, reduce heat to medium-low, and cook until flavors meld, about 5 minutes.

2 Off heat, using back of spoon, make 8 shallow 1½-inch indentations in sauce (seven around perimeter and one in center). Crack 1 egg into each indentation. Spoon sauce over edges of egg whites so that whites are partially covered and yolks are exposed.

3 Return skillet to medium-high heat and bring to simmer. Cover, reduce heat to medium-low, and cook until egg whites are fully set, about 8 minutes, rotating skillet occasionally for even cooking. Sprinkle shakshuka evenly with goat cheese and parsley. Serve, drizzling with extra oil.

Cals 479 | Total Fat 23g | Sat Fat 6g
Chol 379mg | Sodium 1145mg
Total Carb 45g | Dietary Fiber 12g
Total Sugars 16g | Protein 27g

TABIL COUSCOUS
WITH SARDINES

SERVES
4

1 HR

3 tablespoon extra-virgin olive oil, divided, plus extra for drizzling

1½ cups couscous

2 cups frozen pearl onions, thawed

2 tablespoons Tabil (page 15)

4 garlic cloves, minced

¼ teaspoon red pepper flakes

½ preserved lemon, pulp and white pith removed, rind rinsed and minced (2 tablespoons), divided

2¼ cups chicken or vegetable broth, divided

1 tablespoon honey

5 ounces (5 cups) baby kale, chopped

½ cup chopped fresh cilantro

6 ounces canned sardines packed in oil, drained, patted dry, and flaked into 1-inch pieces

2 tablespoons capers, rinsed

Lemon wedges

WHY THIS RECIPE WORKS Couscous is airy and mild, the perfect canvas for bold flavors and ingredients that make it a centerpiece meal. Tabil, a simple and potent combination of cardamom, cumin, and caraway seeds, is a spice blend used in various applications in Tunisia. Here, it seasons our couscous. The warm blend is brightened by preserved lemon and cilantro, and pearl onions bring out its sweeter side. Frozen pearl onions are a fine choice that cuts down on prep and when browned, they add caramelized flavor to our finished dish. To add a briny component, we use capers and canned sardines, which are a pantry staple in the Mediterranean (as we hope they are in your kitchen). The little fillets boast lovely richness, are a great source of protein and healthful fats, and, of course, have a long, stable shelf life. Using skinned and boneless sardines makes flaking them over the dish for plating simple, neat—and spectacular. Be sure to pick through the sardines and discard any lingering skin and bones before flaking.

1 Heat 2 tablespoons oil in 12-inch skillet over medium-high heat until just smoking. Add couscous and cook, stirring frequently, until grains are just beginning to brown, about 5 minutes. Transfer to bowl and wipe skillet clean with paper towels.

2 Heat remaining 1 tablespoon oil in now-empty skillet over medium heat until shimmering. Add onions and cook until beginning to brown, 6 to 8 minutes. Stir in tabil, garlic, pepper flakes, and 1 tablespoon preserved lemon and cook until fragrant, about 30 seconds. Stir in ½ cup broth and honey and bring to simmer. Cover, reduce heat to medium-low, and simmer until onions are tender, 12 to 15 minutes.

3 Stir in toasted couscous, kale, and remaining 1¾ cups broth and bring to simmer. Cover, remove skillet from heat, and let sit until couscous is tender, about 7 minutes. Off heat, add cilantro and fluff couscous and cilantro together with fork to combine. Season with salt and pepper to taste. Top with sardines, capers, and remaining 1 tablespoon preserved lemon. Drizzle with extra oil and serve with lemon wedges.

Cals 510 | Total Fat 14g | Sat Fat 2.5g
Chol 55mg | Sodium 610mg
Total Carb 75g | Dietary Fiber 6g
Total Sugars 9g | Protein 21g

FARRO WITH TOFU, MUSHROOMS, AND SPINACH

SERVES
4 TO 6

1¼ HRS

¼ cup mayonnaise

3 tablespoons red miso

2 tablespoons water

1 tablespoon maple syrup

1 tablespoon plus 2 teaspoons toasted sesame oil, divided

2½ teaspoons sherry vinegar, divided

1½ teaspoons grated fresh ginger

1½ cups whole farro

⅛ teaspoon table salt, plus salt for cooking farro

14 ounces firm tofu, sliced crosswise into 8 equal slabs

⅓ cup cornstarch

¼ cup vegetable oil, divided, plus extra as needed

10 ounces cremini mushrooms, trimmed and chopped coarse

1 shallot, minced

2 tablespoons dry sherry

10 ounces (10 cups) baby spinach

2 scallions, sliced thin

WHY THIS RECIPE WORKS We love vegetable-and-grain dishes, layered in a bowl for dinner, because they give you the freedom to mix things up. This dish is a shining example. Hearty, nutty, good-for-you farro, the base, is associated with Italian flavors, but here we lean into its bold profile, topping it with crispy tofu and a sauté of mushrooms, shallot, and spinach. It's all drizzled with a potent, creamy miso-ginger sauce.

1 Whisk mayonnaise, miso, water, maple syrup, 1 tablespoon sesame oil, 1½ teaspoons vinegar, and ginger together in bowl; set miso-ginger sauce aside until ready to serve. Bring 4 quarts water to boil in large pot. Stir in farro and 1 tablespoon salt, return to boil, and cook until grains are tender with slight chew, 15 to 30 minutes. Drain farro and return to now-empty pot. Drizzle with remaining 2 teaspoons sesame oil and remaining 1 teaspoon vinegar, toss to coat, and cover to keep warm.

2 While farro cooks, spread tofu on paper towel–lined rimmed baking sheet and let drain for 20 minutes. Gently press dry with paper towels.

3 Spread cornstarch in shallow dish. Coat tofu thoroughly in cornstarch, pressing gently to adhere; transfer to plate. Heat 1 tablespoon vegetable oil in 12-inch nonstick skillet over medium-high heat until just smoking. Add tofu and cook until both sides are crisp and browned, about 4 minutes per side, adding more oil and adjusting heat as needed to prevent charring. Transfer to paper towel–lined plate to drain and tent with aluminum foil.

4 In now-empty skillet, heat 2 tablespoons vegetable oil over medium-high heat until shimmering. Stir in mushrooms, shallot, and salt and cook until vegetables begin to brown, 5 to 8 minutes. Stir in sherry and cook, scraping up any browned bits, until skillet is nearly dry, about 1 minute; transfer to bowl. Heat remaining 1 tablespoon vegetable oil over medium-high heat in now-empty skillet until shimmering. Add spinach, 1 handful at a time, and cook until just wilted, about 1 minute. Divide farro among individual bowls, then top with tofu, mushrooms, and spinach. Drizzle with miso-ginger sauce, sprinkle with scallions, and serve.

*Cals 480 | Total Fat 25g | Sat Fat 2g
Chol 0mg | Sodium 540mg
Total Carb 52g | Dietary Fiber 5g
Total Sugars 7g | Protein 15g*

SAFFRON BULGUR WITH FENNEL AND SAUSAGE

SERVES
4

50 MINS

1½ cups medium-grind bulgur

¼ teaspoon table salt, divided, plus salt for cooking bulgur

3 tablespoons extra-virgin olive oil, divided

1 pound Italian turkey sausage

2 fennel bulbs, ¼ cup fronds minced, stalks discarded, bulbs halved, cored, and sliced ¼ inch thick

½ cup dried apricots, chopped

½ teaspoon pepper, divided

¼ teaspoon saffron threads, crumbled

2 tablespoons pomegranate molasses

1 teaspoon grated lemon zest

2 ounces Manchego cheese, shaved

WHY THIS RECIPE WORKS Golden saffron is the flavor—and color palette—for this bright, bold, hearty bulgur dish. Turkey sausage adds deep savor and dinnertime heft to the floral bulgur, given the gold treatment with a saffron-infused pomegranate vinaigrette. Also-floral caramelized fennel deepens the savory notes so we don't need to use too much sausage for flavoring. We cook dried apricots, for contrasting texture and pleasant sweetness, with the fennel and add a little water to plump the apricots. Shaved Manchego on top provides contrasting sharpness and saltiness. When shopping, don't confuse bulgur with cracked wheat, which has a much longer cooking time and will not work in this recipe.

1 Bring 4 quarts water to boil in large pot. Stir in bulgur and 1 teaspoon salt and cook until tender, about 5 minutes. Drain well and set aside.

2 Heat 1 tablespoon oil in 12-inch nonstick skillet over medium heat until shimmering. Add sausage and cook until browned on all sides and registers 160 degrees, 6 to 8 minutes. Transfer to cutting board, cover with aluminum foil, and let rest. Slice sausage ½ inch thick on bias just before serving.

3 Pour off all but 2 teaspoons fat from skillet (or add oil to equal 2 teaspoons). Add sliced fennel, apricots, ½ cup water, ⅛ teaspoon salt, and ¼ teaspoon pepper, cover, and cook over medium heat for 1 minute. Uncover and continue to cook, stirring occasionally, until fennel is spotty brown, 2 to 4 minutes; set aside until ready to serve.

4 Combine saffron with 2 teaspoons water in large bowl and let sit for 5 minutes. Whisk in remaining 2 tablespoons oil, remaining ⅛ teaspoon salt, remaining ¼ teaspoon pepper, pomegranate molasses, and lemon zest, then stir in bulgur to coat. Season with salt and pepper to taste. Divide among individual bowls, then top with fennel mixture and sausage. Sprinkle with fennel fronds and Manchego. Serve.

Cals 610 | Total Fat 26g | Sat Fat 8g
Chol 95mg | Sodium 1050mg
Total Carb 64g | Dietary Fiber 12g
Total Sugars 17g | Protein 33g

BAKED SHRIMP AND ORZO WITH FETA AND TOMATOES

1 tablespoon extra-virgin olive oil

1 red onion, chopped fine

1 red bell pepper, stemmed, seeded, and cut into ½-inch pieces

4 garlic cloves, minced

2 teaspoons minced fresh oregano or ½ teaspoon dried

2 cups orzo

Pinch saffron threads, crumbled

3 cups chicken or vegetable broth

1 (14.5-ounce) can diced tomatoes, drained with juice reserved

1 pound extra-large shrimp (21 to 25 per pound), peeled, deveined, and tails removed

½ teaspoon table salt

¼ teaspoon pepper

½ cup frozen peas

3 ounces feta cheese, crumbled (¾ cup)

2 scallions, sliced thin

Lemon wedges

WHY THIS RECIPE WORKS This dish has a lot going for it, and the sum is an amazing composition of its harmonious parts: creamy pasta, juicy shrimp, fresh-tasting peas, briny feta cheese. Power ingredients like pleasantly assertive oregano, floral saffron, canned tomatoes, and the aforementioned cheese bring plenty of Mediterranean flavor to the dish. To guarantee perfectly cooked shrimp and pasta, we combine stovetop and oven cooking. Sautéing the orzo in the aromatics unlocks its toasty notes; we then stir in chicken broth and the drained juice from a can of diced tomatoes. As the orzo cooks to al dente, its released starch (similar to a risotto) creates a sauce with a subtly creamy texture. To prevent the shrimp from overcooking, we stir them right into the orzo, along with the reserved tomatoes and frozen peas, and transfer the skillet to the oven to cook through gently. Sprinkling on the feta at this point delivers an appealing browned, cheesy crust. Make sure that the orzo is al dente, or slightly firm to the bite; otherwise, it may overcook in the oven. You will need a 12-inch ovensafe nonstick skillet for this recipe.

1 Adjust oven rack to middle position and heat oven to 375 degrees. Heat oil in 12-inch ovensafe nonstick skillet over medium heat until shimmering. Add onion and bell pepper and cook until vegetables are softened, 5 to 7 minutes. Stir in garlic and oregano and cook until fragrant, about 30 seconds. Stir in orzo and saffron and cook, stirring often, until orzo is lightly browned, about 4 minutes.

2 Stir in broth and reserved tomato juice, bring to simmer, and cook, stirring occasionally, until orzo is al dente, 10 to 12 minutes.

3 Pat shrimp dry with paper towels and sprinkle with salt and pepper. Stir shrimp, peas, and tomatoes into orzo mixture in skillet, then sprinkle feta evenly over top. Transfer skillet to oven and bake until shrimp are opaque throughout and feta is lightly browned, about 20 minutes.

4 Carefully remove skillet from oven and sprinkle scallions over top. Serve with lemon wedges.

Cals 560 | Total Fat 11g | Sat Fat 4.5g
Chol 160mg | Sodium 1140mg
Total Carb 79g | Dietary Fiber 4g
Total Sugars 11g | Protein 36g

ESPINACAS CON GARBANZOS

SERVES
4

50 MINS

1   loaf crusty bread, divided

2   (15-ounce) cans chickpeas
    (1 can drained and rinsed,
    1 can undrained)

1½ cups chicken or vegetable
    broth

6   tablespoons extra-virgin
    olive oil, divided

6   garlic cloves, minced

1   tablespoon smoked paprika

1   teaspoon ground cumin

¼   teaspoon table salt

⅛   teaspoon ground cinnamon

⅛   teaspoon cayenne pepper

1   small pinch saffron

2   small plum tomatoes, halved
    lengthwise, flesh shredded
    on large holes of box grater
    and skins discarded

4   teaspoons sherry vinegar,
    plus extra for seasoning

10 ounces frozen chopped
    spinach, thawed and
    squeezed dry

WHY THIS RECIPE WORKS Espinacas con garbanzos is a hyper-regional spinach and chickpea dish native to Seville with strong Arab influence—it's substantive and full of flavor. Briefly simmering canned chickpeas (uniformly tender, well seasoned, and convenient) in a combination of chicken broth and chickpea canning liquid tenderizes them and ensures that the flavor of this main ingredient is extra savory. A picada (a paste of garlic and bread cooked in plenty of olive oil) thickens and seasons the sauce like magic. Smoked paprika and spices such as cumin, cinnamon, and saffron imbue this extra-special picada with heady aromas, and tomatoes and vinegar boost its tang. In Spain, spinach loves chickpeas. Thawed frozen chopped spinach is perfect here; already fine and tender, it disperses beautifully throughout the dish and provides plenty of surface area to hold the flavorful juices in place so the dish isn't soupy. You can top the dish with a fried egg for a heartier meal. Red wine vinegar can be substituted for the sherry vinegar.

1 Cut 1½-ounce piece from loaf of bread (thickness will vary depending on size of loaf) and tear into 1-inch pieces. Process in food processor until finely ground (you should have ¾ cup crumbs). Combine chickpeas and broth in large saucepan and bring to boil over high heat. Adjust heat to maintain simmer and cook until level of liquid is just below top layer of chickpeas, about 10 minutes.

2 While chickpeas cook, heat ¼ cup oil in 10-inch nonstick skillet over medium heat until just shimmering. Add bread crumbs and cook, stirring frequently, until deep golden brown, 3 to 4 minutes. Add garlic, paprika, cumin, salt, cinnamon, cayenne, and saffron and cook until fragrant, 30 seconds. Stir in tomatoes and vinegar and remove from heat.

3 Stir bread mixture and spinach into chickpeas in saucepan. Continue to simmer, stirring occasionally, until mixture is thick and stew-like, 5 to 10 minutes longer. Off heat, stir in remaining 2 tablespoons oil. Cover and let sit for 5 minutes. Season with salt and extra vinegar to taste. Serve with remaining bread.

Cals 430 | Total Fat 25g | Sat Fat 3.5g
Chol 0mg | Sodium 1010mg
Total Carb 36g | Dietary Fiber 11g
Total Sugars 2g | Protein 15g

BULGUR WITH VEGETABLES AND MARINATED TOFU

SERVES 4

1¼ HRS

- 5 tablespoons extra-virgin olive oil, divided
- 3 shallots, sliced into thin rounds
- 1¾ teaspoons plus pinch table salt, divided, plus salt for cooking bulgur
- 3 tablespoons sriracha, divided
- 2 tablespoons honey, divided
- 14 ounces firm tofu, cut into ¾-inch pieces
- ½ cup rice vinegar
- 1½ cups thinly sliced red cabbage
- 1 pound carrots, peeled and sliced on bias ½ inch thick
- 1 pound broccolini, trimmed and cut into 1-inch pieces
- 1¼ cups medium-grind bulgur
- 2 tablespoons mayonnaise

WHY THIS RECIPE WORKS For multidimensional grain dishes, sometimes it's smart to start with the garnish. In this bulgur dish, we like garnishes aplenty: crispy fried shallots, sweet-and-spicy marinated tofu, pickled red cabbage, and roasted broccolini and carrots. We combine a portion of the cabbage pickling liquid with the shallot-infused oil and sriracha to make a zippy dressing for this warm dinner or packed lunch. Stop cooking the shallots once they turn light golden brown; they will continue to darken and crisp as they cool. Placing the broccolini in a pile on the baking sheet creates textural contrast and prevents the broccolini from drying out.

1 Adjust oven rack to middle position and heat oven to 425 degrees. Heat ¼ cup oil and shallots in large saucepan over medium heat, stirring constantly once shallots start to sizzle. Cook until shallots are deep golden, 6 to 10 minutes. Drain shallots in fine-mesh strainer set over bowl; reserve oil. Transfer shallots to paper towel–lined plate and sprinkle with pinch salt; set aside until ready to serve. (Do not wash saucepan or strainer.)

2 Whisk 2 tablespoons sriracha, 1 tablespoon honey, and ½ teaspoon salt together in second bowl. Add tofu and gently toss to coat. Cover and refrigerate until ready to serve. Combine vinegar, ½ teaspoon salt, and remaining 1 tablespoon honey in third bowl. Microwave until simmering, 1 to 2 minutes. Stir in cabbage; set aside until ready to serve, stirring occasionally.

3 Toss carrots with 1½ teaspoons oil and ¼ teaspoon salt and spread on half of rimmed baking sheet. Toss broccolini with remaining 1½ teaspoons oil and remaining ½ teaspoon salt and pile on other half of sheet. Roast until carrots are tender and broccolini is crisp in spots, 15 to 20 minutes, stirring vegetables halfway through roasting.

4 While vegetables roast, add 6 cups water to now-empty saucepan and bring to boil over high heat. Add bulgur and 1 teaspoon salt and return to simmer. Reduce heat to maintain gentle simmer and cook until tender, about 5 minutes. Drain bulgur, then return to saucepan; cover and set aside.

5 Measure out 2 tablespoons cabbage liquid and add to reserved shallot oil. Whisk in mayonnaise and remaining 1 tablespoon sriracha. Mix 3 tablespoons dressing into bulgur. Divide bulgur among individual bowls. Top with tofu, carrots, broccolini, and cabbage (leaving behind pickling liquid), then drizzle with remaining dressing. Sprinkle with shallots and serve.

Cals 664 | Total Fat 33g | Sat Fat 3g Chol 3mg | Sodium 1216mg Total Carb 75g | Dietary Fiber 16g Total Sugars 21g | Protein 27g

PLANT-BASED ALBÓNDIGAS

SERVES 6 TO 8

2½ HRS

Albóndigas

- 2 tablespoons extra-virgin olive oil, divided
- 1 onion, chopped fine
- 4 garlic cloves, minced
- ½ teaspoon paprika
- 1¾ cups water
- 1 cup prewashed white quinoa
- 1 teaspoon table salt
- 2 ounces Monterey Jack cheese, shredded (½ cup)
- 1 ounce Manchego cheese, grated (½ cup)
- 1 large egg plus 1 large yolk, lightly beaten
- 3 tablespoons minced fresh parsley
- 1 teaspoon grated lemon zest

Sauce

- 2 tablespoons extra-virgin olive oil
- 1 onion, chopped fine
- 1 tablespoon tomato paste
- 2 tomatoes, cored, seeded, and chopped
- 1 cup chicken or vegetable broth
- ½ cup dry white wine
- 2 tablespoons minced fresh parsley
- 2 tablespoons finely chopped almonds
- 2 garlic cloves, minced
- ¼ teaspoon saffron threads, crumbled
- ¼ teaspoon paprika
- ¼ teaspoon table salt
- ⅛ teaspoon pepper

WHY THIS RECIPE WORKS In Spain, albóndigas are a quintessential tapas offering, but they can also be served as a main course with a vegetable and potatoes or rice. These vegetarian balls lose the meat and call for quinoa. We cook the quinoa until it's slightly blown out so that the grains are sticky and cohesive. Bready binders are unnecessary; only some cheese and egg are needed for glue. Our delicate quinoa albóndigas are better baked than fried in a pan. We pair them with a saffron-and-paprika-infused wine sauce that is flavored and thickened with one of the most important elements of Catalan cuisine—picada, a lively mixture of fried ground nuts and bread, raw garlic, and parsley.

1 For the albóndigas Heat 1 tablespoon oil in large saucepan over medium heat until shimmering. Add onion and cook until softened, about 5 minutes. Stir in garlic and paprika and cook until fragrant, about 30 seconds. Stir in water, quinoa, and salt and bring to simmer. Cover, reduce heat to low, and simmer gently until quinoa is tender, 16 to 18 minutes. Remove saucepan from heat. Let quinoa sit, covered, until liquid is fully absorbed, about 10 minutes. Spread quinoa onto rimmed baking sheet and let cool for 15 minutes.

2 Line separate rimmed baking sheet with parchment paper and spray with vegetable oil spray. Mix cooled quinoa, Monterey Jack, Manchego, egg and yolk, parsley, and lemon zest in large bowl until thoroughly combined. Portion and shape mixture into twenty-four ¾-inch balls and place on prepared baking sheet. Refrigerate balls, uncovered, until chilled and firm, about 30 minutes.

3 Adjust oven rack to middle position and heat oven to 400 degrees. Gently brush balls with remaining 1 tablespoon oil and bake until browned and slightly crisp, about 20 minutes.

4 For the sauce Meanwhile, heat oil in 12-inch nonstick skillet over medium heat until shimmering. Add onion and tomato paste and cook until onion is softened and lightly browned, 5 to 7 minutes. Stir in tomatoes and cook for 1 minute. Stir in broth and wine, cover, and cook until flavors meld, 8 to 10 minutes.

5 Combine parsley, almonds, garlic, saffron, paprika, salt, and pepper in bowl, then stir into sauce. Continue to simmer sauce until slightly thickened, about 2 minutes. Season with salt and pepper to taste. Transfer quinoa balls to platter, pour sauce over top, and serve.

Cals 250 | Total Fat 15g | Sat Fat 4g | Chol 55mg | Sodium 550mg Total Carb 20g | Dietary Fiber 3g | Total Sugars 3g | Protein 8g

LENTILS WITH ROASTED BROCCOLI AND LEMONY BREAD CRUMBS

SERVES 4 TO 6

1½ HRS

6 tablespoons extra-virgin olive oil, divided, plus extra for drizzling

1 onion, chopped fine

¾ teaspoon table salt, divided

2 garlic cloves, minced

1 teaspoon minced fresh thyme or ½ teaspoon dried

12 ounces (1¾ cups) dried lentilles du Puy (French green lentils), picked over and rinsed

3¾ cups water

½ cup panko bread crumbs

2 teaspoons grated lemon zest

½ cup balsamic vinegar

2 pounds broccoli, florets cut into 1-inch pieces, stalks peeled and sliced lengthwise into ½-inch thick planks

WHY THIS RECIPE WORKS This supersavory dish elevates earthy French green lentils and humble broccoli to a whole new level—an abundant dish that's a company-worthy main. By preheating the sheet pan in a 500-degree oven and laying the broccoli on it in a single layer, we impart deep, flavorful browning to the stalks and florets in a short amount of time so you'll jump to eat your broccoli. While the lentils cook, we quickly make a bright, crispy, lemony bread-crumb topping in a skillet, and we reduce some balsamic vinegar in the same skillet to transform its flavor from sharp and assertive to luxurious, sweet, and drizzleable, a stunning, shining finishing touch. Lentilles du Puy (or French green lentils) hold their shape quite well during cooking; we do not recommend substituting other types of lentils in this dish.

1 Adjust oven rack to lowest position, place aluminum foil–lined rimmed baking sheet on rack, and heat oven to 500 degrees. Heat 1 tablespoon oil in large saucepan over medium heat until shimmering. Add onion and ¼ teaspoon salt and cook until softened, about 5 minutes. Stir in garlic and thyme and cook until fragrant, about 30 seconds.

2 Stir in lentils and water and bring to simmer over high heat. Reduce heat to low, cover, and simmer, stirring occasionally, until lentils are just tender, about 25 minutes. Uncover, increase heat to medium and continue to cook until lentils are completely tender and most of liquid has evaporated, 10 to 15 minutes. Season with salt and pepper to taste, cover to keep warm, and set aside.

3 While lentils cook, combine panko and 2 tablespoons oil in 8-inch skillet, stirring to coat. Cook over medium-low heat, stirring frequently, until light golden brown, 5 to 7 minutes; transfer to bowl and stir in lemon zest. Wipe skillet clean with paper towels. Cook vinegar in now-empty skillet, scraping bottom of skillet with rubber spatula, until thickened and reduced to 2 tablespoons, about 5 minutes.

4 Toss broccoli with remaining 3 tablespoons oil and remaining ½ teaspoon salt in bowl. Working quickly, lay broccoli in single layer, flat sides down, on preheated sheet. Roast until florets are browned, 9 to 11 minutes. Divide lentils among individual bowls and top with broccoli mixture. Sprinkle with panko mixture, drizzle with balsamic reduction, and serve, drizzling with extra oil.

Cals 420 | Total Fat 16g | Sat Fat 2g
Chol 0mg | Sodium 340mg
Total Carb 55g | Dietary Fiber 12g
Total Sugars 11g | Protein 16g

BAKED PUMPKIN KIBBEH WITH FETA

SERVES
4

1¾ HRS

- 3 tablespoons extra-virgin olive oil, divided
- 1 onion, chopped fine
- 2 garlic cloves, minced
- 1 teaspoon ground coriander
- ¼ teaspoon five-spice powder
- 1 (15-ounce) can unsweetened pumpkin puree
- 1½ cups fine-grind bulgur, rinsed
- ½ cup all-purpose flour
- ¼ cup minced fresh cilantro
- 2 tablespoons minced fresh mint
- 1 teaspoon table salt
- ½ teaspoon pepper
- 4 ounces feta cheese, crumbled (1 cup)
- 2 tablespoons pine nuts, toasted and chopped

WHY THIS RECIPE WORKS Middle Eastern kibbeh is a finely ground combination of beef or lamb, bulgur, and onions that can be formed into balls and deep-fried, pressed into a pan and baked, grilled, or served raw. This vegetarian version of the baked variety matches pumpkin with the hearty bulgur and warm spices. We use a 9-inch springform pan, which makes slicing and serving easier—plus the thick slices created by this pan bake up extra moist and tender. Because bulgur soaks up liquid as it cooks, when we stirred raw bulgur into the squash, the kibbeh turned out dry and crumbly. Soaking the bulgur for 10 minutes solves this problem. A garnish of feta and toasted pine nuts adds some creaminess, tang against the squash, and crunch. Serve this hearty meal with a simple salad. You can use medium-grind bulgur here, but the texture of the kibbeh will be more coarse and moist. When shopping, don't confuse bulgur with cracked wheat, which has a much longer cooking time and will not work in this recipe.

1 Adjust oven rack to middle position and heat oven to 400 degrees. Spray 9-inch springform pan with vegetable oil spray. Heat 1 tablespoon oil in 12-inch nonstick skillet over medium heat until shimmering. Add onion and cook until softened, about 5 minutes. Stir in garlic, coriander, and five spice and cook until fragrant, about 30 seconds. Stir in pumpkin puree and cook until slightly thickened, 2 to 4 minutes. Transfer squash mixture to large bowl and let cool.

2 Meanwhile, place bulgur in second bowl and add water to cover by 1 inch. Let sit until tender, about 10 minutes. Drain bulgur through fine-mesh strainer, then wrap in clean dish towel and wring tightly to squeeze out as much liquid as possible.

3 Stir bulgur, flour, cilantro, mint, salt, and pepper into squash mixture until well combined. Transfer to prepared pan and press into even layer with wet hands. Using paring knife, score surface into 8 even wedges, cutting halfway down through mixture. Brush top with remaining 2 tablespoons oil and bake until golden brown and set, about 45 minutes.

4 Sprinkle with feta and pine nuts and continue to bake until cheese is softened and warmed through, about 10 minutes. Let kibbeh cool in pan for 10 minutes. Run thin knife around inside of springform pan ring to loosen, then remove ring. Slice kibbeh into wedges along scored lines and serve.

*Cals 480 | Total Fat 20g | Sat Fat 6g
Chol 25mg | Sodium 860mg
Total Carb 64g | Dietary Fiber 11g
Total Sugars 6g | Protein 14g*

Baked, Broiled, or Fried

Kibbeh is a staple dish of much of the Middle East, and it takes on a great number of unique forms. Kibbeh's bulk ingredients vary from region to region, usually formed with a grain (mostly bulgur) combined with minced meat and onions. A single region could have styles of kibbeh named for different flavorings (Aleppo, Syria, alone is home to upwards of 15). They can look like disks or torpedoes or cakes. And they can be made with almost any cooking technique, fried until crispy, grilled, baked until tender, served raw, much like steak tartare, or even cooked in a soup.

MEATLESS "MEAT" SAUCE WITH CHICKPEAS AND MUSHROOMS

MAKES
6 CUPS
enough for
2 pounds
pasta

1 HR

10 ounces cremini mushrooms, trimmed

6 tablespoons extra-virgin olive oil, divided

1 teaspoon table salt

1 onion, chopped

5 garlic cloves, minced

1¼ teaspoons dried oregano

¼ teaspoon red pepper flakes

¼ cup tomato paste

1 (28-ounce) can crushed tomatoes

2 cups chicken or vegetable broth

1 (15-ounce) can chickpeas, rinsed

2 tablespoons chopped fresh basil

WHY THIS RECIPE WORKS This vegetarian sauce is just as savory and lush as one made with meat. Starting with cremini mushrooms and tomato paste is a big factor—both are rich sources of savory flavor. A generous amount of our favorite ingredient, extra-virgin olive oil, does double duty, enriching the sauce and helping toast the classic aromatics that we still incorporate here: garlic, dried oregano, and red pepper flakes. We bulk up the sauce with chopped chickpeas that are rinsed of their excess starch to maintain their shape and meatiness when mixed in. To thin the sauce without watering down its flavor, we add vegetable broth. Make sure to rinse the chickpeas after pulsing them in the food processor or the sauce will be too thick. You can serve the sauce over pasta or polenta.

1 Pulse mushrooms in 2 batches in food processor until chopped into ⅛- to ¼-inch pieces, 7 to 10 pulses, scraping down sides of bowl as needed. (Do not clean workbowl.) Heat 5 tablespoons oil in Dutch oven over medium-high heat until shimmering. Add mushrooms and salt and cook, stirring occasionally, until mushrooms are browned and fond has formed on bottom of pot, about 8 minutes.

2 While mushrooms cook, pulse onion in food processor until finely chopped, 7 to 10 pulses, scraping down sides of bowl as needed. (Do not clean workbowl.) Transfer onion to pot with mushrooms and cook, stirring occasionally, until onion is softened, about 5 minutes. Combine garlic, oregano, pepper flakes, and remaining 1 tablespoon oil in bowl.

3 Add tomato paste to pot and cook, stirring constantly, until mixture is rust-colored, 1 to 2 minutes. Reduce heat to medium and push vegetables to sides of pot. Add garlic mixture to center and cook, stirring constantly, until fragrant, about 30 seconds. Stir in tomatoes and broth and bring to simmer over high heat. Reduce heat to low and simmer sauce for 5 minutes, stirring occasionally.

4 While sauce simmers, pulse chickpeas in food processor until chopped into ¼-inch pieces, 7 to 10 pulses. Transfer chickpeas to fine-mesh strainer and rinse under cold running water until water runs clear; drain well. Add chickpeas to pot and simmer until sauce is slightly thickened, about 15 minutes. Stir in basil and season with salt and pepper to taste. (Sauce can be refrigerated for up to 2 days or frozen for up to 1 month.)

Cals 180 | Total Fat 11g | Sat Fat 1.5g
Chol 0mg | Sodium 690mg
Total Carb 16g | Dietary Fiber 2g
Total Sugars 6g | Protein 4g

GIGANTES PLAKI

**SERVES
4 TO 6**

2½ HRS
*plus 8¼ hrs
soaking and
cooling*

3 tablespoons table salt
for brining

1 pound (2½ cups) dried
gigante beans, picked over
and rinsed

¼ cup extra-virgin olive oil,
plus extra for drizzling

1 onion, chopped

2 carrots, peeled and chopped

2 celery ribs, chopped

1 teaspoon table salt

2 tablespoons tomato paste

4 garlic cloves, minced

1 tablespoon chopped fresh
oregano or 1 teaspoon dried

¼ teaspoon ground cinnamon

1 (14.5-ounce) can whole peeled
tomatoes, drained with juice
reserved, chopped

1 tablespoon honey

2 bay leaves

2 tablespoons chopped
fresh dill

WHY THIS RECIPE WORKS Gigantes plaki is a popular dish often found both as meze at tavernas throughout Greece and on family dining tables, most often during Lent. The name simply refers to the type of bean (gigantes) and the style of cooking it in a baking dish in the oven (plaki). The beans absorb the juices and flavors of generous amounts of olive oil, tomatoes, and aromatics, becoming creamy, luxurious, and meaty-textured within a scrumptious casserole with caramelized edges and an intoxicating aroma. Onion, celery, carrots, and garlic form the base of the aromatics along with beloved Greek oregano; hints of warmth from cinnamon and sweetness from a touch of honey balance the acidity of the tomato-heavy sauce. Gigantes plaki can be eaten warm or at room temperature, as a hearty side dish or a delicious meal, with a hunk of bread to sop up all of the sauce. If you can't find gigante beans, you can substitute dried large lima beans.

1 Dissolve salt in 4 quarts cold water in large container. Add beans and soak at room temperature for at least 8 hours or up to 24 hours. Drain and rinse well.

2 Bring beans and 3 quarts water to boil in Dutch oven. Reduce heat and simmer, stirring occasionally, until beans are tender, 1 to 1½ hours. (Skim any loose bean skins or foam from surface of liquid as beans cook.) Drain beans and set aside. Wipe out pot with paper towels.

3 Adjust oven rack to middle position and heat oven to 400 degrees. Heat oil in now-empty pot over medium heat until shimmering. Add onion, carrots, celery, and salt and cook until softened and beginning to brown, 7 to 10 minutes. Stir in tomato paste, garlic, oregano, and cinnamon and cook until fragrant, about 30 seconds. Add tomatoes and their juices and 1¼ cups water, scraping up any browned bits. Stir in beans, honey, and bay leaves, and bring to simmer. Season with salt and pepper to taste.

4 Transfer bean mixture to 13 by 9-inch baking dish, smoothing top with rubber spatula. Transfer dish to oven and bake until beans are cooked through and edges are golden brown and bubbling, 30 to 45 minutes. Let cool for 15 minutes, then sprinkle with dill and drizzle with extra oil. Serve.

*Cals 390 | Total Fat 10g | Sat Fat 1.5g
Chol 0mg | Sodium 620mg
Total Carb 60g | Dietary Fiber 16g
Total Sugars 14g | Protein 18g*

GIGANTES PLAKI

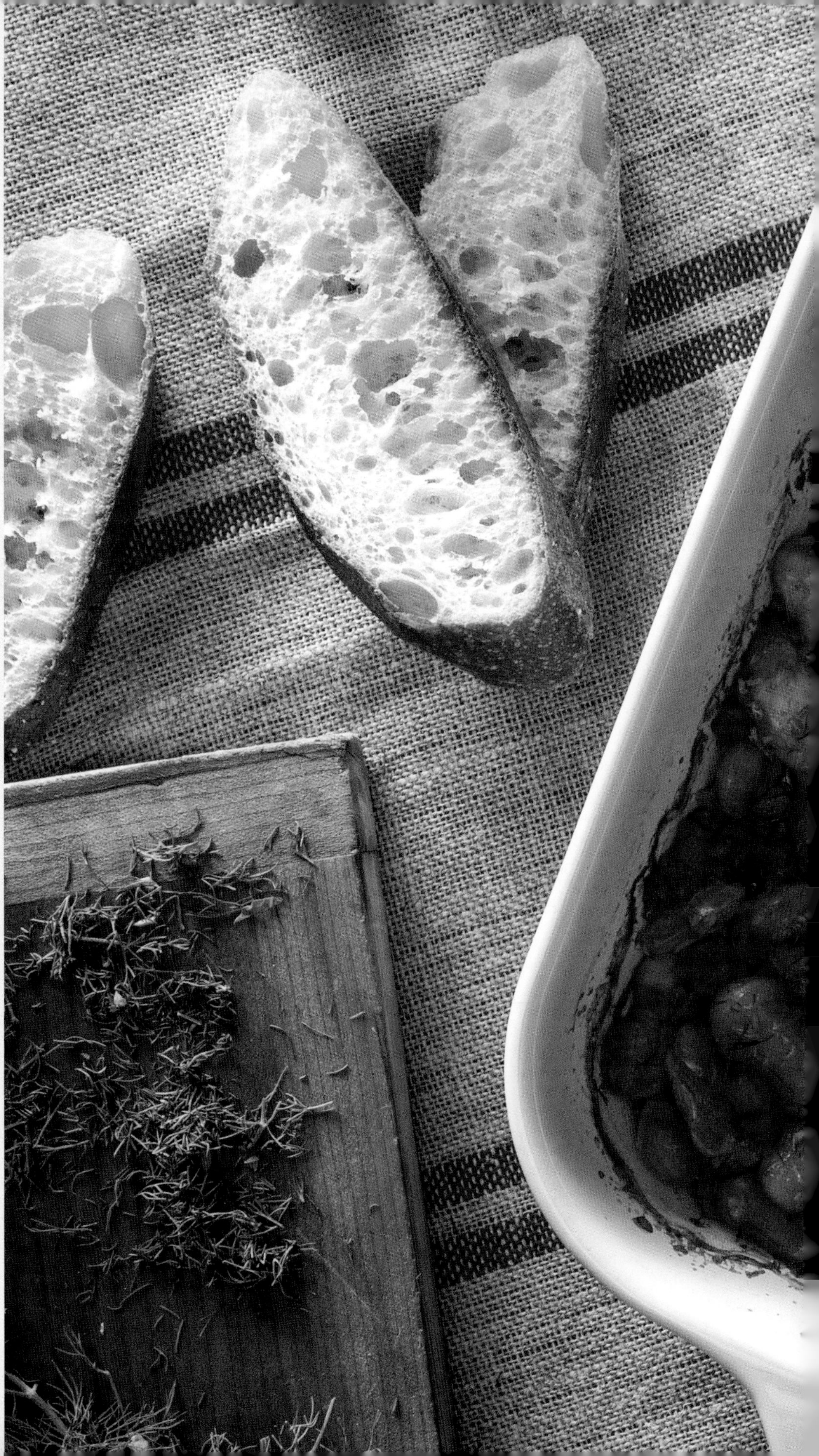

FARRO AND BROCCOLI RABE GRATIN

SERVES
4 TO 6

1¼ HRS

- 3 tablespoons extra-virgin olive oil, divided
- 1 onion, chopped fine
- ¼ teaspoon table salt, plus salt for cooking broccoli rabe
- 1½ cups whole farro
- 2 cups chicken or vegetable broth
- 2 tablespoons white miso
- ½ cup panko bread crumbs
- ¼ cup grated Parmesan cheese
- 1 pound broccoli rabe, trimmed and cut into 2-inch pieces
- 6 garlic cloves, minced
- ⅛ teaspoon red pepper flakes
- 1 (15-ounce) can small white beans or navy beans, rinsed
- ¾ cup oil-packed sun-dried tomatoes, chopped

Cals 410 | Total Fat 13g | Sat Fat 2g
Chol 5mg | Sodium 760mg
Total Carb 61g | Dietary Fiber 9g
Total Sugars 5g | Protein 17g

WHY THIS RECIPE WORKS If you think casseroles are stodgy, or an overly rich side dish, this will feel like a whole new kind of casserole—it's vibrant, fresh, and a perfectly plant-based dinner all on its own. It features creamy white beans, robust broccoli rabe, and farro (the first two a nod to Tuscan greens and beans and the latter a fitting choice to round out the meal). Toasting the farro in the aromatics and oil heighten its very special nuttiness so it shines through the casserole. In addition to adding protein to the dish, the white beans provide creaminess—no milk or cream needed. Sun-dried tomatoes punctuate the casserole with welcome acidity. But the most surprising ingredient is certainly miso; this everyday Japanese ingredient gives the meatless main dish a savory backbone. Combined in a baking dish, the ingredients work well together but still remain distinct beneath a broiled, browned, crunchy Parmesan topping. Do not substitute pearl, quick-cooking, or presteamed farro for the whole farro in this recipe.

1 Heat 1 tablespoon oil in large saucepan over medium heat until shimmering. Add onion and salt and cook until softened and lightly browned, 5 to 7 minutes. Stir in farro and cook, stirring occasionally, until lightly toasted, about 2 minutes. Stir in 2½ cups water, broth, and miso. Bring to simmer and cook, stirring often, until farro is just tender and remaining liquid has thickened into creamy sauce, 25 to 35 minutes.

2 Meanwhile, toss panko with 1 tablespoon oil in bowl and microwave, stirring occasionally, until golden brown, 1 to 2 minutes. Stir in Parmesan and set aside.

3 Bring 4 quarts water to boil in Dutch oven. Add broccoli rabe and 1 tablespoon salt and cook until just tender, about 2 minutes. Drain broccoli rabe and set aside. Combine remaining 1 tablespoon oil, garlic, and pepper flakes in now-empty pot and cook over medium heat until fragrant and sizzling, 1 to 2 minutes. Stir in reserved broccoli rabe and cook until hot and well coated, about 2 minutes. Off heat, stir in beans, tomatoes, and farro mixture. Season with salt and pepper to taste.

4 Adjust oven rack 10 inches from broiler element and heat broiler. Transfer bean-farro mixture to broiler-safe 3-quart gratin dish (or broiler-safe 13 by 9-inch baking dish) and sprinkle with reserved panko mixture. Broil until lightly browned and hot, 1 to 2 minutes. Serve.

WHITE BEAN AND MUSHROOM GRATIN

SERVES 4 TO 6

1½ HRS
plus 20 mins cooling

½ cup extra-virgin olive oil, divided

10 ounces cremini mushrooms, trimmed and sliced ½ inch thick

¾ teaspoon table salt

½ teaspoon pepper, divided

4–5 slices country-style bread, cut into ½-inch pieces (5 cups)

¼ cup minced fresh parsley, divided

1 cup water

1 tablespoon all-purpose flour

1 small onion, chopped fine

5 garlic cloves, minced

1 tablespoon tomato paste

1½ teaspoons minced fresh thyme or ½ teaspoon dried

⅓ cup dry sherry

2 (15-ounce) cans great Northern beans, undrained

3 carrots, peeled, halved lengthwise, and cut into ¾-inch pieces

Cals 427 | Total Fat 19g | Sat Fat 3g
Chol 0mg | Sodium 757mg
Total Carb 50g | Dietary Fiber 10g
Total Sugars 6g | Protein 15g

WHY THIS RECIPE WORKS This cheese-less and dairy-less but still-so-comforting gratin is, unlike many, texturally thrilling, featuring creamy white beans; meaty cremini mushrooms; tender carrots; and a crisp, toasty cubed bread layer. We achieve great flavor from the fond we develop by sautéing mushrooms and aromatics and deglazing the skillet with dry sherry. A combination of flour and starchy bean liquid thickens the sauce. As the gratin bakes, the lower portion of the bread topping merges with the beans, creating a lovely texture, while the upper portion dries. Then a few minutes of broiling browns and crisps the top. We prefer a round rustic loaf (also known as a boule) with a chewy, open crumb and a sturdy crust for this recipe. Cannellini or navy beans can be used in place of great Northern beans, if desired.

1 Adjust oven rack to middle position and heat oven to 300 degrees. Heat ¼ cup oil in 12-inch ovensafe skillet over medium-high heat until shimmering. Add mushrooms, salt, and ¼ teaspoon pepper and cook, stirring occasionally, until mushrooms are well browned, 8 to 12 minutes.

2 While mushrooms cook, toss bread, 3 tablespoons parsley, remaining ¼ cup oil, and remaining ¼ teaspoon pepper together in bowl. Set aside. Whisk water and flour together in second bowl until no lumps of flour remain. Set aside.

3 Reduce heat to medium, add onion to skillet, and continue to cook, stirring frequently, until onion is translucent, 4 to 6 minutes. Reduce heat to medium-low; add garlic, tomato paste, and thyme; and cook, stirring constantly, until bottom of skillet is dark brown, 2 to 3 minutes. Add sherry and cook, scraping up any browned bits.

4 Add beans and their liquid, carrots, and flour mixture. Bring to boil over high heat. Off heat, arrange bread mixture over surface in even layer. Transfer skillet to oven and bake for 40 minutes. (Liquid should have consistency of thin gravy.)

5 Leave skillet in oven and turn on broiler. Broil until crumbs are golden brown, 4 to 7 minutes. Remove gratin from oven and let sit for 20 minutes. Sprinkle with remaining 1 tablespoon parsley and serve.

BAKED ZITI WITH CREAMY LEEKS, KALE, AND SUN-DRIED TOMATOES

SERVES 4 TO 6

1¼ HRS

- ½ cup panko bread crumbs
- ¼ cup grated Parmesan cheese
- ¼ cup extra-virgin olive oil, divided
- ½ teaspoon grated lemon zest, plus lemon wedges for serving
- 2 pounds leeks, white and light green parts only, halved lengthwise, sliced thin, and washed thoroughly
- ¾ teaspoon table salt, divided, plus salt for cooking pasta
- ⅛ teaspoon pepper
- 2 teaspoons minced fresh thyme or ¾ teaspoon dried
- ½ cup dry white wine
- 2 cups chicken or vegetable broth
- 1 pound ziti
- 6 garlic cloves, minced
- ¼ teaspoon red pepper flakes
- 6 cups (6 ounces) baby kale
- ¼ cup oil-packed sun-dried tomatoes, chopped coarse
- 2 tablespoons chopped fresh parsley

Cals 560 | Total Fat 16g | Sat Fat 2g
Chol 0mg | Sodium 930mg
Total Carb 89g | Dietary Fiber 4g
Total Sugars 8g | Protein 15g

WHY THIS RECIPE WORKS This fresh take on baked ziti is substantial and gratifyingly vegetable-forward. We create a creamy, aromatic sauce for baked pasta with vegetables, and the often underestimated leek makes it happen. We sauté 2 pounds of sliced leeks until they begin to caramelize, add some thyme, deglaze with a splash of dry white wine, and then simmer the mixture in chicken broth so it can be blended into a smooth, velvety sauce. Sautéed baby kale and sun-dried tomatoes, flavored with a generous dose of garlic plus red pepper flakes, get baked with the ziti. Parmesan-lemon bread crumbs make a savory, crisp topping. If you can't find baby kale, substitute 8 ounces kale, stemmed and chopped.

1 Adjust oven rack to upper-middle position and heat oven to 450 degrees. Combine panko, Parmesan, 1 tablespoon oil, and lemon zest in bowl; set aside.

2 Heat 2 tablespoons oil in Dutch oven over medium heat until shimmering. Stir in leeks, ½ teaspoon salt, and pepper and cook until softened and lightly browned, 8 to 12 minutes. Stir in thyme and cook until fragrant, about 30 seconds. Stir in wine, scraping up any browned bits, and cook until evaporated, about 2 minutes. Stir in broth and bring to boil. Reduce heat to low, cover, and simmer until leeks are very tender, about 8 minutes. Process leek mixture in blender on high speed until very smooth, about 2 minutes, scraping down sides of blender jar as needed. Season with salt and pepper to taste.

3 Meanwhile, bring 4 quarts water to boil in Dutch oven. Add pasta and 1 tablespoon salt and cook, stirring often, until nearly al dente. Reserve 1½ cups cooking water, then drain pasta. Cook remaining 1 tablespoon oil, garlic, and pepper flakes in now-empty pot over medium heat until fragrant, about 1 minute. Stir in kale, sun-dried tomatoes, and remaining ¼ teaspoon salt and cook, stirring occasionally, until kale is wilted and tomatoes are softened, about 3 minutes. Off heat, stir in cooked pasta, leek mixture, and 1 cup reserved cooking water; season with salt and pepper to taste. Adjust consistency with remaining ½ cup cooking water as needed (sauce should be thick but still creamy).

4 Transfer pasta mixture to broiler-safe 13 by 9-inch baking dish, smoothing top. Cover tightly with aluminum foil and bake until sauce is bubbling, 10 to 12 minutes. Remove baking dish from oven and heat broiler. Remove aluminum foil, sprinkle panko mixture evenly over pasta, and broil until golden brown, about 2 minutes. Sprinkle with parsley and serve with lemon wedges.

MAFTOUL WITH CARROTS AND CHICKPEAS

8 ounces (1⅓ cups) maftoul

½ teaspoon table salt, plus salt for cooking maftoul

2 tablespoons extra-virgin olive oil

1 red onion, sliced ½ inch thick

2 garlic cloves, minced

1 tablespoon Baharat (page 14)

1 pound carrots, peeled, cut crosswise into 1½- to 2-inch lengths, and halved lengthwise or quartered if thick

2 cups chicken or vegetable broth

1 (15-ounce) can chickpeas, rinsed

½ cup minced fresh parsley

1 tablespoon lemon juice

WHY THIS RECIPE WORKS Maftoul, also known as Palestinian couscous, is traditionally made by hand-rolling grains of bulgur wheat in moistened wheat flour (generally a mix of whole wheat and white flours) to create small balls of pasta. Its beige color and extra-nutty flavor make maftoul a unique addition to the hand-rolled pastas of the Mediterranean, like North African couscous (from which maftoul was likely derived) and Sardinian fregula, both made from semolina. While maftoul is traditionally served with a brothy stew of chicken, onions, and chickpeas ("maftoul" refers to both the pasta and the finished dish), our version leans on the inherent heartiness of this nutty and wholesome ingredient, and we instead create a vegetable- and legume-forward dish, fragrant with warm spices. Maftoul is available at well-stocked Middle Eastern grocery stores, or online. If you are unable to find maftoul, you can substitute an equal amount (by weight) of fregula, or moghrabieh. Because the size of maftoul grains can vary considerably, we provide a wide range of cook times; cook until just tender. Choose carrots that are between 1 and 1½ inches in diameter.

1 Bring 2 quarts water to boil in medium saucepan. Add maftoul and 1½ teaspoons salt and cook, stirring occasionally, until just tender, 10 to 25 minutes. Drain and set aside.

2 While maftoul cooks, heat oil in large saucepan over medium-high heat until shimmering. Add onion and cook until softened and beginning to brown, 5 to 7 minutes. Reduce heat to medium, stir in garlic and baharat and cook until fragrant, about 30 seconds. Add carrots, broth, chickpeas, and salt and bring to boil. Reduce heat to maintain simmer and cook, stirring occasionally, until carrots are tender, 8 to 10 minutes.

3 Remove saucepan from heat, stir in reserved maftoul and let sit, covered, until most of broth has been absorbed but dish is still saucy, 3 to 5 minutes. Stir in parsley and lemon juice and season with salt and pepper to taste. Serve.

Cals 410 | Total Fat 9g | Sat Fat 1g
Chol 0mg | Sodium 930mg
Total Carb 70g | Dietary Fiber 7g
Total Sugars 8g | Protein 13g

FIDEOS WITH ARTICHOKES AND SCALLOPS

SERVES
4

1¼ HRS

8 ounces fideos

¼ cup extra-virgin olive oil, divided

1 cup jarred whole baby artichokes packed in water, rinsed, halved, and patted dry

1 fennel bulb, 3 tablespoons fronds minced, stalks discarded, bulb halved, cored, and sliced thin

1 onion, chopped fine

½ teaspoon table salt, divided

1 (14.5-ounce) can whole peeled tomatoes, drained and chopped fine, juice reserved

4 garlic cloves, minced

1½ teaspoons smoked paprika

2¾ cups water

½ cup dry white wine

¼ cup panko bread crumbs

1 pound large sea scallops, tendons removed

¼ cup Anchoïade (page 16)

Cals 600 | Total Fat 26g | Sat Fat 3.5g
Chol 30mg | Sodium 890mg
Total Carb 63g | Dietary Fiber 6g
Total Sugars 7g | Protein 24g

WHY THIS RECIPE WORKS Similar to paella, the Valencian dish fideuà boasts noodles (instead of rice) simmered in a smoky tomato sauce. The noodles, fideos, are short-cut strands. The supporting players get special treatment: Artichokes are seared until they're deeply browned, while scallops are dipped in bread crumbs and scattered over the cooked noodles. A few minutes under the broiler renders the scallops golden and just cooked through and any exposed fideos delectably crispy. You can substitute 3 tablespoons minced parsley for the fennel fronds, if desired. We recommend buying "dry" scallops, which don't have chemical additives and taste better than "wet." Dry scallops will look ivory or pinkish; wet scallops are bright white. Spaghettini or thin spaghetti, broken into 1- to 2-inch lengths may be substituted for fideos.

1 Adjust oven rack 5 to 6 inches from broiler element and heat broiler. Toss pasta and 2 teaspoons oil in 12-inch broiler-safe skillet until pasta is evenly coated. Toast over medium heat, stirring often, until browned and pasta has nutty aroma, 6 to 10 minutes; transfer to bowl. Add 4 teaspoons oil and artichokes, cut side down, to now-empty skillet. Cook, without moving, until well browned, 3 to 5 minutes. Transfer artichokes to plate; set aside.

2 Heat remaining 2 tablespoons oil in again-empty skillet over medium heat until shimmering. Add sliced fennel, onion, and ¼ teaspoon salt and cook until lightly browned, 5 to 7 minutes. Stir in tomatoes and cook until mixture is thickened, dry, and slightly darkened in color, 4 to 6 minutes. Stir in garlic and paprika and cook until fragrant, about 30 seconds. Stir in toasted pasta, water, wine, and reserved tomato juice. Bring to simmer over medium-high heat, then reduce heat to maintain simmer and cook, stirring occasionally, until most of liquid has been absorbed and pasta is just tender, 8 to 10 minutes. Remove skillet from heat.

3 Combine panko and 1 tablespoon fennel fonds in small bowl. Pat scallops dry with paper towels and sprinkle with remaining ¼ teaspoon salt. Working with 1 scallop at a time, press 1 flat side of scallops in panko mixture, pressing gently to adhere. Nestle scallop, crumb side up, into skillet. Repeat with remaining scallops, then nestle reserved artichokes into skillet. Transfer skillet to oven and broil until scallops are golden brown and cooked through, 5 to 7 minutes. Remove skillet from oven (skillet handle will be hot) and let cool for 5 minutes. Sprinkle with remaining 2 tablespoons fennel fronds. Serve with anchoïade.

LINGUINE ALLO SCOGLIO

**SERVES
6**

1 HR

6 tablespoons extra-virgin olive oil, divided

12 garlic cloves, minced

¼ teaspoon red pepper flakes

1 pound littleneck or cherrystone clams, scrubbed

1 pound mussels, scrubbed and debearded

1¼ pounds cherry tomatoes (half of tomatoes halved, remaining tomatoes left whole)

1 (8-ounce) bottle clam juice

1 cup dry white wine

1 cup minced fresh parsley, divided

1 tablespoon tomato paste

4 anchovy fillets, rinsed, patted dry, and minced

1 teaspoon minced fresh thyme or ¼ teaspoon dried

½ teaspoon table salt, plus salt for cooking pasta

1 pound linguine

1 pound extra-large shrimp (21 to 25 per pound), peeled and deveined

8 ounces squid, sliced crosswise into ½-inch-thick rings

2 teaspoons grated lemon zest, plus lemon wedges for serving

WHY THIS RECIPE WORKS To put the seafood in this version of the Italian seafood pasta linguine allo scoglio, we fortify the natural shellfish juices with clam juice and four minced anchovies. We finish cooking the linguine directly in the sauce; the noodles soak up flavor and their starch thickens the sauce. You can omit the clams and squid and increase the amounts of mussels and shrimp to 1½ pounds each; increase the amount of salt in step 1 to ¾ teaspoon. If you can't find fresh squid, it's available frozen at many supermarkets and typically is precleaned; thaw it before cutting and cooking.

1 Heat ¼ cup oil in Dutch oven over medium-high heat until shimmering. Add garlic and pepper flakes and cook until fragrant, about 1 minute. Add clams, cover, and cook, shaking pot occasionally, for 4 minutes. Add mussels, cover, and continue to cook, shaking pot occasionally, until clams and mussels have opened, 3 to 4 minutes. Transfer clams and mussels to bowl, discarding any that haven't opened, and cover to keep warm; leave any broth in pot. Add whole tomatoes, clam juice, wine, ½ cup parsley, tomato paste, anchovies, thyme, and salt to pot and bring to simmer over medium-high heat. Reduce heat to medium and cook, stirring occasionally, until tomatoes have started to break down and sauce is reduced by one-third, about 10 minutes.

2 Meanwhile, bring 4 quarts water to boil in large pot. Add pasta and 1 tablespoon salt and cook, stirring often, for 7 minutes. Reserve ½ cup cooking water, then drain pasta.

3 Add pasta to sauce in Dutch oven and cook over medium heat, stirring gently, for 2 minutes. Reduce heat to medium-low, stir in shrimp, cover, and cook for 4 minutes. Stir in squid, lemon zest, halved tomatoes, and remaining ½ cup parsley. Cover and continue to cook until shrimp and squid are just cooked through, about 2 minutes. Gently stir in clams and mussels. Remove pot from heat, cover, and let sit until clams and mussels are warmed through, about 2 minutes. Season with salt and pepper to taste, and adjust consistency with reserved cooking water as needed. Transfer to large serving dish, drizzle with remaining 2 tablespoons oil, and serve with lemon wedges.

*Cals 702 | Total Fat 19g | Sat Fat 3g | Chol 229mg | Sodium 1505mg
Total Carb 73g | Dietary Fiber 5g | Total Sugars 5g | Protein 51g*

FREGULA WITH CHICKPEAS, TOMATOES, AND FENNEL

**SERVES
4 TO 6**

1 HR

3 tablespoons extra-virgin olive oil, plus extra for drizzling

1 fennel bulb, ¼ cup fronds minced, stalks discarded, bulb halved, cored, and sliced thin

1 onion, chopped fine

3 garlic cloves, minced

2 teaspoons minced fresh rosemary or ¾ teaspoon dried

1 teaspoon fennel seeds

½ teaspoon table salt

½ teaspoon pepper

¼ teaspoon red pepper flakes

4 cups water

2 (15-ounce) cans chickpeas, undrained

10 ounces grape tomatoes

8 ounces (1⅓ cups) fregula

1 tablespoon lemon juice

Grated Pecorino Romano cheese

WHY THIS RECIPE WORKS As befits an Italian island situated in the Mediterranean, the food of Sardinia is at once unique to its isolated, rugged environment and reflective of the influence of the many invaders who reached the island's shores. Fregola sarda, or fregula, is one such example: a sun-dried and toasted spherical pasta, it is hand-rolled from semolina, similar to North African couscous, and frequently paired with clams typical of the area, or with wild fennel foraged from the hillsides. For this fregula recipe, we combine the nutty, chewy pasta with typical Sardinian aromatics: licorice-scented fennel (a fresh bulb for sweetness, and seeds for more intense flavor) and piney rosemary. Chickpeas and grape tomatoes provide heartiness and bursts of sweet acidity to the fregula, along with enough liquid to create a risotto-like texture. A final sprinkling of Pecorino Romano (try Pecorino Sardo, made from the typical sheep's milk of Sardinia, if you can find it) adds just the right amount of richness and salt to complement the dish.

1 Heat oil in Dutch oven over medium heat until shimmering. Add fennel and onion and cook until vegetables are softened, 5 to 7 minutes. Stir in garlic, rosemary, fennel seeds, salt, pepper, and pepper flakes and cook until fragrant, about 30 seconds.

2 Stir in water, chickpeas and their liquid, tomatoes, and fregula and bring to boil. Reduce heat to medium-low and simmer until fregula is al dente, about 25 minutes, stirring occasionally. Stir in lemon juice, fennel fronds, and season with salt and pepper to taste. Serve, drizzling individual portions with extra oil and passing Pecorino separately.

*Cals 557 | Total Fat 14g | Sat Fat 2g
Chol 0mg | Sodium 1094mg
Total Carb 92g | Dietary Fiber 15g
Total Sugars 14g | Protein 19g*

PASTA WITH AVOCADO PESTO AND BROCCOLI

SERVES 4 TO 6

45 MINS

½ teaspoon table salt, plus salt for cooking broccoli and pasta

12 ounces broccoli, florets cut into 1-inch pieces, stalks peeled and sliced ¼ inch thick

1 pound spaghettini or spaghetti

1 ripe avocado, halved and pitted

1 cup fresh basil leaves

½ cup shelled pistachios or walnuts, toasted and chopped, divided

3 anchovy fillets, rinsed

2 teaspoons toasted fennel seeds

1 teaspoon grated lemon zest plus 1 tablespoon juice

1 garlic clove, minced

¼ cup extra-virgin olive oil, plus extra for drizzling

WHY THIS RECIPE WORKS "Pesto" derives from the Italian word for "pounded," and we have pesto recipes featuring other herbs and nuts (see pages 44, 134, 137, and 215) to remind us that delicious pesto isn't just the Genovese basil, pine nuts, and Parmesan version isn't the only one. Here, we make a "pounded" sauce, however, that's incredibly unique because it pumps up the plants with heart-healthy avocados for richness and fiber to boot, and a little cooked broccoli. The avocado carries the creaminess, so this pesto needs just a quarter cup of oil. In place of Parmesan, we combine a classic Southern Italian quartet of anchovies, lemon zest, fennel seed, and garlic to awaken the flavor of the rich sauce. Chopped pistachios keep things green-looking and add contrasting crunch. To make this a full meal, we stir some vividly green blanched broccoli among the strands.

1 Bring 4 quarts water to boil in large pot. Add 1 tablespoon salt and broccoli stalks and cook for 1 minute. Add florets and cook until stalks and florets are tender, 2 to 3 minutes longer. Using slotted spoon, transfer broccoli to colander set over bowl (do not discard boiling water). Let broccoli drain and cool slightly, about 5 minutes, then pat dry with paper towels; set aside.

2 Add pasta to reserved boiling water and cook, stirring often, until al dente. Reserve 1 cup cooking water, then drain pasta and return it to pot.

3 Process 1 cup cooled broccoli, ½ cup pasta cooking water, avocado, basil, ¼ cup pistachios, anchovies, fennel seeds, lemon zest and juice, garlic, and salt in food processor until smooth, about 30 seconds, scraping down sides of bowl as needed. With processor running, slowly add oil until incorporated, about 15 seconds.

4 Add pesto to pasta in pot and toss until sauce evenly coats pasta, adjusting consistency with remaining reserved cooking water as needed. Stir in remaining cooked broccoli and season with salt and pepper to taste. Sprinkle with remaining ¼ cup pistachios and drizzle with extra oil. Serve.

Cals 490 | Total Fat 21g | Sat Fat 2.5g
Chol 0mg | Sodium 280mg
Total Carb 64g | Dietary Fiber 7g
Total Sugars 3g | Protein 14g

FREGULA WITH CLAMS AND SAFFRON

**SERVES
4**

40 MINS

2 tablespoons extra-virgin olive oil, plus extra for drizzling

2 garlic cloves, minced

⅛ teaspoon red pepper flakes

⅛ teaspoon saffron threads, crumbled

2 cups chicken or vegetable broth

2 cups water

⅓ cup oil-packed sun-dried tomatoes, patted dry and chopped coarse

¼ cup minced fresh parsley, divided

1½ cups fregula

2 pounds cockles, scrubbed

1 cup dry white wine

¼ teaspoon grated lemon zest

WHY THIS RECIPE WORKS This soup of pasta and clams is a Sardinian classic that's all about simplicity. It relies chiefly on the flavor inherent in the soup's two main ingredients: chewy, toasty spherical fregula, and arselle, the small, briny, succulent hard-shell clams found along the coast. Broth enriched with tomatoes (in various forms depending on the recipe), parsley, garlic, a touch of fragrant saffron, pepper flakes, and olive oil traditionally constitute the soup base. We cook the pasta using the absorption method, right in our soup's base of chicken broth and water; this way, the fregula soaks up the flavorful broth during cooking. As a substitute for the Sardinian arselle, which aren't widely available in the United States, we landed on diminutive cockles, which are sweet and readily accessible. To cook the clams perfectly, we use our standard test kitchen method of steaming them in a shallow covered skillet and removing the clams as they open. Sun-dried tomatoes, which are found in some traditional versions of this recipe, are our tomato product; given the soup's quick cooking time, their deep, concentrated flavor is a bonus. Cockles are our preferred choice, but if they're unavailable, you can substitute small littleneck clams.

1 Heat oil in Dutch oven over medium heat until shimmering. Add garlic, pepper flakes, and saffron and cook until fragrant, about 30 seconds. Stir in broth, water, tomatoes, and 2 tablespoons parsley and bring to boil. Stir in fregula and cook, stirring often, until al dente.

2 Meanwhile, bring clams and wine to boil in covered 12-inch skillet over high heat. Cook, shaking skillet occasionally, until clams have just opened, 6 to 8 minutes. Using slotted spoon, transfer clams to large bowl. Discard any unopened clams. Cover to keep warm.

3 Strain clam cooking liquid through fine-mesh strainer lined with coffee filter into pot with fregula, avoiding any gritty sediment that has settled on bottom of pan. Stir in lemon zest and remaining 2 tablespoons parsley and season with salt and pepper to taste. Top individual portions with clams and drizzle with extra oil before serving.

*Cals 450 | Total Fat 9g | Sat Fat 1g
Chol 25mg | Sodium 690mg
Total Carb 61g | Dietary Fiber 1g
Total Sugars 3g | Protein 20g*

RIGATONI WITH SWISS CHARD, BELL PEPPERS, AND PANCETTA

8 ounces pancetta, cut into ¼-inch pieces

1 tablespoon extra-virgin olive oil

1 pound rigatoni

1 teaspoon pepper

8 ounces Swiss chard, stemmed and cut into ¼-inch-wide strips

2 ounces Pecorino Romano cheese, grated (1 cup), plus extra for serving

1 cup jarred roasted red peppers, rinsed, patted dry, and cut into ¼-inch-wide strips

WHY THIS RECIPE WORKS This veggie-heavy take on pasta alla gricia, the tasty Roman pasta dish made with just pancetta (or traditional guanciale), Pecorino Romano, and lots of black pepper, hits the spot—with main course fulfillment. The additions of sweet, meaty roasted red peppers and silky Swiss chard are the perfect foil to the richness of the cheese and salty cured meat, which still give this dish a dash of luxury. We cook the pasta in less water than normal; this creates an ultrastarchy cooking liquid to incorporate into the dish for a creamy sauce.

1 Heat pancetta and oil in Dutch oven over medium-low heat, stirring frequently, until fat is rendered and pancetta is deep golden brown, 12 to 15 minutes. Using slotted spoon, transfer pancetta to bowl; set aside. Pour fat from pot into liquid measuring cup. You should have ¼ to ⅓ cup fat; if you don't have enough, add oil to equal ¼ cup. Return fat to Dutch oven.

2 Meanwhile, bring 2 quarts water to boil in large pot. Add pasta and cook, stirring often, until al dente. Reserve 3 cups cooking water, then drain pasta and return it to pot.

3 Add pepper and 2 cups reserved cooking water to reserved fat in Dutch oven and bring to boil over high heat. Boil mixture rapidly, scraping up any browned bits, until reduced to 1½ cups, about 5 minutes. (If you've reduced too far, add more reserved cooking water to equal 1½ cups.) Reduce heat to medium, stir in chard, and simmer until chard begins to wilt, 1 to 3 minutes. Add Pecorino, red peppers, pasta, and pancetta, stirring until cheese is melted and sauce is slightly thickened, about 1 minute. Adjust consistency with remaining reserved cooking water as needed and season with salt and pepper to taste. Serve immediately, passing pepper and extra Pecorino separately.

Cals 450 | Total Fat 14g | Sat Fat 6g
Chol 35mg | Sodium 1030mg
Total Carb 57g | Dietary Fiber 3g
Total Sugars 3g | Protein 21g

PESTO ALLA CALABRESE

SERVES
4

50 MINS

3 red bell peppers, stemmed, seeded, and cut into ¼-inch-wide strips (5 cups)

3 tablespoons extra-virgin olive oil, divided

1 teaspoon table salt, divided, plus salt for cooking pasta

1 small onion, chopped

1 plum tomato, cored, seeded, and chopped

⅓ cup chopped fresh basil

½–¾ teaspoon red pepper flakes

1 teaspoon garlic, minced to paste, divided

4 ounces (½ cup) whole-milk ricotta cheese

¼ cup grated Parmesan cheese, plus extra for serving

¼ teaspoon pepper

1 teaspoon white wine vinegar

1 pound penne

WHY THIS RECIPE WORKS Like many other dishes from the southern Italian region of Calabria—and unlike Genovese-style basil pesto—pesto alla Calabrese is a sauce with red spice. Ricotta, Parmesan, and a combination of sweet and hot peppers are its main ingredients. Here some of the red bell pepper is sautéed for tender texture and nice browning, and some is added to the pesto raw for fresh, fruity bite. The heat comes from chile flakes. Fresh tomato, onion, garlic, and, yes, basil give the pepper mixture further complexity. A modest amount of cheese—a 2:1 ratio of ricotta to Parmesan—adds richness, salty tang, and creamy body without dulling the vegetables' flavor. For a spicier dish, use the larger amount of red pepper flakes. We call for red pepper flakes in this recipe but you can substitute Calabrian chile flakes if you can find them.

1 Toss two-thirds of bell peppers, 1 tablespoon oil, and ¼ teaspoon salt together in 12-inch nonstick skillet. Cover and cook over medium-low heat, stirring occasionally, until bell peppers are softened and just starting to brown, about 15 minutes.

2 Add onion, tomato, basil, pepper flakes, and ½ teaspoon garlic and continue to cook, uncovered, stirring occasionally, until onion is softened and bell peppers are browned in spots, 6 to 7 minutes longer. Remove skillet from heat and let cool for 5 minutes.

3 Process ricotta, Parmesan, pepper, remaining one-third of bell peppers, remaining ¾ teaspoon salt, remaining ½ teaspoon garlic and cooked bell pepper mixture in food processor for 20 seconds. Scrape down sides of bowl. With processor running, slowly add vinegar and remaining 2 tablespoons oil and process for about 20 seconds. Scrape down sides of bowl, then continue to process until smooth, about 20 seconds longer.

4 Bring 4 quarts water to boil in large pot. Add pasta and 1 tablespoon salt and cook, stirring often, until al dente. Reserve ½ cup cooking water, then drain pasta and return it to pot. Add pesto and toss to combine, adjusting consistency with reserved cooking water as needed. Season with salt and pepper to taste. Serve, passing extra Parmesan separately.

Cals 634 | Total Fat 18g | Sat Fat 6g
Chol 21mg | Sodium 672mg
Total Carb 94g | Dietary Fiber 6g
Total Sugars 8g | Protein 22g

SPAGHETTI WITH SPRING VEGETABLES

6 ounces cherry tomatoes, halved

6 tablespoons extra-virgin olive oil, plus extra for drizzling

5 garlic cloves (1 small, minced, 4 sliced thin)

¾ teaspoon table salt, divided, plus salt for cooking pasta

¼ teaspoon pepper

1 pound spaghetti

1 zucchini, halved lengthwise and sliced ¼ inch thick

⅛ teaspoon red pepper flakes

1 pound asparagus, trimmed and cut on bias into 1-inch lengths

1 cup frozen peas, thawed

¼ cup minced fresh chives

1 tablespoon lemon juice

¼ cup grated Pecorino Romano cheese, plus extra for serving

2 tablespoons torn fresh mint leaves

WHY THIS RECIPE WORKS A pasta dish doesn't get much fresher than this. A vibrant herby lemon-oil sauce coats pasta strands that twirl around a farmers' market–full of spring vegetables. The zucchini in the recipe contributes to the sauce; we overcook the squash to create a sauce with a silky texture. Asparagus and peas (frozen for ease) are perfect for signaling spring in our pasta. A final acidic punctuation mark comes from an anytime vegetable: Cherry tomatoes, marinated in garlic and oil, are an eye-pleasing, sweet-tangy flavor addition. The zucchini slices will break down as they cook and create a base for the sauce; do not be alarmed when the slices turn soft and creamy and lose their shape.

1 Toss tomatoes, 1 tablespoon oil, minced garlic, ¼ teaspoon salt, and pepper together in bowl; set aside.

2 Bring 4 quarts water to boil in large Dutch oven. Add pasta and 1 tablespoon salt and cook, stirring often, until al dente. Drain pasta and return it to pot.

3 Meanwhile, heat 3 tablespoons oil in 12-inch nonstick skillet over medium-low heat until shimmering. Add zucchini, pepper flakes, sliced garlic, and remaining ½ teaspoon salt and cook, covered, stirring occasionally, until zucchini softens and breaks down, 10 to 15 minutes. Add asparagus, peas, and ¾ cup water and bring to simmer over medium-high heat. Cover and cook until asparagus is crisp-tender, about 2 minutes.

4 Add vegetable mixture, chives, lemon juice, and remaining 2 tablespoons oil to pasta and toss to combine. Transfer to serving bowl, sprinkle with Pecorino, and drizzle with extra oil. Spoon tomatoes and their juices over top and sprinkle with mint. Serve, passing extra Pecorino separately.

Cals 450 | Total Fat 16g | Sat Fat 2.5g
Chol 0mg | Sodium 520mg
Total Carb 64g | Dietary Fiber 6g
Total Sugars 5g | Protein 14g

PASTA WITH BURST CHERRY TOMATOES AND FRIED CAPER CRUMBS

SERVES 4 TO 6

50 MINS

Topping

2 tablespoons extra-virgin olive oil

¼ cup capers, rinsed and patted dry

1 anchovy fillet, rinsed, patted dry, and minced

½ cup panko bread crumbs

⅛ teaspoon table salt

⅛ teaspoon pepper

¼ cup minced fresh parsley

1 teaspoon grated lemon zest

Pasta

6 tablespoons extra-virgin olive oil, divided

2 garlic cloves, sliced thin

2 anchovy fillets, rinsed and patted dry

2 pounds cherry tomatoes

1½ teaspoons table salt, plus salt for cooking pasta

¼ teaspoon sugar

⅛–¼ teaspoon red pepper flakes

12 ounces penne

1 cup fresh basil leaves, torn if large

Cals 418 | Total Fat 19g | Sat Fat 5g
Chol 12mg | Sodium 574mg
Total Carb 53g | Dietary Fiber 4g
Total Sugars 6g | Protein 10g

WHY THIS RECIPE WORKS Savory-sweet, juicy cherry tomatoes are often enjoyed as a snack or in salads, or as a stir-in for pasta recipes. But they have another application that may surprise you: They're the perfect choice for a quick fresh tomato sauce. You can toss them directly into the pan without any prep, and they don't need lengthy cooking to concentrate their flavor or thicken into a sauce. To keep the sauce bright and tomato-focused, we sauté the tomatoes with slivered garlic, red pepper flakes, and a touch of sugar, along with anchovies that meld into the mix without announcing a fish flavor. We finish the dish with a sprinkle of fresh basil and a gremolata-inspired topping of fried bread crumbs and capers. Be sure to use cherry tomatoes; grape tomatoes won't break down as much and will produce a drier sauce. Our topping contributes crunch and depth, but you can substitute 1 cup (2 ounces) of grated Parmesan cheese for ease, if desired. For a spicier dish, use the larger amount of red pepper flakes.

1 For the topping Heat oil in 10-inch skillet over medium heat until shimmering. Add capers and anchovy and cook, stirring frequently, until capers have darkened and shrunk, 3 to 4 minutes. Using slotted spoon, transfer caper mixture to paper towel–lined plate; set aside. Leave oil in skillet and return skillet to medium heat. Add panko, salt, and pepper and cook, stirring constantly, until panko is golden brown, 4 to 5 minutes. Transfer panko to medium bowl. Stir in parsley, lemon zest, and reserved caper mixture.

2 For the pasta Bring 4 quarts water to boil in large pot. While water is coming to boil, heat ¼ cup oil, garlic, and anchovies in large saucepan over medium heat. Cook, stirring occasionally, until anchovies break down and garlic is lightly browned, 4 to 5 minutes. Add tomatoes, salt, sugar, and pepper flakes to saucepan and stir to combine. Cover and increase heat to medium-high. Cook, without stirring, for 10 minutes.

3 Meanwhile, add pasta and 1 tablespoon salt to boiling water. Cook, stirring often, until al dente. Reserve ½ cup cooking water, then drain pasta and return it to pot. Off heat, add remaining 2 tablespoons oil and tomato mixture to pasta and stir gently until oil and tomato juices combine to form light sauce, about 15 seconds. Adjust consistency with reserved cooking water as needed, adding 2 tablespoons at a time. Stir in basil and season with salt to taste. Serve, passing topping separately.

FARFALLE WITH BEETS, ARUGULA, AND BLUE CHEESE

SERVES
6

45 MINS

1 pound beets, peeled and cut into matchsticks

1 red onion, halved and sliced thin

3 tablespoons extra-virgin olive oil

¼ teaspoon table salt, plus salt for cooking pasta

¼ teaspoon pepper

2 tablespoons lemon juice, divided

1 pound farfalle

5 ounces (5 cups) baby arugula

6 ounces Gorgonzola cheese, crumbled (1½ cups), divided

1 cup walnuts, toasted and chopped

WHY THIS RECIPE WORKS We have fun with the beets' bold color in this recipe by combining farfalle with matchstick-size beets, which give the pasta a vibrant pink color. We precook the beets, along with a little onion, in a skillet while the pasta boils so that the meal takes minutes to come together. Arugula, which we fold in along with Gorgonzola cheese at the end, adds a peppery bite and a contrasting texture and color, while the Gorgonzola contributes a slightly pungent flavor and creamy body. Just before serving, we garnish our pasta with chopped toasted walnuts for crunch and a final sprinkling of more Gorgonzola to pull it together.

1 Combine beets, onion, oil, salt, and pepper in 12-inch nonstick skillet. Add ⅓ cup water, bring to boil, then cover and reduce heat to medium-high. Cook for 10 minutes, then remove lid and continue to cook, uncovered and stirring occasionally, until beets are tender, about 15 minutes. Stir in 1 tablespoon lemon juice and season with salt and pepper to taste.

2 Meanwhile, bring 4 quarts water to boil in large pot. Add farfalle and 1 tablespoon salt and cook, stirring often, until al dente. Reserve ½ cup cooking water, then drain pasta and return it to pot.

3 Stir beets and remaining 1 tablespoon lemon juice into pasta in pot, adjusting consistency with reserved cooking water as needed. Stir in arugula and ¾ cup Gorgonzola and season with salt and pepper to taste. Sprinkle with walnuts and remaining ¾ cup Gorgonzola and serve.

Cals 550 | Total Fat 26g | Sat Fat 3g
Chol 0mg | Sodium 510mg
Total Carb 68g | Dietary Fiber 4g
Total Sugars 2g | Protein 13g

ANGEL HAIR PASTA WITH SUN-DRIED TOMATO AND MINT SAUCE

SERVES 4

35 MINS

½ cup oil-packed sun-dried tomatoes

½ cup fresh mint leaves

⅓ cup extra-virgin olive oil

4 teaspoons white wine vinegar

1 tablespoon tomato paste

2 garlic cloves, minced

¾ teaspoon table salt, plus salt for cooking pasta

½ teaspoon red pepper flakes

⅛ teaspoon sugar

12 ounces angel hair pasta

¼ cup pine nuts, toasted

Grated Pecorino Romano cheese

WHY THIS RECIPE WORKS The delicate, fork-entangling nature of angel hair pasta is a delightful change from spaghetti. Given its slender strands, it has its own set of cooking considerations—or overcooking considerations, as it cooks so quickly that there often isn't time to taste-test it for doneness. Because package directions often result in overcooked pasta, we came up with our own correct cooking times specific to common brands. Instead of tossing the pasta in a pan of bubbling sauce before serving, where it has another chance of overcooking, we toss the delicate pasta with a simple no-cook pesto-like sauce. To allow for the amount of pasta cooking water that's needed (since angel hair pasta absorbs a lot of liquid), we make our sauce extra-potent: Sun-dried tomatoes, white wine vinegar, and tomato paste make it umami-rich and super-tomato-y, while a generous amount of refreshing mint and some garlic give it a complex, lively aroma. Do not follow the cooking time on the pasta box. Boil De Cecco angel hair for 1½ minutes and Barilla and Prince for 3 minutes. Use straight pasta; angel hair curled into nests tends to tangle in the pot.

1 Process sun-dried tomatoes, mint, oil, vinegar, tomato paste, garlic, salt, pepper flakes, and sugar in food processor until smooth, about 1 minute, scraping down sides of bowl as needed. Transfer to large heatproof bowl.

2 Bring 4 quarts water to boil in large pot. Add pasta and 1 tablespoon salt and cook, stirring occasionally, until al dente. Reserve 1½ cups pasta cooking water, then drain pasta. While pasta drains, whisk 1 cup reserved pasta cooking water into sauce. Add pasta to sauce and toss gently with tongs, adjusting consistency with remaining reserved pasta cooking water as needed. Sprinkle with pine nuts. Serve with Pecorino.

Cals 600 | Total Fat 29g | Sat Fat 5g
Chol 7mg | Sodium 359mg
Total Carb 70g | Dietary Fiber 5g
Total Sugars 3g | Protein 16g

GARLICKY SPAGHETTI WITH ARTICHOKES AND HAZELNUTS

SERVES
4

35 MINS

- 2 tablespoons plus ½ teaspoon minced garlic (7 cloves), divided
- ¼ cup extra-virgin olive oil
- 1½ teaspoons fennel seeds, coarsely ground
- ¼ teaspoon red pepper flakes
- 1 pound spaghetti

  Table salt for cooking pasta
- 1 cup jarred whole baby artichoke hearts packed in water, rinsed, patted dry, and chopped
- 1 tablespoon lemon juice
- 1 ounce Parmesan cheese, grated (½ cup), plus extra for serving
- ½ cup hazelnuts, toasted, skinned, and chopped

WHY THIS RECIPE WORKS Garlic is a common pasta dish flavoring, but this pantry-friendly spaghetti makes the most of the allium's nuances. The simple garlic-and-oil sauce starts with garlic toasted over low heat in a quarter-cup of extra-virgin olive oil until pale and golden brown, which brings out the buttery sweet notes (cooked any darker and the flavor becomes bitter and harsh). We cook our spaghetti in just 2 quarts of salted water instead of our usual 4 quarts; this loads the pasta cooking liquid with starch so the garlic oil sauce clings beautifully to the pasta, with no hint of greasiness. Adding ½ teaspoon of raw minced garlic near the end of cooking balances the buttery sweetness of the toasted garlic with the fire of raw garlic. Also benefiting from this garlic duality are pleasantly vegetal baby artichoke hearts and toasty chopped hazelnuts. Floral fennel seeds and spicy red pepper flakes finish the flavor profile.

1 Combine 2 tablespoons garlic and oil in 8-inch nonstick skillet. Cook over low heat, stirring occasionally, until garlic is pale golden brown, 9 to 12 minutes. Off heat, stir in ground fennel seeds and pepper flakes; set aside.

2 Bring 2 quarts water to boil in large pot. Add pasta and 2 teaspoons salt and cook, stirring frequently, until al dente. Reserve 1 cup cooking water, then drain pasta and return it to pot. Add remaining ½ teaspoon garlic, artichokes, lemon juice, reserved garlic-oil mixture, and reserved cooking water to pasta in pot. Stir until pasta is well coated with oil and no water remains in bottom of pot. Add Parmesan and hazelnuts and toss to combine. Season with salt and pepper to taste. Serve, passing extra Parmesan separately.

Cals 450 | Total Fat 18g | Sat Fat 2.5g
Chol 5mg | Sodium 270mg
Total Carb 60g | Dietary Fiber 4g
Total Sugars 2g | Protein 14g

TA'AMEYA WITH TAHINI-YOGURT SAUCE

SERVES 4

1 HR

¾ cup torn pita, plus 2 (8-inch) pitas, halved

½ teaspoon fennel seeds, toasted and cracked

21 ounces frozen shucked fava beans, thawed and outer casing removed

¼ cup chopped fresh cilantro and/or parsley

1 large egg

2 scallions, sliced thin

2 garlic cloves, minced

½ teaspoon baking powder

½ teaspoon ground coriander

½ teaspoon ground cumin

½ teaspoon table salt

¼ teaspoon pepper

2 teaspoons sesame seeds

½ cup extra-virgin olive oil for frying

1 tomato, cored and chopped

2 Persian cucumbers, halved lengthwise and sliced thin

½ red onion, sliced thin (½ cup)

½ cup Tahini-Yogurt Sauce (page 16)

1 teaspoon nigella seeds (optional)

WHY THIS RECIPE WORKS Falafel (balls or patties) nestled into pita bread and adorned with vegetables and tahini sauce is a delectable street cart food across the Mediterranean. While a lot of falafel is made from ground chickpeas, falafel in Egypt, known as ta'ameya there, uses sweet, nutty fava beans. The fried patties have a gorgeous green hue amplified by plentiful fresh herbs and scallions. They're flavored with warm spices and often coated with sesame seeds, which increase the crispness that encases luscious, creamy interiors. Ground pita and an egg are key (and resourceful) binders, and baking powder gives the mash a soft fluffiness. No falafel is complete without toppings, and creamy yogurt-tahini sauce, plus juicy tomatoes, crisp cucumbers, and onions, add richness and freshness. To remove the outer casing of the fava beans, use a paring knife to make a small incision and then squeeze to remove the bean. You can use ¼ of an English cucumber in place of the Persian cucumbers. When taking the temperature of the frying oil, tilt the skillet so the oil pools on one side. We like this falafel served with Pink Pickled Turnips (page 18).

1 Process torn pita pieces and fennel seeds in food processor until finely ground, about 15 seconds. Add fava beans, cilantro, egg, scallions, garlic, baking powder, coriander, cumin, salt, and pepper and pulse until fava beans are coarsely chopped and mixture is cohesive, about 15 pulses, scraping down sides of bowl as needed. Working with 2 tablespoons mixture at a time, shape into 2-inch-wide patties and transfer to large plate (you should have 16 patties). Sprinkle sesame seeds evenly over falafel patties; press lightly to adhere.

2 Set wire rack in rimmed baking sheet and line with triple layer of paper towels. Heat oil in 12-inch nonstick skillet over medium heat to 350 degrees. Add 8 patties and cook until deep golden brown, 2 to 3 minutes per side, using 2 spatulas to carefully flip patties. Transfer falafel to prepared rack to drain and repeat with remaining falafel, adjusting heat as needed if falafel begins to brown too quickly. Stuff each pita half with falafel, tomato, cucumbers, and onion, and top with yogurt-tahini sauce and nigella seeds, if using. Serve.

*Cals 490 | Total Fat 31g | Sat Fat 8g | Chol 55mg | Sodium 330mg
Total Carb 38g | Dietary Fiber 6g | Total Sugars 9g | Protein 18g*

TA'AMEYA
WITH TAHINI-
YOGURT
SAUCE

LENTIL AND MUSHROOM BURGERS

SERVES
12

2 HRS
plus 20 mins
cooling

¾ cup dried brown lentils, picked over and rinsed

1 teaspoon table salt, plus salt for cooking lentils and bulgur

¾ cup medium-grind bulgur, rinsed

½ cup extra-virgin olive oil, divided

2 onions, chopped fine

1 celery rib, chopped fine

1 small leek, white and light green parts only, halved lengthwise, chopped fine, and washed thoroughly

2 garlic cloves, minced

1 pound cremini or white mushrooms, trimmed and sliced ¼ inch thick

1 cup raw cashews

⅓ cup mayonnaise

2 cups panko bread crumbs

12 hamburger buns

WHY THIS RECIPE WORKS Plant-focused burgers can be a satisfying part of a Mediterranean lifestyle, boasting whole grains, legumes, and vegetables in patty form. And they can really be delicious. Lentils give our burgers earthy flavor, and bulgur further bulks them up and absorbs any excess moisture that the lentils retain after cooking. Some well-browned mushrooms add meatiness, and for even more of an umami boost, we include a more surprising ingredient, cashews. When ground into the burger, they add savory richness without disturbing the flavors. Mayonnaise provides cohesion with richness. Don't confuse bulgur with cracked wheat, which has a much longer cooking time and will not work in this recipe. We like to serve the burgers with pickled onions, avocado, and Garlic Yogurt Sauce (page 16).

1 Bring 3 cups water, lentils, and 1 teaspoon salt to boil in medium saucepan over high heat. Reduce heat to medium-low and simmer gently, stirring occasionally, until lentils are just beginning to fall apart, about 25 minutes. Drain lentils, spread out over paper towel–lined baking sheet, and pat dry; let cool completely.

2 Meanwhile, bring 2 cups water and ½ teaspoon salt to boil in small saucepan. Off heat, stir in bulgur, cover, and let stand until tender, 15 to 20 minutes. Drain bulgur, pressing with rubber spatula to remove excess moisture, and transfer to large bowl; let cool slightly.

3 Heat 1 tablespoon oil in 12-inch nonstick skillet over medium-high heat until shimmering. Add onions, celery, leek, and garlic and cook, stirring occasionally, until vegetables begin to brown, about 10 minutes. Spread vegetable mixture onto second baking sheet.

4 Heat 1 tablespoon oil in now-empty skillet over high heat until shimmering. Add mushrooms and cook, stirring occasionally, until golden brown, about 12 minutes; add to baking sheet with vegetables and let cool to room temperature, about 20 minutes.

Cals 410 | Total Fat 17g | Sat Fat 2g
Chol 0mg | Sodium 520mg
Total Carb 54g | Dietary Fiber 5g
Total Sugars 7g | Protein 12g

5 Pulse cashews in food processor until finely chopped, about 15 pulses. Stir cashews into bulgur, then stir in cooled lentils, vegetable-mushroom mixture, and mayonnaise. Working in 2 batches, pulse mixture in now-empty food processor until coarsely chopped, 15 to 20 pulses (mixture should be cohesive but roughly textured); transfer to clean bowl.

6 Stir in panko and salt and season with pepper to taste. Divide mixture into 12 portions, about ½ cup each, shaping each into tightly packed patty about 4 inches in diameter and ½ inch thick. Place patties on paper towel–lined baking sheet. (Patties can be refrigerated for up to 3 days or frozen for up to 1 month. To freeze, transfer patties to 2 parchment paper–lined rimmed baking sheets and freeze until firm, about 1 hour. Stack patties, separated by parchment paper, wrap in plastic wrap, and place in zipper-lock freezer bag. Do not thaw patties before cooking.)

7 Heat 2 tablespoons oil in 12-inch nonstick skillet over medium-high heat until shimmering. Place 4 burgers in skillet and cook until well browned on both sides, about 4 minutes per side; transfer to plate. Repeat with remaining 4 tablespoons oil and remaining burgers. Place burgers on buns and serve.

SPICED SMASHED CHICKPEA WRAPS WITH TAHINI YOGURT

SERVES
4

15 MINS

1   cup plain Greek yogurt

¼   cup tahini

1   teaspoon table salt, divided

2   (15-ounce) cans chickpeas, rinsed

2   tablespoons Asian chili-garlic sauce

2   teaspoons ground cumin

4   (8-inch) pitas, lightly toasted

½   English cucumber, halved lengthwise and sliced thin on bias

½   cup pepperoncini, stemmed and sliced into thin rings

¼   cup thinly sliced red onion

WHY THIS RECIPE WORKS A Greek gyro is a satisfying street food sandwich of warm pita wrapping thin slices of pork or lamb, or sometimes chicken, that cooks on a vertical spit (the word "gyro" loosely translates to "turn"). This quick sandwich is supersatisfying but takes the meat and spit out of the equation: The protein filling is plant-based, the source of spice inspired. We coarsely mash creamy canned chickpeas with Asian chili-garlic sauce and cumin for our filling. The mashing lightly breaks the chickpeas' skins so they can soak up spice. Then we lavish the pitas as richly as we would meat versions, with rich tahini and thick yogurt; zippy, pleasantly acidic pepperoncini; bracing red onion; and crisp cucumber to cool things down. For more heat, serve with extra Asian chili-garlic sauce.

1 Combine yogurt, tahini, and ½ teaspoon salt in small bowl; set aside.

2 Using potato masher, very coarsely mash chickpeas in bowl. Stir chili-garlic sauce, cumin, and remaining ½ teaspoon salt into chickpeas; set aside.

3 Spread reserved yogurt sauce evenly over 1 side of each pita (use all of it). Divide reserved chickpea mixture, cucumber, pepperoncini, and onion evenly among pitas. Fold pitas in half, wrap tightly in parchment paper, and serve.

Cals 588 | Total Fat 19g | Sat Fat 4g
Chol 10mg | Sodium 1021mg
Total Carb 82g | Dietary Fiber 19g
Total Sugars 13g | Protein 28g

ULTRACREAMY HUMMUS

**SERVES
6 TO 8**

makes 3 cups

1 HR

2   (15-ounce) cans chickpeas, rinsed

½   teaspoon baking soda

4   garlic cloves, peeled

⅓   cup lemon juice (2 lemons), plus extra for seasoning

1   teaspoon table salt

¼   teaspoon ground cumin, plus extra for garnish

½   cup tahini, stirred well

2   tablespoons extra-virgin olive oil, plus extra for drizzling

1   tablespoon minced fresh parsley

WHY THIS RECIPE WORKS Hummus is one of the best-known dishes of the Middle East. To achieve a perfectly velvety-smooth, buttercream-like texture, we simmer canned (yes, canned) chickpeas with water and baking soda for 20 minutes, which allows us to quickly remove their grainy skins by gently swishing them under water. Tahini made with heavily roasted seeds can contribute bitterness, so choose a light-colored tahini (avoid versions that look like peanut butter). The hummus will thicken slightly over time; add warm water, 1 tablespoon at a time, as needed to restore its creamy consistency.

1 Combine chickpeas, baking soda, and 6 cups water in medium saucepan and bring to boil over high heat. Reduce heat to maintain simmer and cook, stirring occasionally, until chickpea skins begin to float to surface and chickpeas are creamy and very soft, 20 to 25 minutes.

2 While chickpeas cook, mince garlic. Measure out 1 tablespoon garlic and set aside; discard remaining garlic. Whisk lemon juice, salt, and reserved garlic together in small bowl and let sit for 10 minutes. Strain garlic-lemon mixture through fine-mesh strainer set over bowl, pressing on solids to extract as much liquid as possible; discard solids.

3 Drain chickpeas in colander and return to saucepan. Fill saucepan with cold water and gently swish chickpeas with your fingers to release skins. Pour off most of water into colander to collect skins, leaving chickpeas behind in saucepan. Repeat filling, swishing, and draining 3 or 4 times until most skins have been removed (this should yield about ¾ cup skins); discard skins. Transfer chickpeas to colander to drain.

4 Set aside 2 tablespoons whole chickpeas for garnish. Process garlic-lemon mixture, ¼ cup water, cumin, and remaining chickpeas in food processor until smooth, about 1 minute, scraping down sides of bowl as needed. Add tahini and oil and process until hummus is smooth, creamy, and light, about 1 minute, scraping down sides of bowl as needed. (Hummus should have pourable consistency similar to yogurt. If too thick, loosen with water, adding 1 teaspoon at a time.) Season with salt and extra lemon juice to taste. (Hummus can be refrigerated for up to 5 days; bring to room temperature before serving and stir in 1 tablespoon warm water to loosen hummus texture if necessary.) Transfer hummus to serving bowl and sprinkle with parsley, reserved chickpeas, and extra cumin. Drizzle with extra oil and serve.

*Cals 190 | Total Fat 13g | Sat Fat 2g
Chol 0mg | Sodium 490mg
Total Carb 14g | Dietary Fiber 4g
Total Sugars 0g | Protein 6g*

SWEET POTATO HUMMUS

45 MINS

plus 30 mins sitting

1 pound sweet potatoes, unpeeled

¾ cup water

¼ cup lemon juice (2 lemons)

¼ cup tahini

2 tablespoons extra-virgin olive oil, plus extra for drizzling

1 (15-ounce) can chickpeas, rinsed

1 small garlic clove, minced

1 teaspoon paprika

1 teaspoon table salt

½ teaspoon ground coriander

¼ teaspoon ground cumin

⅛ teaspoon ground cinnamon

⅛ teaspoon cayenne pepper

WHY THIS RECIPE WORKS While we love classic hummus, replacing some of the legumes for a vegetable is a fun and ultranutritious alternative. So in their place, we turn to earthy, vibrant sweet potatoes. To keep things speedy, we opt to microwave rather than bake the sweet potatoes. Happily, microwaving the potatoes results in flavor that is nearly as intense as roasting. Just ¼ cup of tahini is enough to stand up to the spuds without overwhelming the hummus. To round out the flavor of the hummus, we add warm spices: paprika, coriander, and cumin. The addition of cayenne pepper and a clove of garlic curbs the sweetness and accents the spices, while some lemon juice brings the flavors into focus.

1 Prick sweet potatoes several times with fork, place on plate, and microwave until very soft, about 12 minutes, flipping halfway through microwaving. Slice potatoes in half lengthwise, let cool, then scrape sweet potato flesh from skin and transfer to food processor; discard skin.

2 Combine water and lemon juice in small bowl. In separate bowl, whisk tahini and oil together.

3 Process sweet potato, chickpeas, garlic, paprika, salt, coriander, cumin, cinnamon, and cayenne in food processor until almost fully ground, about 15 seconds. Scrape down sides of bowl. With processor running, add lemon juice mixture in steady stream. Scrape down sides of bowl and continue to process for 1 minute. With processor running, add tahini mixture in steady stream and process until hummus is smooth and creamy, about 15 seconds, scraping down sides of bowl as needed.

4 Transfer hummus to serving bowl. Cover with plastic wrap and let sit at room temperature until flavors meld, about 30 minutes. (Hummus can be refrigerated for up to 5 days; bring to room temperature before serving and stir in 1 tablespoon warm water to loosen hummus texture if necessary.) Drizzle with extra oil before serving.

Cals 150 | Total Fat 8g | Sat Fat 1g
Chol 0mg | Sodium 400mg
Total Carb 17g | Dietary Fiber 3g
Total Sugars 4g | Protein 4g

HUMMUS WITH BAHARAT BEEF TOPPING

SERVES 4

35 MINS

2 teaspoons water

½ teaspoon table salt

¼ teaspoon baking soda

8 ounces 85 percent lean ground beef

1 tablespoon extra-virgin olive oil

¼ cup finely chopped onion

2 garlic cloves, minced

2¾ teaspoons Baharat (page 14)

⅓ cup pine nuts, toasted, divided

2 teaspoons lemon juice

3 cups Ultracreamy Hummus (page 294)

1 teaspoon chopped fresh parsley

WHY THIS RECIPE WORKS Hummus makes for a great snack but the hummusiyas of the Middle East show this dish can be a hearty full meal. These restaurants devoted to hummus serve generous dishes of creamy hummus adorned with bright or spiced toppings and served alongside pita and pickles. Toppings can be eggplant, beef, onions, or even shakshuka. This common spiced beef topping is seasoned generously with Baharat adding amazing aroma to the dish. Some lemon juice brightens the beef and spices. Adding pine nuts to the beef and as a garnish gives this satisfying bowl more nutty flavor and crunch. This dish is pictured with Ultracreamy Hummus (page 294), but you can try it with White Bean Hummus (page 299).

1 Combine water, salt, and baking soda in large bowl. Add beef and toss to combine. Let sit for 5 minutes.

2 Heat oil in 12-inch nonstick skillet over medium heat until shimmering. Add onion and garlic and cook, stirring occasionally, until onion is softened, 3 to 4 minutes. Add baharat and cook, stirring constantly, until fragrant, about 30 seconds. Add beef and cook, breaking up meat with wooden spoon, until beef is no longer pink, about 5 minutes. Add ¼ cup pine nuts and lemon juice and toss to combine.

3 Divide hummus among individual bowls. Top with beef mixture, parsley, and remaining pine nuts. Serve.

Cals 400 | Total Fat 30g | Sat Fat 5g
Chol 35mg | Sodium 890mg
Total Carb 18g | Dietary Fiber 5g
Total Sugars 1g | Protein 19g

WHITE BEAN HUMMUS WITH HERB AND OLIVE SALAD

SERVES 8 TO 10
makes 4 cups

2 HRS
plus 8 hrs soaking

½ teaspoon table salt for cooking beans plus 1 teaspoon salt

¼ teaspoon baking soda

8 ounces (1¼ cups) white tepary or cannellini beans, picked over and rinsed

½ cup plus 2 teaspoons lemon juice, divided (3 lemons)

4 garlic cloves, unpeeled

⅔ cup tahini

¼ teaspoon ground cumin

¾ cup chopped fresh parsley

½ cup chopped fresh dill

½ cup pitted kalamata olives, sliced thin

2 tablespoons extra-virgin olive oil, plus extra for drizzling

2 tablespoons roasted pepitas

2 tablespoons roasted sunflower seeds

2 tablespoons white sesame seeds, toasted

Cals 240 | Total Fat 16g | Sat Fat 2g
Chol 0mg | Sodium 290mg
Total Carb 19g | Dietary Fiber 9g
Total Sugars 1g | Protein 9g

WHY THIS RECIPE WORKS This hummus carries the familiar flavors of garlic, lemon, and tahini against a mild, almost sweet, white bean canvas. We soak and then cook dried white tepary beans in a simple solution of baking soda and salt, which helps speed the deterioration of the tough pectin exterior and soften the beans. This results in a smooth puree with a uniform texture. We fancy up the hummus with a fresh herb salad that's simple to make but has complex flavors and textures with parsley and dill, briny kalamata olives, and a trio of nutty, crunchy seeds: pepitas, sunflower, and sesame. This hummus keeps surprisingly well in the fridge, but after one bite, you may find that storage won't be necessary. Skip the herb salad if serving this hummus with the Baharat Beef Topping (page 296) or Crispy Mushrooms and Sumac (page 301).

1 Dissolve salt and baking soda in 8 cups water in large saucepan. Add beans, cover, and soak at room temperature for at least 8 hours or up to 24 hours. Bring beans (still in soaking liquid) to boil over high heat, skimming off any foam that rises to surface. Reduce heat to medium-low and simmer until beans are very tender (some beans will blow out), 1 hour to 1¼ hours. Drain beans and set aside.

2 Pulse ½ cup lemon juice, ⅓ cup water, garlic, and salt in food processor until coarse puree forms, about 20 pulses. Transfer to small bowl and let sit for at least 10 minutes or up to 30 minutes. Strain lemon juice mixture through fine-mesh strainer back into processor; discard solids. Add tahini to processor and process until smooth and well combined, 45 to 60 seconds. Scrape down sides of bowl and add cumin and beans. Process until mixture is very smooth, about 4 minutes. Season with salt to taste and adjust consistency with up to 2 tablespoons additional water as needed. (Hummus can be refrigerated for up to 5 days; bring to room temperature before serving and stir in 1 tablespoon warm water to loosen hummus texture if necessary.)

3 Toss parsley, dill, olives, oil, and remaining 2 teaspoons lemon juice together in small bowl. Season with salt to taste. Transfer hummus to serving bowl and place herb salad in center. Sprinkle pepitas, sunflower seeds, and sesame seeds over top and drizzle with extra oil. Serve.

HUMMUS WITH CRISPY MUSHROOMS AND SUMAC

SERVES
4

35 MINS

12 ounces oyster mushrooms, trimmed and torn into 1½-inch pieces

¼ cup water

2 tablespoons extra-virgin olive oil, divided, plus extra for drizzling

⅛ teaspoon table salt

1 lemon, quartered

1 (15-ounce) can chickpeas, rinsed

2 teaspoons sumac, plus extra for serving

3 cups Ultracreamy Hummus (page 294)

¼ cup fresh parsley leaves

2 tablespoons chopped toasted pistachios

WHY THIS RECIPE WORKS This hummus meal is super-satisfying, as filling as our Hummus with Baharat Beef Topping (page 296) but all about the plants. Here, we opt for sautéed mushrooms, made irresistible by selecting oyster mushrooms; when roughly shredded these mushrooms take on lacy, crispy edges, and you'll want to eat them straight from the pan. Chickpeas tossed in sumac with a squeeze of caramelized lemon offer a bright flavor counterpoint to the rich hummus and well-textured mushrooms. More texture comes from a final sprinkling of chopped slightly sweet pistachios. Just add a spoon and dinner is served. This dish is pictured with Ultracreamy Hummus (page 294), but you can try it with White Bean Hummus (page 299). You can substitute halved portobello mushrooms, sliced thin, for the oyster mushrooms.

1 Cook mushrooms and water in 12-inch nonstick skillet over high heat, stirring occasionally, until mushrooms begin to stick to bottom of skillet, 6 to 8 minutes. Reduce heat to medium-high and stir in 1 tablespoon oil and salt. Cook, stirring occasionally, until mushrooms are crisp and well browned, 8 to 12 minutes. Transfer to plate.

2 Add remaining 1 tablespoon oil and lemon quarters, cut sides down, to now-empty skillet and cook over medium-high heat, until well browned on cut sides, 2 to 3 minutes; transfer to plate with mushrooms. Add chickpeas to oil left in again-empty skillet and cook until lightly browned, about 2 minutes. Off heat, add sumac and toss to coat. Season with salt and pepper to taste.

3 Divide hummus among individual bowls. Top with mushrooms, chickpeas, parsley, and pistachios. Sprinkle with extra sumac and drizzle with extra oil. Serve with seared lemon quarters.

Cals 550 | Total Fat 36g | Sat Fat 5g
Chol 0mg | Sodium 1270mg
Total Carb 44g | Dietary Fiber 13g
Total Sugars 2g | Protein 19g

FAVA BEAN CROSTINI WITH MANCHEGO AND PINE NUTS

24 (¼-inch-thick) slices baguette (1 baguette)

5 tablespoons extra-virgin olive oil, divided, plus extra for drizzling

3 pounds fava beans, shelled (3 cups)

1 shallot, minced

1 garlic clove, minced

½ teaspoon ground cumin

½ teaspoon table salt

3 tablespoons minced fresh parsley

1 tablespoon lemon juice

1 ounce Manchego cheese, shaved

2 tablespoons pine nuts, toasted

WHY THIS RECIPE WORKS Fava beans, also known as broad beans, do require some prep work but the fresh beans popular in the Mediterranean (and beyond) are so special they're well worth it. These artful crostini showcase the rich, creamy-tangy flavor and buttery texture of fava beans. First the beans must be removed from their tough outer pod, and then the translucent waxy sheath covering each bean should also be removed. To preserve the beans' flavor, we simmer them with aromatic shallot, garlic, and cumin. Then we use a potato masher to turn them into a smooth, creamy topping. Stirring in lemon juice and parsley adds more freshness. We spread the puree onto crispy thin toasted baguette slices and garnish them with Manchego cheese and toasted pine nuts. These are lovely as a meal-starter, but you can certainly serve more per person for a nourishing (and fun) lunch. This recipe works best with fresh fava beans, but if you can't find them, you can substitute 1 pound (3 cups) frozen shucked fava beans, thawed. Skip step 2 if using frozen favas.

1 Adjust oven rack to middle position and heat oven to 400 degrees. Place baguette slices in single layer on rimmed baking sheet. Bake until golden and crisp, 8 to 10 minutes, flipping slices halfway through baking. Brush bread with 1 tablespoon oil and season with salt to taste. Let cool completely on sheet, about 30 minutes.

2 Meanwhile, bring 4 quarts water to boil in large pot. Fill large bowl halfway with ice and water. Add fava beans to boiling water and cook for 1 minute. Using slotted spoon, transfer fava beans to ice water and let cool, about 2 minutes. Transfer fava beans to triple layer of paper towels and dry well. Using paring knife, make small cut along edge of each bean through waxy sheath, then gently squeeze sheath to release bean; discard sheath.

3 Heat remaining ¼ cup oil in medium saucepan over medium heat until shimmering. Add shallot and cook until softened, about 3 minutes. Stir in garlic and cumin and cook until fragrant, about 30 seconds. Stir in fava beans, 1 cup water, and salt and bring to simmer. Cook until fava beans are softened and most of liquid has evaporated, 12 to 15 minutes. Off heat, using potato masher, mash bean mixture until mostly smooth. Stir in parsley and lemon juice and let cool completely, about 20 minutes.

4 Spread fava bean mixture evenly over toasted baguette slices and top with Manchego and pine nuts. Drizzle with extra oil. Serve.

*Cals 380 | Total Fat 11g | Sat Fat 2g
Chol 5mg | Sodium 400mg
Total Carb 59g | Dietary Fiber 10g
Total Sugars 14g | Protein 18g*

Meat, Fish, Tofu & More

SHAWARMA–SPICED TOFU WRAPS WITH SUMAC ONIONS

28 ounces firm or extra-firm tofu

½ cup extra-virgin olive oil

6 garlic cloves, minced

1½ tablespoons ground sumac

1 tablespoon ground fenugreek

2 teaspoons smoked paprika

1½ teaspoons ground cumin

1 teaspoon table salt

¼ cup lemon juice (2 lemons)

3 tablespoons honey

4–6 (8-inch) pita, warmed

1 tomato, cored and chopped

½ cup chopped fresh parsley and/or mint

½ cup dill pickle slices

½ cup Sumac Onions (page 19)

½ cup Tahini-Yogurt Sauce (page 16)

WHY THIS RECIPE WORKS Crispy charred tofu fingers burst with bold spices and garlic in this satisfying and texturally varied vegetarian sandwich. The flavors of street cart Middle Eastern shawarma are the inspiration, a marinade to deeply season the tofu relying on classic shawarma spices of sumac, fenugreek, paprika, cumin, and garlic. Lemon juice and honey provide well-rounded, complex flavor, the latter also delivering that impeccable caramelization. The intense heat of the broiler ably blooms the flavors, burnishing them on the crispy tofu. Tossing the finished tofu in some reserved marinade amplifies the smoky flavor. We wrap the tofu in warm, fluffy pita and then pile on some shawarma topping treats: tomatoes, sumac onions, pickles, and fresh herbs, plus a finishing drizzle of cooling, creamy tahini-yogurt sauce. The tofu fingers are delicate and may break while turning; this will not affect the final wraps. We really enjoy the sumac onions here; however, an equal amount of thinly sliced red onion can be substituted. Try using items in these wraps in other contexts; they're great on top of a salad or as a plated meal.

1 Cut tofu crosswise into ½-inch-thick slabs, then slice slabs lengthwise into ½-inch-thick fingers. Spread tofu over paper towel–lined baking sheet, let drain for 20 minutes, then gently press dry with paper towels.

2 Microwave oil, garlic, sumac, fenugreek, paprika, cumin, and salt in medium bowl, stirring occasionally, until fragrant, 30 to 60 seconds. Whisk in lemon juice and honey until honey has dissolved. Measure out and reserve ¼ cup marinade. (Reserved marinade can be refrigerated for up to 24 hours; bring to room temperature and whisk to recombine before using.)

3 Arrange tofu in single layer on second rimmed baking sheet and spoon marinade evenly over top. Using your hands, gently turn tofu to coat with marinade. Cover and refrigerate for at least 1 hour or up to 24 hours.

4 Adjust oven rack 6 inches from broiler element and heat broiler. Line rimmed baking sheet with aluminum foil. Transfer tofu to prepared sheet and arrange in single layer, spaced evenly apart. Broil tofu until well browned on first side, 10 to 15 minutes, rotating sheet halfway through broiling. Gently flip tofu and continue to broil until well browned on second side, 10 to 15 minutes, rotating sheet halfway through broiling. Transfer tofu and reserved marinade to large bowl and gently toss to coat. Divide tofu evenly among pitas and top with tomato; parsley; pickles; sumac onions, and tahini sauce. Serve.

Cals 510 | Total Fat 24g | Sat Fat 3g
Chol 0mg | Sodium 800mg
Total Carb 53g | Dietary Fiber 2g
Total Sugars 10g | Protein 23g

TOFU AND CHICKPEA FLOUR FRITTATA WITH MUSHROOMS

SERVES
6 TO 8

1¼ HRS

28 ounces firm tofu, drained and patted dry

3 tablespoons extra-virgin olive oil, divided

1¼ teaspoons table salt, divided

½ teaspoon ground turmeric

½ teaspoon garlic powder

⅛ teaspoon pepper

¼ cup chickpea flour

8 ounces cremini mushrooms, trimmed and sliced thin

2 shallots, minced

1 garlic clove, minced

1 teaspoon minced fresh thyme

1 tablespoon minced fresh parsley

WHY THIS RECIPE WORKS Simpler and more substantial than omelets and less fussy than quiche, vegetable-filled frittatas are a favorite, so we're delighted to share this plant-based version using tofu instead of eggs. Silken tofu, with its creamy texture, may seem like the obvious starting point, but it's too wet. Firm tofu becomes perfectly smooth and "eggy" after a few seconds in a food processor. For additional structure to balance the frittata's softness, we add some chickpea flour, which also heightens the savory flavor profile. Turmeric gives the frittata a pleasing egg-like color, and garlic powder provides umami flavor depth. After sautéing mushrooms and aromatics until deeply caramelized, we stir the tofu puree into the vegetables and bake the frittata until it's set throughout and lightly golden. Given a 5-minute rest in the pan, the frittata slides right out and slices into neat wedges. Do not use silken, soft, or extra-firm tofu in this recipe. You will need a 12-inch ovensafe nonstick skillet for this recipe.

1 Adjust oven rack to middle position and heat oven to 350 degrees. Process tofu, 1 tablespoon oil, 1 teaspoon salt, turmeric, garlic powder, and pepper in food processor until smooth, about 30 seconds, scraping down sides of bowl as needed. Add chickpea flour and process until well combined, about 15 seconds.

2 Heat remaining 2 tablespoons oil in 12-inch ovensafe nonstick skillet over medium-high heat until shimmering. Add mushrooms and remaining ¼ teaspoon salt and cook until mushrooms have released their liquid and are beginning to brown, 5 to 7 minutes. Stir in shallots and cook until mushrooms are well browned, 5 to 7 minutes. Stir in garlic and thyme and cook until fragrant, about 30 seconds.

3 Off heat, stir in tofu mixture and spread into even layer. Transfer skillet to oven and bake until center is set and surface is slightly puffed, dry, and lightly golden, 30 to 35 minutes, rotating skillet halfway through baking.

4 Using pot holder, remove skillet from oven and let frittata sit for 5 minutes. Being careful of hot skillet handle, use spatula to loosen frittata from skillet and slide onto cutting board. Sprinkle with parsley, cut into wedges, and serve.

Cals 160 | Total Fat 10g | Sat Fat 1g
Chol 0mg | Sodium 370mg
Total Carb 7g | Dietary Fiber 1g
Total Sugars 2g | Protein 10g

GRILLED TOFU AND VEGETABLES WITH ROSE HARISSA

SERVES 4 TO 6

45 MINS

28 ounces firm tofu

¼ cup Rose Harissa (page 18)

2 tablespoons water

1 tablespoon honey

1¼ teaspoon table salt, divided

1 teaspoon pepper, divided

½ teaspoon grated lemon zest plus 2 tablespoons juice

1 large red onion, peeled and cut crosswise into ½-inch-thick rounds

2 red, yellow, or orange bell peppers, halved from pole to pole, stemmed, and seeded

3 tablespoons extra-virgin olive oil, divided

1 head radicchio (10 ounces), quartered

2 cups grape tomatoes, halved

½ cup fresh mint or parsley leaves, torn

Cals 310 | Total Fat 21g | Sat Fat 2.5g
Chol 0mg | Sodium 580mg
Total Carb 17g | Dietary Fiber 4g
Total Sugars 7g | Protein 14g

WHY THIS RECIPE WORKS To assemble a vibrantly flavored tofu dinner platter off the grill we started by thinking about the sauce. Subtly floral, spicy rose harissa complements the char of grilled foods, and tofu slabs are the perfect canvas for the paste's complexity. Brushing the tofu with the mixture after cooking allows us to appreciate this condiment's depth. Alongside the tofu we grill wedges of pleasantly bitter radicchio balanced by sweet bell peppers and red onions. You will need two 12-inch metal skewers for this recipe.

1 Slice each block of tofu lengthwise into 4 slabs (approximately ¾ inch thick). Spread tofu over paper towel–lined baking sheet, let drain for 20 minutes, then gently press dry with paper towels. Whisk harissa, water, honey, ¼ teaspoon salt, ¼ teaspoon pepper, and lemon zest and juice together in bowl; set aside.

2 Thread onion rounds from side to side onto two 12-inch metal skewers. Arrange bell peppers skin side up on cutting board and press to flatten with your hand. Brush tofu with 1 tablespoon oil and sprinkle with ½ teaspoon salt and ¼ teaspoon pepper. Brush radicchio, onions, and bell peppers with remaining 2 tablespoons oil and sprinkle with remaining ½ teaspoon salt and remaining ½ teaspoon pepper.

3A For a charcoal grill Open bottom vent completely. Light large chimney starter filled with charcoal briquettes (6 quarts). When top coals are partially covered with ash, pour evenly over grill. Set cooking grate in place, cover, and open lid vent completely. Heat grill until hot, about 5 minutes.

3B For a gas grill Turn all burners to high; cover; and heat grill until hot, about 15 minutes. Leave all burners on high.

4 Clean cooking grate, then repeatedly brush grate with well-oiled paper towels until grate is black and glossy, 5 to 10 times. Place tofu and vegetables on grill. Cook (covered if using gas), flipping as needed, until radicchio is softened and lightly charred, 5 to 7 minutes, and remaining vegetables and tofu are lightly charred, 10 to 12 minutes. Transfer items to cutting board as they finish grilling and tent with aluminum foil to keep warm.

5 Brush tofu with half of harissa mixture. Using fork, remove onion rounds from skewers. Arrange tofu and vegetables on serving platter. Top with tomatoes, sprinkle with mint, and drizzle with remaining harissa mixture. Serve.

GRILLED
TOFU AND
VEGETABLES
WITH ROSE
HARISSA

SEARED TEMPEH WITH TOMATO JAM

SERVES
4

1 HR
plus 2 hrs marinating and cooling

- 1 pound tomatoes, cored and cut into ½-inch pieces
- 2 tablespoons honey
- ½ cup plus 2 tablespoons red wine vinegar, divided
- 7 garlic cloves, minced, divided
- 1 tablespoon grated fresh ginger
- 1 teaspoon Ras el Hanout (page 15)
- 1 anchovy fillet, rinsed, patted dry, and minced (optional)
- ½ teaspoon ground dried Aleppo pepper, divided
- 1 pound tempeh
- ¼ cup water
- 1 teaspoon dried oregano
- ½ teaspoon table salt
- 3 tablespoons extra-virgin olive oil
- 2 tablespoons chopped fresh cilantro

WHY THIS RECIPE WORKS Since tempeh has such a concentration of protein and is so good at absorbing flavor, we go all in and prepare it as a "meaty" plant-based steak with an umami-rich serving condiment. Marinating the tempeh in a seasoned vinegar-and-water base infuses it with flavor. Patting the marinated tempeh dry and pan-searing it creates a delectably crisp edge and a cohesive interior texture. The tempeh's earthy flavor is well balanced by bright, sweet, meaty tomato jam that gets added depth from an optional anchovy and warm spice from fresh ginger and ras el hanout. Freshness comes at the end in a sprinkling of fresh cilantro. Serve as a steak alongside something verdant, like green beans or sautéed spinach.

1 Combine tomatoes; honey; 6 tablespoons vinegar; half of garlic; ginger; ras el hanout; anchovy, if using; and ¼ teaspoon Aleppo pepper in 12-inch nonstick skillet. Bring to boil over medium-high heat, then reduce to simmer and cook, stirring often, until tomatoes have broken down and begun to thicken, 15 to 20 minutes.

2 Mash jam with potato masher to even consistency. Continue to cook until mixture has thickened and darkened in color, 5 to 10 minutes. Let jam cool completely, about 1 hour. Season with salt and pepper to taste; set aside. (Jam can be refrigerated for up to 4 days; bring to room temperature before serving.)

3 Cut each block of tempeh into 4 even pieces, then halve each piece into approximately ¼-inch-thick slabs. Whisk water, oregano, salt, remaining ¼ cup vinegar, remaining garlic, and remaining ¼ teaspoon Aleppo pepper together in bowl. Transfer marinade to 1-gallon zipper-lock bag. Add tempeh, press out air, seal, and gently toss to coat. Refrigerate tempeh for at least 1 hour or up to 24 hours, flipping bag occasionally.

4 Remove tempeh from marinade and pat dry with paper towels. Heat oil in 12-inch nonstick skillet over medium heat until shimmering. Add 8 pieces tempeh and cook until golden brown on first side, 2 to 4 minutes. Flip tempeh, reduce heat to medium-low, and continue to cook until golden brown on second side, 2 to 4 minutes. Transfer to serving platter and tent with aluminum foil to keep warm. Repeat with remaining tempeh. Serve tempeh steaks with tomato jam, sprinkling individual portions with cilantro.

*Cals 300 | Total Fat 12g | Sat Fat 2g
Chol 5mg | Sodium 710mg
Total Carb 31g | Dietary Fiber 2g
Total Sugars 6g | Protein 17g*

FRITTATA WITH BROCCOLI AND TURMERIC

SERVES
4 to 6

45 MINS

12   large eggs

⅓   cup whole milk

¼   cup grated Parmesan cheese

2   tablespoons extra-virgin olive oil

1   tablespoon minced fresh tarragon

½   teaspoon table salt, divided

12   ounces broccoli florets, cut into ½-inch pieces (4 cups)

1   shallot, minced

1   teaspoon ground turmeric

¼   teaspoon pepper

3   tablespoons water

½   teaspoon grated lemon zest plus ½ teaspoon juice

WHY THIS RECIPE WORKS This golden frittata is substantial and vegetable-packed. How packed? We use a full 4 cups of broccoli in the frittata, chopping the florets small so they're surrounded by the eggs and the frittata comes out a cohesive whole. Adding turmeric and black pepper gives the filling a bold, slightly spicy flavor. A little Parmesan—just ¼ cup—goes a long way to add nutty, cheesy flavor. To ensure that the frittata cooks fully and evenly, we start it on the stovetop, stirring until a spatula leaves a trail in the curds, and then transferring it to the oven to gently finish. Adding milk and salt to the eggs ensures that they stay tender and fluffy, as the liquid makes it harder for the proteins to coagulate and turn rubbery, while the salt weakens their interactions and produces a softer curd. This frittata can be served warm or at room temperature. When paired with a salad, it can serve as a meal.

1 Adjust oven rack to middle position and heat oven to 350 degrees. Whisk eggs, milk, Parmesan, 1 tablespoon oil, tarragon, and ¼ teaspoon salt in bowl until well combined.

2 Heat remaining 1 tablespoon oil in 12-inch ovensafe nonstick skillet over medium-high heat until shimmering. Add broccoli, shallot, turmeric, pepper, and remaining ¼ teaspoon salt and cook, stirring frequently, until broccoli is crisp-tender and spotty brown, 7 to 9 minutes. Stir in water and lemon zest and juice and continue to cook, stirring constantly, until broccoli is just tender and no water remains in skillet, about 1 minute.

3 Add egg mixture and cook, using rubber spatula to stir and scrape bottom of skillet until large curds form and spatula leaves trail through eggs but eggs are still very wet, about 30 seconds. Smooth curds into even layer and cook, without stirring, for 30 seconds. Transfer skillet to oven and bake until frittata is slightly puffy and surface bounces back when lightly pressed, 5 to 8 minutes. Using rubber spatula, loosen frittata from skillet and transfer to cutting board. Let sit for 5 minutes before slicing and serving.

Cals 220 | Total Fat 15g | Sat Fat 4g
Chol 375mg | Sodium 400mg
Total Carb 6g | Dietary Fiber 2g
Total Sugars 2g | Protein 16g

TUNISIAN TAJINE WITH WHITE BEANS

**SERVES
4 TO 6**

1 HR

- 12 large eggs
- ½ cup panko bread crumbs, toasted, divided
- ½ cup minced fresh parsley
- 1 ounce Parmesan cheese, grated (½ cup)
- 3 tablespoons water
- ½ teaspoon table salt, divided
- ½ teaspoon pepper, divided
- 3 tablespoons extra-virgin olive oil
- 1½ pounds boneless, skinless chicken thighs, trimmed and cut into ½-inch pieces
- 1 tablespoon tomato paste
- 6 garlic cloves, minced
- 1 tablespoon Ras el Hanout (page 15)
- ¼ teaspoon cayenne pepper
- 1 cup canned cannellini beans, rinsed
- 4 ounces Monterey Jack cheese, cut into ½-inch pieces (1 cup)

*Cals 500 | Total Fat 29g | Sat Fat 9g
Chol 500mg | Sodium 840mg
Total Carb 15g | Dietary Fiber 3g
Total Sugars 2g | Protein 45g*

WHY THIS RECIPE WORKS The word "tagine"—or "tajine" as in Tunisia—tells a culinary story of history and custom. The classic earthenware vessel used to cook myriad North African dishes, often eponymous stews (see pages 83 and 338), has a unique conical shape that creates moist, delicious results. In Tunisia, the word "tajine" is also the name of a specific satiating egg dish that was originally made in the same pot, despite its looking nothing like a stew. Like frittatas (see page 314) or tortillas (see page 318), these eggs are chock-full, prepared with a wide variety of hearty proteins, herbs, and spices. Now, Tunisians commonly cook the meal in a baking dish; we choose a skillet. We include white beans, which become highly flavorful when cooked with spices and tomato paste, and tender pieces of sautéed chicken thighs. We stir bread crumbs into the eggs; some recipes use this method to absorb extra moisture and set the tajine's texture. Nuggets of mild Monterey Jack cheese melt into satisfying pools along the tajine's surface. The stuffed skillet bakes until the eggs are set up and browned. If purchasing ras el hanout, be sure that your blend features cumin, coriander, and turmeric. Turmeric will create the distinctive yellowish tone typical of traditional Tunisian tajines.

1 Adjust oven rack to upper-middle position and heat oven to 350 degrees. Whisk eggs, ¼ cup panko, parsley, Parmesan, water, ¼ teaspoon salt, and ¼ teaspoon pepper together in bowl; set aside.

2 Heat oil in 12-inch ovensafe nonstick skillet over medium-high heat until shimmering. Add chicken, tomato paste, remaining ¼ teaspoon salt, and remaining ¼ teaspoon pepper and cook, stirring occasionally, until chicken is well browned, 6 to 8 minutes. Stir in garlic, ras el hanout, and cayenne and cook until fragrant, about 1 minute. Stir in beans and cook until heated through, about 5 minutes.

3 Reduce heat to medium-low and stir in egg mixture. Cook, using spatula to scrape bottom of skillet, until large curds form but eggs are still very wet, about 2 minutes. Smooth egg mixture into even layer. Nestle Monterey Jack into egg curds and sprinkle top with remaining ¼ cup panko. Transfer skillet to oven and bake until tajine is slightly puffy and surface bounces back when lightly pressed, 10 to 12 minutes. Using oven mitt, remove skillet from oven. Being careful of hot skillet handle, use rubber spatula to loosen tajine from skillet and transfer to cutting board. Let sit for 5 minutes before slicing and serving.

TUNISIAN TAJINE WITH WHITE BEANS

TORTILLA ESPAÑOLA WITH CELERY ROOT AND PEAS

SERVES
4 TO 6

1 HR

1 pound celery root, peeled, quartered, and sliced thin

5 tablespoons extra-virgin olive oil, divided

1 onion, halved and sliced thin

1 teaspoon table salt, divided

½ teaspoon pepper, divided

8 large eggs

½ cup jarred piquillo peppers, rinsed, patted dry, and cut into ½-inch pieces

½ cup frozen peas, thawed

WHY THIS RECIPE WORKS Tortilla Española, a well-loved tapas bar staple, also makes a simple satisfying dinner at home when the vegetable-filled omelet is sliced and served generously. It consists of potatoes and onions that are simmered in plentiful oil until meltingly tender and then bound with eggs for a dense but creamy omelet. Here we try a celery root version; the texture of this root vegetable is similar to that of potatoes but it carries an intriguing earthy-herbal flavor. We don't use quite so much oil—we microwave the celery root to guarantee it's tender before entering the mix. In addition, piquillo peppers and peas are distributed through the tortilla for more heartiness, texture, and complexity. We love the tortilla on its own—a dollop of anchoïade ups its flavor ante and a salad makes it a very full meal. Look for celery root that is approximately 4 to 5 inches in diameter. If piquillo peppers are unavailable, you can substitute roasted red peppers. Serve the tortilla warm or at room temperature with Anchoïade (page 16).

1 Adjust oven rack to middle position and heat oven to 425 degrees. Microwave celery root in covered bowl, stirring occasionally, until softened and celery root has released its liquid, 8 to 10 minutes. Drain celery root, pat dry with paper towels, and return to now-empty bowl.

2 Heat 3 tablespoons oil in 10-inch ovensafe nonstick skillet over medium heat until shimmering. Add onion, ½ teaspoon salt, and ¼ teaspoon pepper and cook, stirring frequently, until golden brown, 7 to 9 minutes; transfer to bowl with celery root. Whisk eggs, remaining ½ teaspoon salt, and remaining ¼ teaspoon pepper in large bowl until well combined; do not overbeat. Gently fold in celery root mixture, peppers, and peas until thoroughly combined.

3 Heat remaining 2 tablespoons oil in now-empty skillet over medium heat until shimmering. Add egg mixture and cook, using rubber spatula to stir and scrape bottom of skillet until large curds form and spatula leaves trail through eggs, but eggs are still very wet, about 1 minute. Smooth curds into even layer. Transfer skillet to oven and bake until eggs are cooked and surface bounces back when lightly pressed, 9 to 11 minutes. Using pot holder, remove skillet from oven. Being careful of hot skillet handle, use rubber spatula to loosen tortilla from skillet. Place inverted plate on top of tortilla and carefully invert onto plate, then slide tortilla onto cutting board and let cool slightly, about 10 minutes. Slice tortilla into wedges and serve.

Cals 250 | Total Fat 18g | Sat Fat 4g
Chol 250mg | Sodium 600mg
Total Carb 10g | Dietary Fiber 2g
Total Sugars 3g | Protein 10g

NIÇOISE SALAD WITH SMOKED SALMON

4 large eggs

1 pound small red potatoes, unpeeled, halved

¼ teaspoon table salt, plus salt for cooking potatoes and green beans

8 ounces green beans, trimmed

⅔ cup sour cream

2 tablespoons lemon juice

2 tablespoons water

1 tablespoon chopped fresh dill

⅛ teaspoon pepper

10 ounces (10 cups) mesclun

½ cup pitted kalamata olives, halved

8 ounces sliced cold-smoked salmon

WHY THIS RECIPE WORKS French salade niçoise combines light and hearty elements (such as vegetables, hard-cooked eggs, olives, and canned tuna) for a healthful salad and anytime meal. The elements are adaptable so we created a version with flavor-packed smoked salmon. A three-ingredient dressing of sour cream, lemon, and dill (plus salt and pepper) makes a fitting pairing for the smoked salmon and brings this new niçoise together; we toss a small amount with the greens to ensure even distribution and then drizzle the rest over the other components. Use red potatoes measuring 1 to 2 inches in diameter. If you don't have a steamer basket, use a spoon or tongs to gently place the eggs directly in the boiling water.

1 Bring 1 inch water to rolling boil in large saucepan over high heat. Place eggs in steamer basket and transfer to saucepan. Cover, reduce heat to medium-low, and cook eggs for 13 minutes.

2 When eggs are almost finished cooking, fill large bowl halfway with ice and water. Using tongs or slotted spoon, transfer eggs to ice bath and let sit for 15 minutes. Peel and halve cooled hard-cooked eggs.

3 Bring 4 quarts water to boil in now-empty saucepan. Add potatoes and 1½ tablespoons salt, return to boil, and cook for 10 minutes. Add green beans and continue to cook until both vegetables are tender, about 4 minutes. Drain vegetables well and set aside to cool slightly.

4 Whisk sour cream, lemon juice, water, dill, pepper, and salt in large bowl until incorporated; set aside all but ¼ cup dressing. Add mesclun to ¼ cup dressing in bowl and toss to coat, then divide mesclun among individual serving dishes. Top with potatoes, green beans, eggs, olives, and salmon and drizzle with reserved dressing. Serve.

Cals 320 | Total Fat 15g | Sat Fat 5g
Chol 220mg | Sodium 830mg
Total Carb 25g | Dietary Fiber 4g
Total Sugars 5g | Protein 21g

COUSCOUS SALAD WITH SMOKED TROUT, TOMATOES, AND PEPPERONCINI

SERVES
4 TO 6

1 HR

1½ cups couscous

¾ teaspoon table salt

⅓ cup extra-virgin olive oil, plus extra for drizzling

1 cup pepperoncini, stemmed and sliced into thin rings, plus 3 tablespoons brine

1 garlic clove, minced

8 ounces cherry tomatoes, halved

½ cup fresh parsley leaves

3 scallions, sliced thin

6 ounces hot-smoked trout, skin and pin bones removed, flaked

Lemon wedges

WHY THIS RECIPE WORKS Flaking smoked trout into quick-cooking couscous gives this dinner-worthy salad not only a little extra good-for-you protein but also a smoky flavor that complements the semolina pasta. Pepperoncini and cherry tomatoes add spiciness and freshness for a complexly flavored recipe that's remarkably simple. A tangy vinaigrette soaks into and livens up the grains, providing a refreshing counterpoint to the smoky richness of the trout. Much of the punch comes from an ingredient that often goes to waste—we use the brine from the pepperoncini instead of vinegar in the dressing. Tossing the cooked couscous with the dressing while it's still warm helps it absorb the dressing as it cools. Hot-smoked mackerel or hot-smoked salmon also work well here.

1 Bring 2 cups water to boil in medium saucepan. Remove pot from heat, then stir in couscous and salt. Cover and let sit for 10 minutes. Fluff couscous with fork.

2 Whisk oil, pepperoncini brine, and garlic together in large bowl. Transfer couscous to bowl with dressing and toss to combine. Let sit until cooled completely, about 20 minutes.

3 Add cherry tomatoes, parsley, scallions, and pepperoncini rings to cooled couscous and gently toss to combine. Season with salt, pepper, and extra olive oil to taste. Divide salad among individual serving dishes and top with smoked trout. Serve with lemon wedges.

*Cals 360 | Total Fat 16g | Sat Fat 2.5g
Chol 30mg | Sodium 950mg
Total Carb 37g | Dietary Fiber 3g
Total Sugars 1g | Protein 17g*

TUNA AND HEIRLOOM TOMATO SALAD WITH OLIVES AND PARSLEY

- 4 heirloom tomatoes, cored and sliced ½ inch thick
- 1¼ teaspoons table salt, divided
- ⅓ cup extra-virgin olive oil
- 1½ tablespoons lemon juice
- 1 tablespoon Dijon mustard
- 1 garlic clove, minced
- ¼ teaspoon pepper
- 3 (6½-ounce) jars oil-packed tuna, drained (1½ cups)
- 1 cup fresh parsley leaves
- ½ cup pitted kalamata olives, halved
- 1 shallot, sliced thin

WHY THIS RECIPE WORKS Some produce items, when in season, don't need a recipe application; they're ripe for the eating as soon as they're sliced. A juicy, sweet, vibrant peak-season heirloom tomato needs nothing more than a drizzle of olive oil and a sprinkling of salt. But it's also a meaty resting spot for other simple ingredients to make something more filling. This pantry salad places a lightly dressed tuna salad atop the tomatoes. It's rife with whole leaves of refreshing parsley. For the best results, use ripe, in-season tomatoes. Vine-ripened tomatoes can be substituted for the heirlooms. Serve with toasted or grilled bread.

1 Shingle tomatoes on 4 dinner plates and sprinkle with ½ teaspoon salt. Whisk oil, lemon juice, mustard, garlic, pepper, and remaining ¾ teaspoon salt together in large bowl. Reserve 2 tablespoons vinaigrette.

2 Add tuna, parsley, olives, and shallot to remaining vinaigrette in bowl and toss gently to combine. Divide salad evenly among plates on top of tomatoes. Drizzle reserved vinaigrette over salads. Serve.

Cals 330 | Total Fat 24g | Sat Fat 3.5g
Chol 10mg | Sodium 1120mg
Total Carb 8g | Dietary Fiber 2g
Total Sugars 4g | Protein 18g

SHAVED SALAD WITH SEARED SCALLOPS

1½ pounds large sea scallops, tendons removed

1 pound jicama, peeled and shaved into ribbons

1 mango, peeled, pitted, and sliced thin

3 Persian cucumbers or 8 ounces English cucumber, shaved lengthwise into ribbons

4 ounces (4 cups) mesclun

2 radishes, trimmed and sliced thin

1 shallot, sliced thin

1 jalapeño or serrano chile, stemmed, halved, seeded, and sliced thin crosswise

1 teaspoon table salt, divided

¼ teaspoon pepper

6 tablespoons extra-virgin olive oil, divided

1 tablespoon honey

2 teaspoons grated lime zest plus ¼ cup juice (2 limes)

¼ cup fresh cilantro or parsley leaves

3 tablespoons roasted pepitas or sunflower seeds

WHY THIS RECIPE WORKS Serving scallops on a salad is a refreshing and healthful way to feature the sweet seafood. The ingredients in this salad call to mind Mexican antojitos (snacks) of refreshing produce such as sweet mango, crisp cucumber, jicama, peppery radish, and spicy jalapeño showered with chile limon. Here we shave or slice all of them thin into ribbons, and toss them with mesclun to make the salad. Lime dressing, cilantro, and roasted pepitas pull this main course seafood salad together. We recommend buying "dry" scallops, which don't have chemical additives and taste better than "wet." Dry scallops will look ivory or pinkish; wet scallops are bright white. Use a sharp Y-shaped vegetable peeler or mandoline to shave the jicama and cucumbers. For more spice, reserve, mince, and add the ribs and seeds from the jalapeño.

1 Place scallops on clean dish towel, then top with second clean dish towel and gently press to dry. Let scallops sit between towels at room temperature for 10 minutes.

2 Meanwhile, gently toss jicama, mango, cucumbers, mesclun, radishes, shallot, and jalapeño in large bowl, then arrange attractively on individual plates.

3 Line large plate with double layer of paper towels. Sprinkle scallops with ½ teaspoon salt and pepper. Heat 1 tablespoon oil in 12-inch nonstick skillet over medium-high heat until just smoking. Add half of scallops in single layer, flat side down, and cook, without moving them, until well browned, 1½ to 2 minutes. Using tongs, flip scallops and continue to cook until sides of scallops are firm and centers are opaque, 30 to 90 seconds longer. Transfer scallops to prepared plate. Wipe out skillet with paper towels and repeat with 1 tablespoon oil and remaining scallops

4 Divide scallops evenly among salad on prepared plates. Whisk honey, lime zest and juice, and remaining ½ teaspoon salt together in bowl. Whisking constantly, slowly drizzle in remaining ¼ cup oil until emulsified. Drizzle salad and scallops with dressing, then sprinkle with cilantro and pepitas. Serve.

Cals 480 | Total Fat 25g | Sat Fat 4g
Chol 40mg | Sodium 1260mg
Total Carb 38g | Dietary Fiber 8g
Total Sugars 20g | Protein 25g

SHAVED
SALAD WITH
SEARED
SCALLOPS

PAN BAGNAT

SERVES
4 TO 6

45 MINS
plus 1 hr
pressing

1   vine-ripened tomato, cored and sliced thin

1   small red onion, sliced thin

3   tablespoons red wine vinegar

1   garlic clove, minced

¼   teaspoon table salt

1   large baguette, halved horizontally

¾   cup niçoise olives, pitted

½   cup fresh parsley leaves and tender stems

3   tablespoons capers, rinsed

2   tablespoons fresh marjoram leaves

3   anchovy fillets, rinsed and patted dry

½   cup extra-virgin olive oil, divided

2   tablespoons Dijon mustard

¼   teaspoon pepper

2   (6½-ounce) jars oil-packed tuna, drained (1 cup)

3   hard-cooked eggs, sliced thin

Cals 520 | Total Fat 30g | Sat Fat 4.5g
Chol 115mg | Sodium 1260mg
Total Carb 34g | Dietary Fiber 2g
Total Sugars 4g | Protein 27g

WHY THIS RECIPE WORKS Pan bagnat is a Provençal sandwich that shares many ingredients with salade niçoise (see page 321): A crusty baguette is stacked with tuna, olives, capers, tomatoes, hard-cooked eggs, fresh herbs, and a mustardy vinaigrette. Removing the crumb from the bottom half of the loaf creates a trough to pack in the high-flavor ingredients. And as is tradition for a sandwich with a name that translates to "bathed bread," the cut sides of the bread are brushed with fruity olive oil, which helps prevent sogging. Processing the olives, capers, anchovies, and herbs into a coarse salad helps those components hold together. And the tradition of pressing the sandwich (here under a Dutch oven) tamps down the filling so it's compact to bite through; plus, the sandwich is a great make-ahead option. The baguette should be approximately 18 inches long, 3 inches wide, and at least 2 inches tall. Ciabatta will work, as will individual ciabatta rolls. You can substitute 1 tablespoon of oregano for the marjoram and kalamata olives for the niçoise.

1   Adjust oven rack to middle position and heat oven to 350 degrees. Lay tomato slices on paper towel–lined plate and set aside. Place onion, vinegar, garlic, and salt in bowl and toss to combine. Using your hands or metal spoon, remove inner crumb from baguette bottom to create trough, leaving ¼-inch border on sides and bottom. Place baguette halves cut side up on baking sheet and bake until very lightly toasted, 5 minutes.

2   Pulse olives, parsley, capers, marjoram, and anchovies in food processor until coarsely but evenly chopped, 10 to 12 pulses. Transfer olive mixture to bowl with onion mixture. Add ¼ cup oil, mustard, and pepper and toss to combine. Brush inside of each baguette half with 1 tablespoon oil. Place two-thirds of olive mixture in hollow of baguette bottom and spread evenly. Distribute tuna evenly over olive mixture and drizzle with remaining 2 tablespoons oil. Shingle tomato slices over tuna. Shingle egg slices over tomato. Top eggs with remaining olive mixture and cap with baguette top.

3   Press gently on sandwich; slice in half crosswise on bias. Wrap each half tightly in plastic wrap. Place rimmed baking sheet on top of sandwiches and weight with heavy Dutch oven or two 5-pound bags of flour for 1 hour, flipping sandwiches halfway through weighting. (Wrapped sandwiches can be refrigerated for up to 24 hours. Let come to room temperature before serving.) Unwrap sandwiches, slice each sandwich in half (or in thirds to serve 6) on bias, and serve.

GLAZED SALMON WITH BLACK-EYED PEAS, WALNUTS, AND POMEGRANATE

SERVES
4

30 MINS

4 (4- to 6-ounce) center-cut salmon fillets, 1 to 1½ inches thick

¼ cup pomegranate molasses, divided

¾ teaspoon table salt, divided

¼ teaspoon plus ⅛ teaspoon pepper, divided

3 tablespoons extra-virgin olive oil

2 tablespoons lemon juice

2 (15-ounce) cans black-eyed peas, rinsed

2 ounces (2 cups) baby kale

½ cup pomegranate seeds

½ cup walnuts, toasted and chopped

½ cup chopped fresh parsley

3 scallions, sliced thin

WHY THIS RECIPE WORKS Sweet-and-sour pomegranate molasses is the star of this inspired dish, pulling double duty as both an awakening glaze for rich roasted salmon and the main ingredient in a bright vinaigrette for the perfect side salad. In our hybrid salmon-roasting method, preheating the oven to 500 degrees but then turning down the heat to 275 just before placing the fish in the oven firms the exterior and renders fat from the skin, and then finishes cooking the salmon gently. Canned black-eyed peas, along with crunchy toasted nuts, fresh scallions, and tart pomegranate seeds ably complement the salmon with nutty, fresh, sweet, and acidic components. To ensure uniform pieces of salmon that cook at the same rate, buy a whole 1- to 1½-pound center-cut fillet and cut it into four equal pieces. If using wild salmon, cook the fillets to 120 degrees (for medium-rare).

1 Adjust oven rack to lowest position, place rimmed baking sheet on rack, and heat oven to 500 degrees. Pat salmon dry with paper towels, brush with 1 tablespoon pomegranate molasses, and sprinkle with ½ teaspoon salt and ¼ teaspoon pepper.

2 Once oven reaches 500 degrees, reduce oven temperature to 275 degrees. Remove sheet from oven and carefully place salmon skin side down on hot sheet. Roast salmon until center is still translucent when checked with tip of paring knife and registers 125 degrees (for medium-rare), 7 to 13 minutes.

3 Whisk oil, lemon juice, 2 tablespoons pomegranate molasses, remaining ¼ teaspoon salt, and remaining ⅛ teaspoon pepper in large bowl until combined. Add black-eyed peas, kale, pomegranate seeds, walnuts, parsley, and scallions and toss to combine. Season with salt and pepper to taste.

4 Remove sheet from oven and brush salmon with remaining 1 tablespoon pomegranate molasses. Slide fish spatula along underside of salmon fillets and transfer to serving platter, leaving skin behind; discard skin. Serve salmon with black-eyed-pea salad.

Cals 600 | Total Fat 35g | Sat Fat 6g
Chol 60mg | Sodium 930mg
Total Carb 39g | Dietary Fiber 7g
Total Sugars 13g | Protein 56g

SAUTÉED TILAPIA WITH BLISTERED GREEN BEANS AND PEPPER RELISH

SERVES
4
—
45 MINS

4 (4- to 6-ounce) skinless tilapia fillets, halved lengthwise down natural seam

1¼ teaspoons table salt, divided

1 cup jarred roasted red peppers, patted dry and chopped fine

¼ cup whole almonds, toasted and chopped fine

¼ cup extra-virgin olive oil, divided

1 tablespoon chopped fresh basil

1 teaspoon sherry vinegar

⅛ teaspoon plus ¼ teaspoon pepper, divided

1 pound green beans, trimmed

¼ cup water

WHY THIS RECIPE WORKS Readily available, economical, and sustainable, tilapia has a lot going for it even before it hits your plate with a punchy side. The lean, firm fillets are easy to flip during sautéing, and this mild fish becomes golden and crispy on the outside but stays moist on the inside. We split the fish down the seams and separate the thick and thinner halves so they cook evenly. To create a meal centered around this appealing preparation, we first make a simple, flavorful relish of jarred roasted red peppers, crunchy almonds, and basil that adds color, brightness, and contrasting texture to the fish. Then we quickly steam green beans until tender, letting them continue to cook uncovered to get attractive and flavorful browning. Setting the beans aside, we finish our meal by sautéing the tilapia in the same skillet until golden and perfectly cooked. Flounder, sole, or catfish can be substituted for the tilapia. Draining and drying the peppers keeps the relish from becoming watery.

1 Sprinkle tilapia with ½ teaspoon salt and let sit at room temperature for 15 minutes. Meanwhile combine red peppers, almonds, 1 tablespoon oil, basil, vinegar, ⅛ teaspoon pepper, and ¼ teaspoon salt in bowl; set aside relish until ready to serve.

2 Combine green beans, water, 1 tablespoon oil, remaining ½ teaspoon salt, and remaining ¼ teaspoon pepper in 12-inch nonstick skillet. Cover and cook over medium-high heat, shaking pan occasionally, until water has evaporated, 6 to 8 minutes. Uncover and continue to cook until green beans are blistered and browned, about 2 minutes longer. Transfer to platter and tent with foil to keep warm.

3 Pat tilapia dry with paper towels. Heat remaining 2 tablespoons oil in now-empty skillet over high heat until just smoking. Add thick halves of tilapia fillets to skillet and cook, tilting and gently shaking skillet occasionally to distribute oil, until golden brown, 2 to 3 minutes. Using 2 spatulas, flip fillets and cook until second sides are golden brown, 2 to 3 minutes; transfer to platter with green beans.

4 Return skillet to high heat. When oil is just smoking, add thin halves of fillets and cook until golden brown, about 1 minute. Flip and cook until second sides are golden brown, about 1 minute. Transfer tilapia to platter with green beans. Serve with relish.

Cals 330 | Total Fat 20g | Sat Fat 3g
Chol 55mg | Sodium 960mg
Total Carb 12g | Dietary Fiber 4g
Total Sugars 6g | Protein 27g

TUNA AND ONIONS IN AGRODOLCE

SERVES 4

45 MINS

- 1½ pounds red onions, halved and sliced thin
- ⅓ cup water
- ¼ cup extra-virgin olive oil, divided, plus extra for drizzling
- ¾ teaspoon table salt, divided
- ¼ teaspoon red pepper flakes
- 7 teaspoons sugar
- ½ cup red wine vinegar
- ½ cup minced fresh mint, divided
- 4 (4- to 6-ounce) tuna steaks, about 1 inch thick
- ¼ teaspoon pepper

WHY THIS RECIPE WORKS Tuna with sweet-and-sour onions, or tonno con cipolle in agrodolce, was born of the blending of Sicily's natural resources and the regional cuisine's prevalent Arab influence. The waters of Sicily are famed for their tuna and swordfishing industries, while early Arab rule brought North African ingredients and flavors to the island, including agrodolce—the sour-sweet profile. The aim is to build a sauce that has the perfect balance of vinegar and sugar and is bulked up with plenty of sautéed onions. We start with the onions, drawing out their moisture by adding water and cooking them covered; this allows us to get good browning quickly once we lift the lid. Adding the sugar to the onions during the last few minutes of cooking encourages extra caramelization; we then reduce the vinegar to intensify its flavor but mellow its bite. Recipes call for cooking the tuna to varying degrees, from rare to well-done throughout. We typically like our tuna rare, but in this application we prefer it cooked to medium-rare so there is some contrast between the flesh and the soft texture of our onions. If you like your tuna rare, however, cook the tuna just 1 to 2 minutes per side until it's translucent red at center and registers 110 degrees.

1 Bring onions, water, 1 tablespoon oil, ¼ teaspoon salt, and pepper flakes to boil in 12-inch nonstick skillet over high heat. Cover and cook until water has evaporated and onions start to sizzle, 5 to 7 minutes. Uncover, reduce heat to medium-high, and continue to cook until onions begin to brown, 7 to 10 minutes.

2 Sprinkle onions with sugar and cook, stirring occasionally, until well browned, about 3 minutes. Stir in vinegar and cook until mostly evaporated, about 1 minute. Off heat, stir in 2 tablespoons oil and ⅓ cup mint. Transfer to bowl and cover to keep warm. Wipe skillet clean with paper towels.

3 Pat tuna steaks dry with paper towels and season with pepper and remaining ½ teaspoon salt. Heat remaining 1 tablespoon oil in now-empty skillet over medium-high heat until just smoking. Place tuna in skillet and cook until well browned and reddish pink at center when checked with tip of paring knife and registers 125 degrees (for medium-rare), 2 to 3 minutes per side.

4 Transfer onion sauce to serving dish and nestle tuna steaks on top. Drizzle with extra oil and sprinkle with remaining mint. Serve.

Cals 350 | Total Fat 15g | Sat Fat 2g
Chol 45mg | Sodium 500mg
Total Carb 24g | Dietary Fiber 3g
Total Sugars 15g | Protein 30g

CHRAIME

SERVES
4

1 HR

- 3 tablespoons extra virgin olive oil, plus extra for drizzling
- 1 onion, chopped fine
- 1 red bell pepper, stemmed, seeded, and chopped
- 1 jalapeño chile, stemmed, seeded, and minced
- ¾ teaspoon table salt
- ¼ cup tomato paste
- 6 garlic cloves, minced
- 1 tablespoon Tabil (page 15)
- 1 tablespoon ground dried Aleppo pepper
- 2 teaspoons paprika
- ¼ teaspoon pepper
- 1½ cups water
- 1½ pounds skinless haddock fillets, ½ to ¾ inch thick, cut into 3-inch pieces
- 10 ounces cherry tomatoes
- ½ cup chopped fresh cilantro
  Lemon wedges

WHY THIS RECIPE WORKS This spicy, garlicky, saucy, and aromatic tomato-based fish stew was brought to Israel by Libyan and Moroccan Jewish immigrants and commonly appears on Shabbat, Rosh Hashanah, and Passover tables. Libyan versions typically consist of a fiery sauce of tomato paste, hot peppers, and spices, primarily cumin, caraway and paprika, while Moroccan versions include more fresh vegetables (tomatoes and bell peppers) along with generous amounts of herbs. Our take pays homage to both: grassy fresh jalapeños and bright Aleppo pepper bring varied heat, and tomato paste and bell pepper provide balancing sweetness. Cherry tomatoes, tossed in almost at the end of cooking, add fresh pops of sweet acidity. To easily bring in the varied spices with a blend, we incorporate the Tunisian spice blend tabil (see page 15), which adds a range of flavors from earthy muskiness to bright citrus notes. A finishing handful of cilantro and a squeeze of lemon balance all the flavors. Black sea bass, cod, hake, or pollock can be substituted for the haddock. Thin tail-end fillets can be folded to achieve proper thickness. This dish is typically spicy; for a milder dish reduce the amount of Aleppo pepper to 1 or 2 teaspoons. Serve with challah.

1 Heat oil in 12-inch skillet over medium heat until shimmering. Add onion, bell pepper, jalapeño, and salt and cook until vegetables are softened, 5 to 7 minutes. Stir in tomato paste, garlic, tabil, Aleppo pepper, paprika, and pepper and cook until fragrant, about 30 seconds. Stir in water, scraping up any browned bits, and bring to simmer. Reduce heat to low, cover, and cook until flavors meld, about 15 minutes.

2 Nestle haddock into sauce and spoon some of sauce over fish. Sprinkle tomatoes around haddock and return to simmer. Reduce heat to low, cover, and cook until fish flakes apart when gently prodded with paring knife and registers 135 degrees, 5 to 7 minutes. Season with salt and pepper to taste. Sprinkle with cilantro and drizzle with extra oil. Serve with lemon wedges.

Cals 290 | Total Fat 12g | Sat Fat 2g
Chol 90mg | Sodium 930mg
Total Carb 14g | Dietary Fiber 3g
Total Sugars 6g | Protein 31g

FISH TAGINE

1½ pounds skinless cod fillets, 1 to 1½ inches thick, cut into 1½- to 2-inch pieces

¾ teaspoon table salt, divided

½ cup fresh cilantro leaves, plus ¼ cup chopped

4 garlic cloves, peeled

1¼ teaspoons ground cumin

1¼ teaspoons paprika

¼ teaspoon cayenne pepper

1½ tablespoons lemon juice

6 tablespoons extra-virgin olive oil, divided

1 onion, halved and sliced through root end ¼ inch thick

1 green bell pepper, stemmed, seeded, and cut into ¼-inch-wide strips

1 carrot, peeled and sliced on bias ¼ inch thick

1 (14.5-ounce) can diced tomatoes

⅓ cup pitted brine-cured green olives, quartered lengthwise

2 tablespoons rinsed and minced Preserved Lemons (page 18)

WHY THIS RECIPE WORKS The vibrant colors and heady and bright flavors of a tagine give mild white fish a beguiling aroma. The type of fish used in a tagine depends on the region and its available seafood, though white-fleshed fillets are common in Morocco. Regardless of the type of fish, the fillets are typically marinated in chermoula, an herby and warm-spiced sauce; coating the fish in it just before cooking seasons the fish's exterior. Preserved lemon and olives add acidity, complexity, and salty punch to the broth. Black sea bass, haddock, hake, or pollack can be substituted for the cod. Picholine or Cerignola olives work well in this recipe. Serve with flatbread, couscous, or rice.

1 Place cod in bowl and toss with ½ teaspoon salt; set aside.

2 Pulse cilantro leaves, garlic, cumin, paprika, and cayenne in food processor until cilantro and garlic are finely chopped, about 12 pulses, scraping down sides of bowl as needed. Add lemon juice and pulse briefly to combine. Transfer mixture to small bowl and stir in 2 tablespoons oil; set aside.

3 Heat remaining ¼ cup oil in Dutch oven over medium heat until shimmering. Add onion, bell pepper, carrot, and remaining ¼ teaspoon salt and cook, stirring frequently, until softened, 5 to 7 minutes. Stir in tomatoes and their juice, olives, and preserved lemon. Spread mixture in even layer on bottom of pot.

4 Toss cod with cilantro mixture until evenly coated, then arrange cod over vegetables in single layer. Cover and cook until cod starts to turn opaque and juices released from cod are simmering vigorously, 3 to 5 minutes. Remove pot from heat and let sit, covered, until cod flakes apart when gently prodded with paring knife and registers 140 degrees, 3 to 5 minutes. Season with salt and pepper to taste. Sprinkle with chopped cilantro and serve.

Cals 400 | Total Fat 32g | Sat Fat 5g
Chol 75mg | Sodium 1440mg
Total Carb 11g | Dietary Fiber 2g
Total Sugars 3g | Protein 31g

HALIBUT PUTTANESCA

4 (4- to 6-ounce) skinless halibut fillets, 1 inch thick

½ teaspoon table salt

½ teaspoon pepper

¼ cup extra-virgin olive oil, plus extra for drizzling

1 shallot, minced

5 garlic cloves, sliced thin

1 (2-ounce) can anchovies, drained and chopped

2 teaspoons dried oregano

½ teaspoon red pepper flakes

1 (14.5-ounce) can diced tomatoes

½ cup pitted kalamata olives

¼ cup capers, rinsed

¼ cup fresh parsley leaves

WHY THIS RECIPE WORKS Halibut puttanesca—a dish of mild fish simmered in a puttanesca-inspired tomato sauce that's punched up with spicy pepper flakes, garlic, briny olives and capers, and plenty of savory anchovies—brings bold flavor and heft to fish in a flash. We sauté shallot, garlic, anchovies, oregano, and red pepper flakes in the skillet; add canned tomatoes; and then nestle the halibut fillets into the pan of sauce, which we cook gently in the oven. The tomato sauce slowly reduces as it cooks, concentrating its flavor. A mixture of kalamata olives and capers adds pops of savory saltiness to the sauce. Using a whole 2-ounce can of anchovies may sound like a lot, but the anchovies mellow in the sauce and give it an incredible depth of flavor. A shower of parsley before serving adds freshness and color to this bold, simple supper. Note that we do not drain the canned tomatoes before adding them to the sauce. One 2-ounce can of anchovies equals roughly 1½ tablespoons once chopped. Mahi-mahi, red snapper, striped bass, or swordfish can be substituted for the halibut. Serve with crusty bread or couscous and a simple stovetop side, like green beans or pan-roasted cauliflower.

1 Adjust oven rack to middle position and heat oven to 375 degrees. Sprinkle halibut with salt and pepper; set aside. Add oil, shallot, garlic, anchovies, oregano, and pepper flakes to 12-inch ovensafe nonstick skillet and cook over medium-low heat until fragrant and shallot softens, about 4 minutes.

2 Stir in tomatoes and their juice, olives, and capers. Nestle halibut into sauce and bring to simmer over medium-high heat. Transfer skillet to oven and bake until fish flakes apart when gently prodded with paring knife and registers 130 degrees, 10 to 15 minutes.

3 Using spatula, transfer halibut to serving platter. Stir sauce to recombine, then spoon over halibut. Sprinkle with parsley and drizzle with extra oil. Serve.

Cals 310 | Total Fat 18g | Sat Fat 2.5g
Chol 70mg | Sodium 1390mg
Total Carb 9g | Dietary Fiber 3g
Total Sugars 3g | Protein 27g

HALIBUT
PUTTANESCA

ROASTED SALMON WITH WHITE BEANS, FENNEL, AND TOMATOES

- 2 (1-pound) fennel bulbs, stalks discarded, bulbs halved, cored, and sliced ¼ inch thick

- 2 tablespoons extra-virgin olive oil, divided

- 1¼ teaspoons table salt, divided

- ¾ teaspoon pepper, divided

- 2 (15-ounce) cans cannellini beans, rinsed

- 10 ounces cherry tomatoes, halved (2 cups)

- ¼ cup dry white wine

- 3 garlic cloves (2 sliced thin, 1 minced)

- 6 tablespoons unsalted butter, softened

- 1 teaspoon minced fresh thyme

- 1 teaspoon grated lemon zest, plus 1 tablespoon juice

- 4 (4- to 6-ounce) skinless center-cut salmon fillets, 1 to 1½ inches thick

- 2 tablespoons chopped fresh parsley

WHY THIS RECIPE WORKS The vibrant abundance of vegetables packed into this one-pan meal belies its simplicity. We stagger the addition of ingredients to ensure perfect cooking, starting by roasting sliced fennel, which needs some solo oven time to soften and develop tasty browning. After that, we stir in cherry tomatoes, white beans, and garlic and place salmon fillets—which we coat with a tasty compound butter—right on top before roasting everything together. The cherry tomatoes give off flavorful juices, which, with the addition of extra compound butter and some lemon juice, make a luscious sauce that ties the dish together. To ensure uniform pieces of salmon that cook at the same rate, buy a whole 1½-pound center-cut fillet and cut it into four equal pieces. If using wild salmon, cook the fillets to 120 degrees (for medium-rare).

1 Adjust oven rack to middle position and heat oven to 450 degrees. Toss fennel, 1 tablespoon oil, ¼ teaspoon salt, and ¼ teaspoon pepper together on rimmed baking sheet. Spread fennel into even layer and roast until beginning to brown around edges, about 15 minutes.

2 Meanwhile, toss beans, tomatoes, wine, sliced garlic, ½ teaspoon salt, ¼ teaspoon pepper, and remaining 1 tablespoon oil together in bowl. Combine butter, thyme, lemon zest, and minced garlic in small bowl. Pat salmon dry with paper towels and sprinkle with remaining ½ teaspoon salt and remaining ¼ teaspoon pepper. Spread 1 tablespoon butter mixture on top of each fillet.

3 Remove sheet from oven. Add bean mixture to sheet with fennel, stir to combine, and spread into even layer. Arrange salmon on top of bean mixture, butter side up. Roast until centers of fillets register 125 degrees (for medium-rare), 12 to 18 minutes.

4 Transfer salmon to serving platter. Stir lemon juice and remaining 2 tablespoons butter mixture into bean mixture, transfer to serving platter with salmon, and sprinkle with parsley. Serve.

Cals 670 | Total Fat 39g | Sat Fat 15g
Chol 105mg | Sodium 1290mg
Total Carb 43g | Dietary Fiber 15g
Total Sugars 13g | Protein 36g

STEAMED MUSSELS WITH MERGUEZ

SERVES 4 TO 6

45 MINS

- 2 tablespoons extra-virgin olive oil

- 3 shallots, sliced thin

- 8 ounces merguez sausage, casings removed

- 3 garlic cloves, sliced thin

- 1 (28-ounce) can crushed tomatoes

- ½ teaspoon lime zest, plus lime wedges for serving

- 4 pounds mussels, scrubbed and debearded

- ¼ cup fresh cilantro leaves

WHY THIS RECIPE WORKS Mussels are enjoyed across the Mediterranean, from Spain to Israel to North Africa. Steaming mussels is a simple and fast way to enjoy them, as they come with their own built-in, briny-sweet broth that pairs well with a variety of flavors. To start, sweating shallots and garlic provides a nice aromatic base for the mussels. But to build most of our flavor, we turn to merguez sausage, a staple in Maghrebi cuisine. Merguez is a spicy fresh sausage typically made from ground lamb and abundantly spiced with garlic, cumin, and harissa, which gives it its characteristic heat and red color. We crumble and render just a small amount of sausage in the aromatics to release its full flavor potential before adding crushed tomatoes to create a hearty and robust stewy base for steaming the mussels. A final touch of lime zest and cilantro add fresh balance to this savory meal. Discard any raw mussel with an unpleasant odor or with a cracked shell or a shell that won't close. Serve with toasted crusty bread.

1 Heat oil in large Dutch oven over medium heat until shimmering. Add shallots and cook until softened, about 3 minutes. Add sausage, breaking up meat with wooden spoon, and cook until browned, 5 to 7 minutes. Stir in garlic and cook until fragrant, about 30 seconds. Stir in tomatoes and lime zest, bring to simmer, and cook until thickened slightly and flavors meld, 10 to 12 minutes.

2 Increase heat to high and stir in mussels. Cover and cook, stirring occasionally, until mussels open, 4 to 6 minutes. Discard any unopened mussels.

3 Off heat, stir in cilantro. Transfer mussels to individual serving bowls and spoon any remaining broth over top. Serve with lime wedges.

Cals 480 | Total Fat 22g | Sat Fat 6g
Chol 110mg | Sodium 1540mg
Total Carb 25g | Dietary Fiber 3g
Total Sugars 7g | Protein 44g

A Most Prized Fruit

Olive oil is the liquid gold of the Mediterranean. Thus, olive trees and their fruit are beloved and used throughout cuisines of the region. There are far too many olive varieties to list here. But whatever the variety, all olives are harvested from October to January. The time of their harvest determines their color and flavor. A highly bitter, naturally occurring chemical renders olives inedible straight from the tree, so curing is necessary. Some olives are cured with salt, some with salt and water (brine), and others with oil or lye. We use both brine- and oil-cured black and green olives in this book.

BAKED SHRIMP WITH FENNEL, POTATOES, AND OLIVES

1½   pounds Yukon Gold potatoes, peeled and sliced ½ inch thick

2   fennel bulbs, stalks discarded, bulbs halved and cut into 1-inch-thick wedges

3   tablespoons extra-virgin olive oil, divided, plus extra for drizzling

1½   teaspoons table salt, divided

½   teaspoon pepper, divided

2   pounds jumbo shrimp (16 to 20 per pound), peeled, deveined, and tails removed

2   teaspoons dried oregano

1   teaspoon grated lemon zest, plus lemon wedges for serving

4   ounces feta cheese, crumbled (1 cup)

½   cup pitted kalamata olives, halved

2   tablespoons chopped fresh parsley

WHY THIS RECIPE WORKS The bold flavors of oregano and lemon infuse quick-cooking sweet shrimp with big flavor, and adding vegetables to the pan easily turns this dish into a complete sheet pan meal with little fuss and lots of flavor. Since shrimp cook so quickly, we first roast our vegetables—potatoes and fennel—in the oven before scattering the shellfish over the top to roast while the vegetables finish. Complementary choices of briny kalamata olives and salty feta cheese give this simple dish a savory bite, and lemon juice brings it all to life. Don't core the fennel before cutting it into wedges; the core helps hold the wedges together during cooking.

1 Adjust oven rack to lower-middle position and heat oven to 450 degrees. Toss potatoes and fennel with 2 tablespoons oil, 1 teaspoon salt, and ¼ teaspoon pepper in bowl. Spread vegetables in single layer on rimmed baking sheet and roast until just tender, about 25 minutes.

2 Pat shrimp dry with paper towels. Toss shrimp with oregano, lemon zest, remaining 1 tablespoon oil, remaining ½ teaspoon salt, and remaining ¼ teaspoon pepper in now-empty bowl.

3 Using spatula, flip potatoes and fennel so browned sides are facing up. Scatter shrimp and feta over top. Return to oven and roast until shrimp are cooked through, 6 to 8 minutes. Sprinkle olives and parsley over top and drizzle with extra oil. Serve with lemon wedges.

Cals 350 | Total Fat 13g | Sat Fat 4g
Chol 205mg | Sodium 1060mg
Total Carb 29g | Dietary Fiber 3g
Total Sugars 4g | Protein 27g

SALMON EN COCOTTE WITH ROASTED GARLIC AND CHERRY TOMATOES

SERVES 4

45 MINS

¼   cup extra-virgin olive oil, divided

2   garlic cloves, sliced thin

⅛   teaspoon red pepper flakes

    Pinch plus ½ teaspoon table salt, divided

12 ounces cherry tomatoes, quartered

1   tablespoon capers, rinsed

1   teaspoon minced fresh thyme

4   (4- to 6- ounce) skinless salmon fillets, 1 to 1½ inches thick

¼   teaspoon pepper

WHY THIS RECIPE WORKS Cooking en cocotte (in a casserole) is a French technique that's a variation on braising: It uses a covered pot, a low oven temperature, and an extended cooking time to yield tender results to its subject—with no liquid in the pan. Here, meaty, clean-tasting salmon cooks in its own juices along with a punctuating bold, briny sauce of olive oil, garlic, thyme, capers, red pepper flakes, and tomatoes. Cooking sliced garlic in olive oil until browned draws out its flavor for a dish with incredible aroma. Finishing with a splash of extra-virgin olive oil rounds out the flavors and gives the dish a lush feel. To ensure uniform pieces of salmon that cook at the same rate, buy a whole 1½-pound center-cut fillet and cut it into four equal pieces. If using wild salmon, cook the fillets to 120 degrees (for medium-rare).

1 Adjust oven rack to lowest position and heat oven to 250 degrees. Cook 2 tablespoons oil, garlic, pepper flakes, and pinch salt in Dutch oven over medium-low heat until garlic is light golden, 2 to 4 minutes. Off heat, stir in tomatoes, capers, and thyme.

2 Pat salmon dry with paper towels, sprinkle with remaining ½ teaspoon salt and pepper, and lay on top of tomatoes in pot. Place large piece of aluminum foil over pot and cover tightly with lid; transfer pot to oven. Cook until center of salmon is still translucent when checked with tip of paring knife and registers 125 degrees (for medium-rare), 20 to 30 minutes.

3 Transfer salmon to serving platter. Bring tomato mixture to simmer over medium-high heat until slightly thickened, about 2 minutes. Off heat, stir in remaining 2 tablespoons oil and season with salt and pepper to taste. Spoon sauce over salmon and serve.

Cals 380 | Total Fat 29g | Sat Fat 5g
Chol 60mg | Sodium 450mg
Total Carb 4g | Dietary Fiber 1g
Total Sugars 2g | Protein 24g

GRILLED SWORDFISH SKEWERS WITH ZUCCHINI

SERVES 4 TO 6

30 MINS

1½ pounds skinless swordfish steaks, 1¼ inches thick, cut into 1¼-inch pieces

1 tablespoon ground coriander

¾ teaspoon table salt, divided

½ teaspoon pepper, divided

6 tablespoons extra-virgin olive oil, divided

3 zucchini, halved lengthwise

3 tablespoons chopped fresh basil

1 small shallot, minced

WHY THIS RECIPE WORKS Large swordfish have a grand presence in the Mediterranean Sea. The fish, eaten especially frequently in Greece, Italy, and Spain, has a robust taste and calls for seasonings with as much oomph. Grill flavor brings character on its own, and cubing and skewering the swordfish creates more surface area for char. Here the robust flavor comes from a generous coriander spice rub. A quick basil and olive oil mixture lavishes the grilled swordfish and a simple zucchini side freshens the dish. You will need six 12-inch metal skewers for this recipe. Halibut, mahi-mahi, red snapper, or striped bass can be substituted for the swordfish.

1 Pat swordfish dry with paper towels and sprinkle with coriander, ½ teaspoon salt, and ¼ teaspoon pepper. Thread fish onto three 12-inch metal skewers. Brush swordfish with 1 tablespoon oil. Brush zucchini with 1 tablespoon oil and sprinkle with ¼ teaspoon salt and ¼ teaspoon pepper.

2A For a charcoal grill Open bottom vent completely. Light large chimney starter three-quarters filled with charcoal briquettes (4½ quarts). When top coals are partially covered with ash, pour evenly over grill. Set cooking grate in place, cover, and open lid vent completely. Heat grill until hot, about 5 minutes.

2B For a gas grill Turn all burners to high, cover, and heat grill until hot, about 15 minutes. Turn all burners to medium-high.

3 Fold paper towels into compact wad. Holding paper towels with tongs, dip in oil, then wipe grate. Dip paper towels in oil again and wipe grate for second time. Cover grill and heat for 5 minutes. Uncover and wipe grate twice more with oiled paper towels. Place swordfish and zucchini on grill. Cook (covered if using gas), turning as needed, until swordfish flakes apart when gently prodded with paring knife and registers 130 degrees and zucchini is tender and lightly charred, 5 to 10 minutes. Transfer items to serving platter as they finish grilling and tent with aluminum foil to keep warm.

4 Combine remaining ¼ cup oil, basil, and shallot in bowl and season with salt and pepper to taste. Remove swordfish from skewers and drizzle swordfish and zucchini with oil mixture before serving.

Cals 310 | Total Fat 22g | Sat Fat 4g
Chol 75mg | Sodium 390mg
Total Carb 4g | Dietary Fiber 1g
Total Sugars 3g | Protein 24g

GARLICKY ROASTED SHRIMP WITH CILANTRO AND LIME

**SERVES
6 TO 8**

30 MINS

2 pounds shell-on jumbo shrimp
  (16 to 20 per pound)

½ cup extra-virgin olive oil

6 garlic cloves, minced

2 tablespoons coriander seeds,
  cracked

2 teaspoons grated lime zest,
  plus lime wedges for serving

1 teaspoon annatto powder

½ teaspoon table salt

½ teaspoon red pepper flakes

¼ tablespoons minced
  fresh cilantro

WHY THIS RECIPE WORKS Roasting shrimp is an excellent way to concentrate the sweet shellfish's flavor and give it real presence at mealtime along with whatever complementary dishes you choose. We butterfly the shrimp, slicing through the shells but not removing them. The shells protect the delicate shrimp from the oven's heat while also boosting shrimp flavor—they're almost the best part. After tossing the shrimp in olive oil infused with garlic, spices, and herbs, we elevate them on a wire rack set in a rimmed baking sheet and slide them under the broiler. Within minutes, our shrimp emerge tender and deeply fragrant beneath flavorful, browned shells that you can choose to eat or remove. Serve with stovetop greens, grains, or both for a vibrant simple meal. Don't be tempted to use smaller shrimp for this recipe—they will likely end up overseasoned and overcooked. We prefer untreated shrimp; if yours are treated with additives such as sodium tripolyphosphate, omit the salt.

1 Adjust oven rack 4 inches from broiler element and heat broiler. Using kitchen shears or sharp paring knife, cut through shell of shrimp and devein but do not remove shell. Using paring knife, continue to cut shrimp ½ inch deep, taking care not to cut in half completely. Pat shrimp dry with paper towels.

2 Combine oil, garlic, coriander seeds, lime zest, annatto powder, salt, and pepper flakes in large bowl. Add shrimp and cilantro to oil mixture and toss well, making sure oil mixture gets into interior of shrimp. Arrange shrimp in single layer on wire rack set in rimmed baking sheet.

3 Broil shrimp until opaque and shells are beginning to brown, 2 to 4 minutes, rotating sheet halfway through broiling. Flip shrimp and continue to broil until second side is opaque and shells are beginning to brown, 2 to 4 minutes longer, rotating sheet halfway through broiling. Transfer shrimp to serving platter. Serve with lime wedges.

*Cals 190 | Total Fat 15g | Sat Fat 2g
Chol 105mg | Sodium 270mg
Total Carb 2g | Dietary Fiber 0g
Total Sugars 0g | Protein 12g*

GRILLED WHOLE TROUT WITH ORANGE AND FENNEL

SERVES 4

45 MINS

2 teaspoons kosher salt

1 teaspoon ground fennel

1 teaspoon grated orange zest

4 (10- to 12-ounce) whole trout, scaled, gutted, and fins snipped off with scissors

¼ teaspoon pepper

2 tablespoons mayonnaise

½ teaspoon honey

1 (13 by 9-inch) disposable aluminum pan (if using charcoal)

WHY THIS RECIPE WORKS Grill-roasting trout until smoky and crispy-skinned is an impressive way to present whole fish, which is so commonly found on tables throughout the Mediterranean. Cooking whole fish shouldn't be feared, and trout are particularly accessible because they are almost always sold cleaned, scaled, and gutted. And one fish serves one person for nice portioning. We brush mayonnaise and honey over the fish to brown it quickly and enhance the skin. Ground fennel and orange zest are sprinkled inside and perfume the whole fish. A chopped fruit or vegetable salad or a light grain pilaf (maybe Cantaloupe Salad with Olives and Red Onion on page 50 or Barley with Fennel and Dried Apricots on page 188) waiting in the wings would be ideal sides. To take the temperature of the fish, insert the thermometer into the fillets through the opening by the gills.

1 Place salt, fennel, and orange zest on cutting board and chop until finely minced and well combined. Pat trout dry with paper towels inside and out. Open up each fish and sprinkle fennel mixture and pepper evenly over flesh. Close up fish and let sit for 10 minutes. Stir mayonnaise and honey together. Brush mayonnaise mixture evenly over entire exterior of each fish.

2A For a charcoal grill Using kitchen shears, poke twelve ½-inch holes in bottom of disposable pan. Open bottom vent completely and place disposable pan in center of grill. Light large chimney starter two-thirds filled with charcoal briquettes (4 quarts). When top coals are partially covered with ash, pour into even layer in disposable pan. Set cooking grate in place with bars parallel to long side of pan, cover, and open lid vent completely. Heat grill until hot, about 5 minutes.

2B For a gas grill Turn all burners to high, cover, and heat grill until hot, about 15 minutes. Leave all burners on high.

3 Fold paper towels into compact wad. Holding paper towels with tongs, dip in oil, then wipe grate. Dip paper towels in oil again and wipe grate for second time. Cover grill and heat for 5 minutes. Uncover and wipe grate twice more with oiled paper towels. Place trout on grill, perpendicular to grate bars (directly over disposable pan if using charcoal). Cook (covered if using gas) until skin is browned and beginning to blister, 2 to 4 minutes. Gently flip trout and cook until second side is browned and beginning to blister, and fish registers 135 degrees, 2 to 4 minutes. Serve.

Cals 410 | Total Fat 20g | Sat Fat 4g
Chol 175mg | Sodium 920mg
Total Carb 1g | Dietary Fiber 0g
Total Sugars 1g | Protein 57g

PAN-SEARED SHRIMP WITH PISTACHIOS, CUMIN, AND PARSLEY

SERVES
4 TO 6

45 MINS

1½ pounds extra-large shrimp (21 to 25 per pound), peeled, deveined, and tails removed

1 teaspoon kosher salt, divided

1 garlic clove, minced

1 teaspoon ground cumin

1 teaspoon paprika

⅛ teaspoon cayenne pepper

2 tablespoons extra-virgin olive oil, divided

⅛ teaspoon sugar

¼ cup fresh cilantro leaves and tender stems, chopped

¼ cup fresh parsley leaves and tender stems, chopped

1 tablespoon lemon juice

¼ cup shelled pistachios or whole almonds, toasted and chopped coarse

WHY THIS RECIPE WORKS One look at these pan-seared shrimp will tell you that their flavor and texture are superlatively bold. A robust seasoning mixture—fresh garlic, cumin, paprika, and cayenne—blooms in the same pan that was used to cook the shrimp and then gets tossed with the seared shrimp. Once the shrimp are coated in spice, we incorporate lots of freshness with generous amounts of chopped cilantro and parsley and some lemon juice. A crunchy pistachio topping finishes the shrimp with style. For a vegetable, pair with roasted carrots, serve over cauliflower puree (see page 116), or cool things down with a cucumber and tomato salad. We prefer untreated shrimp; if yours are treated with additives such as sodium tripolyphosphate, skip the salting in step 1. You can substitute jumbo shrimp (16 to 20 per pound) for the extra-large shrimp, if desired; if substituting, increase the cooking time by 1 to 2 minutes.

1 Toss shrimp with ½ teaspoon salt in bowl; set aside for 15 to 30 minutes. Combine garlic, cumin, paprika, cayenne, and remaining ½ teaspoon salt in small bowl.

2 Pat shrimp dry with paper towels. Add 1 tablespoon oil and sugar to bowl with shrimp and toss to coat. Add shrimp to cold 12-inch nonstick skillet in single layer and cook over high heat until undersides of shrimp are spotty brown and edges turn pink, 3 to 4 minutes. Remove skillet from heat. Working quickly, use tongs to flip each shrimp; let sit until second side is opaque, about 2 minutes. Transfer shrimp to plate.

3 Add remaining 1 tablespoon oil to now-empty skillet. Add spice mixture and cook over medium heat until fragrant, about 30 seconds. Off heat, return shrimp and any accumulated juices to skillet. Add cilantro, parsley, and lemon juice and toss to combine. Transfer to serving platter, sprinkle with pistachios, and serve.

Cals 140 | Total Fat 8g | Sat Fat 1g
Chol 105mg | Sodium 320mg
Total Carb 3g | Dietary Fiber 1g
Total Sugars 1g | Protein 13g

SIMPLE PROTEIN OPTIONS

This book emphasizes the plant-forward nature of the Mediterranean diet. Sometimes you might want to round out your plate of vegetables or grains with a protein source without making it the centerpiece of the meal—a little shredded chicken to bulk up a salad, some golden slabs of seared tempeh to sit next to braised vegetables, or just a perfectly fried egg to top nearly anything. Here are some simple recipes that will help get a balanced dinner on the table while you focus on building flavor in other dishes from the book.

SEARED TEMPEH

SERVES 4   TOTAL TIME: 20 MINS

Since tempeh has such a concentration of protein and is so good at absorbing flavor, we love using it as a plant-based accompaniment to a meal. Pan-searing the tempeh creates a delectably crispy edge and makes the interior texture cohesive. The tempeh's earthy flavor is well balanced by bright sauces and accompaniments. Try tempeh where you might cook a conventional steak, as a side to salads like Roasted Pattypan Squash Salad with Dandelion Green Pesto (page 44) where it can share its sauce, or to make dishes like Beet Barley Risotto (page 227) extra hearty.

1   pound tempeh
3   tablespoons extra-virgin olive oil

1 Cut each block of tempeh into 4 even pieces, then halve each piece into approximately ¼-inch-thick slabs. Season with salt and pepper.

2 Heat oil in 12-inch nonstick skillet over medium heat until shimmering. Add 8 pieces tempeh and cook until golden brown on first side, 2 to 4 minutes. Flip tempeh, reduce heat to medium-low, and continue to cook until golden brown on second side, 2 to 4 minutes. Transfer to platter. Repeat with remaining tempeh and serve.

CRISPY TOFU

SERVES 6
TOTAL TIME: 40 MINS PLUS 20 MINS DRAINING

Batons of tofu are an excellent topping for a vibrant salad or warm bowl of grains. Dredged in cornmeal and cornstarch, the coating is a crispy-crunchy foil to the custardy interior texture of medium-firm or soft tofu after pan-frying. Try these sensational sticks with Pan-Steamed Kale with Baharat (page 132), atop Brown Rice Salad with Fennel, Mushrooms, and Walnuts (page 176), or even in place of the feta in our Feta, Jicama, and Tomato Salad (page 43).

28   ounces soft tofu, cut into 3-inch-long by ½-inch-thick fingers
¾   cup cornstarch
¼   cup cornmeal
2   tablespoons extra-virgin olive oil

1 Place tofu on paper towel–lined baking sheet; let drain for 20 minutes, then pat dry with paper towels. Adjust oven rack to middle position, place paper towel–lined platter on rack, and heat oven to 200 degrees.

2 Set wire rack in rimmed baking sheet. Whisk cornstarch and cornmeal together in shallow dish. Season tofu with salt and pepper. Working with several pieces of tofu at a time, coat tofu thoroughly with cornstarch mixture, pressing gently to adhere, then transfer to wire rack.

3 Heat 1 tablespoon oil in 12-inch nonstick skillet over medium-high heat until shimmering. Gently add half of tofu to skillet and cook, using spatula to carefully turn pieces, until crisp and lightly golden on all sides, 10 to 12 minutes. Transfer tofu to plate in oven. Repeat with remaining 1 tablespoon oil and remaining tofu. Serve.

2 Increase heat to medium-high and heat until oil is shimmering. Working quickly, pour 1 bowl of eggs into 1 side of skillet and second bowl of eggs into other side. Cover and cook for 1 minute. Remove skillet from heat and let stand, covered, for 15 to 45 seconds for runny yolks (white around edge of yolk will be barely opaque), 45 to 60 seconds for soft but set yolks, or about 2 minutes for medium-set yolks. Slide eggs onto plates and serve.

SOFT-COOKED EGGS

MAKES 4 EGGS   TOTAL TIME: 20 MINS

Soft-cooked eggs like to bathe in a bowl of something warm and creamy, or among twirls of hearty greens. Our foolproof method delivers a set white and a fluid yolk every time. We call for fridge-cold eggs and boiling water: This reduces temperature variables, which provides the steepest temperature gradient to ensure that the yolk at the center stays fluid while the white cooks through. Add soft-cooked eggs to your Triple Pea Salad (page 37), Spiced Eggplant and Kale Soup (page 77), creamy Cauliflower Puree with Blistered Tomatoes and 'Nduja (page 116), or simply a bowl of sautéed spinach (see page 112) or polenta (see page 233). Be sure to use large eggs that have no cracks and are cold from the refrigerator. Because precise timing is vital to the success of this recipe, we strongly recommend using a digital timer. If you have one, a steamer basket does make lowering the eggs into the boiling water easier.

   4   large eggs

1 Bring ½ inch water to boil in medium saucepan over medium-high heat. Using tongs, gently place eggs in boiling water (eggs will not be submerged). Cover saucepan and cook eggs for 6½ minutes.

2 Remove cover, transfer saucepan to sink, and place under cold running water for 30 seconds. Remove eggs from pan and serve, seasoning with salt and pepper to taste.

PERFECT FRIED EGGS

MAKES 4 EGGS   TOTAL TIME: 15 MINS

It's hard to think of anything a fried egg can't top. It's great for adding a little bit extra—extra protein, yes, but also extra richness—to a number of vegetable and grain dishes in this book. Pick one, add an egg, and you have a complete meal with ease. If fried eggs are so versatile, we want them to be perfect—set but not rubbery whites and perfectly runny yolks. We achieve this by starting in a hot nonstick skillet with some oil to crisp and set the bottoms and then covering with the lid and letting the egg finish off heat. And it all takes just a few minutes.

   4   teaspoons extra-virgin olive oil
   4   large eggs

1 Heat oil in 12- or 14-inch nonstick skillet over low heat for 5 minutes. Meanwhile, crack 2 eggs into small bowl and season with salt and pepper. Repeat with remaining 2 eggs and second small bowl.

ROASTED SALMON FILLETS

SERVES 4   TOTAL TIME: 25 MINS

Salmon fillets are one of the top cuts of fish to cook, and there's good reason for that. They're a weeknight workhorse—a rich and satisfying, nutritious addition to your meal. To get dinner on the table with ease, while firing up other dishes for your plate, we turn to a dual-temperature roasting technique; it's a hands-off way to serve up fish with a nicely browned exterior. You can serve a whole fillet next to dishes like Cantaloupe Salad with Olives and Red Onion (page 50), Horta (page 127), or Red Rice and Quinoa Salad with Blood Oranges (page 180), or you can flake the salmon over salads like Beet Salad with Spiced Yogurt and Watercress (page 27). It is important to keep the skin on during cooking; remove it afterward if desired. You can substitute arctic char or wild salmon for farmed salmon; if using them cook the fillets to 120 degrees (for medium-rare) and start checking for doneness after 4 minutes.

4	(4- to 6-ounce) skin-on salmon fillets, 1 inch thick
2	teaspoons extra-virgin olive oil
½	teaspoon table salt
¼	teaspoon pepper

1 Adjust oven rack to lowest position, place aluminum foil–lined rimmed baking sheet on rack, and heat oven to 500 degrees. Make 4 or 5 shallow slashes, about 1 inch apart, on skin side of each fillet, being careful not to cut into flesh. Pat salmon dry with paper towels, rub with oil, and sprinkle with salt and pepper.

2 Reduce oven temperature to 275 degrees and use oven mitts to remove sheet from oven. Carefully place salmon skin side down on hot sheet. Roast until center is still translucent when checked with tip of paring knife and registers 125 degrees (for medium-rare), 8 to 12 minutes. Transfer salmon to platter and serve.

PAN-ROASTED COD

SERVES 4   TOTAL TIME: 20 MINS

There's not much that's more pristine than a perfectly portioned moist white fish fillet sporting a chestnut-brown crust with some crispness—and almost nothing that's more convenient than its minutes-long cooking time. We use a common technique borrowed from professional kitchens: Sear the fillets in a hot pan, flip, then transfer to an oven to continue cooking rather than finishing on the stove. A well-browned crust appeared in around a minute, giving the interior time to turn succulent in the oven. This beautiful piece of fish is the perfect partner to Chopped Vegetable and Stone Fruit Salad (page 32), Riced Cauliflower with Preserved Lemon (page 123), or Spelt Salad with Pickled Fennel, Pea Greens, and Mint (page 162). You can substitute black sea bass, haddock, hake, or pollock for the cod.

- 4   (4- to 6-ounce) skinless cod fillets, 1 inch thick
- ½   teaspoon table salt
- ¼   teaspoon pepper
- ½   teaspoon sugar
- 1   tablespoon extra-virgin olive oil

1 Adjust oven rack to middle position and heat oven to 425 degrees. Pat cod dry with paper towels, sprinkle with salt and pepper, and sprinkle sugar lightly over 1 side of each fillet.

2 Heat oil in 12-inch ovensafe nonstick skillet over medium-high heat until just smoking. Lay fillets sugared side down in skillet and, using spatula, lightly press fillets for 20 to 30 seconds to ensure even contact with skillet. Cook until browned on first side, 1 to 2 minutes.

3 Using 2 spatulas, flip fillets, then transfer skillet to oven. Roast until fish flakes apart when gently prodded with paring knife and registers 135 degrees, 7 to 10 minutes. Transfer cod to platter and serve.

POACHED CHICKEN BREASTS

SERVES 4 TO 6   TOTAL TIME: 55 MINS

Poaching might be the best, most foolproof way to cook lean chicken breasts. And once poached, you can slice the juicy chicken breasts to serve with your dish or shred them into bite-size pieces for a cohesive meal. To ensure moist, judiciously seasoned chicken, we arrange the breasts in a steamer basket, submerge the basket in a Dutch oven filled with salted water, and bring the water up to 175 degrees over medium heat. We then shut off the heat, cover the pot, and let the chicken cook gently via the salted water's residual heat until the chicken registers a perfect 160 degrees. Serve chicken with a side like Roasted Fennel with Crunchy Oil-Cured Olives (page 126) or add shredded chicken to Roasted Cipollini and Escarole Salad (page 49).

- 4   (4- to 6-ounce) boneless, skinless chicken breasts, trimmed
- 2   tablespoons salt

1 Cover chicken with plastic wrap and pound thick ends gently with meat pounder until ¾ inch thick.

2 Whisk 4 quarts cool water with salt in large Dutch oven. Arrange chicken in steamer basket, making sure not to overlap. Submerge steamer basket in pot. Heat over medium heat, stirring occasionally to even out hot spots, until water registers 175 degrees, 15 to 20 minutes. Turn off heat, cover pot, remove pot from burner, and let stand until chicken registers 160 degrees, 17 to 22 minutes. Transfer chicken to cutting board and let cool, for 10 to 15 minutes. Serve.

SEARED FLANK STEAK

SERVES 6   TOTAL TIME: 20 MINS

Just a small amount of steak can increase the richness and protein of a dish for ultimate satiety. Lean flank steak is a good choice that cooks quick—just a hard sear on each side—and slices up nice. Serve with Sweet Potato Salad with Cumin, Smoked Paprika, and Almonds (page 38), Quinoa Pilaf with Olives, Raisins, and Cilantro (page 191), or on top of Roasted Cauliflower and Grape Salad with Chermoula (page 60).

1 (1½-pound) flank steak, trimmed and halved lengthwise
1 tablespoon extra-virgin olive oil

Pat steak dry with paper towels and season with salt and pepper. Heat oil in 12-inch nonstick skillet over medium-high heat until just smoking. Cook steak until well browned and meat registers 120 to 125 degrees (for medium-rare), 5 to 7 minutes per side. Transfer steak to cutting board, tent with foil, and let rest for 5 minutes. Serve.

CHICKEN SALAD WITH PICKLED FENNEL AND MACADAMIA NUTS

**SERVES
4 TO 6**

30 MINS

¾ cup seasoned rice vinegar

¼ cup water

1 garlic clove, peeled and smashed

1 (3-inch) strip orange zest

¼ teaspoon fennel seeds

⅛ teaspoon black peppercorns

⅛ teaspoon mustard seeds

1 fennel bulb, stalks discarded, 2 tablespoons fronds minced and bulb halved, cored, and sliced thin

2 tablespoons extra-virgin olive oil

¼ teaspoon table salt

4 cups shredded cooked chicken

10 ounces (10 cups) watercress, torn into bite-size pieces

½ cup macadamia nuts or cashews, toasted and chopped

WHY THIS RECIPE WORKS A pickled element is a most welcome vegetable meal booster, as the technique imbues fresh, crunchy vegetables with complexity and nuance, tenderizes raw textures, and introduces punchy flavor. And it's not just for cucumbers. Here a quick stint in a spiced, hot brine rounds out the fresh, vegetal flavor of fennel with the more floral notes of fennel seeds. We gently poach some chicken breasts for the salad and then make further use of the flavorful pickling liquid by incorporating it into our vinaigrette. We toss spicy watercress, macadamia nuts, the pickled fennel, and some fennel fronds with our perfectly cooked chicken for a refreshing meal. If your fennel comes without fronds, they can be omitted. We like using Poached Chicken Breasts (page 360) here, but any cooked chicken would work.

1 Microwave vinegar, water, garlic, orange zest, fennel seeds, peppercorns, and mustard seeds in medium bowl until steaming, about 5 minutes. Stir in sliced fennel bulb until completely submerged and let cool completely, about 30 minutes. (Pickled fennel can be refrigerated for up to 1 month.)

2 Drain fennel, reserving ⅓ cup brine; discard garlic and spices. Whisk reserved brine, oil, and salt in large bowl. Add chicken, watercress, pickled fennel, and fennel fronds and toss to combine. Season with salt and pepper to taste. Sprinkle with macadamia nuts and serve.

Cals 280 | Total Fat 16g | Sat Fat 2.5g
Chol 85mg | Sodium 290mg
Total Carb 5g | Dietary Fiber 2g
Total Sugars 2g | Protein 28g

TURMERIC RICE AND CHICKEN SALAD

SERVES
4

1 HR

1 cup long-grain white or jasmine rice

½ teaspoon table salt, plus salt for cooking rice

3 tablespoons extra-virgin olive oil

2 garlic cloves, minced

1 teaspoon ground cumin

1 teaspoon paprika

1 teaspoon ground turmeric

⅛ teaspoon cayenne pepper

Pinch ground cinnamon

3 tablespoons lemon juice

2 cups chopped cooked chicken

6 ounces cherry or grape tomatoes, halved

2 Persian cucumbers, quartered lengthwise and sliced crosswise ¼ inch thick

3 radishes, trimmed, quartered, and sliced thin

1 cup torn fresh cilantro, dill, parsley, or mint

½ cup Garlic Yogurt Sauce (page 16)

WHY THIS RECIPE WORKS We draw inspiration for this salad from Middle Eastern street cart chicken and rice. We use some shawarma seasonings—garlic, turmeric, paprika, cumin, and just a touch of cinnamon—to create a fragrant, flavorful dressing for rice and chopped chicken. Mixing in crunchy sliced cucumbers and radishes and juicy tomatoes freshens the warm-spiced mix. Instead of lettuce, we add herbs—cilantro, parsley, mint, and dill all work, the torn leaves adding intense bursts of flavor in every bite. A lemony-tart herbed yogurt drizzled over the finished salad adds richness and pulls everything together. We like using Poached Chicken Breasts (page 360) here, but any cooked chicken would work. Persian cucumbers (sometimes called "mini cucumbers") are small, slim cucumbers similar to seedless cucumbers in flavor and texture; you can use 6 ounces of English cucumber if Persian cucumbers are not available.

1 Bring 4 quarts water to boil in large pot. Add rice and 1½ teaspoons salt and cook, stirring occasionally, until rice is tender but not soft, about 15 minutes. Drain rice; spread onto rimmed baking sheet; and let cool completely, about 15 minutes.

2 Microwave oil, garlic, cumin, paprika, turmeric, cayenne, and cinnamon in medium bowl until simmering and fragrant, 30 to 60 seconds. Let cool slightly, then whisk in lemon juice and salt.

3 Combine rice, dressing, chicken, tomatoes, cucumbers, radishes, and cilantro in large bowl and toss gently to combine. Season with salt and pepper to taste. Serve with yogurt sauce.

Cals 420 | Total Fat 14g | Sat Fat 3g
Chol 80mg | Sodium 740mg
Total Carb 45g | Dietary Fiber 2g
Total Sugars 4g | Protein 31g

HARISSA WINGS WITH CUCUMBER-TOMATO SALAD

SERVES 4 TO 6

1½ HRS

Chicken Wings

2	pounds chicken wings, halved at joints, wingtips discarded
¼	cup Harissa (page 17), divided
¾	teaspoon table salt
¼	teaspoon pepper
1½	tablespoons honey
1	teaspoon lime zest, plus lime wedges for serving
2	tablespoons cilantro, chopped fine
1	scallion, sliced thin

Cucumber-Tomato Salad

1	English cucumber, quartered lengthwise and sliced ¼ inch thick
2	ripe tomatoes, cored and cut into ¼-inch pieces
½	teaspoon table salt, for salting vegetables
½	cup pitted green olives, chopped coarse
¼	cup fresh mint leaves, shredded
1	tablespoon extra-virgin olive oil
2	tablespoons lemon juice
½	teaspoon pepper

WHY THIS RECIPE WORKS Chicken wings, when combined with a crunchy, refreshing side, can transcend from appetizer to fun and filling main course. Here the chicken is enrobed in harissa for wing-coating heat. We start by roasting the wings with salt and pepper and harissa paste to achieve a layer of deep flavor and lacquering. We combine more harissa with honey (for some balance and requisite sticky goodness) and lime zest and toss the roasted wings in the pool. A final sprinkling of cilantro and scallions provides welcome freshness and an allium bite. Another necessary addition: the cooling counterpoint. A cucumber-and-tomato salad with chopped green olives, fresh mint, lemon juice, and olive oil does the trick and rounds out the plate. We prefer to buy whole chicken wings and butcher them ourselves because they tend to be larger than wings that come presplit. If you can find only presplit wings, opt for larger ones, if possible. This salad is best eaten within 1 hour of being dressed.

1 For the chicken wings Adjust oven rack to middle position and heat oven to 425 degrees. Toss wings with 1 tablespoon harissa, salt, and pepper. Line rimmed baking sheet with aluminum foil and spray with olive oil spray. Arrange wings in single layer, fatty side up, on prepared sheet. Roast until well browned, about 1 hour, rotating sheet halfway through roasting.

2 For the cucumber-tomato salad Meanwhile, toss cucumber, tomatoes, and salt together in colander set over bowl. Let drain for 15 minutes, then discard liquid. Transfer cucumber-tomato mixture to bowl. Add olives, mint, oil, lemon juice, and pepper and toss to combine. Season with salt and pepper to taste.

3 Combine remaining 3 tablespoons harissa, honey, and lime zest in large bowl. Transfer wings to bowl with harissa mixture and toss to combine. Transfer to serving platter and sprinkle with cilantro and scallion. Serve with lime wedges and salad.

Cals 450 | Total Fat 34g | Sat Fat 7g | Chol 135mg | Sodium 1140mg
Total Carb 13g | Dietary Fiber 3g | Total Sugars 7g | Protein 23g

ZA'ATAR CHICKEN SCHNITZEL WITH SWEET POTATO WEDGES

SERVES
4

1 HR

Vinaigrette

- 3 tablespoons minced shallot
- 2 tablespoons red wine vinegar
- 2 tablespoons chopped fresh parsley
- 2 tablespoons chopped fresh tarragon
- 2 tablespoons extra-virgin olive oil
- ⅛ teaspoon table salt

Chicken and Potatoes

- 1½ pounds sweet potatoes, unpeeled, cut lengthwise into 1½-inch-wide wedges
- 1 tablespoon plus ½ cup extra-virgin olive oil, divided
- ¾ teaspoon table salt, divided
- ½ cup all-purpose flour
- 1 large egg
- 1 cup panko bread crumbs
- 2 tablespoons Za'atar (page 15)
- 2 (8-ounce) boneless, skinless chicken breasts, trimmed

Cals 770 | Total Fat 43g | Sat Fat 6g
Chol 130mg | Sodium 700mg
Total Carb 58g | Dietary Fiber 58g
Total Sugars 6g | Protein 34g

WHY THIS RECIPE WORKS A classic Austrian schnitzel is made of veal or pork that's battered and then fried in clarified butter, and the dish is now prevalent, with modifications, in Israeli cuisine. Austrian and German Jews brought the dish to Israel during the 1930s and 40s, but veal was not widely available and pork ran counter to Jewish dietary laws. Chicken and turkey were perfect stand-ins and what you'll commonly find. Often sesame seeds, nigella seeds, or za'atar find their way into the coating in Israeli versions, and they provide appealing extra flavor and crunch. We use za'atar. It's common to find schnitzel served with fries or chips; for a highly nutritious side in that vein, we roast sweet potato wedges until beautifully seared on one side and sweet and fudgy in the center. A zippy, herb-forward vinaigrette balances this sweetness and makes the side just as special as the cutlets. We also enjoy serving this dish with Tahini Sauce (page 16).

1 For the vinaigrette Whisk all ingredients together in bowl; set aside.

2 For the chicken and potatoes Adjust oven rack to middle position and heat oven to 450 degrees. Toss potatoes with 1 tablespoon oil and ¼ teaspoon salt. Arrange potatoes cut side down in even layer on aluminum foil–lined rimmed baking. Roast until potato bottoms are well browned, 20 to 25 minutes. Transfer to serving platter and tent with foil to keep warm.

3 Meanwhile, spread flour in shallow dish. Lightly beat egg in second shallow dish. Combine panko and za'atar in third shallow dish.

4 Halve chicken breasts horizontally to form 4 cutlets of even thickness. Place 1 cutlet between 2 sheets of plastic wrap and pound to ¼-inch thickness. Repeat with remaining cutlets. Pat cutlets dry with paper towels and sprinkle with remaining ½ teaspoon salt. Working with 1 cutlet at a time, dredge in flour, dip in egg, allowing excess to drip off, then coat with panko mixture, pressing gently to adhere.

5 Line second rimmed baking sheet with double layer of paper towels. Heat remaining ½ cup oil in 12-inch nonstick skillet over medium-high heat until shimmering. Place 2 cutlets in skillet and cook until deep golden brown, 2 to 3 minutes per side. Transfer cutlets to prepared sheet and repeat with remaining 2 cutlets. Season with salt and pepper to taste. Drizzle potatoes with vinaigrette. Serve chicken with potatoes.

SKILLET-ROASTED CHICKEN BREASTS WITH HARISSA-MINT CARROTS

**SERVES
4**

1½ HRS

2   (12-ounce) bone-in split chicken breasts, trimmed

1¾ teaspoons kosher salt, divided

    Olive oil spray

1   shallot, sliced thin

2   teaspoons Harissa (page 17)

1½ pounds carrots, peeled and sliced on bias ¼ inch thick

½   cup water

2   teaspoons lemon juice

1   tablespoon chopped fresh mint, divided

WHY THIS RECIPE WORKS The ingredient list for this one-skillet supper may be modest but the flavor is anything but. We skillet-roast chicken breasts until their skin is crispy; then, while they rest, we add shallot, harissa, and salt to the skillet and cook them until the chicken juices have reduced and the aromatics begin to sizzle in the chicken fat and release flavor. Next, we add carrots to the pan along with a little water, cover the pan, and let the carrots cook through. The sweet vegetable becomes bold from the spicy mix. With the skillet uncovered, the chicken-y liquid thickens to coat the carrots making them supersavory. With that, dinner is served. Be sure to remove excess fatty skin from the thick ends of the breasts when trimming.

1 Adjust oven rack to lower-middle position and heat oven to 325 degrees. Working with 1 breast at a time, use your fingers to carefully separate skin from meat. Peel back skin, leaving skin attached at top and bottom of breast and at ribs. Sprinkle ¾ teaspoon salt evenly over chicken (⅜ teaspoon per breast). Lay skin back in place. Using metal skewer or tip of paring knife, poke 6 to 8 holes in fat deposits in skin of each breast. Spray skin with oil spray.

2 Place chicken skin side down in 12-inch ovensafe skillet and set over medium-high heat. Cook, moving chicken as infrequently as possible, until skin is well browned, 7 to 9 minutes. Carefully flip chicken and transfer skillet to oven. Roast until chicken registers 160 degrees, 25 to 30 minutes.

3 Transfer chicken to cutting board; do not discard liquid in skillet. Add shallot, harissa, and remaining 1 teaspoon salt to skillet and cook over medium-high heat, stirring occasionally and scraping up any browned bits, until moisture has evaporated and mixture begins to sizzle, 2 to 4 minutes. Add carrots and water and bring to simmer. Cover skillet and cook until carrots are tender, 10 to 12 minutes, stirring halfway through cooking.

4 Uncover and continue to cook, stirring frequently, until sauce begins to coat carrots, 2 to 4 minutes longer. Add lemon juice, 1½ teaspoons mint, and any accumulated chicken juices to skillet and toss to combine. Season with salt to taste, and sprinkle with remaining 1½ teaspoons mint. Slice chicken ½ inch thick and serve with vegetables.

*Cals 390 | Total Fat 18g | Sat Fat 5g
Chol 110mg | Sodium 740mg
Total Carb 18g | Dietary Fiber 5g
Total Sugars 9g | Protein 37g*

CHICKEN AND SPICED FREEKEH WITH CILANTRO AND PRESERVED LEMON

- 4 (5- to 7-ounce) bone-in chicken thighs, trimmed
- ½ teaspoon table salt
- ¼ teaspoon pepper
- 1 tablespoon extra-virgin olive oil, plus extra for drizzling
- 1 onion, chopped fine
- 4 garlic cloves, minced
- 1½ teaspoons smoked paprika
- ¼ teaspoon ground cardamom
- ¼ teaspoon red pepper flakes
- 2¼ cups chicken broth
- 1½ cups cracked freekeh, rinsed
- ¼ cup plus 2 tablespoons chopped fresh cilantro, divided
- ½ cup shelled unsalted pistachios, toasted and chopped
- 2 tablespoons rinsed and minced Preserved Lemons (page 18)

WHY THIS RECIPE WORKS Freekeh appears often with moist chicken in the Middle East, especially in Lebanon. Freekeh's distinctly toasty flavors play well with both rich spices, like the smoked paprika and intensely floral cardamom, and bright preserved lemon. Here, the high-fiber grain combines with shredded chicken thigh meat, making for a satiating one-pot meal. Freshly chopped cilantro and toasted pistachios offer grassy notes along with a satisfying crunch. We think the fragrant preserved lemon is an important addition to this dish, but if you can't find it you can substitute 1 tablespoon lemon zest. Freekeh is sometimes spelled frikeh or farik. Look for cracked freekeh that is roughly the size of steel-cut oats. Avoid whole freekeh; it will not cook through in time.

1 Adjust oven rack to lower-middle position and heat oven to 350 degrees. Pat chicken thighs dry with paper towels and sprinkle with salt and pepper. Heat oil in Dutch oven over medium-high heat until just smoking. Add chicken and cook until well browned, 8 to 10 minutes.

2 Transfer chicken to plate and discard skin. Add onion to fat left in pot and cook over medium heat until softened, about 5 minutes. Stir in garlic, paprika, cardamom, and pepper flakes and cook until fragrant, about 30 seconds. Stir in broth, scraping up any browned bits, then stir in freekeh.

3 Nestle chicken into freekeh mixture and add any accumulated juices. Cover, transfer pot to oven, and cook until freekeh is tender and chicken registers 195 degrees, 35 to 40 minutes.

4 Remove pot from oven. Transfer chicken to cutting board, let cool slightly, then shred into bite-size pieces using 2 forks; discard bones.

5 Meanwhile, gently fluff freekeh with fork. Lay clean dish towel over pot, replace lid, and let sit for 5 minutes. Stir in chicken, ¼ cup cilantro, pistachios, and preserved lemon. Season with salt and pepper to taste. Sprinkle with remaining 2 tablespoons cilantro and drizzle with extra oil. Serve.

Cals 330 | Total Fat 10g | Sat Fat 1.5g
Chol 45mg | Sodium 440mg
Total Carb 38g | Dietary Fiber 9g
Total Sugars 2g | Protein 23g

MSAKHAN

SERVES
4 TO 6

1¼ HRS

⅓ cup slivered almonds or pine nuts, toasted

5 tablespoons extra-virgin olive oil, divided, plus extra for drizzling

3 pounds bone-in chicken pieces (split breasts cut in half, drumsticks, and/or thighs), trimmed

1½ teaspoons table salt, divided

¾ teaspoon pepper

1½ pounds red onions, chopped

¼ cup sumac, divided

2 teaspoons Baharat (page 14)

3 naans

¼ cup chopped fresh parsley

WHY THIS RECIPE WORKS The dish msakhan is one to "eat with your hands and with your friends," says Palestinian chef and cookbook author Sami Tamimi in his book *Falastin*: Diners tear off pieces of warm, pillowy taboon bread that's slathered with olive oil–simmered onions piled on a communal platter and wrap them around succulent chunks of roast chicken that's sprinkled with tangy sumac. As Palestine's national dish, msakhan's cultural significance runs deep, to the olive tree that's at the heart of both this dish (which is traditionally made to celebrate the olive harvest and test the quality of the oil) and Palestinian identity itself. Traditionally, relates Palestinian chef and historian Awad Awad, olive trees figure into msakhan's every component: The olive oil–enriched flatbread is baked in clay-and-stone taboon ovens that are fueled by olive wood and dried olive pulp, and the chicken and onions are cooked in generous glugs of olive oil. Awad shares a famous Palestinian saying "A good msakhan should have olive oil dripping from your elbows," and this version keeps olive oil central to the dish. Our recipe uses chicken pieces instead of the traditional whole chicken and naan in place of taboon, but we hope you enjoy this marvelous dish as intended: with your hands and with your friends. Afghan or Indian naan and pocketless Greek pita are close substitutes for taboon bread, but any flatbread can be used. Use a good-quality, flavorful extra-virgin olive oil. (Palestinian olive oil can be purchased online.)

1 Line bowl with double layer of paper towels. Cook almonds and 1 tablespoon oil in 12-inch ovensafe skillet over medium heat, stirring frequently, until almonds are golden brown, 3 to 5 minutes. Using slotted spoon, transfer almonds to prepared bowl; set aside.

2 Adjust 1 oven rack to lower-middle and second rack 6 inches from broiler element. Heat oven to 475 degrees. Pat chicken dry with paper towels and sprinkle with 1 teaspoon salt and pepper. Add 1 tablespoon oil to fat left in skillet and heat over medium-high heat until just smoking. Place chicken skin side down in skillet and cook until skin is well browned and crisp, 8 to 10 minutes. Transfer chicken to large plate.

Cals 590 | Total Fat 29g | Sat Fat 7g Chol 115mg | Sodium 910mg Total Carb 37g | Dietary Fiber 3g Total Sugars 8g | Protein 45g

3 Pour off fat from skillet and wipe skillet clean with paper towels. Add onions, remaining 3 tablespoons oil, and remaining ½ teaspoon salt to now-empty skillet. Cook over medium heat, stirring occasionally and scraping up any browned bits, until onions soften and start to stick to bottom of skillet, 8 to 10 minutes. Off heat, stir in 2 tablespoons sumac, and baharat.

4 Arrange chicken skin side up on top of onions and pour any accumulated juices around chicken. Transfer skillet to lower rack in oven and cook until breasts register 160 degrees and drumsticks/thighs register 175 degrees, 15 to 20 minutes.

5 Using pot holder, remove skillet from oven. Being careful of hot skillet handle, transfer chicken to clean plate, tent with aluminum foil, and let rest while preparing naans.

6 Heat broiler. Arrange naans in even layer on rimmed baking sheet (pieces may overlap slightly) and broil on upper rack until lightly toasted, about 2 minutes. Transfer naans to cutting board, spread onions evenly over top, and sprinkle with 1 tablespoon sumac. Cut each naan in quarters and arrange on serving platter. Arrange chicken pieces on top of naan and sprinkle with almonds, parsley, and remaining 1 tablespoon sumac. Drizzle with extra oil and serve.

CUMIN-CORIANDER ROASTED CORNISH GAME HENS

SERVES
8

1 HR
plus 4 hrs
salting

4 (1¼- to 1½-pound) whole Cornish game hens, giblets discarded

2 tablespoons kosher salt

2 teaspoons ground cumin

2 teaspoons ground coriander

1 teaspoon paprika

¼ teaspoon cayenne pepper

¼ teaspoon extra-virgin olive oil

1 teaspoon baking powder

Olive oil spray

1 teaspoon pepper

WHY THIS RECIPE WORKS We adore Mediterranean-inspired spice rubs for their warm, welcoming flavors but also for their practical applications. They liven up dishes without compromising texture—in this case, the crispy skin on Cornish game hens. We split hens in half and poke holes in the skin that allow the fat to drain during cooking, therefore aiding crisping. We add salt and baking powder to our spice rub; the salt helps pull moisture to the skin's surface so that it evaporates quickly, and the baking powder promotes browning. Serve these hens with anything from cauliflower puree to dried fruit–punctuated grain dishes. If your hens weigh 1½ to 2 pounds, cook three instead of four and extend the cooking time in step 4 to 15 minutes. If your hens are frozen, thaw them in the refrigerator for 24 to 36 hours before salting.

1 Working with 1 hen at a time, arrange breast side down on cutting board. Use kitchen shears to cut through bones on either side of backbone. Discard backbone and trim any excess fat or skin at neck. Flip hen and press firmly on breastbone to flatten, then pound breast to be same thickness as leg and thigh. Using sharp chef's knife, cut through center of breast to make 2 halves. Using your fingers, gently separate skin from breast and thighs. Using metal skewer or tip of paring knife, poke 10 to 15 holes in fat deposits on top of breast halves and thighs. Tuck wingtips behind back. Pat hens dry with paper towels.

2 Combine salt, cumin, coriander, paprika, and cayenne in bowl. Sprinkle half of salt mixture on underside (bone side) of hens. Stir oil into remaining salt mixture until evenly coated. Stir in baking powder until well combined. Turn hens skin side up and rub salt mixture evenly over surface. Transfer hens, skin side up, to wire rack set in rimmed baking sheet and refrigerate, uncovered, for at least 4 hours or up to 24 hours.

3 Adjust oven racks to upper-middle and lower-middle positions, place second rimmed baking sheet on lower rack, and heat oven to 500 degrees. Once oven is fully heated, spray skin side of hens with oil spray and sprinkle with pepper. Carefully transfer hens, skin side down, to baking sheet and cook for 10 minutes.

4 Remove hens from oven and heat broiler. Flip hens skin side up. Transfer baking sheet with hens to upper rack and broil until well browned and breasts register 160 degrees and thighs register 175 degrees, about 5 minutes, rotating as necessary to promote even browning. Serve.

Cals 220 | Total Fat 12g | Sat Fat 2g Chol 120mg | Sodium 970mg Total Carb 1g | Dietary Fiber 1g Total Sugars 0g | Protein 27g

POMEGRANATE-GLAZED CHICKEN WITH POTATOES AND MUSTARD GREENS

SERVES 4 TO 6

1¾ HRS
plus 1 hr resting

- 1 (3½- to 4-pound) whole chicken, giblets discarded
- 2 tablespoons extra-virgin olive oil, divided
- 1 tablespoon Baharat (page 14)
- 1½ teaspoons table salt, divided
- 2 pounds Yukon gold potatoes, ends squared off, peeled, and sliced into 1-inch-thick rounds
- ¼ cup pomegranate molasses
- 1 pound mustard greens, stemmed and cut into 1-inch pieces
- 2 tablespoons chopped fresh cilantro

WHY THIS RECIPE WORKS Middle Eastern food embraces bold flavor—pleasant sourness is welcome, warm spices abound—and also celebrates contrasts. This weeknight dish of butterflied roast chicken and vegetables pairs the warmth and subtle heat of baharat seasoning (rubbed under the chicken's skin) with sweet-sour pomegranate molasses brushed on as a complexly flavored glaze. A side of browned potatoes cooks underneath the bird in the skillet and, along with mustard greens, gets flavored with its savory juices.

1 With chicken breast side down, use kitchen shears to cut through bones on either side of backbone. Discard backbone and trim any excess fat or skin at neck. Flip chicken and tuck wingtips behind back. Press firmly on breastbone to flatten, then pound breast to be same thickness as leg and thigh.

2 Combine 1 tablespoon oil, baharat, and 1 teaspoon salt in bowl. Pat chicken dry with paper towels and, using your fingers, gently loosen skin covering breast and thighs. Rub baharat-oil paste evenly under skin. Transfer chicken skin side up to large plate and refrigerate for at least 1 hour or up to 24 hours.

3 Adjust oven rack to middle position and heat oven to 400 degrees. Toss potatoes with remaining 1 tablespoon oil and remaining ½ teaspoon salt. Arrange potatoes flat sides down in single layer in 12-inch ovensafe nonstick skillet. Place skillet over medium heat and cook potatoes, without moving them, until beginning to brown on bottom, 8 to 10 minutes (do not flip). Place chicken breast side up on top of potatoes; transfer skillet to oven. Roast for 30 minutes. Using pot holder, remove skillet from oven. Being careful of hot skillet handle, brush chicken with molasses. Return skillet to oven and cook until chicken breast registers 160 degrees and thighs register 175 degrees, 30 to 45 minutes.

4 Microwave mustard greens and ¼ cup water in large covered bowl until greens are wilted and decreased in volume, 3 to 5 minutes. Remove bowl from microwave and keep covered for 1 minute. Carefully remove cover and transfer greens to colander. Using back of wooden spoon, gently press on greens to release excess liquid.

5 Carefully remove skillet from oven. Transfer chicken to carving board, tent with aluminum foil, and let rest while finishing vegetables. Fold greens into potatoes. Cover, return skillet to oven, and cook until potatoes and greens are tender, 10 to 15 minutes. Season with salt and pepper to taste. Carve chicken and sprinkle with cilantro. Serve chicken with vegetables.

*Cals 600 | Total Fat 31g | Sat Fat 8g
Chol 130mg | Sodium 730mg
Total Carb 41g | Dietary Fiber 2g
Total Sugars 9g | Protein 38g*

Meat, Fish, Tofu & More

TURKEY MEATBALLS WITH LEMONY BROWN RICE AND SUN-DRIED TOMATOES

SERVES 4

1½ HRS

1 slice hearty sandwich bread, torn into 1-inch pieces

1 large egg

4 scallions, white and green parts separated and sliced thin, greens divided

¼ cup chopped fresh parsley, divided

2 teaspoons grated lemon zest, divided, plus 2 tablespoons juice

½ teaspoon table salt

½ teaspoon pepper

1 pound ground turkey

2 tablespoons extra-virgin olive oil

1 cup long-grain brown rice, rinsed

3 garlic cloves, minced

4 cups chicken broth

½ cup oil-packed sun-dried tomatoes, rinsed, patted dry, and sliced thin

¼ cup grated Parmesan cheese

WHY THIS RECIPE WORKS A skillet of meatballs and rice is a simple, hearty meal that's highly adaptable. Here the meat is ground turkey and the rice nutty brown. A heavy dose of lemon, garlic, scallions, and parsley enlivens the pair. Seasoning both the meatballs and the rice with lemon and liberal amounts of herbs gives them corresponding flavor. And cooking the brown rice in chicken broth instead of water intensifies its richness, adding a meaty backbone to the dish. Sliced sun-dried tomatoes scattered atop the finished dish add a beautiful pop of red and a sweet, chewy bite. A mere ¼ cup of Parmesan cheese contributes a salty umami finish. Be sure to use 93 percent lean ground turkey, not 99 percent fat-free ground turkey breast, or the meatballs will be tough.

1 Pulse bread in food processor to fine crumbs, 10 to 15 pulses; transfer to large bowl. Stir in egg, 3 tablespoons scallion greens, 2 tablespoons parsley, 1½ teaspoons lemon zest, salt, and pepper. Add turkey and gently knead with your hands until mixture is combined. Using your lightly moistened hands, pinch off and roll turkey mixture into heaping 1-tablespoon-size meatballs and transfer to rimmed baking sheet. (You should have 20 meatballs.) Cover and refrigerate for at least 15 minutes or up to 24 hours.

2 Heat oil in 12-inch nonstick skillet over medium-high heat until shimmering. Add meatballs and cook until well browned, 5 to 7 minutes. Transfer meatballs to paper towel–lined plate.

3 Stir rice into fat left in skillet. Cook over medium-high heat until edges of rice begin to turn translucent, about 1 minute. Stir in scallion whites and garlic and cook until fragrant, about 1 minute. Stir in broth, remaining ½ teaspoon lemon zest, and lemon juice and bring to boil.

4 Reduce heat to medium-low, cover, and cook for 15 minutes. Return meatballs to skillet and add any accumulate juices. Cover and cook until rice is tender and meatballs are cooked through, about 15 minutes.

5 Off heat, scatter tomatoes over rice and let sit, covered, for 5 minutes. Sprinkle with Parmesan, remaining scallion greens, and remaining 2 tablespoons parsley. Serve.

Cals 470 | Total Fat 15g | Sat Fat 4.5g
Chol 95mg | Sodium 1090mg
Total Carb 47g | Dietary Fiber 3g
Total Sugars 3g | Protein 38g

GRILL-SMOKED BONELESS TURKEY BREAST WITH OLIVES AND SUN-DRIED TOMATOES

SERVES 10 TO 12

2 HRS
plus 1¼ hrs brining and resting time

¼ cup finely chopped pitted kalamata olives

3 tablespoons finely chopped oil-packed sun-dried tomatoes

2 teaspoons table salt

1 garlic clove, minced

1 teaspoon minced fresh thyme

1 anchovy fillet, rinsed, patted dry, and minced

½ teaspoon red pepper flakes

1 (5- to 7-pound) bone-in whole turkey breast, trimmed

½ cup wood chips

1 teaspoon extra-virgin olive oil

1½ teaspoons pepper

WHY THIS RECIPE WORKS There's a lot to do with lean, good-for-you turkey besides roasting it. The smoky fire of a grill can turn turkey into a richly flavored, juicy roast with crisp, well-rendered skin and moist white meat. We start with a bone-in whole turkey breast, remove the skin and bones, and then salt the meat to add flavor and moisture. Next we spread a pungent filling of finely chopped briny kalamata olives; sweet, concentrated sun-dried tomatoes; aromatic garlic and thyme; and salty-nutty anchovy paste on the breast halves and stack them on top of one another, thick end over tapered end, to create an even thickness for even cooking. We drape the halves with the removed turkey skin, and tie the new roast together. The surgery is simple and the skin helps protect the meat from the fire. Each slice through crisp skin and into tender, smoky white meat reveals a generous ribbon of lively olives and tomatoes—a welcome healthful alternative to stodgy gravy. If using a self-basting turkey (such as a frozen Butterball) or a kosher turkey, omit the salt in step 1.

1 Combine olives, tomatoes, salt, garlic, thyme, anchovy, and pepper flakes in bowl.

2 Remove skin from breast meat and then cut along rib cage to remove breast halves; discard bones. Pat turkey breast halves dry with paper towels, then spread olive mixture evenly over cut side of each turkey breast half. Stack breast halves on top of one another with cut sides facing each other, and alternating thick and tapered ends. Stretch skin over exposed meat and tuck in ends. Tie kitchen twine lengthwise around roast, then tie 5 to 7 pieces of twine at 1-inch intervals crosswise around roast. Transfer roast to wire rack set in rimmed baking sheet and refrigerate uncovered for 1 hour.

3 Just before grilling, soak wood chips in water for 15 minutes, then drain. Using large piece of heavy-duty aluminum foil, wrap soaked chips in 8 by 4½-inch foil packet. (Make sure chips do not poke holes in sides or bottom of packet.) Cut 2 evenly spaced 2-inch slits in top of packet.

4A For a charcoal grill Open bottom vent halfway. Light large chimney starter filled with charcoal briquettes (6 quarts). When top coals are partially covered with ash, pour evenly over half of grill. Place wood chip packet on coals. Set cooking grate in place, cover, and open lid vent halfway. Heat grill until hot and wood chips are smoking, about 5 minutes.

Cals 230 | Total Fat 3.5g | Sat Fat 0.5g
Chol 110mg | Sodium 630mg
Total Carb 1g | Dietary Fiber 0g
Total Sugars 0g | Protein 45g

4B For a gas grill Remove cooking grate and place wood chip packet directly on primary burner. Set cooking grate in place, turn all burners to high, cover, and heat grill until hot and wood chips are smoking, about 15 minutes. Turn all burners to medium-low. (Adjust burners as needed to maintain grill temperature around 300 degrees.)

5 Clean and oil cooking grate. Rub surface of roast with oil and sprinkle with pepper. Place roast on grill (on cooler side if using charcoal). Cover (position lid vent over meat if using charcoal) and cook until roast registers 150 degrees, 40 minutes to 1 hour, turning roast 180 degrees halfway through cooking.

6 Slide roast to hotter side of grill (if using charcoal) or turn all burners to medium-high (if using gas). Cook until roast is browned and skin is crisp on all sides, 8 to 10 minutes, rotating every 2 minutes. Transfer roast to carving board and let rest for 20 minutes. Remove twine and slice ½ inch thick. Serve.

RAS EL HANOUT–RUBBED TURKEY BREAST WITH SOUR ORANGE SAUCE

SERVES 10 TO 12

2 HRS
plus 6½ hrs salting and resting time

2   tablespoons extra-virgin olive oil, divided

1   tablespoon table salt

2   tablespoons Ras el Hanout (page 15)

1   (5- to 7-pound) bone-in whole turkey breast

1   shallot, minced

1   garlic clove, minced

2   cups chicken broth

2   cups orange juice (4 oranges)

2   tablespoons white wine vinegar, plus extra for seasoning

1   tablespoon cornstarch

1   tablespoon water

Cals 270 | Total Fat 5g | Sat Fat 1g
Chol 110mg | Sodium 890mg
Total Carb 6g | Dietary Fiber 0g
Total Sugars 4g | Protein 45g

WHY THIS RECIPE WORKS A roasted turkey breast is a great choice of lean protein for a small group and is not often enough paired with bold flavors, like the ras el hanout rub and super-tangy orange sauce in this inspired recipe. Brushing the skin with oil promotes deep browning. We roast the breast in a skillet, instead of a roasting pan, to contain the drippings so they don't scorch. The sauce is simple but potent, made with aromatics and fresh orange juice. If using a self-basting turkey (such as a frozen Butterball) or a kosher turkey, omit the salt; rub the turkey with the spice paste just before roasting.

1   Combine 1 tablespoon oil, salt, and ras el hanout in bowl.

2   Using kitchen shears, cut through ribs following vertical line of fat where breast meets back, from tapered end of breast to wing joint. Using your hands, bend back away from breast to pop shoulder joint out of socket. With paring knife, cut through joint between bones to separate back from breast; discard back. Trim excess fat from breast. Using your fingers, gently loosen skin covering breast. Rub paste evenly over and under skin. Place turkey on large plate, cover with plastic wrap, and refrigerate for at least 6 hours or up to 24 hours.

3   Adjust oven rack to middle position and heat oven to 325 degrees. Arrange turkey breast, skin side up, in 12-inch ovensafe skillet, tucking ribs under breast and arranging so narrow end of breast is not touching skillet. Brush remaining 1 tablespoon oil evenly over turkey. Roast until thickest part of breast registers 130 degrees, 1 to 1¼ hours. Using pot holder, remove skillet from oven and increase temperature to 500 degrees. When oven reaches 500 degrees, return turkey to oven and roast until skin is deeply browned and thickest part of breast registers 160 degrees, 15 to 30 minutes. Transfer to carving board and let rest for 30 minutes.

4   Meanwhile, being careful of hot skillet handle, pour off all but 1 tablespoon fat from skillet. Add shallot to fat left in skillet and cook over medium heat until softened, about 3 minutes. Stir in garlic and cook until fragrant, about 30 seconds. Stir in broth, orange juice, and vinegar, increase heat to high, and bring to boil. Cook, stirring occasionally, until sauce is reduced to 1¼ cups, about 20 minutes. Whisk cornstarch and water together in small bowl. Whisk slurry into sauce and cook until thickened, about 1 minute. Season with salt, pepper, and extra vinegar to taste. Carve turkey and serve with sauce.

KEFTEDES

SERVES
6

1 HR

2 slices hearty white sandwich bread, torn into 1-inch pieces

⅓ cup plain whole-milk yogurt

2 tablespoons water

3 scallions, minced

¼ cup minced fresh mint, dill, and/or cilantro

1 large egg

2 garlic cloves, minced

2 teaspoons ground cumin

1¼ teaspoons table salt, divided

¼ teaspoon pepper

⅛ teaspoon cinnamon

1 pound 93 percent lean ground beef

1 pound ground pork

2 tablespoons extra-virgin olive oil

1½ pounds zucchini, halved lengthwise and cut on bias into 2- to 3-inch lengths

1 cup Garlic Yogurt Sauce (page 16)

WHY THIS RECIPE WORKS Platters full of succulent, herbaceous keftedes are standard fare on a Greek meze spread; the well-spiced meatballs provide welcomed savory bites among all the fresh dishes. This dish makes keftedes the meal, or your own personal meze plate, matching the keftedes with the typical creamy yogurt sauce and also generous planks of zucchini. Different versions use ground lamb, beef, or pork, or a combination. Here, we use equal parts of beef and pork for robust meaty flavor. A healthy dose of garlic, scallions, warm spices, and fresh herbs create the bold yet balanced defining flavor profile for these keftedes. Mashing yogurt, water, and torn bread pieces together creates a panade to bind the meatballs for easier shaping and for keeping them tender and juicy through cooking. To create our very own little meze platter for a filling meal, we sear fresh zucchini pieces in the flavorful rendered fat from the meatballs until nicely charred.

1 Mash bread, yogurt, and water in large bowl to smooth paste. Stir in scallions, mint, egg, garlic, cumin, 1 teaspoon salt, pepper, and cinnamon. Add beef and pork and knead with hands until uniformly combined. Pinch off and roll mixture into 2-inch round meatballs (about 26 meatballs total). Transfer meatballs to large plate, cover loosely with plastic wrap, and refrigerate until firm, 15 to 30 minutes.

2 Heat oil in 12-inch nonstick skillet over medium-high heat until just smoking. Add meatballs and cook, gently shaking skillet and turning meatballs as needed, until browned on all sides and cooked through, 10 to 12 minutes. Using slotted spoon, transfer meatballs to serving platter.

3 Add zucchini to fat left in skillet, cut side down, and sprinkle with remaining ¼ teaspoon salt. Cook over medium-high heat, turning as needed, until tender and deep golden brown, 6 to 10 minutes. Serve meatballs with zucchini and yogurt sauce.

Cals 460 | Total Fat 29g | Sat Fat 10g
Chol 140mg | Sodium 670mg
Total Carb 15g | Dietary Fiber 2g
Total Sugars 6 | Protein 34g

KEFTEDES

MARAK TEMANI

2 pounds bone-in beef short ribs, trimmed

½ teaspoon table salt

1 tablespoon extra-virgin olive oil

1 large onion, halved and sliced thin

6 tablespoons Hawaij (page 15), divided

5 garlic cloves, minced

1 tablespoon tomato paste

4 cups chicken broth

4 cups water

1 (14.5-ounce) can crushed tomatoes

1 pound Yukon Gold potatoes, unpeeled, cut into 1-inch pieces

4 carrots, peeled and cut into 1-inch pieces

½ cup chopped fresh cilantro

WHY THIS RECIPE WORKS Immigrants to Israel bring the many cuisines of their origin countries. This soulful and satisfying soup comes from Israel's Yemeni Jewish population, and it derives from a modest Shabbat chicken soup. This simple chicken soup, typically served on Friday night to celebrate the Sabbath, is redolent with hawaij, the popular Yemeni spice blend, and bolstered with tomatoes and potatoes. In Israel, the soup evolved; unctuous cuts of beef replace the chicken and marrow bones contribute even more richness. Our version uses bone-in beef short ribs; the collagen from the bones helps create the velvety rich broth. They brown and then braise in the hawaij brew. Some of the hawaij is reserved to add later when the vegetables enter the pot to preserve its complexity at the end of cooking.

1 Adjust oven rack to lower-middle position and heat oven to 325 degrees. Pat short ribs dry with paper towels and sprinkle with salt. Heat oil in Dutch oven over medium-high heat until just smoking. Brown ribs on all sides, 8 to 12 minutes, reducing heat if pot begins to scorch; transfer to plate.

2 Add onion to fat left in pot and cook over medium heat until softened, about 5 minutes. Stir in 3 tablespoons hawaij, garlic, and tomato paste and cook until fragrant, about 2 minutes. Stir in broth, water, and tomatoes, scraping up browned bits. Return ribs to pot with any accumulated juices and bring to simmer. Cover, transfer pot to oven, and cook for 1½ hours.

3 Remove pot from oven and stir in potatoes, carrots, and remaining 3 tablespoons hawaij. Return pot to oven and cook, uncovered, until fork slips easily in and out of meat and vegetables are tender, 1 to 1¼ hours.

4 Remove pot from oven. Transfer ribs to cutting board, let cool slightly, then pull beef into large chunks using 2 spoons; discard bones and excess fat. Using large, shallow spoon, skim excess fat from surface of soup. Stir beef and cilantro into soup. Season with salt and pepper to taste. Serve.

Cals 420 | Total Fat 31g | Sat Fat 7g
Chol 75mg | Sodium 660mg
Total Carb 9g | Dietary Fiber 34g
Total Sugars 3g | Protein 27g

SEARED STEAK TIPS WITH CAULIFLOWER AND ZHOUG

SERVES 4 TO 6

1 HR

1 head cauliflower (2 pounds)

1½ pounds sirloin steak tips, trimmed and cut into 2-inch pieces

1¼ teaspoons table salt, divided

1 teaspoon pepper, divided

¼ cup extra-virgin olive oil, divided

2 teaspoons Za'atar (page 15)

1 teaspoon grated lime zest, plus lime wedges for serving

½ teaspoon sumac

6 tablespoons Green Zhoug (page 19)

WHY THIS RECIPE WORKS When pairing flavorful steak tips with a side dish, it's great to choose a vibrantly seasoned vegetable. It's even better if everything is cooked in the same skillet to build flavor. After searing the steak, we cook cauliflower in the fond-coated pan and transform it into a spiced and citrusy delight, seasoned with bloomed lime zest and sumac-supplemented za'atar. We finish our plating with a generous amount of zhoug, the condiment cutting the richness of the meal with clarifying heat. Sirloin steak tips, also called flap meat, are sold as whole steaks, strips, and cubes. To ensure uniform pieces, we prefer to purchase whole steak tips and cut them ourselves.

1 Trim outer leaves of cauliflower and cut stem flush with bottom of head. Turn head so stem is facing down and cut head into ¾-inch-thick slices. Cut around core to remove florets; discard core. Cut large florets into 1½-inch pieces. Transfer florets to bowl, including any small pieces that may have been created during trimming; set aside.

2 Pat meat dry with paper towels and sprinkle with ½ teaspoon salt and ½ teaspoon pepper. Heat 1 tablespoon oil in 12-inch skillet over medium-high heat until just smoking. Add meat and cook until well browned on all sides and registers 120 to 125 degrees (for medium-rare) or 130 to 135 degrees (for medium), 7 to 10 minutes. Transfer to plate, tent with aluminum foil, and let rest while preparing cauliflower.

3 Toss cauliflower with 2 tablespoons oil, remaining ¾ teaspoon salt, and remaining ½ teaspoon pepper in now-empty skillet. Cover and cook over medium-high heat until florets start to brown and edges just start to become translucent (do not lift lid), about 5 minutes.

4 Uncover and stir in 2 tablespoons water, scraping up any browned bits. Reduce heat to medium and cook, stirring every 2 minutes, until florets are tender and turn golden brown, about 12 minutes, adding additional 1 to 2 tablespoons water if skillet begins to scorch. Push cauliflower to edges of skillet. Add remaining 1 tablespoon oil, za'atar, lime zest, and sumac to center and cook, stirring with rubber spatula, until fragrant, about 30 seconds. Stir spice mixture into cauliflower. Serve steak with cauliflower and zhoug, passing lime wedges separately.

Cals 420 | Total Fat 31g | Sat Fat 75g Chol 75mg | Sodium 660mg Total Carb 9g | Dietary Fiber 4g Total Sugars 3g | Protein 27g

BRAISED BEEF SHORT RIBS WITH FENNEL AND PICKLED GRAPES

SERVES
4 TO 6

3 HRS

1½ pounds boneless beef short ribs, trimmed and cut into 2-inch pieces

¾ teaspoon table salt, divided

¼ teaspoon pepper

1 tablespoon extra-virgin olive oil

2 fennel bulbs, 2 tablespoons fronds chopped, stalks discarded, bulb halved and sliced into 1½-inch-thick wedges

1 onion, chopped

4 garlic cloves, minced

2 teaspoons fennel seeds

1½ cups chicken broth

1 sprig fresh rosemary

¼ cup red wine vinegar

1 tablespoon sugar

4 ounces seedless red grapes, halved (½ cup)

WHY THIS RECIPE WORKS This dish combines boneless beef short ribs with aromatic fennel and finishes with sweet-tart pops of quick-pickled grapes, the latter two ingredients seemingly lightening the savory beef. We braise the ribs in an aromatic broth that we build using fennel, onion, garlic, fennel seeds, and rosemary, which later is served with the dish. Look for lean ribs cut from the chuck that are approximately 1½ to 2 inches thick and 4 to 5 inches long. If boneless beef short ribs are unavailable, you can substitute boneless beef chuck-eye roast. Don't core the fennel; the core helps hold the wedges together during cooking.

1 Adjust oven rack to lower-middle position and heat oven to 300 degrees. Pat short ribs dry with paper towels and sprinkle with ¼ teaspoon salt and pepper. Heat oil in Dutch oven over medium-high heat until just smoking. Brown short ribs on all sides, 8 to 12 minutes, reducing heat if pot begins to scorch; transfer to bowl.

2 Add fennel bulb, onion, and ¼ teaspoon salt to fat left in pot and cook over medium heat until softened and lightly browned, 5 to 7 minutes. Stir in garlic and fennel seeds and cook until fragrant, about 30 seconds. Stir in broth and rosemary sprig, scraping up any browned bits, and bring to simmer. Nestle short ribs into vegetable mixture and add any accumulated juices. Cover, transfer pot to oven, and cook until fork slips easily in and out of meat, about 2 hours.

3 Meanwhile, microwave vinegar, sugar, and remaining ¼ teaspoon salt in bowl until steaming, about 1 minute; whisk to dissolve sugar and salt. Add grapes to hot brine and press to completely submerge. Let sit for 20 minutes, then drain grapes and return to now-empty bowl. (Drained grapes can be refrigerated for up to 1 week.)

4 Remove pot from oven. Transfer short ribs to serving dish, tent with aluminum foil, and let rest while finishing sauce. Strain braising liquid through fine-mesh strainer into fat separator. Discard rosemary sprig and transfer vegetables to serving dish with beef. Let braising liquid settle for 5 minutes, then pour ¾ cup defatted liquid over short ribs and vegetables; discard remaining liquid. Sprinkle with grapes and fennel fronds. Serve.

Cals 340 | Total Fat 24g | Sat Fat 10g
Chol 85mg | Sodium 560mg
Total Carb 14g | Dietary Fiber 3g
Total Sugars 9g | Protein 21g

MEHSHI BAZAL

3 large red onions (about
1 pound each)

⅓ cup medium-grain rice, rinsed

12 ounces 85 percent lean
ground beef

¾ teaspoon Baharat (page 14)

1 teaspoon table salt

Pinch cinnamon

2 cups pomegranate juice

1 tablespoon pomegranate
molasses

½ teaspoon ground dried
Aleppo pepper

½ cup pomegranate seeds

2 tablespoons chopped
fresh parsley

WHY THIS RECIPE WORKS Stuffed vegetables of all kinds—kousa squash, vine leaves, cabbage, Swiss chard, eggplant, and more—are standards throughout Lebanon, Syria, and Palestine. Syrian Jewish cook Sheila Sutton introduced us to an impressive variant particular to the cuisine—stuffed onion leaves. Whereas stuffed vegetables in the Middle East tend to be cooked in a savory tomato-based sauce, these onion petals are simmered in pomegranate juice, pomegranate molasses, and Aleppo pepper. As Sutton notes, "The use of cherry and pomegranate is key to the cuisine of Aleppo." This braising medium reduces down to a fruity-sweet-sour sauce that's enriched by the juices of a warm-spiced meat (and rice) filling. The sauce lacquers the onions with its ruby-hued shine. In order to easily separate the onion leaves and render them pliable enough for wrapping around filling, the onions are blanched whole (partially cut so the boiling water can reach the interior). Sometimes the rice (medium-grain for its binding quality) is soaked in advance to prevent the raw rice from wicking away all the moisture from the meat, turning it tough. We give the rice a quick dunk in the onion-blanching water for 5 minutes, which is enough to hydrate it and allow the filling to remain tender. Look for large onions that are approximately 12 to 16 ounces each. If medium-grain rice is unavailable, short grain rice can be substituted; do not use long-grain rice here. Serve onions warm or let rest longer in step 5 and serve at room temperature.

1 Bring 4 quarts of water to boil in Dutch oven. Trim ends of onions and arrange on cutting board with 1 cut side down. Starting at top of each onion with tip of knife at core, cut through 1 side. (Onion should remain intact; do not halve onion completely.) Add onions to boiling water and cook, turning occasionally, until onion layers begin to soften and separate, about 15 minutes.

2 Using slotted spoon, transfer onions to cutting board. Once cool enough to touch, gently separate first 7 layers from each onion. Some layers may tear slightly; only 15 layers are needed. Reserve remaining onion cores for another use.

Cals 310 | Total Fat 9g | Sat Fat 3.5g
Chol 40mg | Sodium 430mg
Total Carb 44g | Dietary Fiber 4g
Total Sugars 23g | Protein 14g

3 Meanwhile, add rice to water left in pot and let sit, off heat, for 5 minutes; drain. Using your hands, gently knead rice, beef, baharat, salt, and cinnamon together in bowl until combined. Arrange 1 onion layer on counter with short side facing you. Place 2 tablespoons of rice mixture about ½ inch from bottom and roll up onion to form torpedo shape with tapered ends. Transfer stuffed onion to plate, seam side down. Repeat with 14 more onion layers and remaining rice mixture. (Stuffed onions can be refrigerated for up to 24 hours.)

4 Whisk pomegranate juice and pomegranate molasses together in 12-inch nonstick skillet. Evenly space 12 stuffed onions seam side down around edge of skillet and place three in center. Sprinkle with Aleppo. Bring to vigorous simmer over medium-high heat. Cover, reduce heat to medium-low, and cook for 25 minutes.

5 Using 2 forks, carefully flip onions. Continue to cook, uncovered, until onions are softened and glaze has thickened slightly, 10 to 15 minutes. Off heat, let rest for at least 10 minutes. Gently turn onions to coat with glaze, then transfer to serving platter. Spoon glaze over top and sprinkle with pomegranate seeds and parsley. Serve.

GRILLED BEEF SHORT RIBS WITH PRESERVED LEMON—ALMOND SAUCE

Short Ribs

1½ pounds boneless beef short ribs, trimmed

2½ teaspoons kosher salt

1 teaspoon pepper

Sauce

5 tablespoons extra-virgin olive oil, divided

¼ cup sliced almonds, chopped

½ cup minced fresh parsley

2 tablespoons rinsed and minced Preserved Lemons (page 18) plus 2 tablespoons brine

2 tablespoons lemon juice

¼ teaspoon sugar

WHY THIS RECIPE WORKS Grilling boneless beef short ribs achieves what is essentially grilled steaks but with superlatively rich, beefy flavor. The richness welcomes a bright counterpart, and we serve the short ribs with a lively, lemony sauce of minced preserved lemon, almonds, lemon juice, and olive oil. Try serving the rich ribs with greens (see page 127) and/ or riced cauliflower (see page 123). Look for lean ribs cut from the chuck that are approximately 1½ to 2 inches thick. Sliced almonds contribute a delicate crunch to the sauce; do not substitute slivered or whole almonds. We like these ribs cooked to about 130 degrees (medium). If you prefer them medium-rare, remove the ribs from the grill when they register 125 degrees.

1 For the short ribs Cut ribs into 3- to 4-inch lengths. Sprinkle with salt and pepper. Let sit at room temperature for 1 hour.

2 For the sauce Combine 1 tablespoon oil and almonds in 8-inch skillet and toast over medium-high heat, stirring constantly, until almonds are golden brown, 1 to 2 minutes. Immediately transfer to bowl. Stir in parsley, preserved lemon and brine, lemon juice, sugar, and remaining ¼ cup oil. Let sit at room temperature for 15 minutes. Stir well before using. (Sauce can be refrigerated for up to 24 hours. Let sit at room temperature for 15 minutes before serving.)

3A For a charcoal grill Open bottom vent completely. Light large chimney starter mounded with charcoal briquettes (7 quarts). When top coals are partially covered with ash, pour evenly over half of grill. Set cooking grate in place, cover, and open lid vent completely. Heat grill until hot, about 5 minutes.

3B For a gas grill Turn all burners to high; cover; and heat grill until hot, about 15 minutes. Turn off 1 burner (if using grill with more than 2 burners, turn off burner farthest from primary burner) and leave other burner(s) on high.

4 Clean and oil cooking grate. Arrange ribs on hotter side of grill. Cook (covered if using gas), flipping ribs every minute, until meat is well browned on all sides and registers about 130 degrees at thickest part, 8 to 14 minutes. (Ribs will be very pale after first flip but will continue to brown as they cook. This cut can quickly overcook; start checking temperature of smaller ribs after 8 minutes.) Transfer ribs to cutting board, tent with aluminum foil, and let rest for 10 minutes. Slice ribs as thin as possible against grain. (Grain runs diagonally, so as long as you slice lengthwise, you will be cutting against grain.) Serve, passing sauce separately.

Cals 364 | Total Fat 29g | Sat Fat 12g
Chol 110mg | Sodium 353mg
Total Carb 0g | Dietary Fiber 0g
Total Sugars 0g | Protein 26g

PORK TENDERLOIN WITH WHITE BEANS AND MUSTARD GREENS

SERVES 4

1 HR

3 tablespoons extra-virgin olive oil, divided

1 (1-pound) pork tenderloin, trimmed and halved crosswise

½ teaspoon table salt

¼ teaspoon pepper

1 onion, chopped fine

1 tablespoon minced fresh thyme or 1 teaspoon dried

2 garlic cloves, minced

¾ cup chicken broth

¼ cup dry white wine

1 pound mustard greens, stemmed and cut into 2-inch pieces

2 (15-ounce) cans navy beans, rinsed

½ cup panko bread crumbs

2 tablespoons chopped fresh parsley

½ teaspoon grated lemon zest, plus 1 teaspoon juice

3 ounces goat cheese, crumbled (1 cup)

WHY THIS RECIPE WORKS The south of France is known for its rich stews that combine creamy white beans, fresh greens, and tender pork. For a slightly less stew-y melange of these ingredients, we turn to tender, quick-cooking pork tenderloin. We first brown the pork and set it aside while we build a flavorful base in a Dutch oven using abundant aromatics: onion, thyme, garlic, and wine. Next, we stir in mustard greens, only wilting them slightly; then navy beans enter the pot. Resting the pork on top of the greens lifts the lean cut of meat out of the braising liquid, which allows it to cook through gently by way of the surrounding moist environment of the pot. During the quick bake time, we make lemon-scented bread crumbs to sprinkle over the completed dish for a bright, textural finish. Finally, a crumble of tangy goat cheese adds pleasant richness.

1 Adjust oven rack to middle position and heat oven to 450 degrees. Heat 2 tablespoons oil in Dutch oven over medium-high heat until just smoking. Pat pork dry with paper towels and sprinkle with salt and pepper. Brown pork on all sides, 5 to 7 minutes; transfer to plate.

2 Add onion to fat left in pot and cook over medium heat until softened, about 5 minutes. Stir in thyme and garlic and cook until fragrant, about 30 seconds. Stir in broth and wine, scraping up any browned bits. Add mustard greens, 1 handful at a time, and cook, stirring constantly, until beginning to wilt, 2 to 3 minutes.

3 Stir in beans. Nestle pork on top of mustard greens mixture. Transfer pot to oven and cook until pork registers 135 degrees and greens are tender, about 15 minutes.

4 Meanwhile, toss panko with remaining 1 tablespoon oil in bowl until evenly coated. Microwave, stirring every 30 seconds, until light golden brown, 2 to 5 minutes. Let cool slightly, then stir in parsley and lemon zest.

5 Remove pot from oven. Transfer pork to cutting board, tent with aluminum foil, and let rest for 5 minutes. Stir lemon juice into mustard greens mixture and season with salt and pepper to taste. Slice pork ½ inch thick and serve with mustard greens mixture, sprinkling individual portions with bread crumbs and goat cheese.

Cals 560 | Total Fat 22g | Sat Fat 8g
Chol 90mg | Sodium 1100mg
Total Carb 43g | Dietary Fiber 11g
Total Sugars 4g | Protein 45g

'NDUJA WITH BEANS AND GREENS

6 ounces 'nduja, casings removed

2 (15-ounce) cans cannellini beans (1 can drained and rinsed, 1 can undrained)

1 pound kale, stemmed and chopped

½ teaspoon pepper, divided

1 ounce Parmesan cheese, grated (½ cup), divided

1 tablespoon extra-virgin olive oil, plus extra for serving

4 large eggs

¼ teaspoon salt

WHY THIS RECIPE WORKS Some meats pack remarkable punch without much treatment at all, perhaps none more so than spicy Italian 'nduja. The spicy, soft cured sausage from Calabria adds heat, acidity and funk, richness, and protein in just a few minutes, needing only a quick sauté to practically melt into the pan and render its spice-infused fat. Combine this with quick-cooking, fortifying canned cannellini beans and kale, and your 20-minute beans and greens reach weeknight superhero status. The crispy lacy edges of a fried egg perched on top offer the perfect contrast to the ingredients below.

1 Cook 'nduja in Dutch oven over medium-high heat, breaking up meat with wooden spoon, until meat darkens in color and fat renders, 3 to 5 minutes. Stir in beans and their liquid, kale, and ¼ teaspoon pepper and bring to simmer. Reduce heat to medium-low, cover, and cook, stirring occasionally, until kale is tender and sauce has thickened slightly, 5 to 7 minutes. Off heat, stir in ¼ cup Parmesan.

2 Meanwhile, heat oil in 12-inch nonstick skillet over medium-high heat until shimmering. Add eggs to skillet and sprinkle with salt and remaining ¼ teaspoon pepper. Cover and cook for 1 minute. Remove from heat and let sit for 15 to 45 seconds for runny yolks, 45 to 60 seconds for soft but set yolks, or about 2 minutes for medium-set yolks. Serve beans and kale with fried eggs, sprinkling individual portions with remaining ¼ cup Parmesan and drizzling with extra oil.

Cals 420 | Total Fat 17g | Sat Fat 5g
Chol 215mg | Sodium 1050mg
Total Carb 38g | Dietary Fiber 12g
Total Sugars 6g | Protein 33g

SPICED PORK TENDERLOIN WITH BUTTERNUT SQUASH AND BRUSSELS SPROUTS

1 teaspoon ground coriander

1 teaspoon ground paprika

¾ teaspoon plus ⅛ teaspoon table salt, divided

¼ teaspoon pepper, divided

1 (1-pound) pork tenderloin, trimmed

3 tablespoons extra-virgin olive oil, divided

8 ounces brussels sprouts, trimmed and halved

8 ounces butternut squash, peeled, seeded, and cut into 1-inch pieces

2 garlic cloves, minced

2 tablespoons chopped fresh parsley

1 tablespoon cider vinegar

¾ teaspoon Dijon mustard

¼ teaspoon brown sugar

WHY THIS RECIPE WORKS This impressive yet simple dinner of warmly spiced pork with hearty roasted butternut squash and brussels sprouts is an ideal example of a balanced meal of satisfying ingredients that aren't all common in the Mediterranean but that fit neatly into the lifestyle. A pork tenderloin is a perfectly portioned roast for four people eating moderate meat portions. After browning the tenderloin, we add the vegetables to the skillet and pop the tenderloin on top to roast in the oven. The vegetables, which finish cooking while the tenderloin rests, get tossed in a mustard-flavored cider vinaigrette for a dish that tastes like fall no matter where you're eating it. Use brussels sprouts no bigger than golf balls, as larger ones are often tough and woody.

1 Adjust oven rack to middle position and heat oven to 475 degrees. Combine coriander, paprika, ¼ teaspoon salt, and ⅛ teaspoon pepper in small bowl. Pat tenderloin dry with paper towels and sprinkle with spice mixture.

2 Heat 1 tablespoon oil in 12-inch ovensafe skillet over medium-high heat until just smoking. Brown tenderloin on all sides, 6 to 8 minutes; transfer to plate.

3 Off heat, add brussels sprouts, squash, garlic, 1 tablespoon oil, and ½ teaspoon salt to now-empty skillet and toss to combine. Place tenderloin on top of vegetables and roast until pork registers 145 degrees, 12 to 15 minutes.

4 Using pot holder, remove skillet from oven. Transfer tenderloin to carving board, tent with aluminum foil, and let rest while brussels sprouts mixture finishes cooking. Being careful of hot skillet handle, gently stir brussels sprouts mixture and continue to roast until tender, about 10 minutes.

5 Whisk parsley, vinegar, mustard, sugar, remaining ⅛ teaspoon salt, remaining ⅛ teaspoon pepper, and remaining 1 tablespoon oil together in large bowl. Transfer vegetables to bowl with vinaigrette and toss to combine. Season with salt and pepper to taste. Slice tenderloin ½ inch thick and serve with vegetables.

*Cals 270 | Total Fat 14g | Sat Fat 2.5g
Chol 60mg | Sodium 600mg
Total Carb 13g | Dietary Fiber 4g
Total Sugars 3g | Protein 25g*

PINCHOS MORUNOS

3 tablespoons table salt
for brining

2 pounds boneless country-
style pork ribs, trimmed

¼ cup extra-virgin olive oil

2 tablespoons lemon juice, plus
lemon wedges for serving

6 garlic cloves, minced

1 tablespoon grated
fresh ginger

2 teaspoons minced fresh
oregano, divided

2 teaspoons smoked paprika

1 teaspoon ground coriander

1 teaspoon table salt

½ teaspoon ground cumin

½ teaspoon pepper

¼ teaspoon cayenne pepper

WHY THIS RECIPE WORKS Pinchos morunos are Spanish pork kebabs influenced by the spices and cuisines of Muslim people from the Maghreb and the Iberian Peninsula that serve as tapas but can certainly serve with an entree. We use country-style ribs; the ribs are convenient and remain juicy when grilled in 1-inch chunks. We coat them with a robust spice paste that includes garlic, lemon, ginger, coriander, smoked paprika, and fresh oregano. And because country-style ribs contain a mix of lighter loin meat and darker shoulder meat, we keep the light meat and dark meat on separate skewers and cook each to its ideal temperature. You will need four or five 12-inch metal skewers for this recipe. If your pork is enhanced, do not brine it in step 1. Grill a vegetable as the skewers cool or serve with a chickpea salad.

1 Dissolve 3 tablespoons salt in 1½ quarts cold water in large container. Submerge ribs in brine and let sit at room temperature for 30 minutes. Meanwhile, whisk oil, lemon juice, garlic, ginger, 1 teaspoon oregano, paprika, coriander, salt, cumin, pepper, and cayenne in small bowl until combined.

2 Remove pork from brine and pat dry with paper towels. Cut ribs into 1-inch chunks; place dark meat and light meat in separate bowls. Divide spice paste proportionately between bowls and toss to coat. Thread light and dark meat onto separate skewers (do not crowd pieces). Place dark meat kebabs on left side of rimmed baking sheet and light meat kebabs on right side.

3A For a charcoal grill Open bottom vent completely. Light large chimney starter filled with charcoal briquettes (6 quarts). When top coals are partially covered with ash, pour evenly over half of grill. Set cooking grate in place, cover, and open lid vent completely. Heat grill until hot, about 5 minutes.

3B For a gas grill Turn all burners to high, cover, and heat grill until hot, about 15 minutes. Leave primary burner on high and turn off other burner(s).

4 Clean and oil cooking grate. Place dark meat on hotter side of grill and cook for 6 minutes. Flip dark meat and add light meat to hotter side of grill. Cook for 4 minutes, then flip all kebabs. Continue to cook, flipping kebabs every 4 minutes, until dark meat is well charred and registers 155 degrees and light meat is lightly charred and registers 140 degrees, 4 to 8 minutes longer. Transfer to serving platter, tent with aluminum foil, and let rest for 5 minutes. Remove pork from skewers, toss to combine, sprinkle with remaining 1 teaspoon oregano, and serve, passing lemon wedges separately.

Cals 230 | Total Fat 14g | Sat Fat 3.5g
Chol 85mg | Sodium 400 mg
Total Carb 2g | Dietary Fiber 0g
Total Sugars 0g | Protein 24g

EMBAKBBKA

1½ pounds lamb shoulder chops (blade or round bone), ¾ to 1 inch thick, trimmed

1 teaspoon table salt, divided

½ teaspoon pepper, divided

4 teaspoons extra-virgin olive oil, divided

1 onion, chopped

2 carrots, peeled, halved lengthwise, and cut into ½-inch pieces

3 garlic cloves, smashed and peeled

½ cup tomato paste

1 tablespoon Baharat (page 14)

2 teaspoons ground turmeric

½ teaspoon ground ginger

⅛–¼ teaspoon cayenne pepper

5 cups water, divided

1 (14.5-ounce) can whole peeled tomatoes, drained with juice reserved, chopped

3 jalapeño chiles, stemmed (1 whole, 2 sliced thin)

8 ounces ditalini or elbow macaroni

½ cup frozen peas

Cals 570 | Total Fat 29g | Sat Fat 13g
Chol 90mg | Sodium 810mg
Total Carb 44g | Dietary Fiber 3g
Total Sugars 6g | Protein 31g

WHY THIS RECIPE WORKS Sounds, in addition to tastes and scents, shape our cooking experiences and enjoyment—the sizzling sear of meat in a skillet, the whisking of a punchy vinaigrette. Here, this is so true that sounds inspire the name of the dish. Embakbbka, a quintessential Libyan dish, is a rich tomatoey pasta dish thought to be named for the "bak bak bak" noise the bubbles make when the stew is boiling. It's pure comfort food and one of the first dishes children learn to cook. Recipes vary from household to household, but the core ingredients of tender meat (usually lamb), pasta, tomatoes, and a myriad of spices remain the same. Including the lamb bones in the braise ensures a robust lamb flavor that stands out just enough from the warmly spiced tomato broth. Embakbbka gets its complex flavor from haharrat, a spice blend in every Libyan kitchen; each cook combines the spices in a slightly different ratio. While it's not readily available to order, baharat, which we use throughout this book, becomes almost identical when combined with turmeric, ginger, and cayenne pepper. Cooking the pasta in the sauce allows it to soak up all the flavor and to release starch into the broth to create a lusciously rich and uniquely velvety sauce. Libyan food is full of heat, and adding a whole jalapeño to the pot infuses the dish with its grassy spice.

1 Pat lamb dry with paper towels and sprinkle with ¼ teaspoon salt and ¼ teaspoon pepper. Heat 2 teaspoons oil in Dutch oven over medium-high heat until just smoking. Brown half of lamb on both sides, 3 to 5 minutes; transfer to plate. Repeat with remaining 2 teaspoons oil and remaining lamb; transfer to plate. Add onion, carrots, and garlic to fat left in pot and cook over medium heat until softened, about 5 minutes. Stir in tomato paste, baharat, turmeric, ginger, cayenne, remaining ¾ teaspoon salt, and remaining ¼ teaspoon pepper and cook until fragrant, about 1 minute. Stir in 3 cups water and tomatoes and reserved tomato juice, scraping up any browned bits; bring to simmer.

2 Nestle lamb and whole jalapeño into pot and add any accumulated lamb juices. Reduce heat to medium-low, partially cover, and simmer gently until lamb is tender, 40 to 45 minutes. Transfer chops to cutting board, let cool slightly, then cut lamb into large chunks; discard bones and excess fat.

3 Stir lamb, pasta, and remaining 2 cups water into pot and bring to simmer. Cook, stirring occasionally, until pasta is tender, 10 to 12 minutes. Off heat, stir in peas and let sit until heated through, about 2 minutes. Season with salt and pepper to taste. Serve, passing sliced jalapeños separately.

LAMB CHOPS WITH TAMARIND PAN SAUCE

SERVES
4

30 MINS

8   (4-ounce) lamb loin or rib chops, ¾ to 1 inch thick, trimmed

½   teaspoon table salt

¼   teaspoon pepper

1   tablespoon extra-virgin olive oil, plus extra as needed

1   shallot, minced

1½ teaspoons ground dried Urfa chile

1   garlic clove, minced

¼   cup tamarind juice concentrate

3   tablespoons water

1   tablespoon chopped fresh mint

WHY THIS RECIPE WORKS Distinctly flavored, ultrarich lamb chops are a fun cut to cook because they stand up to intensely flavored sauces that make even a little meat taste incredibly satisfying. Here, sweet-tart tamarind is the partner. After searing the chops to a browned, perfect medium-rare, we make a quick sauce in the skillet while they rest, starting by sautéing aromatics in some of the rendered lamb fat. Stirring in deeply flavored ground Urfa chile adds complexly smoky heat, a piquant punch that further enlivens the next stir-in of the tamarind concentrate for a tantalizing taste. A few tablespoons of water create the perfect sauce consistency and tame the tartness of the tamarind. Pass these chops around the table along with blistered green beans, rice pilaf, or a sunny beet salad.

1 Pat lamb dry with paper towels and sprinkle with salt and pepper. Heat oil in 12-inch nonstick skillet over medium-high heat until just smoking. Cook chops until well browned and meat registers 120 to 125 degrees (for medium-rare) or 130 to 135 degrees (for medium), 4 to 6 minutes per side. Transfer chops to serving platter, tent with aluminum foil, and let rest while preparing sauce.

2 Pour off all but 2 tablespoons fat from skillet (if necessary, add extra oil to equal 2 tablespoons). Add shallot and cook over medium heat until softened, 2 to 3 minutes. Stir in Urfa and garlic and cook until fragrant, about 30 seconds. Whisk in tamarind concentrate and water and bring to brief simmer. Spoon sauce over chops and sprinkle with mint. Serve.

Cals 270 | Total Fat 13g | Sat Fat 4.5g
Chol 100mg | Sodium 430mg
Total Carb 4g | Dietary Fiber 1g
Total Sugars 3g | Protein 33g

BRAISED LAMB SHOULDER CHOPS WITH BALSAMIC VINEGAR AND RED PEPPER

- 4 (8- to 12-ounce) lamb shoulder chops (blade or round bone), about ¾ inch thick, trimmed

- ½ teaspoon table salt

- ¼ teaspoon pepper

- 2 tablespoons extra-virgin olive oil, divided

- 1 red bell pepper, stemmed, seeded, and cut into ¼-inch pieces

- 1 small onion, chopped fine

- 2 small garlic cloves, minced

- ⅓ cup dry red wine

- 1 cup canned whole peeled tomatoes, chopped

- 2 tablespoons minced fresh parsley

- 2 tablespoons capers, rinsed

- 2 tablespoons balsamic vinegar

WHY THIS RECIPE WORKS Braising robust lamb shoulder chops in a bold sauce creates an incredibly comforting component of your plate. Lamb shoulder chops are magic here—they have chew but they're not particularly tough and so a quick stovetop braise of just 15 to 20 minutes yields fork-tender meat. That bold sauce consists of red wine and tomatoes, sweetened by red bell pepper and accented with capers and balsamic vinegar. We reduce the sauce to a chop-coating consistency. A bed of polenta or pureed cauliflower is a good destination for the chops.

1 Pat chops dry with paper towels and sprinkle with salt and pepper. Heat 1 tablespoon oil in 12-inch skillet over medium-high heat until just smoking. Brown chops, in batches if necessary, 4 to 5 minutes per side; transfer to plate. Pour off fat from skillet.

2 Heat remaining 1 tablespoon oil in now-empty skillet over medium heat until shimmering. Add bell pepper and onion and cook until softened, about 5 minutes. Stir in garlic and cook until fragrant, about 30 seconds. Stir in wine, scraping up any browned bits. Bring to simmer and cook until reduced by half, 2 to 3 minutes. Stir in tomatoes.

3 Nestle chops into skillet and add any accumulated juices; return to simmer. Reduce heat to low, cover, and simmer gently until chops are tender and fork slips easily in and out of meat, 15 to 20 minutes. Transfer chops to serving platter and tent with aluminum foil.

4 Stir parsley, capers, and balsamic into sauce and simmer until sauce thickens, 2 to 3 minutes. Season with salt and pepper to taste. Spoon sauce over chops and serve.

Cals 480 | Total Fat 25g | Sat Fat 9g
Chol 145mg | Sodium 730mg
Total Carb 10g | Dietary Fiber 2g
Total Sugars 6g | Protein 45g

SUMAC LAMB CHOPS WITH CARROTS, MINT, AND PAPRIKA

SERVES
4

35 MINS

- 1 pound carrots, peeled and cut into 1½- to 2-inch lengths, thick pieces quartered lengthwise and medium pieces halved lengthwise

- ½ teaspoon table salt, plus salt for cooking carrots

- 8 (4-ounce) lamb loin or rib chops, ¾ to 1 inch thick, trimmed

- 1 tablespoon ground sumac, plus extra for seasoning

- ¼ teaspoon pepper

- 2 tablespoons extra-virgin olive oil, divided, plus extra for drizzling

- 1 teaspoon lemon juice, plus extra for seasoning

- ½ teaspoon paprika

- 2 tablespoons chopped fresh mint, divided

- ½ cup Tahini-Yogurt Sauce (page 16)

WHY THIS RECIPE WORKS Lamb and sweet carrots love bright flavors, so we use a combination of fresh mint, sweet paprika, and bright, citrusy sumac in this quick meal. We sprinkle the sumac directly onto the lamb chops along with some salt and pepper and then sear the meat in a hot skillet. The carrot component couldn't be simpler; we boil them until they're just tender before combining them with paprika, lemon juice, and mint. This perfect pair is tied together with tahini-yogurt sauce.

1 Bring 2 cups water to boil in medium saucepan over high heat. Add carrots and 2 teaspoons salt, cover, and cook until tender throughout, about 6 minutes (start timer as soon as carrots go into water). Drain carrots; set aside.

2 Meanwhile, pat lamb dry with paper towels and sprinkle with sumac, salt, and pepper. Heat 1 tablespoon oil in 12-inch skillet over medium-high heat until just smoking. Cook chops until well browned and meat registers 120 to 125 degrees (for medium-rare) or 130 to 135 degrees (for medium), 4 to 6 minutes per side. Transfer chops to serving platter, tent with aluminum foil, and let rest while finishing vegetables.

3 Toss carrots with lemon juice, paprika, and remaining 1 tablespoon oil in now-empty skillet. Stir in 1 tablespoon chopped mint. Season with salt, pepper, and lemon juice to taste.

4 Sprinkle remaining 1 tablespoon mint over lamb, drizzle with extra oil to taste, and season with extra sumac to taste. Serve chops with carrots and sauce.

Cals 380 | Total Fat 22g | Sat Fat 6g
Chol 85mg | Sodium 1480mg
Total Carb 16g | Dietary Fiber 4g
Total Sugars 6g | Protein 34g

ARROSTICINI

**SERVES
6 TO 8**

30 MINS

2   pounds boneless lamb shoulder roast, trimmed and cut into ½-inch pieces

1½   teaspoons kosher salt

1   teaspoon pepper

3   tablespoons extra-virgin olive oil

WHY THIS RECIPE WORKS The roots of these grilled lamb skewers are steeped in the long shepherding tradition of the Abruzzo region of Italy; lore has it that the mountain shepherds would roast pieces of mutton over the fire as a quick and easy meal while they traveled. Today, arrosticini is a popular street food—the meat is cut into tiny cubes by machine, cooked over a specialized grill, and eaten directly off the skewer. Arrosticini can be made with lamb or mutton, but either way its exterior should be well browned, with the meat basted in its own flavorful fat and cooked until tender. We use a half-grill fire setup, which produces a concentrated, blazing-hot fire. We cut the lamb into ½-inch chunks and pack it tightly on skewers to prevent it from overcooking. After a quick stint on the grill, it's so flavorful that all it needs is a dash of salt and pepper and some sautéed zucchini or a shaved vegetable salad and it's ready for serving. You can substitute 2½ pounds lamb shoulder chops (blade or round bone) for the lamb shoulder. You will need twelve 12-inch metal skewers for this recipe.

1 Pat lamb dry with paper towels and sprinkle with salt and pepper. Tightly thread lamb onto twelve 12-inch metal skewers, leaving top 3 inches of each skewer exposed. Brush skewers with oil.

2A For a charcoal grill Open bottom vent completely. Light large chimney starter filled with charcoal briquettes (6 quarts). When top coals are partially covered with ash, pour evenly over half of grill. Set cooking grate in place, cover, and open lid vent completely. Heat grill until hot, about 5 minutes.

2B For a gas grill Turn all burners to high, cover, and heat grill until hot, about 15 minutes. Leave all burners on high.

3 Clean and oil cooking grate. Place skewers on hotter side of grill, and cook (covered if using gas), turning frequently, until well browned on all sides, 5 to 7 minutes. Serve.

*Cals 276 | Total Fat 24g | Sat Fat 9g
Chol 65mg | Sodium 221mg
Total Carb 0g | Dietary Fiber 0g
Total Sugars 0g | Protein 15g*

ARAYES

1 onion, cut into 1-inch pieces

1 cup fresh cilantro leaves

¼ cup extra-virgin olive oil

1 tablespoon grated lemon zest plus 3 tablespoons juice

1 tablespoon ground coriander

1 tablespoon ground cumin

1 tablespoon paprika

2 teaspoons table salt

1½ teaspoons pepper

½ teaspoon cayenne pepper

¼ teaspoon ground cinnamon

2 pounds ground lamb

4 (8-inch) pita breads

1 recipe Garlic Yogurt Sauce (page 16)

WHY THIS RECIPE WORKS Seasoned with warm spices, pressed between pita rounds, and grilled until crispy these Middle Eastern lamb sandwiches are a street food that can serve as dinner. You can substitute 85 percent lean ground beef for the ground lamb. This recipe works best with ¼-inch-thick pitas that are fresh and pliable. To determine which side of the pita is thicker, look at the pattern of browning; the fragile side is usually covered with char marks in a dotted-line pattern. Serve with a salad, if desired.

1 Pulse onion and cilantro in food processor until finely chopped, 10 to 12 pulses, scraping down sides of bowl as needed. Transfer mixture to large bowl. Stir in oil, lemon zest and juice, coriander, cumin, paprika, salt, pepper, cayenne, and cinnamon. Add lamb and gently knead with your hands until thoroughly combined.

2 Using kitchen shears, cut around circumference of each pita and separate into 2 halves. Place 4 thicker halves on counter, interior side up. Divide lamb mixture into 4 equal portions and place 1 portion in center of each pita half. Using spatula, gently spread lamb mixture into even layer, leaving ½-inch border around edge. Top each lamb portion with 1 thinner pita half. Press each sandwich firmly until lamb mixture spreads to ¼ inch from edge of pita. Transfer sandwiches to large plate, cover with plastic wrap, and set aside. (Sandwiches can be left at room temperature for up to 1 hour before grilling.)

3A For a charcoal grill Open bottom vent completely. Light large chimney starter two-thirds filled with charcoal briquettes (4 quarts). When top coals are partially covered with ash, pour evenly over grill. Set cooking grate in place, cover, and open lid vent completely. Heat grill until hot, about 5 minutes.

3B For a gas grill Turn all burners to high, cover, and heat grill until hot, about 15 minutes. Turn all burners to medium-high.

4 Clean and oil cooking grate. Place sandwiches on grill, cover, and cook until bottoms are evenly browned and edges are starting to crisp, 7 to 10 minutes, moving sandwiches as needed to ensure even cooking. Flip sandwiches, cover grill, and continue to cook until second sides are evenly browned and edges are crispy, 7 to 10 minutes longer. Transfer sandwiches to cutting board and cut each in half crosswise. Serve with yogurt sauce.

Cals 470 | Total Fat 33g | Sat Fat 14g
Chol 85mg | Sodium 84mg
Total Carb 21g | Dietary Fiber 1g
Total Sugars 2g | Protein 24g

Nutritional Information for Our Recipes

We calculate the nutritional values of our recipes per serving; if there is a range in the serving size, we used the highest number of servings to calculate the nutritional values. We entered all the ingredients, using weights for important ingredients such as most vegetables. We also used our preferred brands in these analyses. We did not include additional salt or pepper for food that's "seasoned to taste."

	CALORIES	TOTAL FAT (G)	SAT FAT (G)	CHOL (MG)	SODIUM (MG)	TOTAL CARB (G)	DIETARY FIBER (G)	TOTAL SUGARS (G)	PROTEIN (G)
Chapter 1: Mostly Plants									
SALADS									
Crispy Artichoke Salad with Lemon Vinaigrette	190	12g	1.5g	0mg	330mg	16g	3g	2g	4g
Carrot and Smoked Salmon Salad	210	11g	1.5g	10mg	710mg	19g	6g	9g	9g
Beet Salad with Spiced Yogurt and Watercress	212	13g	3g	8mg	580mg	19g	5g	13g	9g
Fattoush with Butternut Squash and Apple	310	19g	2.5g	0mg	460mg	33g	4g	7g	4g
Panzanella with Fiddleheads	290	21g	4g	5mg	360mg	17g	0g	1g	8g
Chopped Vegetable and Stone Fruit Salad	110	5g	0.5g	0mg	250mg	15g	3g	11g	2g
Parsley-Cucumber Salad with Feta, Pomegranate, and Walnuts	156	12g	4g	17mg	296mg	10g	2g	6g	4g
Triple Pea Salad	150	12g	2g	2mg	256mg	8g	3g	3g	4g
Sweet Potato Salad with Cumin, Smoked Paprika, and Almonds	309	15g	2g	0mg	473mg	38g	7g	8g	5g
Horiatiki Salata	240	19g	7g	35mg	980mg	10g	3g	6g	7g
Feta, Jicama, and Tomato Salad	250	19g	7g	35mg	530mg	13g	4g	6g	7g
Roasted Pattypan Squash Salad with Dandelion Green Pesto	270	20g	2.5g	0mg	310mg	24g	4g	12g	6g
Harissa Carrot Noodles	320	18g	6g	15mg	550mg	34g	8g	21g	9g
Roasted Vegetable and Kale Salad with Pomegranate Vinaigrette	420	20g	4g	85mg	870mg	37g	7g	16g	26g
Roasted Cipollini and Escarole Salad	290	19g	4.5g	20mg	790mg	21g	3g	5g	10g
Cantaloupe Salad with Olives and Red Onion	54	1g	0g	0mg	266mg	12g	2g	10g	1g
Grilled Peach and Tomato Salad with Burrata and Basil	342	28g	11g	49mg	530mg	14g	2g	11g	11g
Bitter Greens and Fig Salad with Warm Shallot Dressing	431	26g	5g	22mg	817mg	37g	10g	19g	16g
Carrot and Beet Salad with Rose Harissa	250	15g	2g	60mg	410mg	22g	7g	11g	6g
Persimmon and Burrata Salad with Prosciutto	360	23g	10g	55mg	640mg	27g	1g	1g	16g
Roasted Cauliflower and Grape Salad with Chermoula	340	28g	4g	0mg	510mg	22g	6g	11g	6g
Seared Halloumi and Vegetable Salad Bowl	380	26g	10g	30mg	690mg	24g	5g	15g	13g
Salmon, Avocado, Grapefruit, and Watercress Salad	360	26g	4.5g	40mg	370mg	15g	7g	7g	18g

	CALORIES	TOTAL FAT (G)	SAT FAT (G)	CHOL (MG)	SODIUM (MG)	TOTAL CARB (G)	DIETARY FIBER (G)	TOTAL SUGARS (G)	PROTEIN (G)
SOUPS AND STEWS									
Grilled Tomato Gazpacho	270	22g	3g	0mg	630mg	17g	3g	8g	3g
Creamy Hawaij Cauliflower Soup with Zhoug	270	24g	3.5g	0mg	740mg	12g	4g	4g	4g
Pureed Butternut Squash Soup with Fennel	220	17g	6g	25mg	430mg	19g	4g	6g	2g
Hearty Spring Vegetable Soup	300	25g	4.5g	5mg	740mg	12g	4g	6g	8g
Chestnut Soup with Mushrooms and Baharat	290	8g	1.5	5mg	590mg	49g	6g	15g	8g
Spiced Eggplant and Kale Soup	310	27g	6g	5mg	730mg	14g	6g	6g	5g
Patatas a la Riojana	540	25g	9g	50mg	800mg	45g	3g	4g	21g
Eggs in Swiss Chard and Herb Sauce	310	18g	4g	15mg	990mg	21g	8g	7g	18g
Cabbage, Kohlrabi, and Lamb Tagine with Prunes	440	21g	7g	45mg	610mg	47g	6g	21g	17g
VEGETABLE MAINS									
Whole Romanesco with Berbere and Yogurt-Tahini Sauce	260	20g	3.5g	5mg	230mg	16g	5g	6g	7g
Whole Pot-Roasted Cauliflower with Tomatoes and Olives	280	10g	2.5g	5mg	1250mg	37g	8g	21g	12g
Butternut Squash Steaks with Honey-Nut Topping	400	20g	5g	5mg	610mg	55g	8g	19g	7g
Seared Shrimp and Zucchini Noodles with Tomato-Artichoke Sauce	350	23g	5g	15mg	810mg	15g	4g	6g	21g
Corn and Lamb Hash	460	24g	7g	40mg	640mg	48g	5g	6g	17g
Mushroom Bourguignon	420	21g	3g	0mg	840mg	27g	5g	13g	13g
Baharat Cauliflower and Eggplant with Chickpeas	570	28g	3.5	0mg	1220mg	70g	13g	10g	20g
Herb Vegetable and Lentil Bake with Feta	460	28g	7g	25mg	850mg	41g	11g	13g	14g
Hasselback Eggplant with Muhammara	440	25g	3.5g	5mg	800mg	51g	12g	26g	10g
Loaded Sweet Potato Wedges with Tempeh	440	20g	3g	0mg	630mg	54g	9g	14g	12g
Stuffed Portobello Mushrooms with Spinach and Gorgonzola	420	28g	7g	20mg	700mg	29g	6g	7g	15g
Couscous-Stuffed Acorn Squash	440	22g	2g	0mg	450mg	59g	6g	18g	8g
Spiced Stuffed Peppers with Yogurt-Tahini Sauce	520	29g	6g	40mg	510mg	46g	10g	16g	21g
Stuffed Tomatoes with Couscous and Zucchini	420	19g	6g	15mg	560mg	48g	9g	16g	18g
SIMPLE VEGETABLE SIDES									
Boiled Carrots with Fennel and Citrus	80	4g	0.5g	0mg	1240mg	11g	3g	5g	1g
Pan-Roasted Brussels Sprouts with Lemon and Pecorino Romano	240	20g	3.5g	5mg	150mg	10g	4g	3g	7g
Spinach with Garlic and Lemon	100	7g	1g	0mg	110mg	5g	3g	0g	3g
Pan-Roasted Cauliflower with Garlic and Lemon	160	13g	2g	0mg	520mg	9g	4g	3g	5g
Roasted Asparagus with Cilantro-Lime Gremolata	80	6g	1g	0mg	190mg	5g	3g	2g	3g
Sautéed Radishes	80	7g	1g	0mg	140mg	4g	2g	2g	1g
Broiled Broccoli Rabe	120	11g	1.5g	0mg	250mg	4g	3g	0g	4g
Pan-Roasted Parsnips	120	4g	0.5g	0mg	160mg	22g	6g	6g	1g

	CALORIES	TOTAL FAT (G)	SAT FAT (G)	CHOL (MG)	SODIUM (MG)	TOTAL CARB (G)	DIETARY FIBER (G)	TOTAL SUGARS (G)	PROTEIN (G)
HEARTY SIDES OR MORE									
Cauliflower Puree with Blistered Tomatoes and 'Nduja	280	22g	3.5g	10mg	790mg	17g	4g	9g	7g
Patate alla Lucana	480	21g	6g	15mg	910mg	64g	8g	13g	15g
Spiralized Sweet Potatoes with Crispy Shallots, Pistachios, and Urfa	240	9g	2g	5mg	320mg	35g	6g	11g	5g
Riced Cauliflower with Preserved Lemon	100	4g	1g	0mg	540mg	13g	5g	5g	5g
Braised Eggplant with Paprika, Coriander, and Yogurt	150	12g	3g	0mg	630mg	11g	4g	6g	2g
Roasted Fennel with Crunchy Oil-Cured Olives	90	7g	1g	0mg	216mg	6g	3g	3g	1g
Horta	110	8g	1g	0mg	160mg	10g	4g	1g	3g
Charred Green Beans with Coriander, Sesame, and Nigella Seeds	170	14g	2g	0mg	210mg	10g	4g	3g	4g
Skillet-Roasted Carrots with Za'atar Breadcrumbs and Cilantro	162	10g	1g	0mg	489mg	18g	5g	8g	2g
Pan-Steamed Kale with Baharat	200	13g	1.5g	0mg	180mg	18g	4g	10g	6g
Roasted Okra with Fennel and Oregano	100	7g	1g	0mg	105mg	8g	4g	1g	2g
PIZZAS AND PASTRIES									
Whole-Wheat Pizza with Kale and Sunflower Seed Pesto	430	25g	4g	5mg	790mg	41g	5g	3g	12g
Arugula Pesto and Potato Pizza	480	25g	5g	10mg	750mg	49g	2g	6g	15g
Lavash Pizza with Cauliflower, Fennel, and Coriander	400	24g	8g	25mg	610mg	31g	4g	6g	15g
Hortopita	430	27g	8g	85mg	770mg	36g	3g	4g	13g
Eggplant and Tomato Phyllo Pie	410	28g	8g	20mg	800mg	28g	3g	4g	10g
Kataifi-Wrapped Feta with Tomatoes and Artichokes	380	26g	8g	35mg	630mg	27g	2g	5g	10g
SMALL PLATES									
Spiced Cauliflower Fritters	300	20g	6g	100mg	660mg	21g	3g	3g	10g
Spicy Roasted Red Pepper Whipped Feta	110	10g	4.5g	25mg	260mg	3g	0g	2g	4g
Shishito Peppers with Mint, Poppy Seeds, and Orange	80	7g	0.5g	0mg	140mg	3g	1g	1g	1g
Beet Muhammara	150	12g	1.5g	0mg	330mg	9g	2g	6g	2g
Butternut Squash Tartlets with Almonds, Pomegranate, and Mint	110	4.5g	0g	0mg	220mg	16g	2g	2g	2g
Chapter 2: Mainly Grains & Beans									
GRAIN SALADS AND PILAFS									
Spelt Salad with Quick-Pickled Fennel, Pea Greens, and Mint	190	9g	1.5g	5mg	210mg	26g	4g	4g	5g
Tabbouleh with Garlicky Tofu	160	10g	1.5g	0mg	300mg	12g	2g	2g	7g
Farro Salad with Butternut Squash and Radicchio	530	21g	4.5g	10mg	680mg	78g	10g	8g	14g
Quinoa Lettuce Wraps with Feta and Olives	420	27g	6g	20mg	600mg	35g	5g	6g	11g
Pearl Couscous with Chorizo and Chickpeas	600	21g	6g	35mg	1190mg	78g	6g	14g	25g
Wheat Berry Salad with Chickpeas, Spinach, and Orange	230	6g	0.5g	0mg	340mg	38g	7g	6g	7g

	CALORIES	TOTAL FAT (G)	SAT FAT (G)	CHOL (MG)	SODIUM (MG)	TOTAL CARB (G)	DIETARY FIBER (G)	TOTAL SUGARS (G)	PROTEIN (G)
GRAIN SALADS AND PILAFS (CONTINUED)									
Marinated Eggplant and Barley Salad	430	20g	3.5g	10mg	520mg	57g	11g	12g	9g
Brown Rice Salad with Fennel, Mushrooms, and Walnuts	560	29g	3.5g	0mg	920mg	65g	6g	7g	11g
Kamut with Carrots and Pomegranate	190	8g	1g	0mg	160mg	27g	5g	5g	6g
Red Rice and Quinoa Salad with Blood Oranges	260	8g	1g	0mg	75mg	44g	3g	18g	4g
Pesto Farro Salad with Cherry Tomatoes and Artichokes	460	27g	4g	5mg	460mg	46g	7g	5g	13g
Wheat Berry Salad with Radicchio, Dried Cherries, and Pecans	200	11g	2g	5mg	190mg	22g	4g	3g	5g
Bulgur Salad with Spinach, Chickpeas, and Apples	580	29g	3.5g	0mg	530mg	72g	14g	15g	14g
Barley with Fennel and Dried Apricots	230	4g	0.5g	0mg	190mg	44g	9g	11g	5g
Brown Rice Pilaf with Dates and Pistachios	200	5g	1g	0mg	380mg	34g	3g	5g	4g
Quinoa Pilaf with Olives, Raisins, and Cilantro	180	6g	0.5g	0mg	300mg	26g	3g	5g	5g
LEGUME DISHES									
Red Lentil Kibbeh	450	19g	3g	5mg	760mg	60g	13g	6g	16g
White Bean and Tuna Salad	190	10g	1.5g	10mg	440mg	16g	5g	2g	12g
Lentil Salad with Oranges, Celery, and Feta	260	14g	2.5g	5mg	350mg	26g	6g	6g	8g
Modern Succotash with Fennel and Scallions	209	7g	4g	15mg	461mg	32g	6g	6g	8g
Crispy Lentil and Herb Salad	240	17g	5g	10mg	220mg	16g	3g	5g	7g
Cannellini Beans with Roasted Red Peppers and Kale	220	10g	1.5g	0mg	480mg	24g	7g	5g	8g
SOUPS AND STEWS									
Chorba Frik	270	13g	2.5g	40mg	850mg	25g	7g	3g	13g
Garlicky Wild Rice Soup with Artichokes	420	12g	1.5g	5mg	1220mg	58g	7g	7g	20g
Harira	390	15g	2g	0mg	780mg	51g	11g	9g	17g
Pasta e Ceci	506	19g	4g	10mg	905mg	67g	13g	10g	19g
Butternut Squash and White Bean Soup with Sage Pesto	520	27g	4g	5mg	1210mg	55g	14g	9g	19g
Lablabi	420	19g	2.5g	0mg	610mg	49g	14g	9g	15g
Shrimp, Tomato, and White Bean Stew	260	10g	1.5g	95mg	660mg	24g	6g	8g	17g
Creamy White Bean Soup with Pickled Celery	220	11g	2g	0mg	640mg	23g	5g	3g	9g
RISOTTOS AND PORRIDGES									
Miso Mushroom Risotto	600	17g	2g	0mg	1090mg	90g	4g	9g	20g
Shrimp Risotto	560	22g	3.5g	110mg	920mg	62g	4g	4g	23g
Mushroom Farrotto	430	17g	3.5g	10mg	930mg	53g	6g	2g	18g
Beet Barley Risotto	500	11g	2g	5mg	1000mg	77g	17g	10g	17g
Creamy Polenta with Radicchio Agrodolce	370	25g	6g	20mg	860mg	20g	2g	15g	15g

	CALORIES	TOTAL FAT (G)	SAT FAT (G)	CHOL (MG)	SODIUM (MG)	TOTAL CARB (G)	DIETARY FIBER (G)	TOTAL SUGARS (G)	PROTEIN (G)
SIMPLE GRAIN AND BEAN SIDES									
Basmati Rice Pilaf	180	3g	0g	0mg	100mg	34g	0g	1g	3g
Basmati Rice Pilaf with Currants and Cinnamon	190	3g	0g	0mg	100mg	39g	1g	5g	3g
Baked Brown Rice with Parmesan, Lemon, and Herbs	260	9g	2.5g	5mg	440mg	37g	2g	1g	8g
Baked Wild Rice	150	1.5g	1g	5mg	290mg	28g	3g	0g	5g
Creamy Parmesan Polenta	150	7g	4g	20mg	710mg	15g	2g	0g	8g
Quinoa Pilaf with Lemon and Herbs	210	7g	1g	0mg	300mg	29g	3g	2g	6g
Simple Couscous	260	5g	0.5g	0mg	490mg	45g	3g	0g	8g
Warm Farro with Orange and Herbs	180	1.5g	0g	0mg	290mg	38g	4g	3g	6g
Chickpea Salad with Carrots, Raisins, and Almonds	250	13g	1.5g	0mg	580mg	28g	6g	12g	6g
Lentil Salad with Pomegranates and Walnuts	220	11g	1.5g	0mg	290mg	23g	9g	4g	10g
HEARTY MAINS									
Shakshuka with Chickpeas	479	23g	6g	379mg	1145mg	45g	12g	16g	27g
Tabil Couscous with Sardines	510	14g	2.5g	55mg	610mg	75g	6g	9g	21g
Farro with Tofu, Mushrooms, and Spinach	480	25g	2g	0mg	540mg	52g	5g	7g	15g
Saffron Bulgur with Fennel and Sausage	610	26g	8g	95mg	1050mg	64g	12g	17g	33g
Baked Shrimp and Orzo with Feta and Tomatoes	560	11g	4.5g	160mg	1140mg	79g	4g	11g	36g
Espinacas con Garbanzos	430	25g	3.5g	0mg	1010mg	36g	11g	2g	15g
Bulgur with Vegetables and Marinated Tofu	664	33g	3g	3mg	1216mg	75g	16g	21g	27g
Plant-Based Albóndigas	250	15g	4g	55mg	550mg	20g	3g	3g	8g
Lentils with Roasted Broccoli and Lemony Bread Crumbs	420	16g	2g	0mg	340mg	55g	12g	11g	16g
Baked Pumpkin Kibbeh with Feta	480	20g	6g	25mg	860mg	64g	11g	6g	14g
Meatless "Meat" Sauce with Chickpeas and Mushrooms	180	11g	1.5g	0mg	690mg	16g	2g	6g	4g
Gigantes Plaki	390	10g	1.5g	0mg	620mg	60g	16g	14g	18g
Farro and Broccoli Rabe Gratin	410	13g	2g	5mg	760mg	61g	9g	5g	17g
White Bean and Mushroom Gratin	427	19g	3g	0mg	757mg	50g	10g	6g	15g
PASTAS									
Baked Ziti with Creamy Leeks, Kale, and Sun-Dried Tomatoes	560	16g	2g	0mg	930mg	89g	4g	8g	15g
Maftoul with Carrots and Chickpeas	410	9g	1g	0mg	930mg	70g	7g	8g	13g
Fideos with Artichokes and Scallops	600	26g	3.5g	30mg	890mg	63g	6g	7g	24g
Linguine allo Scolio	702	19g	3g	229mg	1505mg	73g	5g	5g	51g
Fregula with Chickpeas, Tomatoes, and Fennel	557	14g	2g	0mg	1094mg	92g	15g	14g	19g
Pasta with Avocado Pesto and Broccoli	490	21g	2.5g	0mg	280mg	64g	7g	3g	14g
Fregula with Clams and Saffron	450	9g	1g	25mg	690mg	61g	1g	3g	20g
Rigatoni with Swiss Chard, Bell Peppers, and Pancetta	450	14g	6g	35mg	1030mg	57g	3g	3g	21g
Pesto alla Calabrese	634	18g	6g	21mg	672mg	94g	6g	8g	22g

	CALORIES	TOTAL FAT (G)	SAT FAT (G)	CHOL (MG)	SODIUM (MG)	TOTAL CARB (G)	DIETARY FIBER (G)	TOTAL SUGARS (G)	PROTEIN (G)
PASTAS (CONTINUED)									
Spaghetti with Spring Vegetables	450	16g	2.5g	0mg	520mg	64g	6g	5g	14g
Pasta with Burst Cherry Tomatoes and Fried Caper Crumbs	418	19g	5g	12mg	574mg	53g	4g	6g	10g
Farfalle with Beets, Arugula, and Blue Cheese	550	26g	3g	0mg	510mg	68g	4g	2g	13g
Angel Hair Pasta with Sun-Dried Tomato and Mint Sauce	600	29g	5g	7mg	359mg	70g	5g	3g	16g
Garlicky Spaghetti with Artichokes and Hazelnuts	450	18g	2.5g	5mg	270mg	60g	4g	2g	14g
SANDWICHES									
Ta'ameya with Tahini-Yogurt Sauce	490	31g	8g	55mg	330mg	38g	6g	9g	18g
Lentil and Mushroom Burgers	410	17g	2g	0mg	520mg	54g	5g	7g	12g
Spiced Smashed Chickpea Wraps with Tahini Yogurt	588	19g	4g	10mg	1021mg	82g	19g	13g	28g
HUMMUS DISHES									
Ultracreamy Hummus	190	13g	2g	0mg	490mg	14g	4g	0g	6g
Sweet Potato Hummus	150	8g	1g	0mg	400mg	17g	3g	4g	4g
Hummus with Baharat Beef Topping	400	30g	5g	35mg	890mg	18g	5g	1g	19g
White Bean Hummus with Herb and Olive Salad	240	16g	2g	0mg	290mg	19g	9g	1g	9g
Hummus with Crispy Mushrooms and Sumac	550	36g	5g	0mg	1270mg	44g	13g	2g	19g
Fava Bean Crostini with Manchego and Pine Nuts	380	11g	2g	5mg	400mg	59g	10g	14g	18g
Chapter 3: Meat, Fish, Tofu & More									
TOFU AND TEMPEH									
Shawarma-Spiced Tofu Wraps with Sumac Onions	510	24g	3g	0mg	800mg	53	2g	10g	23g
Tofu and Chickpea Flour Frittata with Mushrooms	160	10g	1g	0mg	370mg	7g	1g	2g	10g
Grilled Tofu and Vegetables with Rose Harissa	310	21g	2.5g	0mg	580mg	17g	4g	7g	14g
Seared Tempeh with Tomato Jam	300	12g	2g	5mg	710mg	31g	2g	6g	17g
EGGS									
Frittata with Broccoli and Turmeric	220	15g	4g	375mg	400mg	6g	2g	2g	16g
Tunisian Tajine with White Beans	500	29g	9g	500mg	840mg	15g	3g	2g	45g
Tortilla Española with Celery Root and Peas	250	18g	4g	250mg	600mg	10g	2g	3g	10g
FISH									
Niçoise Salad with Smoked Salmon	320	15g	5g	220mg	830mg	25g	4g	5g	21g
Couscous Salad with Smoked Trout, Tomatoes, and Pepperoncini	360	16g	2.5g	30mg	950mg	37g	3g	1g	17g
Tuna and Heirloom Tomato Salad with Olives and Parsley	330	24g	3.5g	10mg	1120mg	8g	2g	4g	18g
Shaved Salad with Seared Scallops	480	25g	4g	40mg	1260mg	38g	8g	20g	25g
Pan Bagnat	520	30g	4.5g	115mg	1260mg	34g	2g	4g	27g
Glazed Salmon with Black-Eyed Peas, Walnuts, and Pomegranate	600	35g	6g	60mg	930mg	39g	7g	13g	56g

	CALORIES	TOTAL FAT (G)	SAT FAT (G)	CHOL (MG)	SODIUM (MG)	TOTAL CARB (G)	DIETARY FIBER (G)	TOTAL SUGARS (G)	PROTEIN (G)
FISH (CONTINUED)									
Sautéed Tilapia with Blistered Green Beans and Pepper Relish	330	20g	3g	55mg	960mg	12g	4g	6g	27g
Tuna and Onions in Agrodolce	350	15g	2g	45mg	500mg	24g	3g	15g	30g
Chraime	290	12g	2g	90mg	930mg	14g	3g	6g	31g
Fish Tagine	400	32g	5g	75mg	1440mg	11g	2g	3g	31g
Halibut Puttanesca	310	18g	2.5g	70mg	1390mg	9g	3g	3g	27g
Roasted Salmon with White Beans, Fennel, and Tomatoes	670	39g	15g	105mg	1290mg	43g	15g	13g	36g
Steamed Mussels with Merguez	480	22g	6g	110mg	1540mg	25g	3g	7g	44g
Baked Shrimp with Fennel, Potatoes, and Olives	350	13g	4g	205mg	1060mg	29g	3g	4g	27g
Salmon en Cocotte with Roasted Garlic and Cherry Tomatoes	380	29g	5g	60mg	450mg	4g	1g	2g	24g
Grilled Swordfish Skewers with Zucchini	310	22g	4g	75mg	390mg	4g	1g	3g	24g
Garlicky Roasted Shrimp with Cilantro and Lime	190	15g	2g	105mg	270mg	2g	0g	0g	12g
Grilled Whole Trout with Orange and Fennel	410	20g	4g	175mg	920mg	1g	0g	1g	57g
Pan-Seared Shrimp with Pistachio, Cumin, and Parsley	140	8g	1g	105mg	320mg	3g	1g	1g	13g
SIMPLE PROTEIN OPTIONS									
Seared Tempeh	270	15g	2g	0mg	40mg	20g	0g	0g	15g
Crispy Tofu	220	10g	0.5g	0mg	0mg	20g	0g	0g	11g
Perfect Fried Eggs	110	9g	2g	185mg	70mg	0g	0g	0g	6g
Soft-Cooked Eggs	70	5g	1.5g	185mg	70mg	0g	0g	0g	6g
Roasted Salmon Fillets	260	18g	4g	60mg	360mg	0g	0g	0g	23g
Pan-Roasted Cod	130	4.5g	0.5g	50mg	350mg	1g	0g	1g	20g
Poached Chicken Breasts	90	2g	0g	55mg	230mg	0g	0g	0g	17g
Seared Flank Steak	210	12g	4g	75mg	160mg	0g	0g	0g	24g
CHICKEN									
Chicken Salad with Pickled Fennel and Macadamia Nuts	280	16g	2.5g	85mg	290mg	5g	2g	2g	28g
Turmeric Rice and Chicken Salad	420	14g	3g	80mg	740mg	45g	2g	4g	31g
Harissa Wings with Cucumber-Tomato Salad	450	34g	7g	135mg	1140mg	13g	3g	7g	23g
Za'atar Chicken Schnitzel with Sweet Potato Wedges	770	43g	6g	130mg	700mg	58g	6g	6g	34g
Skillet-Roasted Chicken Breasts with Harissa-Mint Carrots	390	18g	5g	110mg	740mg	18g	5g	9g	37g
Chicken and Spiced Freekeh with Cilantro and Preserved Lemon	330	10g	1.5g	45mg	440mg	38g	9g	2g	23g
Msakhan	590	29g	7g	115mg	910mg	37g	3g	8g	45g
Cumin-Coriander Roasted Cornish Game Hens	220	12g	2g	120mg	970mg	1g	1g	0g	27g
Pomegranate-Glazed Butterflied Chicken with Potatoes and Mustard Greens	600	31g	8g	130mg	730mg	41g	2g	9g	38g

	CALORIES	TOTAL FAT (G)	SAT FAT (G)	CHOL (MG)	SODIUM (MG)	TOTAL CARB (G)	DIETARY FIBER (G)	TOTAL SUGARS (G)	PROTEIN (G)
TURKEY									
Turkey Meatballs with Lemony Brown Rice and Sun-Dried Tomatoes	470	15g	4.5g	95mg	1090mg	47g	3g	3g	38g
Grill-Smoked Boneless Turkey Breast with Olives and Sun-Dried Tomatoes	230	3.5g	0.5g	110mg	630mg	1g	0g	0g	45g
Ras el Hanout–Rubbed Turkey Breast with Sour Orange Sauce	270	5g	1g	110mg	890mg	6g	0g	4g	45g
BEEF									
Keftedes	460	29g	10g	140mg	670mg	15g	2g	6g	34g
Marak Temani	420	31g	7g	75mg	660mg	9g	34g	3g	27g
Seared Steak Tips with Cauliflower and Zhoug	420	31g	75g	75mg	660mg	9g	4g	3g	27g
Braised Beef Short Ribs with Fennel and Pickled Grapes	340	24g	10g	85mg	560mg	14g	3g	9g	21g
Mehshi Bazal	310	9g	3.5g	40mg	430mg	44g	4g	23g	14g
Grilled Beef Short Ribs with Preserved Lemon–Almond Sauce	364	29g	12g	110mg	353mg	0g	0g	0g	26g
PORK									
Pork Tenderloin with White Beans and Mustard Greens	560	22g	8g	90mg	1100mg	43g	11g	4g	45g
'Nduja with Beans and Greens	420	17g	5g	215mg	1050mg	38g	12g	6g	33g
Spiced Pork Tenderloin with Butternut Squash and Brussels Sprouts	270	14g	2.5g	60mg	600mg	13g	4g	3g	25g
Pinchos Morunos	230	14g	3.5g	85mg	400mg	2g	0g	0g	24g
LAMB									
Embakbbka	570	29g	13g	90mg	810mg	44g	3g	6g	31g
Lamb Chops with Tamarind Pan Sauce	270	13g	4.5g	100mg	430mg	4g	1g	3g	33g
Braised Lamb Shoulder Chops with Capers, Balsamic Vinegar, and Red Pepper	480	25g	9g	145mg	730mg	10g	2g	6g	45g
Sumac Lamb Chops with Carrots, Mint, and Paprika	380	22g	6g	85mg	1480mg	16g	4g	6g	34g
Arrosticini	276	24g	9g	65mg	221mg	0g	0g	0g	15g
Arayes	470	33g	14g	85mg	840mg	21g	1g	2g	24g

Conversions & Equivalents

Some say cooking is a science and an art. We would say that geography has a hand in it, too. Flours and sugars manufactured in the United Kingdom and elsewhere will feel and taste different from those manufactured in the United States. So we cannot promise that the loaf of bread you bake in Canada or England will taste the same as a loaf baked in the States, but we can offer guidelines for converting weights and measures. We also recommend that you rely on your instincts when making our recipes. Refer to the visual cues provided. If the dough hasn't "come together in a ball" as described, you may need to add more flour—even if the recipe doesn't tell you to. You be the judge.

The recipes in this book were developed using standard U.S. measures following U.S. government guidelines. The charts below offer equivalents for U.S. and metric measures. All conversions are approximate and have been rounded up or down to the nearest whole number.

Example

1 teaspoon	=	4.9292 milliliters, rounded up to 5 milliliters
1 ounce	=	28.3495 grams, rounded down to 28 grams

Volume Conversions

U.S.	METRIC
1 teaspoon	5 milliliters
2 teaspoons	10 milliliters
1 tablespoon	15 milliliters
2 tablespoons	30 milliliters
¼ cup	59 milliliters
⅓ cup	79 milliliters
½ cup	118 milliliters
¾ cup	177 milliliters
1 cup	237 milliliters
1¼ cups	296 milliliters
1½ cups	355 milliliters
2 cups (1 pint)	473 milliliters
2½ cups	591 milliliters
3 cups	710 milliliters
4 cups (1 quart)	0.946 liter
1.06 quarts	1 liter
4 quarts (1 gallon)	3.8 liters

Weight Conversions

OUNCES	GRAMS
½	14
¾	21
1	28
1½	43
2	57
2½	71
3	85
3½	99
4	113
4½	128
5	142
6	170
7	198
8	227
9	255
10	283
12	340
16 (1 pound)	454

Conversions for Common Baking Ingredients

Baking is an exacting science. Because measuring by weight is far more accurate than measuring by volume, and thus more likely to produce reliable results, in our recipes we provide ounce measures in addition to cup measures for many ingredients. Refer to the chart below to convert these measures into grams.

INGREDIENT	OUNCES	GRAMS
Flour		
1 cup all-purpose flour*	5	142
1 cup cake flour	4	113
1 cup whole-wheat flour	5½	156
Sugar		
1 cup granulated (white) sugar	7	198
1 cup packed brown sugar (light or dark)	7	198
1 cup confectioners' sugar	4	113
Cocoa Powder		
1 cup cocoa powder	3	85
Butter†		
4 tablespoons (½ stick or ¼ cup)	2	57
8 tablespoons (1 stick or ½ cup)	4	113
16 tablespoons (2 sticks or 1 cup)	8	227

* U.S. all-purpose flour, the most frequently used flour in this book, does not contain leaveners, as some European flours do. These leavened flours are called self-rising or self-raising. If you are using self-rising flour, take this into consideration before adding leaveners to a recipe.

† In the United States, butter is sold both salted and unsalted. We generally recommend unsalted butter. If you are using salted butter, take this into consideration before adding salt to a recipe.

Oven Temperatures

FAHRENHEIT	CELSIUS	GAS MARK
225	105	¼
250	120	½
275	135	1
300	150	2
325	165	3
350	180	4
375	190	5
400	200	6
425	220	7
450	230	8
475	245	9

Converting Temperatures from an Instant-Read Thermometer

We include doneness temperatures in many of the recipes in this book. We recommend an instant-read thermometer for the job. Use this simple formula to convert Fahrenheit degrees to Celsius:

Subtract 32 degrees from the Fahrenheit reading, then divide the result by 1.8 to find the Celsius reading.

Example

"Roast chicken until thighs register 175 degrees."

To convert:

$$175°F - 32 = 143°$$
$$143° ÷ 1.8 = 79.44°C, \text{ rounded down to } 79°C$$

Further Readings

Cookbooks and online resources from authors of the Mediterranean helped deepen our knowledge of the countries and diverse cuisines of the Mediterranean Basin. They guided our learning, research, and development for many of the recipes in this book. As you enjoy making the dishes, we highly recommend you explore this selection. This list isn't exhaustive, but it represents some sources we were particularly inspired by. They're excellent for supplementing your cooking and learning.

- Admony, Einat and Janna Gur. *Shuk: From Market to Table, the Heart of Israeli Home Cooking.*

- Akin, Engin. *Essential Turkish Cuisine.*

- America's Test Kitchen, Julia Croce, Eugenia Bone, and National Geographic. *Tasting Italy: A Culinary Journey.*

- Barbarigou, Argiro. argirobarbarigou.com

- Barrenechea, Teresa. *The Cuisines of Spain: Exploring Regional Home Cooking.*

- Benkabbou, Nargusse. mymoroccanfood.com

- Casas, Penelope. *Tapas: The Little Dishes of Spain.*

- Conistis, Peter. *Greek Cuisine: The New Classics.*

- Hal, Fatema. *Food of Morocco: Authentic Recipes from the North African Coast.*

- Helou, Anissa. *Feast: Food of the Islamic World.*

- Helou, Anissa. *Levant: Recipes and Memories from the Middle East.*

- Hirigoyen, Gerald. *The Basque Kitchen: Tempting Food from the Pyrenees.*

- Kadé-Badra, Dalal and Elie Badra. *Flavours of Aleppo: Celebrating Syrian Cuisine.*

- Kalla, Joudie. *Palestine on a Plate: Memories from My Mother's Kitchen.*

- Kassis, Reem. *The Palestinian Table.*

- Kochilas, Diane. dianekochilas.com

- Kochilas, Diane. *Ikaria: Lessons on Food, Life, and Longevity from the Island Where People Forget to Die.*

- Massoud, Shahir. *Eat, Habibi, Eat!: Fresh Recipes for Modern Egyptian Cooking.*

- Mousawi, Dina and Itab Azzam. *Our Syria: Recipes from Home.*

- Ottolenghi, Yotam. *Plenty: Vibrant Vegetable Recipes from London's Ottolenghi.*

- Ottolenghi, Yotam and Sami Tamimi. *Jerusalem: A Cookbook.*

- Psilakis, Michael. *How to Roast a Lamb: New Greek Classic Cooking.*

- Qsuda, Khalid. *The Most Delicious Libyan Recipes: Top 10 Step-by-Step Traditional Libyan Recipes.*

- Sharif, Dima. dimasharif.com

- Shaya, Alon. *Shaya: An Odyssey in Food, My Journey Back to Israel.*

- Sourligo, Christos. *My Big Fat Greek Cookbook: Classic Mediterranean Soul Food Recipes.*

- Solomonov, Michael. *Zahav: A World of Israeli Cooking.*

- Tamimi, Sami. *Falastin: A Cookbook.*

- "Taste of Maroc." tasteofmaroc.com

Index

Note: Page references in *italics* indicate photographs.

T

Ta'ameya with Tahini-Yogurt Sauce, 287, *288*

Tabbouleh with Garlicky Tofu, *164,* 165

Tabil

about, 11, 15

Couscous with Sardines, *238, 239*

recipe for, 15

Tagines

Cabbage, Kohlrabi, and Lamb, with Prunes, *82,* 83

Fish, 338

Tunisian, with White Beans, 315, *316*

Tahini

Sauce, 16

Sauce and Crispy Lentils, Spicy Sweet Potato Wedges with, 13, *13*

and Sweet Potato Dip, 295

Ultracreamy Hummus, 294

White Bean Hummus with Herb and Olive Salad, *298,* 299

Yogurt, Spiced Smashed Chickpea Wraps with, 292, *293*

-Yogurt Sauce, 16

-Yogurt Sauce, Spiced Stuffed Peppers with, 106–7, *107*

-Yogurt Sauce and Berbere, Whole Romanesco with, 84–85, *85*

Tamarind Pan Sauce, Lamb Chops with, *404,* 405

Tartlets, Butternut Squash, with Almonds, Pomegranate, and Mint, 159

Tempeh

Loaded Sweet Potato Wedges with, 100, *102*

Seared, 357, *357*

Seared, with Tomato Jam, 312, *313*

Textures and flavors, balancing, 12

Thin-Crust Pizza Dough, 147

Thyme

Za'atar, 15, *15*

Tilapia, Sautéed, with Blistered Green Beans and Pepper Relish, *332,* 333

Tofu

and Chickpea Frittata with Mushrooms, 308

Crispy, 357

Garlicky, Tabbouleh with, *164,* 165

Marinated, and Vegetables, Bulgur with, 247

Tofu cont'd

Mushrooms, and Spinach, Farro with, 240, *241*

Shawarma-Spiced, Wraps with Sumac Onions, 306, *307*

and Vegetables, Grilled, with Rose Harissa, 309, *310*

Tomato(es)

about, 67

and Artichokes, Kataifi-Wrapped Feta with, 144, *145*

-Artichoke Sauce, Seared Shrimp and Zucchini Noodles with, *90,* 91

Blistered, and 'Nduja, Cauliflower Puree with, 116, *117*

Braised Lamb Shoulder Chops with Balsamic Vinegar and Red Pepper, 406

Burst Cherry, and Fried Caper Crumbs, Pasta with, 280, *281*

Cherry, and Artichokes, Farro Salad with, 182, *183*

Cherry, and Roasted Garlic, Salmon en Cocotte with, 348

Chickpeas, and Fennel, Fregula with, 270, *271*

Chorba Frik, 208, *209*

Chraime, 336, *337*

-Cucumber Salad, Harissa Wings with, 366, *367*

and Eggplant Phyllo Pie, *142,* 143

Embakbbka, 402, *403*

Farro and Broccoli Rabe Gratin, 258, *259*

Feta, and Jicama Salad, *42,* 43

and Feta, Baked Shrimp and Orzo with, *244,* 245

Fideos with Artichokes and Scallops, 266, *267*

Fish Tagine, 338

Gigantes Plaki, 255, *257*

Grilled, Gazpacho, 66, *67*

and Grilled Peach Salad with Burrata and Basil, 52–53, *53*

Grilled Tofu and Vegetables with Rose Harissa, 309, *310*

Halibut Puttanesca, 339, *340*

Harira, 212, *213*

Herb Vegetable and Lentil Bako with Feta, 96, *97*

Horiatiki Salata, 40, *41*

Jam, Seared Tempeh with, 312, *313*

Linguine allo Scoglio, 268, 269

Tomato(es) cont'd

Loaded Sweet Potato Wedges with Tempeh, 100, *102*

Marak Temani, *388,* 389

Meatless "Meat" Sauce with Chickpeas and Mushrooms, 254

and Olives, Whole Pot-Roasted Cauliflower with, *86,* 87

Panzanella with Fiddleheads, 30, *31*

Pasta e Ceci, 214

Patate alla Lucana, *118,* 119

Plant-Based Albóndigas, 248, *249*

Quinoa Lettuce Wraps with Feta and Olives, 168, *170*

Roasted Pattypan Squash Salad with Dandelion Green Pesto, 44, *45*

Shakshuka with Chickpeas, *236,* 237

Shrimp, and White Bean Stew, 218, *219*

Smoked Trout, and Pepperoncini, Couscous Salad with, 322, *323*

Spaghetti with Spring Vegetables, *278,* 279

Steamed Mussels with Merguez, 344, *345*

Stuffed, with Couscous and Zucchini, 108, *109*

Sun-Dried, and Lemony Brown Rice, Turkey Meatballs with, *380,* 381

Sun-Dried, and Mint Sauce, Angel Hair Pasta with, *284,* 285

Sun-Dried, and Olives, Grill-Smoked Boneless Turkey Breast with, 382–83, *383*

Sun-Dried, Creamy Leeks, and Kale, Baked Ziti with, *262,* 263

Tabbouleh with Garlicky Tofu, *164,* 165

Turmeric Rice and Chicken Salad, 364, *365*

White Beans, and Fennel, Roasted Salmon with, 342, *343*

Whole-Wheat Pizza with Kale and Sunflower Seed Pesto, 134–35, *135*

Tortilla Española with Celery Root and Peas, 318, *319*

Triple Pea Salad, *36,* 37

Trout

Grilled Whole, with Orange and Fennel, 352, 353

Smoked, Tomatoes, and Pepperoncini, Couscous Salad with, 322, *323*

U

V

W

Y

Z